DIXIE LOOKS ABROAD

DIXIE LOOKS ABROAD

The South and U.S. Foreign Relations, 1789–1973

JOSEPH A. FRY

LOUISIANA STATE UNIVERSITY PRESS
Baton Rouge

11   10   09   08   07   06   05   04   03   02
5   4   3   2   1

Designer: Amanda McDonald Scallan
Typeface: Adobe Caslon
Typesetter: Coghill Composition Co. Inc.
Printer and binder: Thomson-Shore, Inc.

Library of Congress Cataloging-in-Publication Data

Fry, Joseph A., 1947–
    Dixie looks abroad : the South and U.S. foreign relations,
1789–1973 / Joseph A. Fry.
        p.   cm.
    Includes bibliographical references and index.
    ISBN 0-8071-2745-0 (alk. paper)
    1. Southern States—Politics and government—1775–1865.   2.
Southern States—Politics and government—1865–   3. Southern
States—Relations—Foreign countries.   4. United States—Foreign
relations—1783–1865.   5. United States—Foreign
relations—1865–   I. Title.
F209 .F79   2002
975—dc21   2001005166

The paper in this book meets the guidelines for permanence and durability of the Committee on Production Guidelines for Book Longevity of the Council on Library Resources. ∞

For Lois, Sandy, and Bryan Fry

CONTENTS

ILLUSTRATIONS

following page 174

ACKNOWLEDGMENTS

I have received indispensable assistance over the many years I have worked on this book. Tennant S. McWilliams graciously shared his insights on the South and U.S. foreign relations, the notes from his own book on the subject, and his spare bedroom. Ed Crapol's probing criticism of the entire manuscript suggested numerous areas in need of clarification or elaboration. More generally, Ed's friendship has long afforded me a wonderful example of a person truly committed to colleagues and students. Alan Bromberg, also a friend of long standing, read the manuscript with a keen eye for both factual errors and interpretive opportunities. Randall B. Woods provided a similarly acute assessment and incisive blueprint for improvement. Lawrence S. Kaplan gave chapter 1 a careful and helpful reading, and George Herring applied his vast knowledge of U.S. involvement in Vietnam to a critique of chapter 8.

Several of my UNLV colleagues have also provided essential support. Colin Loader, Tom Wright, and Gene Moehring have variously read portions of the book, helped me overcome computer nightmares, and listened patiently to my musings over southerners and foreign policy. I am much in the debt of all these colleagues and friends, near and far, for their personal and professional help. Of course, neither they nor any of the other persons and institutions I have thanked in other portions of these acknowledgments, are responsible for any errors that remain in this book. There is, after all, only so much that friends and editors can do to save an author from himself!

The University of Nevada, Las Vegas, has been consistently supportive of my scholarly endeavors. A sabbatical leave facilitated much of the initial research and conceptualization, and I have received generous travel support to investigate sources and present aspects of my research at professional meetings. The Interlibrary Loan Department (recently renamed Document Delivery Services) of our library has rendered indispensable assistance in locating and securing materials. And the UNLV Department of History has long provided an environment highly conducive to the pursuit of excellence in both teaching and scholarship. I found stimulating and sustaining friends and colleagues on my arrival in 1975, and I have benefited immeasurably from the steady addition over the interim of historians who devote their efforts to intellectual pursuits and students rather than to endless squabbling over peripheral matters. These priorities have made this a wonderful place to teach and write.

Several other institutions have aided my research and granted me permission to draw on and quote from their holdings. Included among these libraries are the Lyndon Baines Johnson Library; the John Fitzgerald Kennedy Library; the Library of Congress Manuscripts Division, Newspaper Division, and Photographic Division; and the Margaret I. King Library at the University of Kentucky. The excellent staffs at each of these libraries directed me to materials that I would never have found on my own and enabled me to take full advantage of research trips.

My experience with the Louisiana State University Press has been exceedingly positive. Sylvia Frank Rodrique, the acquisitions editor, oversaw the process of manuscript submission and approval with sensitivity and dispatch. Jean C. Lee, the editor with whom I worked, skillfully identified mistakes and inconsistencies of fact and form. She also possessed an artful ability to enhance the clarity of my arguments and prose without altering my voice as the author.

My greatest thanks go to my family. By exhibiting genuine concern for others, unwavering faith, and indomitable spirit, my mother, Lois M. Fry, inspires all who know her. My son Bryan, who was still in high school when I conceived of this book, has now completed a graduate degree and become an impressive professional. His instructive perspective on balancing work and personal happiness and his insightful opinions on the characteristics of superior college teachers have been ongoing revelations. Most of all, I am pleased to have the opportunity to thank my wife, Sandy. Her intelligence, strength of character, and unqualified love and support have sustained me during this project, as well as in all other facets of our life together over the past thirty-two years.

DIXIE LOOKS ABROAD

INTRODUCTION

In 1951, Richard W. Leopold, one of the first true specialists in the history of United States foreign relations, asserted that "high on the list of topics worthy of future investigation is the role played by sectionalism in our thinking and our actions toward other countries." More recently in his presidential address to the Southern Historical Association, Carl N. Degler urged that Dixie be viewed as a "co-creator of the nation's history" rather than an "outsider" or an "obstacle" to national development, and he offered foreign policy as a prime example: "What is called *American* foreign policy has often been heavily influenced if not molded by the South. . . . Without the South, in short, American activities in the world would have been different, and perhaps in some instances even reversed."[1]

Although Degler's assertion is accurate, neither historians of the American South nor students of U.S. foreign relations have appreciated or investigated Dixie's influence sufficiently. Numerous excellent monographs, book sections, biographies, and articles examine specific persons, issues, or time frames, but there is no comprehensive overview of the South's response to and influence on U.S. foreign relations. This study treating the years from 1789 (the initiation of foreign policy under the Constitution) through 1973 (the end of U.S. military involvement in Vietnam) is meant to fill that historiographical void. An examination of the South's role in the formation of

1. Richard W. Leopold, "The Mississippi Valley and American Foreign Policy, 1890–1941: An Assessment and an Appeal," *Mississippi Valley Historical Review* 37 (March 1951): 625; Carl N. Degler, "Thesis, Antithesis, Synthesis: The South, the North, and the Nation," *Journal of Southern History* 53 (February 1987): 6, 17.

U.S. foreign policy illuminates one of the principal "internal . . . determinants" of American foreign relations. Peter Trubowitz has argued persuasively that "America's *regional* diversity" has been "the most important source of tension and conflict over foreign policy." Trubowitz contends that "place matters": "When viewed over time and across a wide range of issues, sectional interests emerge as a powerful and consistent force shaping the nation's foreign policy."[2]

For the years from 1789 to 1960, this book is a synthesis and interpretation of the extensive secondary literature. Secondary sources treating the years 1960 to 1973 are less comprehensive and more historiographically diffuse; therefore, I have supplemented the existing historical works by consulting oral histories and other documentary materials from the Lyndon Baines Johnson and John Fitzgerald Kennedy presidential libraries and analyzing public opinion data from the *Gallup Opinion Index* and congressional debates and votes from the *Congressional Quarterly Almanac.*

I have defined the South as including Alabama, Arkansas, Georgia, Florida, Louisiana, Mississippi, North Carolina, South Carolina, Tennessee, Texas, Virginia, and Kentucky. The first eleven states composed the Con-

2. For a discussion of the critical importance of studying the domestic background of policy formation, see Robert J. McMahon, "The Study of American Foreign Relations: National History or International History?" in *Explaining the History of American Foreign Relations,* eds. Michael J. Hogan and Thomas G. Paterson (New York, 1991), 11–23, 16 (internal . . . determinants); Peter Trubowitz, *Defining the National Interest: Conflict and Change in American Foreign Policy* (Chicago, 1998), 4, 12. For a complete listing of the sources I have consulted, see the notes and bibliographic essay. The following studies are representative of high-quality works focused specifically on the South and foreign policy or biographies in which significant attention has been devoted to the subjects' activities in this area: Alfred O. Hero Jr., *The Southerner and World Affairs* (Baton Rouge, 1965); Robert E. May, *The Southern Dream of a Caribbean Empire, 1854–1861* (Athens, Ga., 1989); Tennant S. McWilliams, *The New South Faces the World: Foreign Affairs and the Southern Sense of Self, 1877–1950* (Baton Rouge, 1988); Frank L. Owsley, *King Cotton Diplomacy: Foreign Relations of the Confederate States of America,* 2d ed., revised by Harriet Chappell Owsley (Chicago, 1959); Randall B. Woods, *Fulbright: A Biography* (New York, 1995); Gilbert C. Fite, *Richard B. Russell Jr., Senator from Georgia* (Chapel Hill, 1991); Robert Dallek, *Flawed Giant: Lyndon Johnson and His Times, 1961–1973* (New York, 1998). Edward W. Chester's *Sectionalism, Politics, and American Diplomacy* (Metuchen, N.J., 1975) covers the same chronological span as this study but does not focus specifically on the South; both Richard F. Bensel, *Sectionalism and American Political Development, 1880–1980* (Madison, Wis., 1984), and Trubowitz, *Defining the National Interest,* have emphasized the role of sectionalism in the formation of U.S. foreign policy; and Paul A. Varg, *New England and Foreign Relations, 1789–1850* (Hanover, N.H., 1983), examines a different region and shorter time frame.

federacy. Kentucky is included on the bases of geographic proximity, long dependence on staple agriculture and low-wage industries, parallel racial attitudes, concern for personal and national honor, and devotion to territorial expansion prior to the Civil War and economic expansion generally. This definition of the South has been employed while calculating all of the individual congressional votes cited. Where secondary sources have been unclear or define the South differently, I have consulted the *Congressional Globe, Congressional Record,* or *Congressional Quarterly Almanac.* I have drawn on several informative secondary sources for larger aggregate voting analyses.[3]

The chronological starting point in 1789 coincides with the initiation of the new government under the Constitution and its provision of the institutional and domestic political frameworks for the formation of American foreign policy. The conclusion of active U.S. involvement in Vietnam in 1973 constituted an important turning point in U.S. foreign relations. It marked the first time that the United States had lost a war and the last prolonged military intervention of the twentieth century. When combined with Richard Nixon's simultaneous pursuit of détente with the Soviet Union and China, 1973 ended the most intense and dangerous period of the cold war. More important for this study, significant changes in the South and the nation eroded many of the region's peculiar characteristics and the bases for its distinctive responses to U.S. foreign policy. The impact of the Civil Rights movement, the demise of the solid Democratic South, and the rise of the Sunbelt economy have, according to some observers, resulted in the "Americanization of Dixie," or the South's strong influence in the shaping of "American values, politics, and culture." Although the extent of change in the South's economic conditions and racial and political attitudes should not be exaggerated, the regional distinctiveness on which this analysis is based became much less salient as the Vietnam War concluded, and these processes have continued over the remainder of the century.[4]

3. For example, Harold T. Butler, "Partisan Positions on Isolationism vs. Internationalism, 1918–1933" (D.S.S. dissertation, Syracuse University, 1963); Malcolm E. Jewell, *Senatorial Politics and Foreign Policy* (1962; reprint, Westport, Conn., 1974); George L. Grassmuck, *Sectional Biases in Congress on Foreign Policy* (Baltimore, 1951).

4. John Egerton, *The Americanization of Dixie: The Southernization of America* (New York, 1974); Peter Applebome, *Dixie Rising: How the South Is Shaping American Values, Politics, and Culture* (New York, 1996); James C. Cobb, "An Epitaph for the North: Reflections on the Politics of Regional and National Identity at the Millennium," *Journal of Southern History* 66 (February 2000): 3–24.

Over the more than 180 years examined in this study, the South quickly developed a self-conscious sectionalism and, acting from a perceived sense of regional interest, exercised a vast and often decisive influence on U.S. foreign policy. Southern leadership and public support were predominant and formative during the Jeffersonian ascendancy and were critical to the relocation of Native Americans from the 1830s through the 1850s and to expansion at the expense of Mexico during the 1840s. Dixie provided dependable and decisive support for the activist, often interventionist foreign policies of Woodrow Wilson and Franklin D. Roosevelt—policies that led to the United States's emergence as the world's most powerful nation. With the onset of the cold war, southerners ardently backed containment, greatly expanded defense spending, and military and diplomatic interventions abroad. This cold warrior mentality was particularly prominent during the Vietnam War, when Lyndon Johnson and Dean Rusk formulated overall policy, William C. Westmoreland implemented its military aspects, and key southerners such as Richard Russell and John C. Stennis ensured the necessary congressional funding.

Other periods found the South assuming a minority perspective that conformed more closely to Degler's "outsider" image, but even while opposing national actions, southerners contributed significantly to the process that yielded a domestically negotiated foreign policy. During both the Federalist era of the 1790s and the period of Republican domination of the presidency from 1865 to 1912, the South constituted a minority but still influential opposition to U.S. policies; and with the formation of the Confederacy, southerners fashioned the ultimate opposition by attempting to formulate a completely independent foreign policy.

Even while exercising this often crucial influence, southerners seldom presented a completely united front on foreign policy questions. For example, during the 1840s, southern Democrats led the movement to annex Texas and southern Whigs articulated many of the most compelling objections to territorial expansion. Similarly, during both the Gilded Age and the 1960s, first John Tyler Morgan and then J. William Fulbright emerged as Dixie's most forceful and prominent foreign policy spokesmen. Ironically, both Morgan's aggressive advocacy of territorial expansion and Fulbright's adamant opposition to the Vietnam War embodied positions that ultimately prevailed nationally even though they were decidedly minority viewpoints below the Mason-Dixon Line. Southern African Americans presented an additional dimension to the South's frequently contested foreign policy perspective. As the victims of systematic racial oppression in the American South, blacks pointedly noted the contradiction between the abuse of minorities at home and foreign policies ostensibly devoted to the promotion of freedom and democracy abroad.

While disagreeing among themselves, white southerners consistently viewed the world through a distinctly southern lens and acted on a variety of perceived sectional interests. Although the southern assessment of regional interests produced varying responses at different historical moments, the issues prompting the South to formulate and act on sectional perspectives remained rather constant. As early as the Constitutional Convention, southerners expressed apprehensions about becoming a minority section in the anticipated Union. Conditioned by adherence to the ideology of republicanism, by the experience of a colonial economy based on staple agriculture, and by the felt need to defend slavery, southerners feared for their liberties, jealously guarded the prerogatives of states' rights, and warned of the threat posed by "foreigners"—be they from beyond national or regional boundaries. Just as this attachment to states' rights and aversion to centralized governmental power remained influential over the next two centuries and prompted the South periodically to oppose an assertive foreign policy that might enhance greater national power, economic calculations and race continued to be central southern considerations. The quest for export markets and for low-priced manufactured goods dictated commercial expansion and low tariffs until the 1960s, when the South continued to covet exports but became increasingly sympathetic to protectionism. The aggressive and successful pursuit of national defense spending after 1898 added another economic dimension to the South's increasing inclination to endorse an activist foreign policy. Racial assumptions exercised a similarly persistent influence on the white South, whether as a justification for Indian removal and territorial expansion prior to the Civil War, opposition to the acquisition of an island empire at the turn of the century, growing distress at membership in a United Nations increasingly populated by Africans and Asians in the 1960s, or chronic hostility to immigration in the twentieth century.

Partisan politics has also been fundamental to the South's response to U.S. foreign policy. Political considerations coincided with other sectional interests in eliciting the strong opposition to Federalist foreign policies in the 1790s and to Republican initiatives in the four decades after the Civil War and during the 1920s. Jeffersonian Republicans believed Dixie's interests were being neglected by pro-British northern political adversaries; and an overwhelmingly Democratic South harbored identical apprehensions when assessing the policies of Republicans who had led the North to victory in the Civil War and imposed Reconstruction. Conversely, Democratic politics go far toward explaining Dixie's backing for the foreign policies of Woodrow Wilson and Franklin Roosevelt. Southerners would never have provided decisive congressional and popular support during these eras for initiatives that dramatically expanded executive, federal, and military power and that greatly extended U.S. commitments abroad had these departures been introduced by Republican presidents.

Southern concern for honor and patriotism and a proclivity for personal violence have also shaped the region's foreign policy perspectives. Although the South's peculiar devotion to formal militarism and its possession of pronounced martial skills have been exaggerated, the region's heightened sensitivity to matters of personal, sectional, and national honor has been crucial. Since the antebellum period, demonstrated manhood and bravery and a refusal to tolerate challenges to honor have inclined southern society to the acceptance and use of violence both at home and abroad. In the wake of the Civil War, the Lost Cause ideology reinforced these tendencies and conditioned southerners to emulate the alleged courage and devotion to duty of their Confederate forebears. After 1865, sons of Dixie also felt compelled to demonstrate patriotism by supporting the reconstituted Union in times of crisis.

Finally, the South's devotion to Woodrow Wilson and his policies framed much of the region's response to U.S. foreign relations from 1913 through at least the mid-1950s and remained vitally important to many southerners, such as Dean Rusk and J. William Fulbright, through the end of the Vietnam War. Southerners viewed Wilson as one of their own and rallied behind his policies, ranging from the pursuit of an open commercial world to aggressive intervention in Mexico and participation in World War I, but especially to his call for a new international order and U.S. membership in the League of Nations. When nonsoutherners blocked American entry into the League, Dixie made the institutional enactment of Wilson's international aspirations into a second "Lost Cause." Championing their fallen hero and arguing for U.S. membership in an international organization provided southerners a respectable platform for attacking Republicans on a topic that promised to benefit the nation. This debate simultaneously enabled Dixie to avoid less palatable domestic matters such as segregation or southern poverty.

Southerners were instrumental in the American decision to join the United Nations, and at the height of the cold war, Rusk and Fulbright, despite their diametrically opposed foreign policy positions, both believed that they were faithfully upholding Wilson's principles. Indeed, the Wilson presidency was a pivotal juncture in the South's relation to U.S. foreign relations. While following its southern leader, Dixie reversed its pattern over the previous fifty years of opposing an aggressive foreign policy based on a strong executive and military. Thereafter, the South provided decisive domestic support for the nation's involvement in World War II and cold war strategy of containment that formed the basis for the United States's rise to the most powerful nation in world history. But Wilsonianism had its limits. It was one thing to wax eloquent about lost opportunities and Republican and northern blunders; it was quite another to actually sacrifice national sovereignty, to cooperate after 1945 with emerging nations, and to refrain from interventions in Latin America or Asia. When confronted with these choices, Dixie opted for continued and extensive international involvement but on independent, primarily unilateralist terms. In so doing, the South helped establish and sustain a foreign policy pattern that extended well beyond 1973.

CHAPTER 1

Resisting Dependence, 1789–1815

REACTING TO THE PROSPECT of a treaty with Great Britain in 1794, a Virginia Republican declared, "To submit to this and to become the felons of our own constitution, would be synonymous terms. It would be on the one hand, a tyranny unread in the annals of the most despotic government, and on the other, a passive obedience unfound among our African slaves." Other, more prominent Virginians echoed this fear of dependence during the early years of the Republic. Thomas Jefferson was convinced that "dependence begets subservience and venality, suffocates the germ of virtue, and prepares fit tools for the designs of ambition." Although Jefferson referred more to personal than to national liberties, he agreed completely with James Madison, who complained in 1789 that the British had "bound us in commercial manacles, and very nearly defeated the object of our independence." This persistent concern for individual, sectional, and national liberties was not peculiar to the South during the early national period, but the strength and tenacity of these apprehensions were deeply rooted in the southern experience and psyche. Together with the growing influence of party politics, economic considerations, and nascent sectionalism, they provide the keys to understanding Dixie's response to foreign affairs from the 1790s through 1815.[1]

The origins of these attitudes can be traced to the colonial period, during

---

1. Richard R. Beeman, *The Old Dominion and the New Nation, 1788–1801* (Lexington, Ky., 1972), 139 (Va. Republican); Joseph J. Persky, *The Burden of Dependency: Colonial Themes in Southern Economic Thought* (Baltimore, 1992), 35 (Jefferson); Drew R. McCoy, *The Elusive Republic: Political Economy in Jeffersonian America* (New York, 1982), 138 (Madison).

which "liberty" became the region's "central political idea." The southern colonies identified liberty with local control, and they effectively established this control by persistently enlarging the powers of the lower houses of their colonial assemblies. By the 1760s, these lower houses regulated local finances, defined their own memberships, and employed the principle of direct representation to justify their existence. Therefore, as southerners revolted against Great Britain, they were defending de facto liberties embodied in relatively mature and independent political institutions and ideology.[2]

To this political evolution must be added the South's long experience with staple agriculture and production for the market. From early in their history, southerners concentrated more than any other American region on the cultivation of a few staple crops for export. Over the course of the antebellum period, southern economic growth resulted principally from the expanded cultivation and sale of these staples rather than from the development of a more sophisticated industrial or technological infrastructure. This pattern of growth left the South burdened with "semi-colonial economic relations under which increased staple production masked continued structural backwardness." Within this colonial context, coping with both the vagaries of international markets and the alleged conspiracies of merchant factors further sensitized southerners to the value of personal and regional autonomy. On the eve of the American Revolution, Virginia's Tidewater planters complained of "Vassalage & Dependence" and identified debt with the loss of personal liberty, honor, and integrity. Similar expressions of mistreatment by malignant forces from within and beyond the region would echo forth from Dixie well into the twentieth century.[3]

By the time of the Revolution, African American slavery had long been the foundation of this staple agricultural economy. In 1770, black slaves constituted approximately 40 percent of the southern population, and nine times more slaves lived in the southern colonies than in their northern counterparts. Twenty years later, in 1790, the first federal census found one-third of the South's people were black slaves, a proportion that persisted

2. William J. Cooper Jr. and Thomas E. Terrill, *The American South: A History* (New York, 1996), 54 (quote); Jack P. Greene, "The Role of the Lower Houses of Assembly in Eighteenth-Century Politics," *Journal of Southern History* 27 (November 1961): 451–74.

3. Peter Kolchin, *American Slavery, 1619–1877* (New York, 1993), 179 (backwardness); T. H. Breen, *Tobacco Culture: The Mentality of the Great Tidewater Planters on the Eve of Revolution* (Princeton, 1985), 134 (vassalage).

until the outbreak of the Civil War. Owning slaves had become closely identified in Dixie with upward social mobility, and the institution was already tied to westward expansion and viewed as crucial to southern welfare. Given the centrality of slavery to the southern political economy and social system, defending the peculiar institution, often via the vehicle of states' rights, assumed a high priority among southern leaders. According to historian Kenneth S. Greenberg, "From 1776 to 1860 the liberty white southerners celebrated always included the freedom to preserve the slavery of blacks." Ironically, living with the institution of slavery provided a constant, graphic reminder of the dangers of dependence, oppression, and loss of freedom. Slavery was the mirror image of liberty, the "condition most cherished by Southerners."[4]

Taken cumulatively, these colonial experiences rendered southerners particularly receptive to the tenets of republicanism. Adapted from the opposition, or anticourt, groups in Great Britain, the republican vision emphasized the maintenance of civic virtue and the protection of political liberty. As interpreted by the leaders of majority opinion in the South, civic virtue depended upon citizens possessing economic, social, and political freedom. These conditions hinged in turn on the widespread ownership of property within an agricultural society. The alternative of a more urbanized and industrialized society, such as had evolved in Great Britain and would develop in New England, threatened to produce greater disparities of income, impoverished and dependent factory workers, and dangerous concentrations of wealth. The latter led to improper pressures on government and institutional corruption. Rather than expanding through time and enduring such perils of modernization, southern republicans such as Jefferson and Madison advocated expanding through space. They sought to accomplish this by acquiring new agricultural lands and markets and thereby prolonging the nation's status as an overwhelmingly agrarian republic. Although uneasy with certain facets of modernization, southerners were never anticommercial. Rather, theirs was a "hybrid," or "modified," republicanism that equated civic virtue with individual industry and frugality and considered "economic development . . . the precondition of true independence." Finally, southern republicans also stood guard against a host of other potential

4. Cooper and Terrill, *American South,* 92 (1776 to 1860); Kenneth S. Greenberg, *Masters and Statesmen: The Political Culture of American Slavery* (Baltimore, 1985), 87 (slavery and liberty).

abuses of power and threats to political liberties. Like their British counterparts, they were apprehensive of centralized governmental authority, standing armies, public debt, bloated and corrupt bureaucracies, and moneyed aristocracies.[5]

Even as the nation looked ahead in 1789 to a viable and coherent foreign policy under the new Constitution, the South had developed a self-conscious sectionalism derived from these economic, social, and ideological perspectives. In the Virginia ratifying convention, Patrick Henry described "a striking difference, and great contrariety of interests" between the "carrying and productive states." Madison further located southern distinctiveness in the institution of slavery rather than in geographic size or an agricultural economy; the difference between northern and southern states, he argued, arose "principally from the effects of having or not having slaves." Other southerners emphasized the South's lesser population and, hence, minority status in the national legislature. During the debates at the Constitutional Convention, George Mason worried that the "Southern States" would be "the *minority* in both Houses," and in 1790 Governor Henry Lee of Virginia asserted that he could tolerate no arrangement that forced the South to bow before "the rule of a fixed and insolent majority" in the North and East.[6]

5. The literature on republicanism is vast. I have drawn particularly on McCoy, *Elusive Republic;* Lance Banning, *The Jeffersonian Persuasion: Evolution of a Party Ideology* (Ithaca, N.Y., 1978); Banning, "Jeffersonian Ideology Revisited: Liberal and Classical Ideas in the New American Republic," *William and Mary Quarterly,* 3d ser., 43 (January 1986): 1–19; and Lacy K. Ford, "Republican Ideology in a Slave Society: The Political Economy of John C. Calhoun," *Journal of Southern History* 54 (August 1988): 405–24. For the quotes, see Ford, "Republican Ideology," 422, and Cathy Matson and Peter S. Onuf, "Toward a Republican Empire: Interest and Ideology in Revolutionary America," *American Quarterly* 37 (fall 1985): 531. Also useful are Rowland Berthoff, "Independence and Attachment, Virtue and Interest: From Republican Citizen to Free Enterpriser, 1787–1837," in *Uprooted Americans: Essays to Honor Oscar Handlin,* eds. Richard L. Bushman et al. (Boston, 1979), 97–124; Joyce Appleby, *Capitalism and a New Social Order: The Republican Vision of the 1790s* (New York, 1984); Appleby, "Republicanism and Ideology," *American Quarterly,* 37 (fall 1985): 461–73; Appleby, "Republicanism in Old and New Contexts," *William and Mary Quarterly,* 3d ser., 43 (January 1986): 20–34; Daniel T. Jordan, "Republicanism: The Career of a Concept," *Journal of American History* 79 (June 1992): 11–38; James Oakes, "From Republicanism to Liberalism: Ideological Change and the Crisis of the Old South," *American Quarterly* 37 (fall 1985): 551–71; Robert E. Shalhope, "Thomas Jefferson's Republicanism and Antebellum Southern Thought," *Journal of Southern History* 42 (November 1976): 529–56.

6. Jesse T. Carpenter, *The South as a Conscious Minority, 1789–1861: A Study in Political Thought* (1930; reprint, Columbia, S.C., 1990), 8, 9, 26.

Indeed, the geopolitical framework created by the new Constitution combined with these indigenous southern apprehensions and commitment to republican ideology to reinforce the region's sectional perspective. Historian Peter S. Onuf has argued incisively that "both before and after independence, vigilant republicans sought to guard against dangerous concentrations of power." In the absence of a "great metropolis, a privileged central place" that dominated the new nation's wealth and power, the fears of outside domination were "conceptualized in spatial, geographical terms." Southerners and other Americans feared that the essential equality of all parts of the country would be destroyed by "selfish politicians" who "would promote the parochial concerns of one region at the expense of the others." As southerners looked north for such threats after 1789, they identified themselves with legitimate unionism and national interest. It was their equality, liberty, and independence that was synonymous with a correct reading of the Constitution, a healthy political economy, and a viable foreign policy. To the extent that domestic opponents seemed to be allied with foreign threats to southern interests, these adversaries within the United States were similarly viewed as "foreigners."[7]

From the implementation of the new Constitution in 1789 through the War of 1812, these southern fears of dependence translated into aggressive territorial and economic expansion. Both land and markets were deemed crucial to a growing and prosperous agricultural society and economy. Most southerners viewed Great Britain as the primary obstacle to this preferred form of development. Whether intriguing with Native Americans on the frontier, refusing to remove soldiers from American territory, denying the United States a generous commercial treaty, or harassing U.S. trade, the British seemed always to obstruct southern prosperity and independence. As a result, a bitter Anglophobia characterized southern opinion throughout the period, and this hatred and fear of Great Britain frequently translated into support for France, Britain's principal European rival. Southerners also viewed Native Americans as an impediment to expansion into Kentucky, Tennessee, Georgia, and Mississippi. Frontiersmen in these regions ignored governmental policies of restraint and often pursued alter-

7. Peter S. Onuf, "Federalism, Republicanism, and the Origins of American Sectionalism," in *All over The Map: Rethinking American Regions,* Edward L. Ayers et al. (Baltimore, 1996), 13, 15; Onuf, "Thomas Jefferson and the Origins of American Sectionalism" (paper presented at the Southern Historical Association Meeting, Atlanta, Ga., November 6, 1997), 8.

native strategies aimed at Indian removal. Despite such aggressive stands toward both the British and the Native Americans, majority southern opinion never endorsed the creation of a military establishment consistent with such policies. Opposed to a standing army and a genuine oceangoing navy, southerners reluctantly approved of scaled-down frontier forces and vetoed incorporation of state militias into a viable national organization.

These political, economic, and territorial considerations also led to the formation of the nation's first political parties in the early 1790s. Organized initially in the national capital among U.S. congressmen, the party structure was subsequently extended to the states. Supporters of Thomas Jefferson and James Madison and their policies, as well as pro-French Americans, gravitated to the Jeffersonian Republican or Republican Party; backers of Alexander Hamilton, George Washington, and John Adams and their agendas, along with pro-British Americans, adopted the party designation of Federalists. While both parties had national constituencies, over the period from the mid-1790s until 1815, the Republican Party grew dominant in the South and the Federalists for most of these years controlled New England. This partisan political identification in turn led southerners to support Republican foreign policies.

As the First Congress gathered in 1789, a clear majority of southerners continued to view Great Britain as the principal foreign enemy. Much of this Anglophobia carried over from the Revolution. Jefferson observed in 1788, that "history will never relate the horrors committed by the British army in the *southern* states of America," and Madison agreed that "no description" could convey "an adequate idea of the barbarity with which the enemy . . . conducted the war" in the South. Planters remained embittered over the loss of slaves freed by invading British soldiers, and the British refusal to allow American ships and goods entry into its Caribbean possessions angered both Virginia wheat growers and aspiring southern merchants, such as the Blounts of North Carolina. Finally, debts owed to British citizens rankled southerners. To these pre–Revolutionary War obligations, planters had added mounting postwar liabilities.[8]

Indeed, Madison and Jefferson were convinced that ongoing British eco-

8. Lawrence S. Kaplan, *Thomas Jefferson: Westward the Course of Empire* (Wilmington, Del., 1999), 19 (Jefferson); Jerald A. Combs, *The Jay Treaty: Political Battleground of the Founding Fathers* (Berkeley, Calif., 1970), 21 (Madison); Lisle A. Rose, *Prologue to Democracy: The Federalists in the South, 1789–1800* (Lexington, Ky., 1968), 105–6; J. C. A. Stagg, *Mr. Madison's War: Politics, Diplomacy, and Warfare in the Early Republic, 1783–1830* (Princeton, 1983), 14.

nomic domination threatened American political independence and the very survival of the new nation's republican experiment. Madison contended that conducting more than 60 percent of the nation's commerce with the British Empire and depending on the former mother country for the great bulk of America's international credit left Britain with an unacceptable influence over the U.S. economy. This influence circumscribed access to foreign markets, denied the profits that could accrue from the competitive sale of American products, and hindered the growth of an American merchant marine. It also raised the specter of British intervention in domestic politics and the possible promotion of monarchy at the expense of republicanism.

From 1789 through 1794, Madison and Jefferson actively promoted commercial discrimination against the British as the means of escaping this dependent condition and of stimulating American agricultural prosperity. With the meeting of the First Congress, Madison introduced legislation mandating higher tariffs and tonnage duties for countries that had no commercial treaty with the United States. Since the 1778 treaty with France was still in effect, this legislation was aimed unmistakably at Great Britain. Commercial retaliation, Madison and Jefferson argued, would force Britain to treat the United States more fairly and to grant Americans access to the carrying trade of the West Indies. They also anticipated that this legislation would reduce dependence on the British by diverting trade to France and by aiding the construction of American shipping, thereby lessening reliance on British bottoms. Despite the doubts of numerous contemporaries, Madison was confident that the United States could coerce the British. Ironically, he deemed them more dependent on the United States for the "necessaries" of food and raw materials than were Americans on the imports of "superfluities" or manufactured goods from Britain.[9]

The two Virginians never managed to test this formula for greater economic and political independence during the 1790s. Operating from a distinctly different vision for American development, Secretary of the Treasury Alexander Hamilton sought to build the new nation in Britain's image. To fund the national debt and promote a diversified manufacturing economy, he perceived continued access to British credit and the revenues from nondiscriminatory duties on British imports essential. Therefore, Madison's

9. McCoy, *Elusive Republic,* 140 (necessaries); Combs, *Jay Treaty,* 76; Merrill D. Peterson, "Thomas Jefferson and Commercial Policy, 1783–1793," *William and Mary Quarterly,* 3d ser., 22 (October 1965): 584–610; Stagg, *Mr. Madison's War,* 8–16.

legislation and the accompanying threat of commercial war with Great Britain were unthinkable, and Hamilton lobbied artfully against discrimination within both Congress and the Washington administration. Hamilton's decision for a neocolonial economic position within the British Empire was anathema to Madison and Jefferson, and they were further distressed that the New Yorker derived his principal domestic support from northern merchants, bankers, shipping interests, and property owners—in short, from nonagricultural and nonsouthern groups. The Virginia legislature shared these fears and in 1790 warned that Hamilton sought "the prostration of agriculture at the feet of commerce, or a change in the present form of federal government, fatal to the existence of American liberty." From the Virginians' southern vantage point, both national and sectional independence appeared at risk.[10]

Not all southerners adopted the Madison-Jefferson perspective. During the 1780s, the South, particularly North Carolina, Georgia, and South Carolina, had opposed discriminatory tariffs. Southerners feared an over-concentration of power in the Continental Congress, and without a regional merchant marine, they anticipated higher shipping costs for agricultural exports. Congressman William Loughton Smith reiterated the later argument while opposing Madison's discriminatory legislation in 1789–90. Speaking on behalf of both Charleston merchants and British factors, the South Carolina Federalist also warned that New England merchants could provide neither the essential credit nor the all-important international business contacts. Representative James Jackson of Georgia was more blunt. He stressed that British counterdiscrimination would leave southern "produce . . . on our hands" and "annihilate in a great measure" Georgia's and North Carolina's trade in the West Indies. The final House vote on Madison's 1789 bill reflected these Deep South reservations. Six of Georgia's and South Carolina's seven representatives voted against discrimination, while Upper South congressmen from Virginia, North Carolina, and Maryland provided much greater support for Madison's strategy for economic independence.[11]

Over the course of the early 1790s, the great majority of southerners put

10. Alexander DeConde, *Entangling Alliance: Politics and Diplomacy under George Washington* (Durham, N.C., 1958), 49; Carpenter, *South as a Conscious Minority,* 55 (Va. legislature).

11. Combs, *Jay Treaty,* 83; George C. Rogers Jr., *Evolution of a Federalist: William Loughton Smith of Charleston (1758–1812)* (Columbia, S.C., 1962), 173–75; Rudolph M. Bell, *Party and Faction in American Politics: The House of Representatives, 1789–1801* (Westport, Conn., 1973), 135–37 (Jackson).

such reservations aside in favor of Madison's and Jefferson's analysis. Ongoing British depredations against American commerce and territory and the close association of the Federalist Party with British and northern interests seemed to dictate a policy aimed at national independence and regional prosperity. The French Revolution and particularly the outbreak of war between France and Great Britain in 1793 accelerated this conversion process. Within the Washington administration, Secretary of State Jefferson advocated a pro-French neutrality. He urged the president to seek concessions from Great Britain before declaring neutrality, to remain silent concerning American obligations under the Franco-American Alliance of 1778, and to receive and thereby officially recognize any diplomatic representative from the French republic. By leaning toward France, Jefferson hoped to obtain greater independence from Britain. Save the acceptance of a French diplomat, President Washington rejected Jefferson's proposals. Acting instead on Hamilton's advice, he issued a formal declaration of neutrality in April 1793 and thereby continued the country's pro-British economic and political stance. Jefferson condemned the proclamation for offering "our breech to every kick which Great Britain may chuse to give it," and Madison worried that this "plan connecting" the United States with Great Britain constituted "one great leading step towards assimilating our Government to the form and spirit of the British Monarchy."[12]

Although their reasons were less rational and calculating, most southerners agreed with Jefferson's and Madison's pro-French orientation. To the southern public, the war pitted an old enemy against an old friend—a longstanding monarchical nemesis against the world's newest republic. Southerners expressed this preference unmistakably in their lavish greeting for Edmond-Charles Genet, French minister to the United States, who landed in Charleston, South Carolina, on April 8, 1793. After cordial treatment from important South Carolinians, Genet received enthusiastic receptions at every town on his three-week overland journey to Philadelphia. Even such normally staunch Federalist enclaves as Richmond and Alexandria demonstrated great enthusiasm for the gallant Frenchman.[13]

Genet quickly discovered that neither southern public sympathy nor Jefferson's search for economic autonomy translated into toleration of a chal-

---

12. Combs, *Jay Treaty*, 110 (Jefferson); Beeman, *Old Dominion*, 128–29 (Madison).

13. Harry Ammon, *The Genet Mission* (New York, 1973), 45, 52, 54; Beeman, *Old Dominion*, 121; John H. Wolfe, *Jeffersonian Democracy in South Carolina* (Chapel Hill, 1940), 73–75.

lenge to Washington's neutrality policy. When the minister recruited volunteers on American soil and dispatched privateers from American ports, Jefferson and Madison disavowed his actions. Virginians more generally retained their sympathy for France and hatred of Great Britain but were unprepared for war with the latter. Hamilton seized on Genet's indiscretions as an opportunity to discredit not only the minister but also Madison and Jefferson and their pro-French foreign policy. At the treasury secretary's instigation, meetings to denounce Genet's actions and to endorse Washington's stand on neutrality were organized in New York, New Jersey, and Delaware and also in Maryland and Virginia.[14]

The first of these Federalist-directed meetings in the South assembled in Richmond on August 17, 1793, and others followed in Williamsburg, Norfolk, Fredericksburg, and Petersburg. Prodded by Madison and Jefferson, members of the emerging Republican Party countered with gatherings in Caroline, Shenandoah, Albemarle, and Culpeper Counties. These Republican gatherings produced resolutions in accord with Madison's instructions to distinguish carefully between Genet and support for the French Revolution and to criticize Federalist dependence on the British; more extreme Republicans went even farther and endorsed Genet as well. By late fall 1793, neither side had clearly won this battle of resolutions in the public arena, but the criticism had so offended President Washington that his commitment to a pro-British foreign policy was reinforced rather than weakened.[15]

This commitment grew especially unpopular in the South the following year when a combination of British actions produced the "War Cloud of 1794." Ignoring the stipulations of the peace settlement of 1783, British troops continued to occupy a series of forts on U.S. soil and to collaborate with Native Americans living around the Great Lakes to block American settlement and control. Britain's maritime policies in its war with France also injured U.S. interests. The British rejected the American contention that goods carried on neutral, or "free," ships also became neutral; instead, they enforced their "Rule of 1756," which forbade trade in time of war that had been illegal in time of peace. Acting on these premises in late 1793, the British navy seized 250 American ships bound for the French West Indies with French goods. And in an even more galling affront to U.S. sovereignty and self-respect, British naval vessels regularly stopped American ships to

14. Beeman, *Old Dominion*, 132–33; Ammon, *Genet Mission*, 133–42.
15. Rose, *Prologue to Democracy*, 74–77; Beeman, *Old Dominion*, 126–37.

search for alleged deserters from His Majesty's Service. These searches often resulted in American citizens being wrongfully impressed into the British navy.[16]

These British actions reinforced southern Anglophobia. The naval blockade hindered the sale of southern flour and grain, and the British practice of impressing American seamen impinged on the livelihood of southern merchants and shipowners. Norfolkers complained that the British were also impressing slaves owned by Virginians, and British search parties frequently came ashore in pursuit of deserters. One of these forays led to the arrest of the captain of the Norfolk Town Guard. Such actions confirmed the fears of persons already uneasy about British domination and incursions on their liberties. Residents of both Baltimore and Norfolk responded during the spring of 1794 by attacking and on occasion tarring and feathering both British sailors and pro-British Americans.[17]

Farther south, prominent public figures in both North and South Carolina grew increasingly hostile toward Great Britain. In North Carolina, leading merchants, such as Thomas Blount, had anticipated that a strengthened government under the Constitution of 1787 would bring access to the West Indies, and these ambitious businessmen joined Virginia farmers in blaming Britain for the ongoing restrictions. Less prominent men gathered in Halifax, Edenton, and Warrenton taverns to drink to French victories. In South Carolina, perceived British impositions led Edward Rutledge, Charles C. Pinckney, and their influential families to break with the Washington administration and to weaken the strongest Federalist outpost in the South. The Rutledge-Pinckney forces resented not only the British maritime depredations but also the economic and political influence of British merchants in Charleston. These merchants had intervened actively in state politics and helped elect William L. Smith, one of Hamilton's principal spokesmen in the U.S. House of Representatives, to four terms. Hostility toward the British was complemented by pro-French enthusiasm, which led to the founding of a French theater in Charleston and, according to one observer, to the "tri-colored cockade of France" becoming "the great badge of honour" and "'Vive la republique Francaise!' the universal shout."[18]

16. Samuel Flagg Bemis, *Jay's Treaty: A Study in Commerce and Diplomacy* (New Haven, 1962), 253.

17. Beeman, *Old Dominion*, 125; DeConde, *Entangling Alliance*, 98.

18. Rose, *Prologue to Democracy*, 103–12; Delbert H. Gilpatrick, *Jeffersonian Democracy in North Carolina, 1789–1816* (New York, 1931), 63; Wolfe, *Jeffersonian Democracy in South Carolina*, 76 (cockade).

When news of the British seizure of American ships and negotiations with the Indians on the northwest frontier reached Philadelphia, Madison was again attempting to enact his policy of commercial discrimination. To avert the complete embargo of British goods and a possible war, Hamilton and the Federalists recommended dispatching John Jay, chief justice of the Supreme Court, on a special diplomatic mission to settle the differences between the two nations. Federalists also advocated enhanced military preparedness through the construction of six frigates and the raising of a regular army of twenty thousand and a militia numbering eighty thousand.[19]

Southern Republicans denounced both recommendations. Jefferson dismissed the Jay mission as humiliating, as purely political, and as a Federalist attempt to "bind up the hands" of Congress "from ever restraining the commerce of their patron nation." Madison and William Branch Giles of Virginia led the opposition to an augmented military. They did so for two reasons. First, Madison was convinced that the Republican policy of commercial discrimination would force British concessions without war and thereby safeguard national autonomy. Second, the Republicans worried that an enlarged military provided a crucial component in the growth of centralized authority and heavier taxes—a pattern that traditionally had threatened local autonomy and individual liberties. In 1792, southerners had opposed movement toward a national militia with federal authority over the arming of soldiers and calls to active duty. They preferred instead the continued predominance of state authority. A standing army was even more objectionable. Madison warned the delegates to the Constitutional Convention, "A standing military force, with an overgrown Executive will not long be safe companions to liberty. . . . Throughout all Europe, the armies kept up under the pretext of defending, have enslaved the people." Republicans agreed grudgingly to a frontier constabulary of three thousand to five thousand in the 1793–96 period; both the cost and the fear of a centralized military force rendered more ambitious Federalist initiatives unpalatable.[20]

The results of Jay's negotiations confirmed southern apprehensions. The New York Federalist preserved peace with the world's principal economic and military power while securing British evacuation of the forts in the

19. Combs, *Jay Treaty*, 123–24, 128–29.

20. Ibid., 128 (Jefferson); Lawrence Delbert Cress, *Citizens in Arms: The Army and the Militia in American Society to the War of 1812* (Chapel Hill, 1982), 112, 37; Walter LaFeber, "The Constitution and United States Foreign Policy," *Journal of American History* 74 (December 1987): 697 (Madison).

Northwest and gaining commercial access to India. These were no mean accomplishments, but other portions of the treaty infuriated the South. By granting most-favored-nation status to the British and agreeing not to raise tonnage duties on British ships for twelve years, the Jay Treaty rejected the Jeffersonian policy of commercial discrimination and left intact the nation's neocolonial relationship with Great Britain. By referring pre–Revolutionary War debts to a mixed tribunal and providing for possible recovery of property confiscated from Loyalists, the agreement threatened potential restitution and loss of land throughout Virginia and North Carolina. By ignoring the question of slaves confiscated or freed by the British during the Revolution, the treaty compounded the discomfort of those fearing payments to British citizens and former Loyalists. By limiting access to the British West Indies to American ships of seventy tons or less and specifically excluding cotton and sugar, Jay's negotiations were particularly harmful to the South's staple export trade. By effectively surrendering the principle of "free ships" make "free goods" and essentially agreeing to the British interpretation of maritime law, the compact violated the spirit, if not the letter, of the Franco-American Alliance of 1778.[21]

Shrill protests reverberated throughout the South. In Charleston, South Carolina, unruly mobs dragged a British flag about the town before burning it outside the British consulate, and they later constructed a gallows from which were hung effigies of Jay, John Adams, and William L. Smith. In Camden, a public meeting resolved that "war, with all its horrors, ought to be preferred to peace upon such disgraceful and dishonorable terms." More significantly, virtually all of South Carolina's political elite either condemned the treaty or fell into a sullen silence, unwilling to defend Jay's efforts. Only Federalist congressmen Smith and Robert Goodloe Harper braved the crowds to argue the commercial and strategic merits of a close Anglo-American connection. Public meetings throughout North Carolina castigated Jay's efforts, and the pact found few defenders in Virginia. Jefferson characterized the treaty as an "execrable thing," as "nothing more than a treaty of alliance between England and the Anglomen of this country against the Legislature & people of the United States." Denunciations rang forth from every commercial center save Alexandria, and the Virginia legis-

21. Thomas J. Farnham, "The Virginia Amendments of 1795: An Episode in the Opposition to Jay's Treaty," *Virginia Magazine of History and Biography* 75 (January 1967): 75–82; Combs, *Jay Treaty*, 137–88.

lature adopted resolutions criticizing both the treaty and President Washington. Some Virginians even toasted "A speedy Death to General Washington," and "Atticus" in the *Alexandria Gazette* concluded simply, "YES, Sir, you have bitched it; you have indeed put your foot in it Mr. Jay."[22]

When this public clamor failed to dissuade the Senate from ratifying the treaty in June 1795, Madison and Jefferson sought to derail the agreement by denying the necessary funding in the House. In August the Virginia General Assembly voted to propose four amendments to the Constitution as a means of forcing the House to debate and vote on the treaty. The strategy of forcing debate succeeded, but the attempt to block funding failed narrowly. The sectional distribution of the 51 to 48 vote was revealing. Of the 51 yeas only 5 were from the South, and 35 of the 48 nays were southern. The vast majority of southerners agreed with Jefferson and Madison that the treaty embodied an ongoing alliance between northern Federalists and Great Britain at the expense of the South's interests and independence.[23]

Although ratification of the Jay Treaty defused the crisis with Great Britain, the agreement heightened tensions with France. The French deemed U.S. concession on the "free ships, free goods" doctrine and acceptance of Britain's broad definition of contraband to be violations of the Franco-American agreements of 1778. In retaliation, France captured 316 American ships in the West Indies by June 1797 and refused to grant diplomatic credentials to Charles C. Pinckney, who had been sent by President Washington in 1796 to replace James Monroe as the U.S. minister in Paris. Seeking to mend diplomatic relations and to avoid war, President John Adams dispatched a special mission composed of Pinckney; Elbridge Gerry, a Massachusetts Republican; and John Marshall, a Virginia Federalist. The three Americans arrived in Paris in October 1797 but had no success in initiating serious negotiations with Charles-Maurice de Talleyrand, the French foreign minister. Instead, Talleyrand's agents, subsequently identified as X, Y, and Z, informed the Americans that bribes to the foreign minister and loans to France were prerequisites to discussion of the nations' differences. De-

22. Wolfe, *Jeffersonian Democracy in South Carolina,* 85 (Camden); Rogers, *Evolution of a Federalist,* 280 (Jefferson); DeConde, *Entangling Alliance,* 115 (Atticus), 133 (death); Beeman, *Old Dominion,* 139–46; Rose, *Prologue to Democracy,* 115–18, 120–22.

23. Bell, *Party and Faction,* 146–47; Farnham, "Virginia Amendments of 1795," 82–88; Rose, *Prologue to Democracy,* 146 n. 2; Beeman, *Old Dominion,* 146, 150; Paul A. Varg, *New England and Foreign Relations, 1789–1850* (Hanover, N.H., 1983), 28. The 35 no votes included 2 from Kentucky.

spairing of substantive talks, the Americans rejected the conditions in April 1798, and Marshall and Pinckney returned to the United States.[24]

News of the XYZ affair sent shock waves through American politics. Federalists seized on the incident and the national outrage as the occasion for making France rather than Britain the national enemy. During the summer of 1798, Congress adopted John Adams's recommendations to arm American merchant ships, construct additional naval vessels, and resist French warships and privateers. Congress also voted to add ten thousand soldiers to the regular army and to raise a ten-thousand-man provisional force for use in case of invasion. To these military measures, Federalists added the Alien and Sedition Acts, which made criticism of the government grounds for deportation or imprisonment. Hamilton and his most extreme followers unsuccessfully sought to use the conflict to secure a declaration of war against France, a formal alliance with Great Britain, and imperial expansion at the expense of Spain in Louisiana and the Southwest.[25]

Based almost exclusively on this foreign policy crisis and the ensuing "quasi," or limited, naval war with France in the West Indies, southern Federalists significantly rejuvenated their activities and influence. Throughout the region, Federalists emphasized French corruption and the threat to American independence and accentuated the defense of national honor and autonomy. Virginia Federalists declared that Americans had to choose "between submission to the will of a foreign nation, and the maintenance of our independence," and the state's first Federalist newspaper depicted the party as "the only all-efficient Guardian of National Independence." Ironically, the party's temporary successes reflected the same southern fear of dependence and loss of liberties to which the Republicans customarily appealed. In addition to the threat of dependence, southern Federalists warned of a possible French attack from Saint-Domingue against the adjacent American coast. Were the French to seize Savannah or Charleston, Robert Goodloe Harper was convinced "they might do immense mischief" by inciting slave rebellions in an "ideal location for guerrilla activities." The excitable Harper further highlighted the alleged threat from "Southern Jacobins" supposedly prepared to aid the French.[26]

24. Alexander DeConde, *The Quasi-War: The Politics and Diplomacy of the Undeclared War with France, 1797–1801* (New York, 1966).

25. Cress, *Citizens in Arms*, 137; Varg, *New England and Foreign Relations*, 33.

26. Rose, *Prologue to Democracy*, 174–80, 184–85, 194–95, 214, 223 (Virginia quotes); Joseph W. Cox, *Champion of Southern Federalism: Robert Goodloe Harper of South Carolina* (Port Washington, N.Y., 1972), 126–27 (Harper); Stanley Elkins and Eric McKitrick, *The Age of Federalism*

The reversal of Federalist political fortunes was evident in the post–XYZ affair congressional elections. South Carolina's delegation went from 3 Republicans and 3 Federalists to 5 Federalists and 1 Republican, North Carolina's from 9 Republicans and 1 Federalist to 7 Federalists and 3 Republicans, Georgia's from 2 Republicans to 2 Federalists, and Virginia's from 13 Republicans and 4 Federalists to 9 Republicans and 8 Federalists. Collectively, Federalists captured 22 of 38 congressional seats in 1798–99. The North Carolina legislature's 51 to 38 endorsement of President Adams and his policies further demonstrated the newly established Federalist dominance. And in graphic illustrations of the popular reaction, Charleston residents raised $100,000 in the summer of 1798 to build the sloop-of-war *John Adams*, and a North Carolina militia company of 7,294 men unanimously signed a petition volunteering their services.[27]

Politically moderate, most southern Federalists identified more closely with the Adams than the "High" or Hamiltonian wing of the party. They endorsed the breaking of diplomatic relations with France and the measures for military preparedness but preferred ongoing efforts at negotiation rather than all-out war, and their anti-French diatribes were not equivalent to a pro-British stance or sympathy for an Anglo-American alliance. Nor were they enthusiastic over the Alien and Sedition Acts. For example, the same North Carolina legislature that had endorsed Adams by 51 to 38 censured the Alien and Sedition Acts by 58 to 21. Once again, southern fears for personal liberties and centralized government proved bipartisan.[28]

Southern Republicans continued to act from this perspective. Blaming the Federalists and the Jay Treaty for the nation's difficulties with France, the Republicans supported Adams's decision to send a special diplomatic mission. When it ended disastrously, Republicans adopted the Federalist stance relative to Britain four years earlier—they condemned French actions but warned that war would be a calamity. Jefferson and Madison continued to view British monarchy and imperialism as the principal threats to Ameri-

---

(New York, 1993), 597–99, 645; Thomas M. Ray, "'Not One Cent for Tribute': The Public Addresses and American Popular Reaction to the XYZ Affair, 1798–1799," *Journal of the Early Republic* 3 (winter 1983): 391, 393, 399, 401, 407.

27. Bell, *Party and Faction*, 255–59; John W. Kuehl, "Southern Reaction to the XYZ Affair: An Incident in the Emergence of American Nationalism," *Register of the Kentucky Historical Society* 70 (January 1972): 29–36; Rose, *Prologue to Democracy*, 176; Wolfe, *Jeffersonian Democracy in South Carolina*, 121–22; Ray, "'Not One Cent for Tribute,'" 407.

28. DeConde, *Quasi-War*, 213, 261; Rose, *Prologue to Democracy*, 199–203, 211.

can autonomy and republicanism and France as the primary international counterweight to the British. Therefore, an alliance with Britain or war with France was unthinkable. The former, declared James Monroe, would render the United States "a feeble contemptible satellite" of the former mother country; the latter could only weaken France's position as a balancer of British power.[29]

Jefferson and Madison also responded to the Alien and Sedition Acts by writing the Virginia and Kentucky Resolutions, which declared the Federalist laws unconstitutional. While these resolutions raised the specter of a major constitutional crisis and even secession, the Republican leaders had sought to channel the rising protests of some of their more extreme followers into the legal and political realm. Students at the College of William and Mary had burned President Adams in effigy, and the Virginia legislature had established an armory in Richmond to resist any Federalist-led army's entrance into the commonwealth. This domestic discord and southern Republican protests helped forestall High Federalist hopes for a declaration of war against France in 1798.[30]

Reinforcing the southern Republican break on policy was the influence of moderate southern Federalists, especially George Washington, the newly named commander of the army. Still the most influential person in the region, Washington rejected Hamilton's suggestion to tour the South and stimulate war sentiment in 1798 and vetoed his former treasury secretary's plan for a frontier war against the Spanish. When President Adams responded to the startling domestic strife and reciprocated French overtures for peace by opting for a second and ultimately successful diplomatic mission, Washington endorsed the decision. He was joined by John Marshall, Patrick Henry, and the great majority of southern Federalists. When combined with the adamant opposition of southern Republicans, Dixie's Federalists played a crucial role in avoiding a declaration of war against France and alliance with Great Britain and in securing a satisfactory end to the "quasi-war."[31]

Ironically, these actions led to the effective demise of southern Federalism. The party's transitory revival had resulted directly from the crisis with

29. Lawrence S. Kaplan, *"Entangling Alliances with None": American Foreign Policy in the Age of Jefferson* (Kent, Ohio: 1987), 92–93 (quote); Beeman, *Old Dominion*, 169–70, 176–77.

30. DeConde, *Quasi-War*, 91–92, 107, 192; Rose, *Prologue to Democracy*, 221.

31. DeConde, *Quasi-War*, 107, 113, 122–23, 179, 183.

France. As the crisis subsided, the Federalist-sponsored standing army, higher taxes, and Alien and Sedition Acts became fatal political liabilities. Long-standing southern fears of centralization and loss of personal and sectional liberties resurfaced with a vengeance. Republicans scored solid victories in state legislative races in Virginia, Georgia, Kentucky, and Tennessee in 1799, and Jefferson carried the South handily in the 1800 presidential election.[32]

Upon grasping the reins of government, Jefferson and Madison sought to consolidate and perpetuate their conception of a proper republican political economy. They continued to consider individual liberty, industry, and loyalty to government dependent on prosperity—on access to land and markets for agricultural exports. Land and markets in turn provided the essential foundation for an agricultural republic free from economic dependence on Great Britain and the liabilities that accompanied the growth of manufacturers. In short, economic and territorial expansion remained central. The Republican leadership also retained its abhorrence of high taxes, government bureaucracy, and a strong military. These concerns led to a reduction of the regular army to only thirty-five hundred, an ongoing refusal to reform and invigorate the militia, and the construction of a navy of coastal gunboats rather than oceangoing vessels. This feeble military establishment ultimately jeopardized portions of the Jeffersonians' ambitious expansionist agenda and the safeguarding of the republican experiment.[33]

Significantly, Jefferson did not reduce the power of the executive in foreign policy. Rather his actions in ordering naval attacks on the Barbary pirates, purchasing the Louisiana Territory, and enforcing the Embargo Act of 1807 enhanced presidential power over foreign policy. His actions were consistent with a general southern inclination to endorse consolidated national authority in foreign (versus domestic) affairs and to recognize and follow the president as the principal national leader in the international realm. Jefferson had argued in 1786 that a revised constitution needed "to make us one nation as to foreign concerns, & keep us distinct in Domestic ones," and he saw himself as the nation's "prime mover" in the foreign

32. Rose, *Prologue to Democracy*, 227–28, 236, 249, 259–60, 267, 280–82, 287; James H. Broussard, *The Southern Federalists, 1800–1816* (Baton Rouge, 1978), 68.

33. McCoy, *Elusive Republic*, 136–208; Cress, *Citizens in Arms*, 151–71; Stagg, *Mr. Madison's War*, 130–35; Bradford Perkins, *Prologue to War: England and the United States, 1805–1812* (Berkeley, Calif., 1961), 50–51.

arena. Over the subsequent 173 years, majority southern opinion continued to accord presidents this position.[34]

Jefferson's assertive philosophy was crucial to the Louisiana Purchase, the era's greatest expansionist achievement. Skillfully exploiting Napoleon's difficulties in Europe and Haiti and the bellicosity of Federalists and settlers in the Mississippi Valley, Jefferson secured this immense tract at bargain rates without resorting to force. His concerns and objectives spoke directly to the essence of Republican foreign policy, and they provide insights into the South's ongoing support for this policy. Most immediately, Jefferson and the residents of the Mississippi Valley, especially Kentucky and Tennessee, sought to safeguard use of the Mississippi River and the right of deposit and transshipment of goods at New Orleans. Both the navigation of the river and the use of the port were crucial to the export of agricultural produce and hence to the prosperity and independence associated with viable republicanism. Jefferson cogently asserted that since the "produce of three-eights of our territory" currently passed through New Orleans and "more than half our whole produce . . . and inhabitants" would soon be dependent on Mississippi River commerce, any country controlling this key port was America's "natural and habitual enemy." By removing the French from the country's western border, Jefferson also reduced the need for either foreign alliances or a stronger military and seemed to secure a virtually unlimited supply of land for agricultural expansion and the maintenance of an agrarian republic. Finally, the persistent concern for the protection of slavery once more motivated southern Republicans. Madison explained that France's presence along the Mississippi would create "inquietude . . . in the Southern States, whose numerous slaves [had] been taught to regard the French as the patrons of their cause."[35]

For a South sensitive to its liberties, all of these considerations elicited support. Not even Jefferson's choice of the land over a strict interpretation of the Constitution or his assertion of strong executive authority in estab-

34. Carpenter, *South as a Conscious Minority*, 35 (Jefferson); Kaplan, *Jefferson*, 128 (prime mover).

35. John R. Nelson Jr., *Liberty and Property: Political Economy and Policymaking in the New Nation, 1789–1812* (Baltimore, 1987), 139 (Jefferson); James E. Lewis Jr., *The American Union and the Problem of Neighborhood: The United States and the Collapse of the Spanish Empire, 1783–1829* (Chapel Hill, 1998), 26 (Madison); Alexander DeConde, *This Affair of Louisiana* (New York, 1976); McCoy, *Elusive Republic*, 195–208; Robert W. Tucker and David C. Hendrickson, *Empire of Liberty: The Statecraft of Thomas Jefferson* (New York, 1990), 87–135.

lishing a temporary government in Louisiana occasioned criticism beyond the handful of surviving southern Federalists. In addition to recognizing these benefits, southerners acted from party loyalty and the assumption that westward expansion benefited them at the expense of the Northeast. New western states seemed destined to be Republican. Northern Federalists shared and voiced the same assumption in criticizing the wisdom and the constitutionality of the purchase. Stephen Higginson of Massachusetts complained, "The Virginia faction have certainly formed a deliberate plan to govern and depress New England; and this eagerness to extend our territory and create new States is an essential part of it." Writing to the *Boston Columbia Centinel*, "Fabricus" agreed and worried that "imperial *Virginia*" was attempting to confirm "dominion over the rest of the states."[36]

Ironically, Toussaint-Louverture and his army of former black slaves had decisively aided Jefferson by repulsing French efforts to reassert control over Santo Domingo (renamed Haiti in 1804). The French defeat in 1803 dashed Napoleon's hopes of establishing an empire in Louisiana and convinced him to sell the magnificent tract to the United States. U.S. policies toward the ongoing Haitian revolution after 1791 had derived from a combination of racial assumptions, economic interest, and realpolitik, and revealed much about the increasingly important place of slavery in the South's response to national diplomacy.

Southerners had been immediately apprehensive that the slave rebellion might offer an explosive example to their own chattels. In 1791 Governor Charles Pinckney of South Carolina warned President Washington that if left unchecked, the black revolt would become a "flame which will extend to all the neighboring islands, and may prove not a very pleasing or agreeable example to the Southern States." Washington agreed, deeming the revolt "alarming" and overseeing the extension of some $726,000 in aid to the French planters' unsuccessful attempts to check the uprising. Following the destruction of Cap-Français, the island's principal port, in 1793, fifteen thousand French refugees fled to the United States, often with their slaves in tow. Their emigration reinforced southern trepidation. Five years later when Congress adopted legislation opening trade with Toussaint, Jefferson

36. Reginald Horsman, "The Dimensions of an 'Empire for Liberty': Expansion and Republicanism, 1775–1825," *Journal of the Early Republic* 9 (spring 1989): 8 (Higginson); Jerry W. Knudson, "Newspaper Reaction to the Louisiana Purchase: 'This New, Immense, Unbounded World,'" *Missouri Historical Review* 58 (January 1969): 199 (Fabricus); see also Varg, *New England and Foreign Relations*, 43.

expressed these fears while worrying, "We may expect therefore black crews, and supercargoes and missionaries thence into the southern states. . . . If this combustion can be introduced among us under any veil whatever, we have to fear it." Acting on these fears, several southern states passed laws forbidding the entry of free blacks or slaves from the West Indies. The ominous example of this successful black revolution, combined with unsuccessful contemporary attempts at rebellion in the southern states, prompted southerners to solidify the institution of slavery and to reject any public discussion of its validity or standing.[37]

Despite the South's racial fears, economics and power politics most influenced U.S. policy. After the Federalists had negotiated between alternating British and French attacks on U.S. commerce through much of the 1790s, the Adams administration cooperated with London in opening trade with Haiti in 1799. This trade furnished Toussaint valuable matériel for his campaign, and U.S. naval ships aided the black leader by capturing vessels en route to ports controlled by his rivals. During these years, southern Federalists such as Robert Goodloe Harper of South Carolina favored Santo Domingo's independence from France, but opposed extending any official U.S. recognition of that independence. Southern Republicans also rejected any formal recognition because of their pro-French leanings and their fear of the precedent of a black nation achieving independence.

By the time Jefferson took office in 1801, Toussaint had established control over Haiti. The U.S. president was unwilling to continue cooperation with the hated British or to aid a black rebellion so overtly. To avoid endangering French ratification of the Treaty of Mortefontaine in 1800 ending the "quasi-war," Jefferson recognized French sovereignty over Santo Domingo and in 1801 suggested to the French chargé d'affaires that the United States could not abide "another Algiers in the seas of America." But Jefferson, consistent with his pursuit of the broadest possible export trade and his understanding of the implications of the struggle in Haiti for the French emperor's Louisiana aspirations, did not impede crucial U.S. commerce with Toussaint, nor did he extend aid to Napoleon when the French armies sought to reconquer the colony. Only after the French forces had fallen to

37. Timothy M. Matthewson, "George Washington's Policy toward the Haitian Revolution," *Diplomatic History* 3 (summer 1979): 324 (Pinckney), 327 (Washington); Winthrop D. Jordan, *White over Black: American Attitudes toward the Negro, 1550–1812* (Chapel Hill, 1968), 381 (Jefferson); see also Donald R. Hickey, "America's Response to the Slave Revolt in Haiti, 1791–1806," *Journal of the Early Republic* 2 (winter 1982): 361–79.

their black adversaries and yellow fever in 1803 and Haiti had declared its independence in 1804, did Jefferson endorse the Logan Bill interdicting all commerce sailing to rebel-controlled ports. Jefferson hoped that this measure would induce Napoleon to persuade the Spanish to sell the Floridas and to assuage the strong anti-Haitian temper of southern opinion, but he also realized that the law was unenforceable.[38]

While southerners agreed with Jefferson's pursuit of trade and the Floridas, Dixie effectively forestalled recognition of Haiti. Senator James Jackson of Georgia not only endorsed the embargo, he further recommended that the Haitian state be "destroyed." Jefferson's son-in-law, Congressman John W. Epps, was aghast that "some gentlemen would declare St. Domingo free." To do so meant endorsing a "system that would bring immediate and horrible destruction on the fairest portion of America." Horrified at even the suggestion of recognition, Epps agreed with Jackson that "the Negro government should be destroyed." But Epps broke with most southern Republicans by denouncing the Logan Bill as cravenly subservient to France. He cautioned his father-in-law that signing the bill would "seal the degradation of your country. . . . While we thus yield obedience to France, we shall become the object of her contempt, and the pawn of Europe." Although Jefferson shared Epps's fear of dependence, the president recognized that the Logan Bill imposed no such condition; moreover, the temporary appearance of subservience could be tolerated if it helped obtain the Floridas.[39]

Jefferson and Madison coveted the Floridas from the same ideological, racial, and strategic perspectives that had led to the acquisition of Louisiana; access to land and markets was again their primary consideration. Non-American ownership of West Florida endangered control of the lower Mississippi and unfettered access to New Orleans. In addition, the important Pearl, Perdido, and Alabama Rivers flowed through Spanish territory to the Gulf (the Alabama to the significant port of Mobile), and goods shipped over these waterways incurred a burdensome 12 percent duty. Residents of Georgia and the Orleans and Mississippi Territories complained of Spanish complicity in Indian raids, agonized over the refuge afforded runaway slaves

38. Timothy M. Matthewson, "Jefferson and Haiti," *Journal of Southern History* 61 (May 1995): 209–48; Merrill D. Peterson, *Thomas Jefferson and the New Nation: A Biography* (New York, 1970), 749.

39. Charles C. Tansill, *The United States and Santo Domingo, 1798–1873: A Chapter in Caribbean Diplomacy* (1938; reprint, Gloucester, Mass., 1967), 105 (Jackson and Epps); Jordan, *White over Black*, 385 (Epps); Peterson, *Jefferson*, 824 (Epps); Kaplan, *Jefferson*, 139–42.

by the Native Americans, and considered expulsion of the Spanish and Indians both a vital security issue and essential to the opening of new agricultural lands.[40]

Acting on these interests, Jefferson threatened the Spanish and unsuccessfully solicited French aid in attempts to purchase the Floridas. In 1805 the president secured a $2 million appropriation from Congress designed to both bribe the French and to compensate the Spanish for all lands east of the Perdido, but to no avail. Not until 1810 was Madison able to exploit an American-inspired revolt in Baton Rouge to seize West Florida to the Perdido, and he did so via the constitutionally dubious route of a secret executive proclamation. Two years later, Madison and Secretary of State James Monroe disavowed the capture of Amelia Island and the seizure of Saint Augustine, directed by Governor George Mathews of Georgia. Imminent war with Great Britain was most responsible for this restraint, but northern opposition to what was seen as a purely southern project also influenced the decision. As Secretary of the Treasury Albert Gallatin warned, war to capture East Florida would "disgust every man north of Washington." Acquisition of the remainder of Florida was postponed until 1819, but relentless pressure from southerners against the Spanish borderlands and covert Jeffersonian machinations were characteristic of other actions, such as U.S. meddling in the Green Flag revolt in Texas from 1810 to 1814.[41]

Unlike Jefferson's purchase of Louisiana, his pursuit of Florida provoked shrill dissent from parts of the South. Southern Federalists denounced the ill-concealed $2 million appropriation designed for bribing France in 1805 and questioned the constitutionality of Madison's annexation of West Florida in 1810; however, southern Federalist representation had shrunk to only one congressman by 1805 and therefore offered no obstacle to Republican policy. More troublesome were the objections of John Randolph and his "old Republican" allies. Randolph and his small band of fellow ideologues, particularly John Taylor of Virginia and Nathaniel Macon and Richard Stanford of North Carolina, were acutely sensitive to any hint of executive centralization or corruption, and they located both in Jefferson's scheme for obtaining West Florida. With Randolph leading the opposition, Jefferson

40. Robert V. Haynes, "The Southwest and the War of 1812," *Louisiana History* 5 (winter 1964): 43–44; McCoy, *Elusive Republic*, 207–8; Tucker and Hendrickson, *Empire of Liberty*, 138; Frank L. Owsley Jr. and Gene A. Smith, *Filibusters and Expansionists: Jeffersonian Manifest Destiny, 1800–1821* (Tuscaloosa, 1997), 21–26.

41. Owsley and Smith, *Filibusters and Expansionists*, 80.

was forced to obtain more than half of the 77 to 54 majority for the $2 million allocation from northern Republicans, and Virginia's delegation divided 12 to 10 against the president. This House vote proved anomalous; the old Republicans commanded "scant public support," and the measure passed easily in the Senate with only 2 southerners and 1 Kentuckian in the negative column. As was true of virtually all Republican administration foreign policy objectives, the South provided solid partisan support.[42]

The same Jeffersonian concern for national autonomy and prosperity and their crucial link to national honor and the preservation of Republican Party predominance provided the bases for the United States response to war in Europe after 1803. With the resumption of fighting between Britain and France, American exports rebounded dramatically from a post-1801 slump. By 1804 foreign sales had risen to $77 million and in 1806 exceeded $100 million for the first time. Both the British and the French considered this American trade detrimental to their war efforts. In 1806 the British outlawed the American practice of carrying goods from the French West Indies to the United States for a brief stop, acquiring the status of the goods having been produced domestically, then sailing on to Europe. Napoleon in turn condemned any ship coming to the Continent after stopping in England.[43]

While Jefferson and Madison contemplated a response to these infringements on American commerce, the *Leopard,* a British naval vessel, attacked the U.S.S. *Chesapeake* in June 1807 off the Virginia coast, killing three Americans, wounding eighteen, and taking four alleged British deserters into custody. The *Chesapeake* affair was only the latest and most outrageous example of the British practice of impressing Americans into the royal navy. The following November, Britain enacted its most comprehensive set of orders in council for the governance of international commerce. Moving beyond the ban on the carrying trade from the French West Indies and the sale of obvious contraband, the orders declared that direct trade in all American domestic products would have to pass through Britain and pay a tax before going to France. Moreover, a prohibitive duty excluded cotton completely. When Napoleon further tightened the "continental system," American exporters and shipowners were left with few agreeable alternatives.[44]

42. Broussard, *Southern Federalists,* 70–71, 81; Norman K. Risjord, *The Old Republicans: Southern Conservativism in the Age of Jefferson* (New York, 1965), 25 (scant), 48–50, 287 n. 23.

43. Clifford L. Egan, *Neither Peace nor War: Franco-American Relations, 1803–1812* (Baton Rouge, 1983), 6.

44. Perkins, *Prologue to War,* 200; Egan, *Neither Peace nor War,* 101–2.

Possessing neither the military capacity nor the inclination for war, Jefferson and Madison resorted to economic coercion as the means for protecting American commerce, sailors, and sovereignty. They first tried the Embargo Act of 1807, which prohibited the export of American goods and precluded American shipping beyond the coastal trade. When this measure proved unenforceable and failed to alter British policies, it was replaced by the Nonintercourse Act of 1809. Even less enforceable and no more influential with the British, this law allegedly halted all trade with the belligerents while resuming commerce with the remainder of the world. Finally in 1810, the Republicans resorted to Macon's Bill No. 2, which ended all restrictions, but promised to reapply them to the belligerent that refused to drop its restrictions on American trade. The most feeble and embarrassing of the three attempts at coercion, the Macon Bill also came to naught, leaving Madison and the Republicans with the choice of submission or war. The president and his party chose war.

The essential feature of this Republican choice was the gradual consolidation of a southern consensus on the impossibility of maintaining national prosperity, honor, and autonomy without resorting to force. In the House vote of June 1812, the South Atlantic states of Virginia, North Carolina, South Carolina, and Georgia provided 31 of the 79 votes for war and only 8 of 49 against. Kentucky and Tennessee added 8 for and none against, and Maryland voted 6 to 3 with the majority. Unformed in 1805, this consensus had evolved as southerners came increasingly to fear British neocolonial control, to blame economic depression on British trade restrictions, to see war as a way to banish the Spanish and the Native Americans from the Old Southwest, and to accept party discipline in time of crisis.[45]

Southern ambivalence was evident in 1805 as Congress debated how best to respond to the British *Essex* decision outlawing the carrying trade of goods from the French West Indies. Representative Andrew Gregg of Pennsylvania offered a resolution calling for a complete boycott of British goods. Although this proposal was consistent with Madison's long-standing contention that the United States possessed the economic leverage to coerce the British, many southerners demurred. They distinguished between the carrying trade and direct trade in domestic goods with Britain and asserted that only the latter was crucial to sustaining the sale of southern agricultural products. In 1805, to-

45. Bradford Perkins, ed., *The Causes of the War of 1812: National Honor or National Interest* (New York, 1962), 9.

bacco, rice, tar, pitch, and resin had constituted $11 million of $22.7 million in American exports to Great Britain, and 30 percent of the South's cotton was exported to the former mother country. Representative Peter Early of Georgia concisely summarized the southern opposition: "Do not gentlemen ask too much when they require us to jeopardize the whole agricultural interest of the nation for the sake of that which in our opinion produces no benefit to that interest? Is it not expecting too much of us to suppose that we will consent to surrender the certainty of good markets and high prices for our produce, and brave danger of total stagnation, for the purpose of embarking on a hazardous contest with Great Britain for the carrying trade?"[46]

Even if the carrying trade did not warrant such a risk, most southerners concluded that the *Chesapeake* affair and the 1807 British orders in council did. The kidnaping of U.S. citizens from a government naval vessel consti-tuted a blatant disregard for American sovereignty, and the British maritime regulations effectively reimposed pre-Revolution colonial restrictions. Like Madison, Jefferson was confident that Britain could not survive without U.S. food and raw materials, and he responded by proposing and receiving con-gressional authorization for the embargo. In the absence of a firm response, the president feared that all American commerce would fall under British control and that the new nation would invite international contempt. Na-tional autonomy and honor compelled action. Jefferson recognized that the embargo actually aided Napoleon, but he deemed Great Britain the more im-mediate threat to American security and hoped that the French leader might at last be persuaded to pressure Spain into yielding the Floridas. In August 1807 Jefferson observed, "I never expected to be under the necessity of wishing success to Bonaparte. But the English being equally tyrannical at sea as he is on land & that tyranny bearing on us in every point of either honor or inter-est, I say, 'down with England' and as for what Bonaparte is then to do with us, let us trust to the chapter of accidents. I cannot, with the Anglomen, pre-fer a certain present evil to a future hypothetical one."[47]

Although the embargo failed either to coerce the British or to cultivate the French, it proved ruinous to southern commerce. Prices for staple crops plunged precipitously, and complaints of business stagnation and failure arose from throughout the region. In Norfolk, Richmond, and Petersburg,

46. Burton Spivak, *Jefferson's English Crisis: Commerce, Embargo, and the Republican Revolu-tion* (Charlottesville, Va., 1979), 41.

47. Kaplan, *"Entangling Alliances with None,"* 116.

the tobacco market collapsed; in Charleston, the nation's fifth largest city, commercial activity ground to a halt; and in Georgia, a congressman complained that his "nearly 100 bales of cotton . . . commonly worth 10,000 dollars, [were] now worth little more than nothing." While deeply resented, this economic dislocation harmed primarily staple planters and farmers and merchants; the majority of southern farmers still practiced subsistence agriculture and suffered fewer ill effects. This buffered economic impact, together with the influence of party regularity, persisting Anglophobia, and the sense that the embargo offered the best means for protecting the nation without war, produced toleration of the measure as a "necessary burden." South Carolinian Wade Hampton observed that it was "difficult to imagine the pecuniary effect and the individual distress, occasioned by the embargo. . . . Yet, notwithstanding this distress, . . . there is everywhere an acquiescence in the measure proceeding from a confidence in the government." In contrast to other sections of the nation, there were virtually no antiembargo meetings in the South; "from Virginia to Georgia there was silence."[48]

By early 1809, the embargo's deleterious effect on the American economy and its failure to bring the British to heel had elicited protests from northern Republicans and threats to party unity. While circumstances dictated a change in policy, southerners were more resistant to repeal of the Embargo Act than were representatives from New England or the Middle States. Ultimately eighteen southerners cast the crucial votes for repeal, but the debate also demonstrated that southerners were most inclined to replace the embargo with more aggressive measures, such as letters of marque and reprisal or the seizure of British territory and ships as hostages or prizes. Led by Wilson Cary Nicholas and John G. Jackson of Virginia and Thomas Blount of North Carolina in the House and William Branch Giles of Virginia and William Crawford of Georgia in the Senate, southern Republican "militants" attempted unsuccessfully to convince their more conservative colleagues of the need for a firmer stand. Nonintercourse provided the compromise between those seeking to continue the embargo and those endorsing limited warfare.[49]

48. Broussard, *Southern Federalists,* 96 (distress), 108 (burden and silence); Wolfe, *Jeffersonian Democracy in South Carolina,* 222 (Hampton); Egan, *Neither Peace nor War,* 94, 100–1.

49. Reginald C. Stuart, "James Madison and the Militants: Republican Disunity and Replacing the Embargo," *Diplomatic History* 6 (spring 1982): 145–67; Ronald L. Hatzenbuehler and Robert L. Ivie, *Congress Declares War: Rhetoric, Leadership, and Partisanship in the Early Republic* (Kent, Ohio, 1983), 102–3.

Over the ensuing three years, the majority of southerners gradually came to agree with the militants and in so doing forged the vote for war in 1812. Several considerations prompted the formation of this prowar coalition. Residents of South Carolina, Kentucky, Tennessee, the Orleans and Mississippi Territories particularly, and southerners more generally attributed their economic difficulties after 1807 primarily to British trade restrictions. As prices for staple crops such as cotton, tobacco, and hemp steadily eroded, southerners blamed the duties on exports to the British Isles and British interference with the flow of American goods to the Continent. John C. Calhoun declared that southerners "see in the low price of the produce, the hand of foreign injustice," and Nathaniel Macon of North Carolina viewed the war's "object . . . to obtain the privilege of carrying the produce of our lands to a market." But, as historian Drew R. McCoy has demonstrated, this concern for markets did not derive merely from the narrow objective of profits. It was also crucial to the maintenance of the viable agricultural political economy for which Jefferson and Madison had been working since the Revolution: "Restricted markets inevitably meant glutted markets, which in turn meant falling prices, idle American farmers, and a debilitating social malaise. To this extent, indeed, the basic integrity of America's republican political economy was at stake."[50]

Georgians and settlers in the Orleans and Mississippi Territories also deemed Spanish control of the Floridas as obstructing the free flow of commerce to the Gulf, and Orleans Governor W. C. C. Claiborne even eyed the seizure of Cuba in a war against Britain and her ally Spain. Cuba, Claiborne asserted, constituted "the real mouth of the Mississippi" and controlled the "trade of the Western States." These southwesterners also railed at alleged Spanish incitement of the Indians and anticipated the removal of additional Native Americans from the path of white settlement. Thus, the southern perspective once again fused commercial and landed expansion.[51]

These concerns for markets and land blended easily into more general southern Republican anxieties over national honor and autonomy. In the face

50. Reginald Horsman, *The Causes of the War of 1812* (New York, 1962), 232, 236 (Calhoun and Macon); McCoy, *Elusive Republic*, 234; Roger Brown, *The Republic in Peril: 1812* (New York, 1971), 70. See also Margaret K. Latimer, "South Carolina—A Protagonist of the War of 1812," *American Historical Review* 61 (July 1956): 914–29; George Rogers Taylor, "Agrarian Discontent in the Mississippi Valley preceding the War of 1812," *Journal of Political Economy* 39 (August 1931): 471–505.

51. Haynes, "Southwest and the War of 1812," 50 (Claiborne); Brown, *Republic in Peril*, 127.

of ongoing British abuses, most southerners gradually concluded that the only choices were war or submission and accompanying disgrace for both their party and country. John Clopton of Virginia articulated this sentiment in April 1812: "The outrages in impressing American seamen exceed all manner of description. Indeed the whole system of aggression now is such that the real question between G. Britain and the U. States has ceased to be a question merely relating to certain rights of commerce . . . it is now clearly, positively, and decidedly a *question of independence,* that is to say, whether the U. States are really an independent nation." Mississippian George Poindexter agreed that the United States could "submit to abject, servile colonization, or call into action the national energies to vindicate the rights, and redress the wrong and insults which have been inflicted on us by that haughty and faithless government." Speaking for the Madison administration in June 1812, Secretary of State James Monroe asserted that since only "unconditional submission" would satisfy the British, "the only remaining alternative, was to get ready for fighting, and to begin as soon as we were ready."[52]

Acting from these motives, together with the pressures of party loyalty and regularity, representatives from below the Potomac voted 45 to 11 for war in the House and 12 to 2 in the Senate. Still, they did so reluctantly. William B. Bibb of Georgia spoke for the majority of his southern colleagues in admitting "great difficulty in bringing my mind to the 'sticking place.'" He and others worried that the United States was aiding Napoleon and that war would result in the very growth of the military and centralized bureaucracy that so frightened adherents of republicanism. The newly converted southern conservatives also apprehended that war would bring great destruction and burdensome national debt. Easily the most shrill exponent of these fears was John Randolph, who bitterly opposed the war and further charged that the conflict was unnecessary, was sure to cause additional damage to the U.S. economy, and was being fought for the unsavory objective of conquering Canada. Although Randolph counted no more than two or three allies in the Congress and failed to convince his own constituents, many of his strictures differed only in degree from the reservations of the southern majority. This ongoing ambivalence was evident in southern re-

52. Norman K. Risjord, "1812: Conservatives, War Hawks, and the Nation's Honor," *William and Mary Quarterly,* 3d ser., 18 (April 1961): 205 (Clopton); Egan, *Neither Peace nor War,* 142 (Poindexter); Brown, *Republic in Peril,* 45–46 (Monroe).

fusal to vote for a frigate navy in 1812 and the region's aversion to paying the taxes necessary to wage the conflict. Within Virginia and North Carolina, at least a quarter of the citizens, primarily Federalists and Old Republicans, opposed the decision for war.[53]

In the last analysis, Dixie's determination to avoid submission and dependence and its devotion to the Republican Party overcame these reservations. Ironically, while war went far toward redeeming national honor and self-respect, neither the South nor the nation escaped Britain's neocolonial economic grasp. Both the panics of 1819 and 1837 revealed the United States's continuing dependence on British credit and capital, and resentment of Britain's economic influence remained prominent in the South. Moreover, the war stimulated the growth of manufactures, helped produce a strengthened and more centralized national financial structure, and spurred government-sponsored internal improvements—all of which seemed antithetical to Jefferson's and Madison's prewar vision of the ideal republican political economy.[54]

Despite these rather mixed results, the war's "most decisive and most significant victory" came in the South with Andrew Jackson's defeat of the Creek Indians. Throughout the Jefferson and Madison years, Americans in the Old Southwest had pressed into Creek lands, calling for the construction of roads and defying feeble administration efforts to restrain them. With the outbreak of war, southerners hoped to expel Spain from West Florida and to gain unobstructed access to the Gulf, but they feared that Britain might employ its alliance with Spain to occupy the region and to present a much greater obstacle to American ambitions. Whether opposing the actual Spanish presence or a potential British invasion, the Madison ad-

53. Brown, *Republic in Peril,* 66–67 (quote); Perkins, *The Causes of the War of 1812,* 9 (vote by states); Ronald L. Hatzenbuehler, "Party Unity and the Decision for War in the House of Representatives, 1812," *William and Mary Quarterly,* 3d ser., 29 (July 1972): 367–90; Risjord, "Conservatives, War Hawks, and the Nation's Honor," 196–210. See also Sarah McCulloh Lemmon, *Frustrated Patriots: North Carolina and the War of 1812* (Chapel Hill, 1973), 6–23; James Wallace Hammack Jr., *Kentucky and the Second American Revolution: The War of 1812* (Lexington, Ky., 1976), 5–15.

54. Drew R. McCoy, "An Unfinished Revolution: The Quest for Economic Independence in the Early Republic," in *The American Revolution: Its Character and Limits,* ed. Jack P. Greene (New York, 1987), 146; Steven Watts, *The Republic Reborn: War and the Making of Liberal America, 1790–1820* (Baltimore, 1987), 277–82, 305–9, 317–18.

ministration and General Jackson deemed it essential to defeat anti-American Creek and Seminole townships.[55]

As with the South's responses to the "quasi-war" with France, the Haitian revolution, the Louisiana Purchase, and the persistent pursuit of the Floridas, southerners again sought to safeguard their peculiar institution. They were disturbed by the southern "underground railroad," which carried escaped slaves to safety among the Seminoles in Florida. These black Muscogulges and their "maroon" settlements embodied an unacceptable example that southern slaves might seek to emulate. Fearful of taking their slaves into areas near these settlements, southerners urged Jackson to capture or kill these blacks while waging the larger war against the Creeks. The freed slaves understood that American expansion into Alabama, Georgia, and Florida threatened both their liberty and survival, and they fought fiercely as a part of the Indian resistance. Southerners were greatly relieved when U.S. forces destroyed an armed maroon settlement at the "Negro Fort" at Prospect Bluff in West Florida in August 1816 and drove the surviving black Muscogulges into central Florida. Jackson's victory on the Tallapoosa River in March 1814 accomplished the larger goal of removing the Creeks as an impediment to subsequent expansion. His defeat of the British ten months later at New Orleans precluded a possible British occupation and eliminated potential British objections to the validity of the Louisiana Purchase or to Madison's annexation of portions of West Florida in 1810.[56]

The removal of the Creeks and the British from the path of southern empire symbolized the South's persistent pursuit of economic and territorial expansion, designed to ensure personal, sectional, and national liberty. Conditioned by its successful assertion of local legislative autonomy during the colonial period, by its early and ongoing commitment to staple agriculture for export, and by the centrality of slavery to its economy and society, the South viewed the world through the lens of republicanism and favored a foreign policy aimed at achieving liberty and avoiding domination by other sections or nations. When combined with its predominant loyalty to the Republican Party, these influences led the South to furnish the principal backing for Jefferson's and Madison's efforts to escape British domination and to employ

55. Stagg, *Mr. Madison's War,* 352–62 (quote), 485–86; Robert V. Remini, *Andrew Jackson and the Course of American Empire, 1767–1821* (New York, 1977), 187–223, 298–300; Owsley and Smith, *Filibusters and Expansionists,* 84–102.

56. J. Leitch Wright, *Creeks and Seminoles: The Destruction of the Muscogulge People* (Lincoln, Neb., 1986), 163–65, 190, 197–99.

territorial and commercial expansion as the means to safeguard the existence of an agrarian republic. Even as southern Republicans provided the legislative majorities leading to war with Great Britain in 1812, their fears of an overly strong central government and military blocked adequate military preparation. Indeed, the pattern of the South furnishing first Jefferson and then Madison decisive majorities for their foreign policies but remaining ambivalent about central authority and military power would be repeated a century later under the first post–Civil War southern president, Woodrow Wilson.

In adopting these foreign policy positions, the South frequently stood in direct contrast to New England. The South's northern neighbors agreed on the appropriateness of a republican vision but foresaw a political economy based on banking, shipping, manufacturing, and free labor rather than on agriculture, commerce, and slavery. This alternative vision led northerners to be much less anxious about domination by Great Britain and much more solicitous of the close economic ties needed to guarantee access to British capital and markets. These conservative Yankees were also much more apprehensive of the French Revolution and Napoleon and considered France the greater threat to U.S. independence. Finally, while sharing the South's desire for commercial expansion, New England came to oppose the acquisition of new territory when, according to John Cabot of Boston, it became "obvious that the influence of our part of the Union must be diminished by the acquisition of more weight at the other extremity."[57]

Cabot was correct. Prior to 1815, the South had definitely benefited from territorial expansion. Even as southerners worried about sectional autonomy and liberty during these years, they were very much in the majority. Even as southern attitudes on slavery hardened and southern willingness to tolerate discussion of the peculiar institution declined, slavery only occasionally emerged as a predominant consideration in foreign policy. All this would change with the debate over Missouri's entry into the Union in 1819, which abruptly dashed southern assumptions that new territories would automatically enhance the South's political power or political economy. Rather, both the debate and the compromise demonstrated that slavery and the South's autonomy and ongoing political power were "inextricably bound up with the future path of territorial admissions."[58]

57. Varg, *New England and Foreign Relations,* 43.
58. Robert E. May, "Epilogue to the Missouri Compromise: The South, the Balance of Power, and the Tropics in the 1850s," *Plantation Society* 1 (June 1979): 216; Horsman, "Dimensions of an 'Empire for Liberty,'" 19–20.

CHAPTER 2

Lurching toward the Abyss, 1815–1861

WHILE CONDEMNING the northern-inspired tariff bill of 1824, John Randolph of Roanoke characterized the measure as "an attempt to reduce the country south of Mason and Dixon's line, and east of the Allegheny Mountains, to a state worse than colonial bondage; a state to which the domination of Great Britain was, in my judgment, far preferable." In the 1840s, Peter V. Daniel, also a Virginian and an associate justice of the U.S. Supreme Court, employed similar language to reject the Wilmot Proviso's recommendation to exclude slavery from territory acquired in the Mexican War: The measure embodied "an insulting exclusiveness or superiority on the one hand, and denounces a degrading inequality or inferiority on the other." In effect southerners were being told, "You are not my equal, and hence are to be excluded as carrying a moral taint with you." In 1851 an Alabamian decried the exclusion of slavery from the nation's trans-Mississippi empire as an assertion "that a free citizen of Massachusetts was a better man and entitled to more privileges than a free citizen of Alabama." He demanded to know whether Dixie would "submit to be bridled and saddled and rode under whip and spur" or southerners would defend "the great doctrine of *Equality*: Opposition to ascendancy in any form, either by classes, by way of monopolies, or of sections, by means of robbery." In the years from 1815 to the outbreak of the Civil War in 1861, southern concerns about liberty, independence, honor, and centralized authority continued to condition the section's attitudes toward U.S. foreign relations.[1]

1. Joseph J. Persky, *The Burden of Dependency: Colonial Themes in Southern Economic Thought* (Baltimore, 1992), 54 (Randolph); for Daniel, see Kenneth S. Greenberg, *Masters and*

In the four decades preceding secession, "republicanism" remained the formative context for southern politics. Even as political and economic conditions changed in the 1820s and after the second American party system of Jacksonian Democrats versus Whigs evolved, much of the language and substantive assumptions of the pre-1815 polity retained a decisive influence. Southerners continued to evidence acute concern for personal and regional liberty and independence, to worry that centralized authority jeopardized their liberties, to denounce political corruption and the abuses of factions or irresponsible parties, and to brook no assaults on their honor. While Democrats and Whigs interpreted these concepts quite differently than did their Jeffersonian and Hamiltonian forebears, intense political partisanship provided another crucial facet of the southern foreign policy perspective well into the 1850s. During that crucial decade, the second American party system disintegrated as sectionalism and the debate over the extension of slavery came to dominate national and southern perspectives. Neither southern republicanism, political partisanship, nor rabid sectionalism produced anticommercial attitudes. To the contrary, hard work and individual economic independence were viewed as essential to maintaining civic virtue and regional autonomy.

Given the South's economic expansion after 1815, an anticommercial bias would have been decidedly incongruous. Tobacco production in Virginia, North Carolina, Maryland, Kentucky, and Tennessee increased from 200 million pounds in 1839 to 347 million pounds in 1859, an increase of more than 73 percent. Sugar yields climbed from 30 million pounds in the mid-1820s to 244 million in 1860, more than a 713 percent jump. But, of course, cotton was king, and its growth dwarfed all other crops—exploding from 335 bales in 1820 to 4.5 million in 1860. The bulk of this raw cotton was exported in 1859–60, with 2.34 million bales going to Great Britain and 1.07 million bales to continental Europe, compared to the .96 million bales sold to domestic manufacturers. Crucial to Dixie's agricultural expansion was the simultaneous growth of the institution of slavery. From 1800 to 1860, the slave population expanded from 1 to 4 million, and slaves constituted 33 percent of the region's overall population throughout the period. This dramatic

Statesmen: The Political Culture of American Slavery (Baltimore, 1985), 140, and Chaplain W. Morrison, *Democratic Politics and Sectionalism: The Wilmot Proviso Controversy* (Chapel Hill, 1967), 65; J. Mills Thornton III, *Politics and Power in a Slave Society: Alabama, 1800–1860* (Baton Rouge, 1978), 58 (Alabamian).

growth of staple agriculture reinforced republicanism's rationale for landed and commercial expansion. Ideological goals of personal liberty and civic virtue and the accompanying pursuit of personal and sectional prosperity and autonomy dictated ever larger territorial acquisitions and export markets.[2]

The crisis over Missouri's entry into the Union served to crystallize many of these southern perspectives. The furor arose in February 1819 in response to New York representative James Tallmadge Jr.'s amendments aimed at blocking Missouri's entry into the Union as a slave state. Tallmadge and his supporters challenged both southern interests and honor and in so doing expressed long-standing northern resentments. Southerners were told that slavery was "abhorrent to every noble and honorable feeling" and "contrary to the spirit of our republican institutions." But northern declarations were not solely humanitarian. New York senator Rufus King denounced the practice of counting three-fifths of the slaves in determining representation in Congress and votes in the electoral college. He declared that this provision of the Constitution gave the South an additional twenty representatives and electors and that the "extension of this disproportionate power to the new states" such as Missouri "would be unjust and odious." It would deprive northerners of all "political power or influence in the Union. The slave region will parcel out the great offices, will determine all questions," and will "remain our Masters."[3]

Southerners also understood the implications of containing the expansion of slavery. For the first time since the American Revolution, territorial expansion threatened to come at Dixie's expense. If the federal government could bar slavery from Missouri, it would set an injurious precedent for southern interests and simultaneously signal the strengthening of the federal government at local expense. The *Richmond Enquirer* asserted that the Tallmadge amendments would block southern access to the New West; were this strategy successful, "'the sceptre will depart from Judah:' and Virginia influence . . . will be heard of no more." Charles C. Pinckney of South Carolina dismissed the professed northern concern for "liberty, humanity, or

2. Douglas R. Egerton, "Markets without a Market Revolution: Southern Planters and Capitalism," *Journal of the Early Republic* 16 (summer 1996): 207–21.

3. Charles S. Sydnor, *The Development of Southern Sectionalism, 1819–1848* (Baton Rouge, 1948), 122 (contrary); for King, see William W. Freehling, *Secessionists at Bay, 1776–1854*, vol. 1 of *The Road to Disunion* (New York, 1990–), 148, and Glover Moore, *The Missouri Controversy, 1819–1821* (1953; reprint, Gloucester, Mass., 1967), 58.

religion"; Tallmadge and his cohorts acted instead from the "love of power" and the aim of controlling the "honors and offices of the Government." And Freeman Walker of Georgia declared that "to expect such submission from the free born sons of America, upon whose birth the genius of liberty smiled, . . . 'Tis to expect from freedmen the conduct of slaves."[4]

This ominous sectional confrontation was averted when Maine applied for statehood, thereby facilitating a compromise that incorporated Missouri as a slave state and Maine as a free state. Effected in early 1820, this arrangement also stipulated that slavery would be excluded from the remainder of the Louisiana Purchase north of 36°30'. Southerners voted almost unanimously against the Tallmadge amendments and almost unanimously in favor of the overall settlement, but were much less united on the 36°30' provision. Dissenters argued that Missouri was being purchased at a dear price. Arkansas was the only prospective slave state south of this boundary, while several free states could be formed from the area north of the line. This portion of the compromise passed the House by 134 to 42, with the South opposed 35 to 23. Subsequent developments through 1861 confirmed the dissenters' fears when Minnesota, Iowa, and ultimately Kansas became free states and easily outweighed the entry of Arkansas.[5]

The vote on the 36°30' boundary embodied the diverse southern responses elicited by the Missouri crisis. Accustomed to dominating government during the Virginia Dynasty, southerners recognized that greater northern population would lead to control of the House of Representatives. This prospect prompted the South to pursue a balance of power by retaining parity in the Senate. Southerners also shuddered at northerners linking the moral condemnation of slavery to their political arguments against the addition of new slave states. Most southerners were as yet unprepared to defend slavery as a positive good or a perpetual institution. Instead, they responded apologetically and propounded arguments that foreshadowed debates in the 1840s. Led by Representative John Tyler of Virginia, they asserted that the expansion or diffusion of slavery would lessen racial tensions, promote re-

4. Sydnor, *Development of Southern Sectionalism*, 128 (*Enquirer* and Pinckney); Michael A. Morrison, *Slavery and the American West: The Eclipse of Manifest Destiny and the Coming of the Civil War* (Chapel Hill, 1997), 50 (Walker); Robert E. May, "Epilogue to the Missouri Compromise: The South, the Balance of Power, and the Tropics in the 1850s," *Plantation Society* 1 (June 1979): 201–25.

5. *Annals of Congress*, 16th Cong., 1st sess., 1587–88; Don E. Fehrenbacher, *The South and Three Sectional Crises* (Baton Rouge, 1980), 18–19.

form, and speed the institution's demise. But even as he articulated the diffusion argument, Thomas Jefferson perceived the potentially disastrous implications of the sectional confrontation over expansion. He likened the northern attack to a "fire bell in the night," which had "awakened and filled me with terror. I considered it at once as the death knell of the Union." Congressman Thomas W. Cobb of Georgia stated his fear: "We have kindled a fire which all the waters of the ocean cannot put out, which seas of blood can only extinguish." President James Monroe agreed it was "evident, that the further acquisition of territory, to the West and South, involves difficulties of an internal nature which menace the Union itself." Perhaps, he theorized, "no step" should be taken "in that direction, which is not approved by all the members, or at least a majority of those who accomplished our Revolution."[6]

Even as southerners displayed apprehension over future territorial expansion and its implications for the institution of slavery and the regional balance of power, they simultaneously moved to expel Native Americans and to consolidate formal control over all lands east of the Mississippi and subsequently of Arkansas and Texas. Although historians have long been reluctant to view native-settler interactions as a facet of U.S. foreign relations, the United States negotiated more than 350 formal treaties with Native Americans between 1776 and 1871. These treaties not only duplicated in form those concluded with European states, they also served as the "vehicle" for expanded "colonial empire." Indeed, the southern arguments for seizing tribal lands paralleled the arguments for holding allegedly inferior African Americans in bondage and foreshadowed the imperial ideology subsequently directed at Mexicans, Spaniards, Cubans, Puerto Ricans, and Filipinos. Native Americans, like other less-powerful groups who possessed territory coveted by white Americans, were declared racially inferior and incapable of productive use of the land. Waddy Thompson of South Carolina, who served as U.S. minister to Mexico in the early 1840s, articulated the southern view of nonwhites, be they Native Americans, African Americans, or Mexicans. He predicted that "the Indian race of Mexico" would "recede before us," just as "our own Indians" had done. Thompson further described blacks in Mexico as "the same lazy, filthy, and vicious creatures that they inevitably become where they are not held in bondage," and the general

---

6. Sydnor, *Development of Southern Sectionalism,* 131 (Jefferson and Cobb); Harry Ammon, *James Monroe: The Quest for National Identity* (New York, 1971), 444 (Monroe).

Mexican population as "lazy, ignorant, and, of course, vicious and dishonest."[7]

Southern incursions upon tribal lands and successful demands for support from Washington paralleled the formation of European empires. Actions on the periphery greatly influenced (even periodically determined) imperial decision making in the capitol. White southerners on the frontier were "the actual empire builders," and it was ultimately their determination to have "all of the land and none of the Indians" that dictated the policy of removal applied from Florida through Texas. This southern hunger for Indian land reflected Dixie's "republican" concern for acquiring additional agricultural resources, its economic desire to raise more cotton, and its political drive to organize states in Mississippi, Alabama, Louisiana, Arkansas, and Texas. Slavery was integral to both the economic and political motivation to acquire these lands and to the ability of southern whites to exploit them profitably. Ironically, black chattels provided much of the labor that enabled southerners to argue that they used the land more constructively than Native Americans.[8]

In the wake of the War of 1812, southern developments set the tone for U.S. Indian policy. More than sixty thousand Native Americans inhabited the Southeast, and the Mississippi Territory's twenty-three thousand Native Americans nearly equaled the North's total Native American population. General Andrew Jackson spearheaded this southern campaign. Charged with negotiating peace with the Creeks following the Battle of Horseshoe Bend in 1814, Jackson exacted 23 million acres from his dispirited foes in August of that year. Over the next six years, Old Hickory forced agreements upon the Cherokees, Chickasaws, and Choctaws and opened another 27 million acres—or most of Alabama, western Tennessee, and southern Mis-

7. John R. Wunder, *"Retained by the People": A History of American Indians and the Bill of Rights* (New York, 1994), 18 (vehicle); Reginald Horsman, *Race and Manifest Destiny: The Origins of American Racial Anglo-Saxonism* (Cambridge, Mass., 1981), 98–116, 190–207, 212 (Thompson); Horsman, "American Indian Policy and Manifest Destiny," *University of Birmingham Historical Journal* 11 (1968): 128–40; see also Arthur N. Gilbert, "The American Indian and United States Diplomatic History," *History Teacher* 8 (February 1975): 229–41; James O. Gump, *The Dust Rose Like Smoke: The Subjugation of the Zulu and the Sioux* (Lincoln, Neb., 1994).

8. Horsman, *Race and Manifest Destiny,* 105 and 199 (quotes); Randolph B. Campbell, *An Empire for Slavery: The Peculiar Institution in Texas, 1821–1865* (Baton Rouge, 1989), 59–61, 63; Theda Perdue, *Slavery and the Evolution of Cherokee Society, 1540–1866* (Knoxville, Tenn., 1979), 40–41.

sissippi—to white settlers and speculators. The 1817 agreement with the Cherokees established the precedent for "removal" by calling for the Native Americans to be compensated "acre for acre" with lands west of the Mississippi for the territory forfeited in Georgia, Tennessee, and Alabama. Jackson deemed the "Principle Established" of "great importance" compared to the "cession of land," and he boasted of opening the "whole southern country." According to historian Robert V. Remini, Jackson had "assembled a veritable Kingdom. The Cotton Kingdom!"[9]

As Jackson moved from military to political battlefield during the 1820s, southerners maintained the pressure for removal. In Georgia, Governor George M. Troup defied federal authority and the threat of federal military intervention while forcing the Creeks to surrender the last remnants of their territory. In Alabama, Governor John Murphy and the legislature extended the state's sovereign jurisdiction over Creek lands and prohibited the Native Americans from hunting, trapping, or fishing on lands "to which the Indian title had been extinguished." And in 1827, Mississippi congressman William Haile summoned a meeting of other southern representatives from North Carolina, Georgia, Florida, Tennessee, and Alabama who had called for complete Indian removal from the Southeast.[10]

While alternately pressuring the federal government to pursue that end or acting unilaterally in the face of contrary national policy, southerners repeatedly linked their actions to the states' rights philosophy employed to defend slavery. Alabamian Dixon Hall Lewis declared "locality the proper measure of jurisdiction" and warned that if Congress could "invade the jurisdiction of a State" on behalf of Native Americans, it could by "a similar exercise of municipal power . . . say that Negroes shall not be slaves." Still clinging to his nationalist perspective, John C. Calhoun decried those southerners who were combining "the Slave with the Indian question, in order, if possible, to consolidate the whole South."[11]

When virtually the entire South voted to elect Andrew Jackson president and helped return Democratic congressional majorities in 1828, the U.S.

9. Robert V. Remini, *Andrew Jackson and the Course of American Empire, 1767–1821* (New York, 1977), 306, 331, 335. See also Grace Steel Woodward, *The Cherokees* (Norman, Okla., 1963), 159, passim.

10. Michael D. Green, *The Politics of Indian Removal: Creek Government and Society in Crisis* (Lincoln, Neb., 1982), 146.

11. Green, *Politics of Indian Removal*, 146–47 (Dixon); Charles G. Sellers, *The Market Revolution: Jacksonian America, 1815–1846* (New York, 1991), 272 (Calhoun).

government adopted a decidedly southern Indian policy. Jackson agreed completely with his fellow southerners regarding the racial inferiority of Native Americans and the necessity of forcing them to emigrate west of the Mississippi. Practical politics also played a crucial role. One historian has characterized Jackson's victory as a "southern mandate for Indian removal," and the new president certainly moved to compensate the southern wing of the party. In addition, when Jackson decisively rejected South Carolina's call for nullification of federal tariff laws, Indian policy provided an opportunity for reasserting his commitment to states' rights.[12]

Soon after his inauguration in March 1829, Jackson warned the southern tribes, "The arms of this country can never be employed, to stay any state of this Union, from the exercise of those legitimate powers which attach, and belong to their sovereign character." The following year, secretary of war and fellow Tennessean John Eaton elaborated: "Congress has no power over the subject [Indian affairs]. Your Great Father has none. It belongs to the State in which your lands are situated, to regulate and direct all affairs within her limits; and nothing can prevent it." Acting on these assumptions, the Jackson administration offered no opposition when Georgia, Alabama, and Mississippi extended state jurisdiction over Indian lands and deprived Native Americans of political, civil, and property rights or when whites swarmed over Indian lands, seizing them by force and fraud. When the U.S. Supreme Court overruled Georgia's claim of sovereignty over the Cherokees, Jackson refused to enforce this rebuke to states' rights.[13]

Nor was the administration's policy confined to passive toleration of actions on the periphery of the empire. Jackson also dispatched emissaries to urge the Indians of the Southeast to move west, and most important, the administration sponsored and enforced the Indian Removal Act of 1830. With Tennessee allies of the president chairing both the House and Senate Committees on Indian Affairs and Jackson marshaling strict Democratic Party discipline, the measure passed the Senate 28 to 19 and the House 102 to 97 in consistent party votes. When viewed in sectional terms, the South and West aggressively supported the bill and the North and East opposed it. Southern proponents of removal reiterated their states' rights perspective, sounded the section's usual determination to maintain equality with the

---

12. Green, *Politics of Indian Removal,* 155.

13. Ronald N. Satz, *American Indian Policy in the Jacksonian Era* (Lincoln, Neb., 1975), 13 (Jackson); Green, *Politics of Indian Removal,* 163 (Eaton).

North, and charged northerners with attempting to forestall Dixie's territorial unity. According to the editor of the *Charleston Southern Patriot,* "One of the reasons why certain people of the North are so strongly opposed to the Indian emigration . . . is that it will give the Southern and Southwestern states . . . an influence in the councils of the Nation which they do not now possess, while their territory is inhabited by savages."[14]

Armed with this legislation empowering the president to exchange public lands west of the Mississippi River for lands held by Native Americans in the East and aided by the relentless pressure of southern state governments and settlers, the Jackson administration negotiated nearly seventy treaties with Indian groups—a record of formal diplomatic interaction far surpassing any other single presidency. Almost forty-six thousand Indians were driven west, leaving behind about 100 million acres of land for white ownership, settlement, and cultivation. When added to the other Indian lands acquired by the federal government after the War of 1812 and sold cheaply to southern whites, this territory constituted a substantial subsidy to "the expansion of the cotton industry and the slave system along with it." The acquisition of this portion of the nineteenth-century American empire had proven of great benefit to the South.[15]

The same imperial dynamic and ultimate displacement of Native Americans by aggressive southern whites and their black slaves unfolded in Arkansas and Texas. Treaties with the Cherokees in 1817 and the Choctaws in 1820 led to the resettlement of more than three thousand Cherokees and ceded approximately five counties of fertile farmland to the titular ownership of the Choctaws in the Arkansas Territory. The white response was immediate and shrill. Arkansans demanded that these "numerous hoards of Savages" be expelled and that the title to the Choctaw reserve be returned to Arkansas and the white settlers already occupying the land. When congressional relief was slow in coming, Arkansas's delegate to Congress protested that northerners were using the Native Americans to slow the territory's progress toward statehood. Arkansas did not become a state until 1836, but familiar southern pressure yielded revised treaties in 1825 and 1828. The first reclaimed the great bulk of the Choctaw land; the second forced the Cherokees to move farther west into Indian Territory.[16]

14. Arthur H. De Rosier Jr., *The Removal of the Choctaw Indians* (Knoxville, Tenn., 1970), 109 (*Southern Patriot*); Satz, *American Indian Policy in the Jacksonian Era,* 25, 30.

15. Anthony F. C. Wallace, *The Long, Bitter Trail: Andrew Jackson and the Indians* (New York, 1993), 11.

16. S. Charles Bolton, *Territorial Ambition: Land and Society in Arkansas, 1800–1840* (Fayetteville, Ark., 1993), 25–28, 26 (savages).

Native-settler conflict in Texas was both more violent and more pro-longed than in Arkansas. By the late 1820s, Cherokees, Alabamas, and Creeks had migrated to East Texas, where they joined more indigenous peoples such as the Caddos and Wichitas. A decade later the combined Native American population of the territory east of the Trinity River had grown to forty-five hundred. The customary pattern of white encroachment, frontier violence, and illicit trade, particularly in liquor, ensued. Following the Texas revolution in 1836, Native American conditions deteriorated steadily. In December 1838 Texas president Mirabeau Buonaparte Lamar voiced the sentiments of the overwhelming majority of his constituents by proclaiming that the "proper policy" was to wage a "rigorous war" against all Indians until they recognized "that flight from our borders without hope of return" was their only recourse. Although subsequent government policy was not so systematic, the absolute refusal of whites to tolerate reservations demonstrated their determination to expel these East Texas Indians. The fate of the most able and conscientious of the federal Indian agents working for a Texas reservation spoke volumes. After conceding failure and leading his charges to Indian Territory in 1859, he was shot in the back by a disgruntled Texan.[17]

The expulsion of these relatively sedentary agricultural Indian peoples did not bring peace to the Texas frontier, since the much more mobile and warlike Comanches and Kiowas continued to contest the territory west of 98° latitude until the mid-1870s. Armed, mounted, and relentless, these "red niggers," in the parlance of contemporary Texans, inspired both fear and hatred with their raids on white settlements. Only with the conclusion of the Red River Indian War of 1874–75 were these Native Americans subdued, their principal chiefs banished to prisons in Florida, and the final portion of the U.S. continental empire rendered secure. As had been the case prior to the Civil War, southerners spearheaded this process.[18]

The South's aggressive, often violent, displacement of the Native Americans has been cited as evidence of Dixie's pronounced martial spirit. Proponents of a martial South have variously attributed the region's proclivity for war to its long exposure to the Indian frontier, to the fear of slave revolts,

17. T. R. Fehrenbach, *Lone Star: A History of Texas and the Texans* (New York, 1968), 453 (Lamar); Robert M. Utley, *The Indian Frontier of the American West, 1846–1890* (Albuquerque, 1984), 55–56; Dianna Everett, *The Texas Cherokees: A People between Two Fires, 1819–1840* (Norman, Okla., 1990), 67; F. Todd Smith, *The Caddos, the Wichitas, and the United States, 1846–1901* (College Station, Tex., 1996), 25, 30, 53, 65.

18. Fehrenbach, *Lone Star,* 452.

and to the plantation gentry's focus on "honor, bravery, and physical prowess, including riding, shooting, and other field sports." According to this interpretation, these influences placed the South and southerners in the forefront of war with Britain in 1812 and Mexico in 1846, made southerners the dominant influence at antebellum West Point, and led the South to support more military schools and militia units than other sections prior to 1860.[19]

Recent students have disputed the region's peculiar martial character during the antebellum period; and other political, economic, and racial explanations better explain the coming of war with Great Britain, Mexico, and the North. For example, R. Don Higginbotham argues persuasively that New England was much more martial than the South during the colonial and Revolutionary War eras and maintained a more viable nineteenth-century militia. Similarly, Marcus Cunliffe has asserted that nineteenth-century cities were as violent and disorderly as the southern frontier, that military academies began in the North and retained a presence comparable to that in the South, especially if the Virginia Military Academy and the Citadel are not given inordinate prominence. Cunliffe also stipulates that many more northerners than southerners died fighting Mexico, and both he and James L. Morrison Jr. demonstrate that southerners did not exercise a disproportionate influence at the U.S. Military Academy as instructors, students, or graduates.[20]

But to question Dixie's propensity for institutional militarism or influence at West Point is not to refute the South's intense concern for honor and its relation to demonstrated manhood, personal bravery, and devotion to family and country—concepts that have persisted (albeit in altered form) to the latter part of the twentieth century. Antebellum southern men acted from a strong need for both a sense of self-worth and recognition of that worth by others. Real or perceived slights or insults to one's family or region were intolerable if honor were to be properly maintained. These attitudes

19. R. Don Higginbotham, "The Martial Spirit in the Antebellum South: Some Further Speculations in a National Context," *Journal of Southern History* 58 (February 1992): 4; Robert E. May, "Dixie's Martial Image: A Continuing Historiographical Enigma," *Historian*, 40 (February 1978): 213–34.

20. Higginbotham, "Martial Spirit in the Antebellum South," 6–14; Marcus Cunliffe, *Soldiers and Civilians: The Martial Spirit in America, 1775–1865* (Boston, 1968), 335–84; James L. Morrison Jr., *"The Best School in the World": West Point, the Pre–Civil War Years, 1833–1866* (Kent, Ohio, 1986), 131–34; see also Robert E. May, "John A. Quitman and the Southern Martial Spirit," *Journal of Mississippi History* 41 (May 1979): 155–81.

helped to make violence a distinguishing characteristic of pre–Civil War southern life. Although limited in scope, quantitative studies indicate that physical assault and murder were significantly more common in the South than the North, and duels provided the most conspicuous individual examples of violence that occurred "because one antagonist cast doubt on the manliness and bearing of the other." In addition, southern concern with "courage as a social value" and the "most efficacious means of exhibiting and defending personal, family, and national honor" elevated military service to the level of planter, lawyer, or doctor among southerners.[21]

Neither the southern proclivity for personal violence nor respect for military careers decisively influenced the region's response to U.S. foreign policy prior to 1860, but these inclinations did become fundamental to southern society and helped to shape post–Civil War attitudes on international relations. Concern for personal and sectional honor, the bases for these other attitudes, proved much more critical to the region's foreign policy perspective as the nation acquired and sought to incorporate a North American empire. For example, the "culture of honor . . . helped define how Mississippians comprehended and reacted to the Mexican War." The editor of the *Yazoo Democrat* declared that "*submission whether as regards individuals or nations provokes insult and aggression,*" and his counterpart at the *Jackson Mississippian* lectured his readers that true men would be prepared "to yield up their lives as a sacrifice for their country's honor." Young Mississippi volunteers agreed. Following the battle of Buena Vista, Charles Dabney observed that defending the "glory" of Mississippi had proven exceedingly costly, "but to have lost her honor would have been an expense far greater." In their personal declarations, Mississippi women also endorsed this code of honor and called for their men to demonstrate personal bravery. Eliza Quitman, the wife of John A. Quitman, who returned a hero, bluntly avowed that she "would rather be the *widow* of a man who had fallen fighting in the battles of his country, than the *wife of a living coward.*"[22]

Although the South's culture of honor helped shape the region's foreign policy perspective, it was within the context of second American party sys-

21. Bertram Wyatt-Brown, *Southern Honor: Ethics and Behavior in the Old South* (New York, 1982), 17, 34, 191 and 360 (quotes), 366–67; see also Greenberg, *Masters and Statesmen,* 23–41; William R. Taylor, *Cavalier and Yankee: The Old South and American National Character* (New York, 1961).

22. Gregory S. Hospodor, " 'Bound by all the ties of honor': Southern Honor, the Mississippians, and the Mexican War," *Journal of Mississippi History* 61 (spring 1999): 2, 6, 11, 21.

tem that the South reacted to the annexation of Texas and Oregon and war with Mexico. Both the Jacksonian Democrats and their opponents, the Whigs, continued to view the world, albeit a rapidly changing one, through the lens of republicanism. Personal liberty and equality remained the ultimate end of southern politics, and both parties persisted in issuing dire warnings against tyranny and corruption, even as they adopted a more modern, positive attitude toward the very existence of permanent political organization. The two groups differed markedly, however, in locating the sources of these dangers.

Fundamentally apprehensive of modernization, the Democrats feared industrialization, urbanization, and centralized power. Jackson's neo-Jeffersonian southern followers worried that industrial growth and urban crowding would recreate a British environment in America, replete with class conflict and the loss of independence associated with land ownership. The Democrats denounced the Whigs' advocacy of a protective tariff, the second Bank of the United States, and corporate growth. Democratic spokesmen sounded a common refrain: "Enormous profits" from the tariff benefited the "moneyed manufacturer" rather than the "toiling operatives"; "our population has become comparatively dense"; "we are separating more and more, capital and labor, and have the beginnings of a constantly increasing *operative* class." Just as the Jacksonian diagnosis of the polity's illness sounded quite Jeffersonian, the suggested remedy was equally familiar—commercial and landed expansion. Plentiful supplies of new land and trading outlets would sustain an agricultural-based economy, the widespread ownership of property, and individual liberty and equality.[23]

The Whigs, by contrast, located their political and social specters in Jackson's abuse of executive power and patronage, in Democratic-induced class conflict, and in the concentrated governmental power and social dislocation that would accompany rapid expansion. Whereas the Democrats emphasized negative government, the Whigs placed greater value on harmony

23. Thomas R. Hietala, *Manifest Design: Anxious Aggrandizement in Late Jacksonian America* (Ithaca, N.Y., 1985), 101; Michael A. Morrison, "Westward the Curse of Empire: Texas Annexation and the American Whig Party," *Journal of the Early Republic* 10 (summer 1990): 226. See also Major Wilson, "Republicanism and the Idea of Party in the Jacksonian Period," *Journal of the Early Republic* 8 (winter 1988): 419–42; Marc W. Kruman, "The Second American Party System and the Transformation of Revolutionary Republicanism," *Journal of the Early Republic* 12 (winter 1992): 509–37; Harry L. Watson, *Liberty and Power: The Politics of Jacksonian America* (New York, 1990), 43–51, 238–53.

and a unified society; and whereas the Democrats viewed the future with dread, the Whigs embraced modernization and touted progress. But Whigs believed that change needed to be controlled and orderly; if properly paced, national progress would yield the southern goal of "expanded opportunities and an extension of personal liberty." The proper pace and mode of change also required less expansion over space, as the Democrats preached, and more qualitative improvement over time: Senator Alexander Barrow of Louisiana questioned whether "it was the duty and right of this government by treaty, by war, and by every other means, to extend the area of freedom." Instead, he advocated bettering the condition of the American society and polity by elevating the nation on the "scale of intelligence and morality." In short, he sought change over time rather than space. Working from this philosophical perspective, southern Whigs endorsed expanded trade but raised a host of political, social, economic, and racial objections to landed expansion.[24]

Although the foregoing considerations distinguished Dixie's Democrats and Whigs, a final political-economic reality undergirded all southern politics from the 1830s until 1861 and gradually relegated economic issues to secondary standing. William J. Cooper Jr. has identified this all-embracing influence as the "politics of slavery," and William W. Freehling labeled the phenomenon "southern loyalty politics." Slavery, Cooper asserts, was the "central axis of political debate in the South" and the "cherished visible symbol of [personal and sectional] independence, honor, and equality." Southern Democrats and Whigs served as the "advocates and guardians" of southern rights and interests on the national scene and demanded that their northern counterparts accede to their demands. Political survival in the South increasingly turned on being perceived as the most effective defender of southern interests and honor, and slavery's expansion into the territories west of the Mississippi became the ultimate issue by which Dixie's voters evaluated their leaders.[25]

The debate over the annexation of Texas cast all of these perspectives

24. Morrison, "Westward the Curse of Empire," 233–34 (quotes); Major Wilson, "Ideological Fruits of Manifest Destiny: The Geopolitics of Slavery Expansion in the Crisis of 1850," *Journal of the Illinois State Historical Society* 77 (summer 1970): 132–57; Michael F. Holt, *The Rise and Fall of the American Whig Party: Jacksonian Politics and the Onset of the Civil War* (New York, 1999), 176.

25. William J. Cooper Jr., *The South and the Politics of Slavery, 1828–1856* (Baton Rouge, 1978), xi–xii, xiv; Freehling, *Secessionists at Bay*, 553.

into stark focus. This "ramshackle republic" maintained a tenuous independence for more than a decade after its successful revolt against Mexico in 1835–36. While Mexico never made good on its threats to reconquer its former province, it was clear that "Texas was too weak to stand alone for long." Still, the seemingly logical annexation to the United States of the more than thirty thousand Americans led by Andrew Jackson's old friend Sam Houston went unconsummated into the 1840s. Jackson feared the abolitionist outcry against the addition of an area that could spawn five to six slave states. His Democratic successor, Martin Van Buren, harbored similar apprehensions but was even more concerned with the economic and social dislocation caused by the panic of 1837. When combined with Houston's enigmatic leadership in Texas, these domestic U.S. concerns relegated Texas to secondary status on the national agenda and left the fledgling country independent but vulnerable.[26]

In 1843 President John Tyler and his fellow Virginian and secretary of state Abel Upshur abruptly rescued Texas from this somnolent status and pushed annexation to the forefront of American politics. Tyler's motives were complex. A former Jacksonian who had broken with Old Hickory over the nullification controversy, Tyler had switched to the Whig Party and joined William Henry Harrison's ticket as the vice-presidential candidate in 1840. When Harrison died in office in April 1841, "His Accidency" assumed the presidency, but he did not share majority Whig devotion to a protective tariff, national bank, or internal improvements. Following two years of squabbling with Henry Clay and congressional Whigs, Tyler turned to Texas as the issue around which to build a new states' rights political coalition and to gain election as president. Secretary of State Upshur articulated the strategy: by championing the annexation of Texas, Tyler hoped to attract states' rights "individuals of *both parties*" to a new "party of his own." Texas, Upshur asserted, was "the only matter, that will take sufficient hold of the South to rally it on a southern candidate and weaken Clay & Van Buren so much there as to bring the election into the House."[27]

Tyler did not seek purely personal or partisan ends; he also sought to safeguard southern interests and to promote "national greatness . . . by

<hr/>

26. Bradford Perkins, *The Creation of a Republican Empire, 1776–1865,* vol. 1 of *The Cambridge History of American Foreign Relations,* ed. Warren I. Cohen (New York, 1993), 179.

27. Upshur quoted in Freehling, *Secessionists at Bay,* 391, and Sellers, *Market Revolution,* 413.

expansion"—objectives he deemed entirely compatible. He hearkened back to the Jeffersonian period, when national expansion simultaneously enhanced national power and the southern political economy. In the fall of 1841 Tyler had dispatched Duff Green of Maryland to London as a confidential executive agent, ostensibly to promote reciprocal trade relations. Green considered Great Britain the United States's principal commercial rival and Texas as the crucial point of contention. In a series of alarmist reports, he contended that the British government, in league with English abolitionists, was working to ensure Texas's independence, to abolish slavery there, and in so doing to hasten abolitionism in the United States, to secure a source of raw cotton other than the U.S. South for its manufacturers, and to block subsequent U.S. territorial expansion into the Southwest.[28]

Although largely inaccurate, Green's contentions impressed Upshur and Tyler. Upshur declared that Texas had to be "a *Southern* question, and not one of Whiggism and Democracy." Texas was merely a matter of "interest" to the North; for the South it was "a question of *safety*," and slaveholders needed to recognize Texas "as indispensable to their security."[29] Tyler agreed that an independent, free-soil Texas jeopardized U.S. security and southern slavery and would "most seriously threaten the existence of this happy Union." Senator John C. Calhoun, the president's confidant, echoed these concerns and cited another critical dimension. If slavery were abolished in the United States, it "would transfer the production of cotton, rice, and sugar . . . to [Britain's] colonial possessions, and would consummate the system of commercial monopoly, which she has been so long and systematically pursuing."[30]

Senator Calhoun's attention to commercial expansion reflected a long-standing southern preoccupation and another basic component of Tyler's foreign policy formulation. An aggressive economic expansionist, the president searched worldwide for markets to dispose of the U.S. "surplus of production beyond the home demand" and consciously acted to secure a U.S.

28. Edward P. Crapol, "John Tyler and the Pursuit of National Destiny," *Journal of the Early Republic* 17 (fall 1997): 475; David M. Pletcher, *The Diplomacy of Annexation: Texas, Oregon, and the Mexican War* (Columbia, Mo., 1973), 123–24.

29. Freehling, *Secessionists at Bay*, 401; Sam W. Haynes, "Anglophobia and the Annexation of Texas: The Quest for National Security," in *Manifest Destiny and Empire: American Antebellum Expansion*, eds. Sam W. Haynes and Christopher Morris (College Station, Tex., 1997), 127.

30. Hietala, *Manifest Design*, 23–24.

monopoly over the growing of raw cotton and to outpace British commercial competition. Tyler's search for markets was multifaceted: he and Upshur attempted to bolster the U.S. Navy and its capacity to defend and extend American commerce; he dispatched the first U.S. diplomatic official to Hawaii, favored the establishment of a naval base there, and warned other nations (and specifically the British) against colonizing or taking possession of the islands; he appointed Caleb Cushing as special U.S. commissioner to China, and Cushing negotiated the Treaty of Wanghia, opening five ports to American merchants and extending extraterritorial rights to American citizens in China; and he obtained a reciprocity treaty with the German customs union, or *Zollverein* (which the Senate rejected).[31]

Although Tyler and his southern advisers deemed each of these initiatives significant, the annexation of Texas commanded preeminent attention. By adding Texas as a slave state, the United States would simultaneously safeguard Dixie's peculiar institution against British abolitionist designs, avoid any British-controlled obstacles to subsequent expansion, and obtain U.S. domination of the world's production of raw cotton. To allow the British to gain mastery over Texas's potentially vast cotton crops would forfeit commercial supremacy and bring ruin to both southern planters and emerging northern manufacturers. Voicing both the Anglophobia long characteristic of southern foreign policy makers and the confidence in King Cotton that would guide subsequent sons of Dixie, Tyler claimed that he acted not to perpetuate slavery but to prevent the British from gaining an "absolute control over the trade of Texas" and escaping "all dependence upon us for the supply of cotton." By acquiring Texas and retaining "the monopoly of the cotton plant," the United States placed "all other nations at our feet." "An embargo of a single year," Tyler asserted in 1850, "would produce in Europe a greater amount of suffering than a fifty years' war." Another Virginian boasted that the United States held "England by a cotton string."[32]

With these several objectives in view, Tyler, Upshur, and Calhoun, who became secretary of state in April 1844, negotiated a treaty of annexation with Texas. Upon assuming office, Calhoun, long vexed at the dependence of American cotton and commercial interests on the British and worried that the British sought to destroy the U.S. economy, fired off a scathing

31. Ibid., 60; see also Crapol, "John Tyler," 476–77.

32. Hietala, *Manifest Design*, 69–70 (Tyler); Walter LaFeber, *The American Age: United States Foreign Policy at Home and Abroad since 1750* (New York, 1994), 113 (Virginian).

letter of rebuke to Richard Pakenham, England's minister to the United States. Continuing Upshur's strategy of stimulating the unity of the South and the formation of a states' rights party around the Texas issue, Calhoun excoriated British abolitionist activities in Texas and warned that English successes there would threaten slavery in the American South. Since slavery was a great benefit to the American "negro race," the United States was bound to act in "obedience" to racial "obligation," block British aggression, and safeguard American slavery by annexing Texas.[33]

Tyler and his lieutenants had pushed Texas, and with it slavery and sectionalism, to the forefront of American politics and diplomacy. But they did not elicit a unified southern states' rights party; nor could they control the Texas issue, which was appropriated by the Democrats and their presidential nominee, James K. Polk. While rejecting the treaty by a 35 to 16 vote, the U.S. Senate demonstrated the lack of southern unity. Southern Democrats voted 9 to 0 in favor; southern Whigs voted 8 to 1 in opposition. Party rather than section prevailed, and Texas became a (perhaps, the) key issue in the 1844 presidential contest.[34]

Henry Clay, the eventual Whig nominee for president, denounced the failed annexation treaty in April. Voicing the general Whig uneasiness with territorial expansion, he opposed annexing Texas in the face of opposition by Mexico or a "considerable and respectable portion" of the United States. To do so without Mexican assent would bring war and dangerous concentration of governmental authority; to do so without northern assent would incite sectional crisis and destroy the harmony necessary for progress. Southern Whigs added a host of more specific reservations. They asserted that this "lust for dominion" undermined the true constitutional process for adding new states and impugned America's international standing, that Texas cotton and sugar would provide injurious competition for the existing South, that the rich new lands would drain both white and black population away from the Southeast and thereby weaken its economy and the institution of slavery, that the entire issue was a narrowly partisan Democratic political ploy designed to divide southern Whigs and promote class strife, and that acquiring Texas set the dangerous precedent of adding a nonwhite pop-

33. Freehling, *Secessionists at Bay,* 409 (Calhoun); John Niven, *John C. Calhoun and the Price of Peace: A Biography* (Baton Rouge, 1988), 275.

34. *Congressional Globe,* 28th Cong., 1st sess., 652; Freehling, *Secessionists at Bay,* 431. Kentucky's two Whigs, who voted against passage, are not reflected in this total.

ulation to the body politic. Even while pressing these arguments, southern Whigs feared that they were in an untenable position, caught between unbending northern Whig opposition to the extension of slavery and persuasive Democratic arguments for Texas's benefits for Dixie. Southern Whigs attempted to escape this dilemma by arguing for delaying annexation until the country truly required the territory, but in so doing they ran the risk of being "damned as soft on Texas, therefore soft on slavery."[35]

When Martin Van Buren also attempted to finesse and delay on Texas, southern and western Democrats led the party's turn to Tennessee's James K. Polk, an unapologetic expansionist who ran for president on a platform seeking Texas, Oregon, and Pacific markets. Unfettered by unified and unalterably antiexpansionist northern colleagues, southern Democrats constructed a persuasive brief specifying the benefits Dixie would derive from annexation. By acquiring Texas, the United States and the South would confound British abolitionists and protect American slavery, gain access to cheap land and new markets, safeguard its monopoly over the growing of cotton, and gain at least one and perhaps several additional slave states. Mississippian Robert Walker's influential pamphlet echoed John Tyler's slavery "diffusion" position at the time of the Missouri crisis. In a twenty-six-page letter, reprinted nationally, Walker appealed to both southern and northern racial anxieties by contending that Texas would facilitate the immediate "diffusion" and ultimate elimination of slavery. Slaves sold from the older South would reduce the concentration and threat of rebellion and, because of their smaller number and the greater necessity for agricultural productivity, be treated more humanely in Texas. Walker further asserted that slavery would naturally die away as the soil was exhausted and the institution lost its profitability. Therefore, acquiring the Lone Star Republic would promote abolition and funnel newly free blacks into Mexico and away from the North. These contentions struck a most responsive chord among northern Democrats, who could simultaneously assuage their humanitarian concerns for slaves without the fear of having to live among them if and when they were freed. Most important, Walker helped solidify southern Democratic support for annexation and for Polk.[36]

35. Robert V. Remini, *Henry Clay: Statesman for the Union* (New York, 1991), 639–41, 659–60; Douglas A. Ley, "Expansionists All? Southern Senators and American Foreign Policy, 1841–1860" (Ph.D. dissertation, University of Wisconsin, 1990), 16 (lust); Freehling, *Secessionists at Bay*, 437 (damned); Holt, *Rise and Fall of the American Whig Party*, 176–77 (requires); Morrison, *Slavery and the American West*, 22–25.

36. Hietala, *Manifest Design*, 26–32.

By May 1844, a Virginia Whig reported with distress that many of his fellow party members appeared "to think that honor, prosperity, happiness & even the very salvation of the United States depended on the immediate acquisition of Texas," and the *Richmond Enquirer* proclaimed, "The cause of Texas is flying like wildfire over that whole region." While it is far from clear that the Democratic call for the annexation of Texas and Oregon produced Polk's narrow defeat of Clay, historian John H. Schroeder has argued persuasively that "Polk most certainly would neither have received his party's nomination nor won the election without the Texas issue."[37]

Southern Whigs concurred with this analysis. A Georgian believed that the "preposterous humbug of Texas . . . ruined" his party, and another southerner asserted, "For anyone now to say that the Texas question had no influence on the Presidential election only makes a fool or an ass of himself." Democrats benefited in the South from Texas as a symbolic issue tied to the institution of slavery but even more from its potential as a source of cheap land for ambitious southern nonslaveholders. Fittingly, Tyler rather than Polk consummated the acquisition. In January 1845 the lame-duck president turned to the device of a joint resolution, requiring a simple majority vote in each house of Congress. The Senate's 27 to 25 affirmative vote on February 27 demonstrated the ongoing party division. Southern Democrats voted 9 to 0 for Texas, and southern Whigs 7 to 2 against. Only Henry Johnson of Louisiana and John Henderson of Mississippi crossed party lines and in so doing provided the margin needed for annexation.[38]

This victory for the southern Democratic preference on Texas hardly signified a united southern vision on foreign policy in the mid-1840s. The South's partisan political divisions remained more influential than agreed-upon regional interests. Indeed, Dixie's response to the Oregon question demonstrated that Texas's ostensible advantages had made even the Democrats appear more united than they actually were. During the campaign, President Polk had called for the "whole of the Oregon territory," which stretched to 54°40'; but upon taking office, he offered the British a compro-

37. Morrison, "Westward the Curse of Empire," 245 (acquisition); John McCardell, *The Idea of a Southern Nation: Southern Nationalists and Southern Nationalism, 1830–1860* (New York, 1979), 233 (*Enquirer*); John H. Schroeder, "Annexation or Independence: The Texas Issue in American Politics, 1836–1845," *Southwestern Historical Quarterly* 89 (October 1985): 160.

38. Holt, *Rise and Fall of the American Whig Party*, 198–201 (quotes, 199); Morrison, *Slavery and the American West*, 35–36; *Congressional Globe*, 28th Cong., 1st sess., 362; Freehling, *Secessionists at Bay*, 446–48. Kentucky's two Whigs were opposed.

mise boundary at the 49th parallel in July 1845. When the British minister to Washington, Richard Pakenham, foolishly rejected this overture without even forwarding it to London, Polk reverted back to 54°40′, which was much more popular with northern and western Democrats. As midwestern Democrats screamed for "Fifty-Four Forty or Fight," Polk urged Congress in December 1845 to rescind the 1827 agreement with Britain for the joint occupation of Oregon, to declare American laws in force there, and to approve the military preparations necessary to look "John Bull . . . straight in the eye."[39]

Facing the prospect of war with Great Britain, both southern Whigs and many southern Democrats demurred. Although both groups agreed with Polk's search for viable ports on the Pacific and Asian markets, neither was eager to fight to obtain a future northern state that would further weaken Dixie's leverage in the Senate. Nor were the Whigs willing to endorse the aggressive actions of a Democratic president. War with Great Britain would not only destroy commerce with America's principal trading partner but also result in greater bureaucratic and military centralization. Far better, argued all Whigs, to negotiate in good faith while profiting from the steady migration of U.S. citizens into the disputed territory. Senator William Archer of Virginia declared: "On peace depended the expansion of commerce; on this expansion depended the growth and application of productions; on these the developments of prosperity, improvement, and power—the verification of visions, the highest interests and the best hopes of humanity." Given the Whigs' strong partisanship, ambivalence about territorial expansion, commitment to foreign commerce and good relations with the British, and ongoing concerns about republicanism, their cautious stance was hardly surprising.[40]

Many contemporaries were more puzzled by the actions of John C. Calhoun and his contingent of southeastern Democratic followers. Senator Edward Hannegan of Indiana charged his fellow Democrats with bad faith; he argued that they had supported Oregon until Texas and slavery were secured, after which these "peculiar friends of Texas turned, and were doing all they could to strangle Oregon!" The reality was far more complex. Calhoun and other southeastern Democratic dissenters concurred with the

39. Norman A. Graebner, *Empire on the Pacific: A Study in American Continental Expansion* (New York, 1955), 123.
40. Ley, "Expansionists All?" 25.

Whig fear that war with England would induce dreaded federal centralization, obliterate southern commerce, and produce unwanted financial burdens. Unlike the Whigs, Calhoun and his followers perceived free trade as a great boon to the South and refused to imperil the evolving and ultimately successful movements in both Great Britain and the United States to reduce trade barriers. Referring to the westward U.S. migration, Calhoun asserted that "*Time*" was "acting for us; . . . it will assert and maintain our right with resistless force, without costing a cent of money, or a drop of blood." All that was needed was "'a wise and masterly inactivity.'" George McDuffie, Calhoun's senate colleague from South Carolina, was more blunt, rejecting Oregon as not worth "a pinch of snuff," as "a strip of barren land never worth fighting about."[41]

Calhoun and four of his southeastern Democratic followers joined with the Whigs to force Polk and Democratic extremists to accept the 49° compromise. After more than two months of acrimonious debate, Congress passed a resolution in April 1846 abrogating the 1827 agreement for joint occupation, but it also attached conciliatory language that signaled its members' desire for a moderate negotiated solution. Recognizing that the Congress would support neither extreme demands nor war preparations and faced with the prospect of simultaneous hostilities with both Mexico and Britain, Polk capitulated. When the British proposed a settlement at 49° in late May, the president forwarded the treaty to the Senate for its prior approval. On June 18, the Senate voted 41 to 14 for ratification. Only one southerner, Democrat James Westcott of Florida, voted no. As with Texas, a prosouthern outcome had emerged: an excellent port was obtained at San Juan de Fuca, access to Asian markets was enhanced, commerce with Great Britain and the prospects for freer trade were preserved, and war was avoided.[42]

President Polk's pursuit of California precluded such a pacific outcome with Mexico. The president's territorial ambitions extended beyond Texas and Oregon; he also coveted Mexico's northernmost province with its vast agricultural potential and superb ports at San Francisco and San Diego. He first offered Mexico $25 million for California and New Mexico and the territory between the Nueces River (which Mexico considered the boundary) and the Rio Grande (which Texas claimed as its southern limit). When

41. Ibid., 36–37, 65, 78.

42. Ibid., 69–83; Hietala, *Manifest Design*, 81–82; Graebner, *Empire on the Pacific*, 130–49.

Mexico refused, Polk ordered U.S. troops into this disputed region, where they blockaded Mexican soldiers at Matamoros. The virtually inevitable clash of arms ensued in late April, and the president and his cabinet employed the incident as the justification for a war they had already decided to wage. "The cup of forbearance," Polk proclaimed, "had been exhausted" even before this outrage. "But . . . now Mexico . . . has invaded our territory and shed American blood upon the American soil." Presented with the loss of American life and an army under attack, Congress approved the declaration of war 174 to 14 in the House and 40 to 2 in the Senate. The votes were deceiving. John C. Calhoun abstained from the vote and confided to his son, "Never was so momentous a measure adopted, with so much precipitancy; so little thought; or forced through by such objectionable means." The grizzled South Carolinian's reservations foreshadowed the Whig opposition to and southern ambivalence over this patently aggressive war.[43]

Although Whigs had not blocked the declaration of war, they promptly denounced Polk's actions and intentions. Southern Whigs such as Alexander H. Stephens and John M. Berrien of Georgia and James A. Pearce of Maryland sounded familiar concerns and criticisms and in so doing anticipated southern objections to the acquisition of an island empire in 1898–99. By forcing war on a weaker neighbor, the United States sacrificed its national honor and international standing as a republican exemplar. "No warrant" could be found "in the Constitution" for governing new territories "as *subject provinces*." Hostilities promised to inflate federal spending, debt, and bureaucracy and to expand executive and military power—all of which ran counter to southern values and interests. Annexing California and New Mexico would bring a "sickening mixture" of "debased population," "an ignorant, a fanatic, a disorderly people," whose presence would threaten republican government. Southern Whigs warned that there were no guarantees that slavery would be safeguarded in any new territories and worried correctly that the sectional struggle to control the New West could shatter both the Whig Party and the nation. To avoid these objectionable, even disastrous, outcomes, they advocated the policy of "no territory" through conquest. This prescription allowed them to attain the maximum partisan advantage from opposing an increasingly unpopular war while simultaneously preserving party unity and avoiding the deadly Democratic charge of

43. Pletcher, *Diplomacy of Annexation,* 385–86 (Polk); Perkins, *Creation of a Republican Empire,* 191 (Calhoun).

failing to protect slavery and southern equality. Working from the same re-publican belief system, southern Democrats shared many of their Whig rivals' racial, fiscal, bureaucratic, and constitutional fears. But party regularity and the ongoing conviction that territorial and commercial expansion were essential to republicanism and the South's political economy kept the overwhelming majority of them supportive of Polk and the war and receptive to his call for territorial expansion.[44]

Significantly, the "politics of slavery" and devotion to the peculiar institution led both groups to at least temporarily put aside partisan and policy differences in favor of sectional solidarity. In August 1846 Congressman David Wilmot, a hitherto obscure Pennsylvania Democrat, offered a proviso stipulating that "neither slavery nor involuntary servitude" should be allowed in any territory acquired from Mexico. No southerner could abide such a restriction, and southern Democrats and Whigs united to block its passage. As with the Missouri crisis, the sectional balance of power was at stake. Calhoun warned that if deprived of the fruits of national expansion, the South would be left "a mere handful" of circumscribed states with their fate "entirely . . . in the hands of the nonslaveholding States." The minority and hence dependent status that southerners had feared and decried as early as 1789 appeared to be materializing. A southern Democrat warned, "The South is a minority, a weakening minority. . . . She, therefore, cannot injure the North. They alone have the weapon of aggression in their hands." Perhaps as alarming to southerners as the threat to their political and economic interests was the challenge to their honor and equality. Georgia Whig Alexander Stephens rejected this "*insult* to the South," this "expression to the world" that Dixie warranted "public censure and national odium." Francis Pickens, a Calhoun follower, agreed that the South could not accept this restriction "without *feeling* our *degradation*." "Death," declared another Democrat, "is preferable to acknowledged inferiority."[45]

Even as southern Whigs and Democrats agreed on the need to safeguard slavery in the territories, they continued to clash over the efficacy of extracting territorial compensation from Mexico. When negotiations with Mexico

44. John H. Schroeder, *Mr. Polk's War: American Opposition and Dissent, 1846–1848* (Madison, Wis., 1973), 53, 55; Ley, "Expansionists All?" 123; Morrison, *Slavery and the American West,* 74.

45. Freehling, *Secessionists at Bay,* 461 (Stephens), 462 (Calhoun); Morrison, *Slavery and the American West,* 61 (southern Democrat); Cooper, *South and the Politics of Slavery,* 239 (Pickens and death); see also Morrison, *Democratic Politics and Sectionalism,* 199 n. 43.

faltered and U.S. forces occupied Mexico City in the fall of 1847, a number of northern and midwestern Democrats advocated the retention of "All Mexico" to pay the expenses of the war. Whigs, north and south, responded with their "No Territory" platform; to the motives outlined above, southern Whigs added the growing apprehension that slavery was unlikely to prosper in either the desert Southwest or Mexico. Regular southern Democrats exhibited slight enthusiasm for "All Mexico" and only grudgingly conceded that Polk might need to occupy the country to end the war. John C. Calhoun and at least six other Senate Democrats broke openly with the Polk administration and cooperated with the Whigs, much as they had done over Oregon.

Calhoun had called in February 1847 for military withdrawal to a "defensive line" along the Rio Grande and extending west from El Paso to the Pacific Ocean. In January 1848 he introduced resolutions denouncing the military occupation or annexation of Mexico and delivered a spirited critique of the president's policies. Calhoun feared the centralization and expenses that would result from an extended war and occupation. The expenses could be used to justify a protective tariff, with all of its injurious effects on the South. But most of all, Calhoun opposed the annexation of the vast, nonwhite Mexican population, the incorporation into the Union of "any but the Caucasian race. To incorporate Mexico would be the first departure of the kind. . . . Ours is the government of the white man," and it should not commit "the fatal error of placing the colored race on an equality with the white." He did not, however, oppose annexing the thinly populated areas of the Southwest and California, with its excellent ports. Calhoun, like Polk and most Democrats, coveted additional territory for republican ends, but he and ultimately the nation faced the "dilemma of balancing imperialism with racism."[46]

Nicholas Trist, Polk's peace envoy to Mexico, rescued the president and the nation from this potential military and political quagmire. Even though Polk had ordered his recall several months before, Trist delivered a most auspicious agreement in February 1848. In return for a payment of $15 million and the commitment to assume $3.25 million in American claims

---

46. Hietala, *Manifest Design*, 162, 164; see also Schroeder, *Mr. Polk's War*, 68–74, 131–33; Ernest M. Lander Jr., *Reluctant Imperialists: Calhoun, The South Carolinians, and the Mexican War* (Baton Rouge, 1980), 153, 159–60, 162, 174; Lacy K. Ford, "Republican Ideology in a Slave Society: The Political Economy of John C. Calhoun," *Journal of Southern History* 54 (August 1988): 409–24.

against the Mexican government, Mexico surrendered New Mexico and California and consented to the Rio Grande border with Texas. Presented with the opportunity to acquire the less-populated and less-nonwhite half of Mexico (including Texas) and confronted with the prospect of renewed war if the treaty were rejected, Senate Democrats and Whigs ratified the pact for different reasons. The racial barrier of all Mexico had been circumvented, and a grand addition to the American empire had been annexed on terms agreeable to the vast majority of southerners.

Tyler's and Polk's striking territorial acquisitions failed to yield any of the outcomes predicted by Democrats in general or southern Democrats in particular. Slaves were not drawn toward Mexico and Central America, thereby producing a magical transformation in U.S. race relations. Excellent ports on the Pacific did not result in an immediate expansion of commerce with Asia and greater southern prosperity. And the vast new territories did not preserve agrarian republicanism in competition with nineteenth-century urban and industrial development. Whig predictions proved more accurate—particularly in terms of the internal discord occasioned by the new empire. In the wake of war with Mexico, sectional competition for control of the New West grew ever more bitter. Territorial expansion had not secured either southern security or equality. To the contrary, southern apprehensions and alienation intensified as the North decisively rejected the old nationalism that had combined the growth of the national domain and slavery. Indeed, the South's fears, first raised by the Missouri crisis, that territorial expansion could be detrimental to Dixie, were realized in the decade leading to secession.

Several crucial events in the early 1850s contributed to the southern sense of embattlement and simultaneously led to the demise of the Whig Party and the second American party system. President Zachary Taylor's commitment to accepting California as a state without slavery and to popular sovereignty, or allowing the settlers in Utah and New Mexico to decide on the legality of slavery, and northern Whig opposition to a strengthened fugitive slave law impugned the ability of southern Whigs to defend sectional interests. In 1854 southern Whigs, practicing the politics of slavery, challenged the Democrats to repeal the Missouri Compromise with its stipulation prohibiting slavery north of 36°30' in the Louisiana Purchase and guaranteeing the institution's existence south of that boundary. The Kansas-Nebraska Act, which repealed the compromise, also created the Kansas and Nebraska Territories and specified that popular sovereignty be applied in these areas.

What initially appeared as the recognition of southern equality and slavery's access to all of the New West proved to be an utter disaster for the Whig Party and the nation. The passage of this prosouthern law convinced northerners of the reality of a slave-power conspiracy and led to the formation in 1854–55 of the Republican Party, dedicated to the containment of slavery within the states where it then existed.

The Republican rise as a purely northern party coincided with the demise of the Whigs, who could not compete with the Republicans' antislavery stance in the North or the Democrats' proslavery advocacy in the South. These developments marked a crucial step in the realignment of American politics in terms of sectional loyalties and commitment to slavery rather than allegiance to party. This transformation was completed over the ensuing six years, as northern and southern loyalists killed one another in "Bleeding Kansas," as the Supreme Court endorsed the southern position on popular sovereignty in the Dred Scott case, as John Brown led an antislavery attack on the federal arsenal at Harpers Ferry, and as Republican Abraham Lincoln won the 1860 presidential election with a purely northern vote.

Increased southern alienation in the 1850s did not immediately yield a unified sectional perspective on expansion and foreign policy. Southerners could come together in opposition to the Wilmot Proviso and remain committed to the republican ends of individual and sectional liberty and equality and to the maintenance of honor—all of which demanded and produced a solid sectional demand for equal access to the New West. But southerners continued to disagree over the appropriate foreign policy tactics for achieving these goals. Southwestern Democrats sustained their demands for territorial expansion and frequently endorsed filibustering expeditions aimed at annexing new slave areas; southern Whigs and their successors in the American Party reiterated their opposition to territorial expansion and argued instead for internal development and commercial expansion; many Upper South and South Carolina Democrats demonstrated a similar devotion to economic expansion and anxiety regarding overly aggressive pursuit of territorial acquisitions in the tropics. Only as the decade ended and the frustration of northern opposition to all southern and slave expansion became indisputable did Dixie move closer to a unified foreign policy position.

While disagreeing on the merits of territorial expansion, southerners evidenced considerable coherence and caution concerning Europe's midcentury revolutions. Always concerned with the implications for slavery, southerners particularly abhorred establishing any precedent for interference in the internal affairs of another country or for endorsing radical actions that overthrew established governments and placed morality over legal order. From the southern perspective, these were the same frightening implications of abolitionist actions and demands. When Ohio senator William Allen offered a joint resolution in 1848 lauding the new republican government in France, John C. Calhoun attempted to table the measure. Calhoun not only doubted the French ability to sustain a republican government and opposed intervention in France, he also wanted no part of commending a revolution of too great a "rapidity, extent, and too thorough and radical . . . character" or a government that had only recently abolished slavery in its Caribbean possessions. In a series of votes on Allen's resolution, a majority of southern Whigs and nearly half of Dixie's Democrats consistently demurred.[47]

By the summer of 1849, all of the European revolutions had failed, including the campaign led by Louis Kossuth to free Hungary from Austrian rule. Although Governor Henry Foote of Mississippi was among Kossuth's most enthusiastic partisans, most southerners were again wary. When Lewis Cass advocated the suspension of diplomatic relations with Austria in 1850 as a sign of support for the Hungarians, Senator R. M. T. Hunter of Virginia questioned the "right of one Government to interfere in the domestic affairs of another, a right which would be dangerous, in the last degree, to the peace and liberties of mankind." Domestic calculations also dictated Dixie's cool response to the dashing Kossuth's visit to the United States in 1851–52 following his military defeat and confinement in a Turkish prison. When Kossuth headed south in March–April 1852, he attracted small and unresponsive crowds, and in Jackson, Mississippi, an irate citizen even swore out a warrant for his arrest. The southern press warned that northern support for intervention shrouded an abolitionist plot. The *Baltimore Clipper* condemned antislavery papers for urging "this Government to commit itself to a principle which can hereafter be applied to internal interests." The *New Orleans Bulletin* added, "If we sanction interference, we will be the first who will be interfered with; if we become a consenting party to the project

47. Richard C. Rohrs, "American Critics of the French Revolution of 1848," *Journal of the Early Republic* 14 (fall 1994): 363–71.

of overthrowing European forms of government, our own institutions will be the first crushed beneath the juggernautic wheels of unlicensed, unconfined radicalism."[48]

Similar concerns regarding the elevation of morality over law combined with familiar partisan perspectives and planter anxieties over potential economic competition to prompt mixed southern reactions through much of the 1850s about the prospect and means of annexing Cuba. Among traditional, expansionist Democrats, Cuba had long been a coveted prize. Figures such as Senators John Slidell and Judah P. Benjamin of Louisiana and Albert Gallatin Brown of Mississippi deemed the addition of Cuba as a slave state critical to balancing northern power in the U.S. Senate and rebutting antislavery initiatives. This aspiration assumed even greater strength and urgency following the incorporation of California as a free state in 1850 and the explosive northern response to the passage of the Kansas-Nebraska Act in 1854. Southern equality and liberty appeared directly at issue. The Spanish threat in the early 1850s to abolish slavery on the island also heightened southern anxieties that the example of emancipation would stimulate slave unrest in Dixie and negate any political or economic advantage that would accompany annexation. John A. Quitman of Mississippi, perhaps the South's most enthusiastic proponent of U.S.-based filibustering against Cuba, worried that the potential of freeing slaves on the island would force whites to flee and create another "hideous St. Domingo," a "mongrel empire." Only a filibustering strike could ensure "safety to the South & her institutions." In 1854, A. Dudley Mann, a Virginian and assistant secretary of state, concluded that the foregoing considerations made Cuba "essential to the South both in a political and geographical point of view."[49]

Southerners of this stripe were inclined to support the filibustering expeditions of Narciso López, who landed in Cuba in both 1850 and 1851, ostensibly to liberate the island from Spain and facilitate its annexation to the United States. López attracted his most significant southern support among Gulf Coast Democrats, particularly from New Orleans' maritime and mer-

48. Tom Chaffin, "'Sons of Washington': Narciso López, Filibustering, and U.S. Nationalism, 1848–1851," *Journal of the Early Republic* 15 (spring 1995): 104 (Hunter); Donald S. Spencer, *Louis Kossuth and Young America: A Study of Sectionalism and Foreign Policy, 1848–1852* (Columbia, Mo., 1977), 103 (*Clipper* and *Bulletin*).

49. Robert E. May, *The Southern Dream of a Caribbean Empire, 1854–1861* (Athens, Ga., 1989), 37 (Mann); May, *John A. Quitman: Old South Crusader* (Baton Rouge, 1985), 277–78 (Quitman); see also May, "Manifest Destiny's Filibusters," in *Manifest Destiny and Empire*, 156–57.

cantile groups, who eyed Cuba and increased trade in the Caribbean and Asia via Central American transit as the vehicle for compensating for lost trade with the Midwest and for enhancing the city's economy relative to the Northeast. Louisiana authorities covertly furnished arms to López, and the New Orleans press severely criticized the federal government under President Zachary Taylor for acting to forestall the attacks on Cuba. Following López's capture and execution by Spanish authorities in August 1851, rampaging mobs destroyed the Spanish consulate and Spanish-owned businesses in New Orleans. John A. Quitman, López's staunchest supporter, worked energetically from 1853 to 1855 to mount a filibustering expedition of his own. The former Mississippi governor and soon-to-be congressman discarded this project only after President Franklin Pierce indicated his unalterable opposition.[50]

Pierce also frustrated expansionist southern Democrats when he backed away from the Ostend Manifesto. In response to the Pierce administration's directive to purchase Cuba for $130 million, Pierre Soulé, John Y. Mason, and James Buchanan, U.S. ministers to Spain, France, and Great Britain, respectively, met in Ostend, Belgium, in October 1854. Soulé from Louisiana, Mason from Virginia, and Buchanan, a southern sympathizer from Pennsylvania, recommended confidentially to Pierce that if attempts to buy Cuba failed, "then by every law human and divine, we should be justified in wresting it from Spain, if we possess the power." When the manifesto became public in March 1855, northerners castigated it as another abuse by the advocates of slavery, and Pierce abandoned the scheme. The actions of López and Quitman, the support they commanded, the failed purchase project, and the inflammatory manifesto have led historian Robert E. May to conclude that "annexation of Cuba had become a sectional goal around the time of the Kansas-Nebraska Act."[51]

Still, southern unity on this issue should not be overstated. Southern Whigs, many of whom moved to the American Party during the middle 1850s, had not modified their opposition to territorial expansion. Whig-Americans contended that Cuban sugar and cotton would be injuriously

50. Chaffin, "Narciso López," passim; Richard Tansey, "Southern Expansionism: Urban Interests in the Cuba Filibusters," *Plantation Society* 1 (June 1979): 227–51; Chester Stanley Urban, "New Orleans and the Cuba Question during the López Expeditions of 1849–1851: A Local Study in 'Manifest Destiny,'" *Louisiana Historical Quarterly* 22 (January 1939): 1095–155.

51. Edward W. Chester, *Sectionalism, Politics, and American Diplomacy* (Metuchen, N.J., 1975), 82 (wresting); May, *Southern Dream of a Caribbean Empire*, 51.

competitive with southern staple crops and the annexation of large numbers of free mestizos and blacks would endanger southern racial order. These southern Whigs recognized that supporting or even tolerating filibustering sanctioned extralegal actions and jeopardized regular legal order. Once again, morality could not be made superior to law—which the South had come to count on as the ultimate defender of slavery. Important southern Democrats, who otherwise favored territorial annexation and the acquisition of Cuba, agreed. Senator James M. Mason of Virginia rejected filibustering and instead called for either the purchase of Cuba from Spain or waiting until the "fruit will ripen, and fall from the parent stem" into the U.S. lap. As Mason explained concerning extralegal proslavery actions in Kansas, "The South of all the sections is most deeply interested, in vindicating and insisting on submission to law." Senators Andrew P. Butler and R. M. T. Hunter concurred in the need for the peaceful acquisition of the "Ever Faithful Isle," while emphasizing the centralizing effects of war.[52]

Only as the decade neared its end and southerners became acutely apprehensive about their lack of equality within the Union and offended by northern attacks on their honor did these divisions within Dixie diminish. Southern Democrats and the remnants of the Whig-Americans in the Senate voted nearly unanimously in 1859 for President Buchanan's initiative to purchase Cuba for $30 million. The Senate debate over the bill "bared sectional enmities" and elicited strident Republican denunciations of any project calculated to add a slave state or to perpetuate slavery in Cuba. After the failure even to bring the measure to a vote, southern frustration and determination not to be rendered dependent were evident. Former Whig Alexander Stephens declared that of "all these acquisitions" an independent South might secure, "the most important to the whole country is that of Cuba." Stephens's longtime political adversary Jefferson Davis echoed this assessment: Cuba's possession, he asserted, would be "indispensable" to the "Southern States if formed into a separate confederacy." With access to the New West blocked, southerners had looked abroad to protect their equality and honor, only to have their fears intensified when areas such as Cuba also proved to be beyond Dixie's grasp.[53]

52. Robert W. Young, *Senator James Murray Mason: Defender of the Old South* (Knoxville, Tenn., 1998), 69 (Cuba); Ley, "Expansionists All?" 287 (submission).

53. May, *Southern Dream of a Caribbean Empire,* 176, 186, 188 (Stephens and Davis); Ley, "Expansionists All?" 383–84; Thomas D. Schoonover, "Foreign Relations and Kansas in 1858," *Kansas Historical Quarterly* 48 (winter 1976): 345–52; Ebba and Thomas D. Schoonover, "Docu-

The South's response to William Walker's filibustering campaigns in Nicaragua revealed similar patterns of partisan and regional reactions and produced comparable frustrations. Between June 1855 and September 1860, Walker mounted four expeditions aimed at controlling and exploiting Nicaragua. He realized this control from November 1855 until May 1857, when he was deposed by a combination of indigenous forces and transit magnate Cornelius Vanderbilt's influence. Although Walker had not acted originally from prosouthern or proslavery motives, he expediently claimed such a mantle in 1856 by reinstating slavery in Nicaragua. Walker declared his intention to tie "the Southern states to Nicaragua as if she were one of themselves," and he subsequently assured southerners that he hoped to "extend your institutions" into Central America. These actions and declarations, together with vocal support form Pierre Soulé of Louisiana and John H. Wheeler of North Carolina, U.S. minister to Nicaragua under President Pierce, confirmed both northern suspicions and southern hopes that Walker was promoting the South's interests. Domestic sectional positions hardened in November 1857 when Commodore Hiram Paulding of the United States Navy intervened in Nicaragua to quash Walker's second expedition. In so doing, Paulding enforced U.S. neutrality laws beyond American jurisdiction. By 1859, Walker had become another "sectional symbol" in the bitter confrontation leading to Civil War.[54]

As with Cuba, political and strategic influence over Nicaragua and Central America had obvious appeal to the South. Additional southern states were needed to balance northern power in the U.S. Senate, and southerners, such as Matthew Fontaine Maury, clearly recognized the potential commercial benefits of interoceanic transit for their section's trade with Asia. Nevertheless, within this regional understanding, regular Democrats, especially those from the Lower South and the Gulf Coast, were much more aggressively pro-Walker, while Upper South and South Carolina Democrats and Whig-Americans were again more restrained. For example, Democrats James M. Mason of Virginia and Andrew Butler of South Carolina and former Whigs John Bell of Tennessee and John J. Crittenden of Kentucky rejected an overly assertive Central American policy in the mid-1850s.

---

ments: Bleeding Kansas and Spanish Cuba in 1857, A Postscript," *Kansas History* 11 (1988–89): 240–42.

54. William Earl Weeks, *Building the Continental Empire: American Expansion from the Revolution to the Civil War* (Chicago, 1996), 159–60 (Walker); May, *Southern Dream of a Caribbean Empire,* 125 (sectional symbol); McCardell, *Idea of a Southern Nation,* 271.

Against the backdrop of mounting domestic tensions, Commodore Paulding's arrest of Walker elicited general southern condemnation. Practicing the politics of slavery, Whig and American Party papers charged the Buchanan administration with opposing the expansion of the peculiar institution and questioned whether the Democratic Party was the best defender of southern welfare. In the Senate, Albert Brown and his Gulf Coast allies were the most outspoken in denouncing Paulding and arguing the merits of new slave states in Central America. By contrast, Mason and Crittenden maintained their previous restraint and defended Paulding's actions. Mason's arguments recalled the Virginian's concerns over the implications of Narciso López's actions for legal order. In January 1858 the chairman of the Committee on Foreign Relations defended Buchanan and Paulding. He praised the administration's arrest of Walker as an unprecedented "instance of wisdom and expediency" in employing the neutrality laws to preserve the "public peace." Once more, however, the entire issue acquired decisive sectional symbolism. In 1859 the House belatedly voted on a year-old resolution congratulating Paulding. The measure passed 99 to 85 with only 3 affirmative votes cast by slave-state senators. Democrat William T. Avery of Tennessee summarized the ultimate southern perspective regarding Paulding's actions: "A heavier blow was never struck at southern rights, [and] southern interests" than the commodore's "highhanded outrage."[55]

The failure of the Crittenden Compromise further demonstrated this same acute sectionalism and the resulting obsolescence of the older American nationalism that combined territorial expansion and the extension of slavery. As the nation moved toward war in the spring of 1861, Senator Crittenden sought to resolve the conflict over slavery in the New West. The former Whig's solution was to redraw the Missouri Compromise line of 36°30′ and to extend it to the Pacific Ocean. Slavery would be prohibited to the north and protected to the south of the boundary. Significantly, Crittenden would have applied this demarcation both to territory currently possessed by the United States and to that "hereafter acquired." Republicans decisively rejected this proposal and its possibility of the future extension of slavery either on the North American continent or in the tropics. As early as 1856, John Murray Forbes had worried not just about southern determination to introduce "slavery into our own territories" but also to employ the

55. May, *Southern Dream of a Caribbean Empire*, 120, 125–26 (quotes). The three were Francis P. Blair (Mo.), H. Winter Davis (Md.), and John H. Reagan (Tex.).

"whole power of the confederacy . . . for buying or conquering all the islands north of Panama for the mere extension" of the peculiar institution. The party's newly elected president, Abraham Lincoln, harbored the same fears. In an argument that forecast with remarkable clarity the concerns of U.S. policy makers one hundred years later regarding the deleterious effects of racial discrimination on the nation's international standing, Lincoln wrote that "slavery deprives our republican example of its just influence in the world—enables the enemies of free institutions to taunt us as hypocrites." Turning specifically to the "hereafter" dimension of Crittenden's proposal, Lincoln predicted that the South would "repeat the experiment ad libitum. A year will not pass, till we shall have to take Cuba as a condition upon which they will stay in the Union."[56]

The most ardent southern secessionists were equally negative. "Fire-eaters" such as William Lowndes Yancey of Alabama, Robert Barnwell Rhett of South Carolina, Edmund Ruffin of Virginia, and Albert Brown of Mississippi rejected all compromise and sought slavery's preservation and expansion outside the Union. Southerners more generally, especially those from the Upper South, who appeared receptive to Crittenden's plan, were unwilling to tolerate the Republican containment policy and the accompanying implication of southern inferiority and dependence. As with the South's failure to expand its influence and institutions into Cuba, Central America, or the New West north of Texas, this final northern statement in the area of "foreign affairs" served only to hasten the tragic war.

By 1861 southerners had concluded that their political, economic, and social equality, their material interests, and their personal and sectional honor were no longer safe within the Union. The region's loss of control over foreign policy and its benefits contributed significantly to this conclusion. Prior to the controversy over Missouri in 1819–20, American nationalism and accompanying expansion had consistently benefited the South. Although the immediate extension of slavery into Missouri appeared prosouthern, the bitter national debate over slavery in this new state served notice that the older nationalism, which had incorporated the extension of slavery into national expansion, might not remain functional. Over the ensuing thirty-five years, northern opposition to the extension of slavery hardened, first denying the

56. Ibid., 219, and Weeks, *Building the Continental Empire*, 163 (Lincoln); Morrison, *Slavery and the American West*, 169 (Forbes); Albert D. Kirwan, *John J. Crittenden: The Struggle for the Union* (Lexington, Ky., 1962), 375–421.

South equal access to the New West acquired from Mexico and then to the tropics. Moreover, the practical workings of the Missouri Compromise yielded three northern states but only one southern slave state.

Along with the demise of the old nationalism came the death of the second American party system. By the mid-1850s, the Whigs had succumbed nationally to the sectional controversy over slavery and within the South to the ongoing politics of slavery. By the end of the decade, the latter had left the region much more unified on foreign policy than at any time during the previous four decades. Throughout the foregoing period of partisan debate, southerners, conditioned to think in terms of republicanism, had consistently agreed that foreign policy should help promote regional and individual liberty, equality, and honor. With the old nationalism and expansionist foreign policy rendered obsolete, the South's fears for the loss of these cherished conditions became acute. Jefferson Davis's condemnation of the Republican position on expansion spoke directly to the South's independence and equality. He lectured Republican senators, "Your platform . . . denies us equality . . . . without which we should be degraded if we remained in the Union." Ironically, the Whig warnings had been vindicated; persistent southern Democratic expansionism had failed to offset urbanization or centralization or to mitigate economic dependence on the North or Great Britain. Rather, expansion had accentuated sectional insecurity when the nation could not peacefully allocate the empire of the New West. The South's dread of dependence and rule by "foreigners," expressed as early as the Constitutional Convention, seemed to be at hand. Complementing these fears and alienation and also pushing Dixie toward the abyss was the supreme confidence that King Cotton provided the basis for an independent and triumphant foreign policy.[57]

57. Morrison, *Slavery and the American West*, 255.

CHAPTER 3

Forging an Independent Foreign Policy, 1861–1865

IN THE HEAT of the Senate debate over admitting Kansas into the Union in March 1858, Senator James H. Hammond of South Carolina defiantly proclaimed the power of the South and its principal crop of cotton: "Without firing a gun, without drawing a sword," the South "could bring the whole world to our feet." Should southerners withhold cotton from international commerce, "England . . . and . . . the whole civilized world" would fall prostrate. "No," Hammond thundered, "you dare not make war on cotton. No power on earth dares to make war upon it. Cotton is king!" J. D. B. De Bow, editor of the region's primary economic periodical, concurred. De Bow exhorted fellow southerners "to teach our children to hold the cotton plant in one hand and a sword in the other, ever ready to defend it as the source of commercial power abroad and through that, of independence at home."[1]

Hammond and De Bow cogently articulated the fundamental assumptions underlying Confederate diplomacy. Southerners left the Union confident that their domination of the world's supply of raw cotton could be employed to obtain political independence. This reliance upon economic means to secure political ends recalled the unsuccessful facets of Jefferson's and Madison's diplomacy. Similarly, De Bow's reference to independence at home and the very act of secession highlighted the South's long-standing concern for liberty and honor and fear of dependence—traits that remained

1. Frank L. Owsley, *King Cotton Diplomacy: Foreign Relations of the Confederate States of America*, 2d ed., revised by Harriet Chappell Owsley (Chicago, 1959), 16–17.

central to the South's diplomacy during the life of the Confederacy. Indeed, the region's faith in its economic leverage and its ongoing apprehension of central authority and dependence contributed to several unfortunate patterns in Confederate diplomacy. Confederate leaders were reluctant initially to pursue political and military alliances, preferring instead to utilize economic coercion. In so doing, they squandered potential commercial and political opportunities early in the war, failed to use their limited resources to best advantage, and delayed pursuing more fundamental and essential goals. Reflecting the sectional anxiety about central authority, Confederate diplomatic, economic, and purchasing operations were habitually plagued by a lack of coordination and clear lines of authority. When neither King Cotton nor its successor strategies gained the European support necessary for Confederate victory, the South cried foul in terms that echoed the region's claims of mistreatment and persecution prior to the war. Although harshly critical of Napoleon III and France, these complaints also revealed Dixie's persistent Anglophobia.

These shortcomings in Confederate foreign policy were particularly injurious given the aspiring nation's relative weakness in population, fiscal resources, and manufacturing capacity. At the outset of the war in April 1861, the North had twice as many people and railroad mileage, three times as much bank capital, and ten times as many manufacturers. Northern industrial workers outnumbered southern laborers by 1,300,000 to 110,000 and produced thirteen times as much cotton and woolen cloth, thirty times as many boots and shoes, twenty-four times as many railroad locomotives, and thirty-two times as many firearms. Such yawning discrepancies in physical resources placed a high premium on the South's ability to utilize efficiently its scarce economic resources and to secure European aid. The King Cotton strategy accomplished neither.[2]

As the war began, southern production of raw cotton ostensibly provided a solid basis for Confederate foreign policy. Both Britain and France appeared dependent on Dixie for the cotton needed to fuel the key textile branches of their economies. Britain imported more than 80 percent of its cotton from the South, France more than 90. More than 900,000 British

2. Emory M. Thomas, *The Confederate Nation: 1861–1865* (New York, 1979), 105; Richard N. Current, "God and the Strongest Battalions," in *Why the North Won the Civil War,* ed. David Herbert Donald (New York, 1960), 15; Richard E. Beringer et al., *Why the South Lost the Civil War* (Athens, Ga., 1986), 8–9.

workers and four million people, a fifth of the total population, depended on the cotton textile industry for their livelihood. Although cotton textiles were much less crucial to the French economy, the mills still employed over 250,000 operatives. Cotton also seemed essential to northern prosperity. In 1859 nearly $200 million out of a total of $278 million in U.S. exports had derived from southern products—principally cotton, but also tobacco and rice—and Yankee textile mills consumed 650,000 bales of cotton per year.[3]

Given these trade patterns, southerners confidently assumed that by withholding, or by threatening to withhold, cotton from export that the northern economy would be ruined and that Britain and France would be compelled to help secure Confederate independence. Confederates also offered virtually free trade to the Europeans and contended that an autonomous South would provide a healthier balance of power in North America and block subsequent northern expansion. Finally, southerners assumed a decisive cultural affinity with aristocratic European ruling classes in opposition to the aggressive, contentious northern democracy.

Armed with this package of negative and positive incentives, southerners were supremely confident of diplomatic success and its corollary, political independence. They could not conceive of Britain and France failing to support the Confederacy. In retrospect, this southern confidence, even arrogance, was naive and unfounded and reflected an inability to appreciate the workings of either the contemporary international system or the interests of the European nations. The historian D. P. Crook ties the region's "fatal ignorance of European conditions" to the "cultural isolation in which the south had sought redemption from sectional tensions," and Emory M. Thomas detects a "worldly provincialism," which allowed southerners to read classic European authors and travel on the Continent, all the while acquiring little understanding of contemporary Europeans. John W. Daniel, editor of the *Richmond Examiner* and an intellectual who read Latin classics, Swift, and Voltaire, characteristically wrote home from Italy in the early 1850s:

The real comforts of Europe don't compare with those of the United States. The people are no where as good as ours. The women are ug-

3. Owsley, *King Cotton Diplomacy,* 1–23; D. P. Crook, *The North, the South, and the Powers, 1861–1865* (New York, 1974), 16–17, 19–21; Gordon H. Warren, "The King Cotton Theory," in *Encyclopedia of American Foreign Policy: Studies of the Principal Movements and Ideas,* ed. Alexander DeConde (New York, 1978), 2: 515–20.

lier; the men have fewer ideas. . . . I am busily learning to speak French and studying what is popularly, but most falsely, termed the "great world" and "polite society." I have dined with dukes, jabbered bad grammar to countesses, and am sponged on for seats in my opera-box by counts who stink of garlic, as does the whole country. I receive visits from diplomats with titles as long as a flagstaff, and heads as empty as their hearts, and find the whole concern more trashy than I have ever imagined.[4]

This combination of confidence and naivete led southerners to underestimate the value of diplomacy. The appointment of key diplomatic personnel demonstrated Confederate assumptions. Not until March 1862, nearly a year after the firing on Fort Sumter, did President Jefferson Davis secure a competent secretary of state in Judah P. Benjamin. In the interim, Davis had appointed Robert Toombs of Georgia and R. M. T. Hunter of Virginia. Neither exhibited a grasp of his duties or deemed the office worthy of his abilities; Toombs left for a generalship and Hunter for the Confederate Senate. Similarly, historians have agreed almost unanimously that William Lowndes Yancey, A. Dudley Mann, and Pierre A. Rost, who composed the first set of Confederate commissioners to Europe, were a sorry lot—either because of overly close association with slavery or lack of ability. As with Toombs and Hunter, these men were not replaced until early 1862 by John Slidell in France and James M. Mason in Great Britain. Slidell spoke French fluently, maintained close communications with Napoleon III's government, and participated effectively in Confederate shipbuilding and financial policies. But "he was self-deluding, misjudged French self-interests and purposes, and failed completely to understand the political relationships existing between the emperor and the ministers." Mason contributed even less to the Confederate cause. Arrogant and opinionated, he demonstrated his lack of affinity for British sensitivities by spitting tobacco juice on the carpet of the House of Commons while loudly cheering prosouthern speakers. When compared with Secretary of State William H. Seward and Union representative Charles Frances Adams in London and even William L. Dayton in Paris, this cast of characters fell far short of compensating for southern deficiencies in physical strength.[5]

4. Crook, *The North, the South, and the Powers,* 24–25; Thomas, *Confederate Nation,* 168 (Daniel).

5. Warren F. Spencer, *The Confederate Navy in Europe* (University, Ala., 1983), 14 (quote); Clement Eaton, *A History of the Southern Confederacy* (New York, 1954), 71; for a more favorable

Finally to Mexico, characterized by historian Frank L. Owsley as "in many respects the most vital foreign problem with which the Confederacy had to deal," Davis sent John T. Pickett, previously U.S. consul at Vera Cruz. Pickett variously threatened to summon "at least thirty-thousand Confederate diplomatic agents [soldiers]" into Mexico and dismissed a rumor that Mexican officers might join the northern army with the "hope that they would all go and only regretted that the entire U.S. Army is not officered by Mexico." Were these officers taken prisoner by the South, Pickett declared they would "find themselves for the first time in their lives usefully employed in agricultural pursuits—i.e. hoeing corn and picking cotton." As if his offensive statements had not damaged the Confederacy sufficiently, Pickett was jailed for thirty days for physically assaulting a northerner in Mexico City and was released only after bribing a judge.[6]

Not only did the Confederate diplomatic corps embody the South's relative disregard for diplomacy, Davis initially eschewed political and military alliances. First Yancey, Mann, and Rost and subsequently Mason and Slidell were authorized to request recognition of southern independence but were not empowered to negotiate more formal political alliances or to solicit foreign aid. In early 1862, Hunter declared that "we seek no such interventions" and harbor "no doubt about our abilities to achieve our own independence and to free our soil from the invaders' tread." Mason thereafter informed Lord John Russell, the British foreign secretary, on February 10, 1862, that the South sought neither a military alliance nor more general foreign support. Recognizing the probable futility of this approach, South Carolinian Robert Barnwell Rhett told Yancey, "[You have] no business in Europe, you carry no arguments that Europe cares to hear. My counsel is . . . to stay at home, or to go prepared to conciliate Europe by irresistible proffers of trade."[7]

Most southerners disagreed, assuming that King Cotton and the obvious merits of their claims to nationhood would compel Europe to acknowledge

portrayal of Mason, see Robert W. Young, *Senator James Murray Mason: Defender of the Old South* (Knoxville, Tenn., 1998), 120.

6. Owsley, *King Cotton Diplomacy*, 87; Charles M. Hubbard, *The Burden of Confederate Diplomacy* (Knoxville, Tenn., 1998), 46–47; James W. Daddysman, *The Matamoros Trade: Confederate Commerce, Diplomacy, and Intrigue* (Newark, Del., 1984), 41–42 (Pickett).

7. Douglas B. Ball, *Financial Failure and Confederate Defeat* (Urbana, 1991), 64 (Hunter); Crook, *The North, the South, and the Powers*, 28 (Rhett); Howard Jones, *Union in Peril: The Crisis over British Intervention in the Civil War* (Chapel Hill, 1992), 102.

Confederate independence and to break the northern blockade of southern ports. This inflated sense of southern power led one southerner to recommend as the Confederate seal a man in his own canoe with the inscription, "D——n England and France." And in January 1862, the *New Orleans Daily Picayune* expressed regret at the theretofore minimal expectations of aid from the European nations: "Much harm has been done to the cause of the Southern Confederacy by relying, with absorbing confidence, on the relief in our struggle . . . by the early interposition of foreign powers." Self-reliance was clearly preferable.[8]

The peaceful settlement of the *Trent* affair, the most significant diplomatic crisis of the war's first year, reinforced the *Daily Picayune* editor's bitter disdain for foreign aid. The crisis occurred as James Mason and John Slidell traveled to Europe to replace Yancey, Mann, and Rost. After eluding the northern blockade outside Charleston in early October 1861, Mason and Slidell sailed to Cuba and subsequently departed from Havana on November 7 aboard the *Trent*, a British mail steamer. The following day, Captain Charles Wilkes, commander of the USS. *San Jacinto*, forcibly stopped the *Trent* and took Mason and Slidell prisoner. When Wilkes allowed the *Trent* to sail on to England rather than claiming it as a prize, he seemed to have adopted the British practice of impressment that had figured prominently in the American decision for war in 1812.

Wilkes's actions produced the real possibility of war between the United States and Great Britain and with it the European intervention that might have secured Confederate independence. When popular opinion in the North applauded Wilkes's audacious decision and the British demanded the release of the Confederate envoys and prepared for hostilities, southerners assumed that Great Britain would "resent and punish" such a blatant attack upon their "jurisdiction" and "flag." From the South's perspective, national honor permitted no other response. Lincoln and Seward dashed these southern hopes for a virtual British alliance by deciding on Christmas Day to free the hated Confederates.[9]

As would repeatedly be the case over the ensuing three and one-half years, southerners were deeply chagrined at this lost foreign policy opportunity. From Richmond, the French consul reported that Dixie was "greatly

8. E. Merton Coulter, *The Confederate States of America, 1861–1865* (Baton Rouge, 1950), 192 (D——n); Crook, *The North, the South, and the Powers*, 171 (*Picayune*).

9. Brian Jenkins, *Britain and the War for the Union* (Montreal, 1974–80), I: 198–99.

upset." Davis and his government had expected war since Great Britain had "not obtained all the satisfactions" it had "a right to demand for the honor of its flag." The editor of the *New Orleans Daily Picayune* was similarly appalled at Lincoln's "cowardice" and dismissed the North's decision as a "sickening, contemptible and disgusting exhibition of diplomacy."[10]

Unfounded Confederate expectations and subsequent disappointment and bitterness were not the only revealing aspects of the *Trent* affair. It was also instructive that the South played no meaningful role in either the initiation or the resolution of the crisis. Some scholars have argued that the Confederate envoys acted as bait and even facilitated their own capture with the goal of inciting a U.S.-British conflict. Neither direct evidence nor other contemporary examples of shrewd Confederate diplomatic calculation substantiate this contention. The South was unprepared in terms of either appropriately placed diplomatic personnel or a follow-up strategy to influence events after the capture of Mason and Slidell. Whitehall and Washington resolved their differences while the South watched from afar. Both northern diplomatic flexibility and British caution and reluctance to intervene were prescient and ominous omens for the Confederacy. Finally, in a telling early commentary on the diplomatic liability the institution of slavery imposed on the South, the *Times of London* assured Mason and Slidell that Britain would "have done just as much to rescue two of their own Negroes," and *Punch* referred to the South as "Slaveownia."[11]

In the absence of fatal northern miscalculation or British adventurism, the South was left to act on its professions of independence and strength and to embargo exports of raw cotton. Summarizing southern thinking, the *Charleston Mercury* proclaimed, "The cards are in our hands," and "we intend to play them out to the bankruptcy of every cotton factory in Great Britain and France or the acknowledgement of our independence." Although President Davis concurred with the *Mercury*'s strategy, he preferred that the Confederate government avoid an official endorsement of an embargo and the accompanying appearance of blackmailing the Europeans. Rather, southern newspapers, planters, cotton factors, and state govern-

10. Ibid., 1: 229 (*Picayune*); Lynn M. Case and Warren F. Spencer, *The United States and France: Civil War Diplomacy* (Philadelphia, 1970), 193–94 (French consul).

11. Jenkins, *Britain and the War for the Union*, 1: 81 (*Punch*); Alexander DeConde, *A History of American Foreign Policy*, 3d ed. (New York, 1978), 2: 227 (*Times*); for the Confederate trap, see Case and Spencer, *United States and France*, 190–94; Crook, *The North, the South, and the Powers*, 106 n. 14; and Hubbard, *Burden of Confederate Diplomacy*, 64–65.

ments acted with amazing unanimity in effecting a largely extralegal prohibition on cotton sales during the first year of the war. Building on the logic of the embargo and enforced scarcity in Europe, the Confederate Congress passed joint resolutions in the spring of 1862 urging that no cotton be planted that year and that any cotton in danger of falling into Yankee hands be burned. Hundreds of thousands of bales were put to the torch, and cotton yields fell from 4.5 million bales in 1861 to 1.5 million in 1862, 449,059 bales in 1863, and 299,372 in 1864. Aided, ironically, by the northern blockade and capture of southern ports and territory, the South had enacted the King Cotton strategy with a vengeance.[12]

To southern dismay, King Cotton's sense of independence and strength was "founded on a grave financial misconception." As Lord Richard B. P. Lyons, British minister to the United States commented in 1860: "The very exaggerated and very false ideas they have in the South about cotton will lead to very foolish conduct. It is true that cotton is almost a necessity to us, but it is still more necessary for them to sell it than it is for us to buy it." With far stronger economies than the Confederacy, both Great Britain and France were better equipped to endure the dislocation of the international cotton trade. Indeed, as the American war began, the larger British and French cotton manufacturers had amassed an oversupply of both raw cotton and finished goods. Therefore, southern withholding of cotton actually aided the efforts of these manufacturers to adjust their inventories. Problems of scarcity did not arise until mid-1862, and even then, the real question may have been the apprehension of inadequate supplies of raw cotton rather than the reality. Thousands of cotton operatives lost jobs in Britain and France during 1862 and after, but in neither nation did textile interests or the majority of the unemployed workers have the inclination or the influence to force their governments to intervene on behalf of the Confederacy and risk war with the Union. The London *Times* noted correctly "that it would be cheaper to keep all Lancashire on turtle and venison than to plunge into a desperate war with the Northern States of America."[13]

12. Owsley, *King Cotton Diplomacy*, 23–50 (*Mercury*, 24).

13. Richard I. Lester, *Confederate Finance and Purchasing in Great Britain* (Charlottesville, Va., 1975), 6 (misperception); Norman R. Ferris, *Desperate Diplomacy: William H. Seward's Foreign Policy, 1861* (Knoxville, Tenn., 1976), 40 (Lyons); Frank J. Merli, *Great Britain and the Confederate Navy, 1861–1865* (Bloomington, Ind., 1970), 258 (*Times*); Eugene A. Brady, "A Reconsideration of the Lancashire 'Cotton Famine,'" *Agricultural History* 37 (July 1963): 156–62; Crook, *The North, the South, and the Powers*, 199–206; Case and Spencer, *United States and France*, 158–89, 374–81; Philip S. Foner, *British Labor and the American Civil War* (New York,

Both the British and French economies were far more complex than the South understood. Although British textile workers suffered, cotton manufacturers, munitions makers, shipbuilders, and linen and wool producers profited from the war. Moreover, the North had long been a valued consumer of British steel and metal goods, liquor, pottery, and investment capital; and Britain had imported massive quantities of corn and wheat from the United States during the 1850s. While the war may not have been of overall benefit to the British economy, the impact hardly dictated government aid to the South and opposition to the North—which was a better customer, a principal provider of foodstuffs, and a potentially formidable military adversary. Similarly, the influence of France's watchmaking, silk, glass, lace, chinaware, wine, and shipbuilding concerns far outweighed the cotton textile makers and their allies. Deeming peace essential to their prosperity, those other French groups may have favored mediation with Union approval but were unprepared for blatantly prosouthern steps. And as in Great Britain, the linen, wool, and hemp industries did well. In short, the two principal European economies were far too diverse to be compelled to bow before King Cotton. Like its Jeffersonian forebears, the Confederate generation had greatly overestimated its ability to coerce the major European nations through economic pressure.[14]

The King Cotton strategy not only failed to compel European intervention, it also squandered the South's principal financial resource. Having begun the war without a treasury, supplies of bullion, or established credit, the South needed to parlay its cotton into a functional commercial asset. Embargoing, burning, and curtailing the planting of cotton accomplished precisely the opposite. During the war's crucial first year, Alexander H. Stephens and Robert Toombs recommended shipping 100,000 bales of cotton to Europe for use in the purchase of badly needed military matériel. Subsequent students have observed that extensive cotton shipments would have been easier in 1861 and 1862 before the Union naval blockade became more efficient and that utilizing cotton as collateral for significant foreign loans would have facilitated Confederate purchasing operations in Europe and

1981), 1–78; Thomas D. Schoonover, *The United States in Central America, 1860–1911: Episodes of Social Imperialism and Imperial Rivalry in the World System* (Durham, N.C., 1991), 1–27, 175–79; Ball, *Financial Failure and Confederate Defeat,* 65–69, 91.

14. Owsley, *King Cotton Diplomacy,* 545–57; Case and Spencer, *United States and France,* 158–89; Crook, *The North, the South, and the Powers,* 268–69; Henry Blumenthal, *A Reappraisal of Franco-American Relations, 1830–1871* (Chapel Hill, 1959), 153–56.

might have helped align the European states on the side of the South. When Davis and the overwhelming majority of southerners disagreed with Stephens and Toombs, such possibilities, like so much of Confederate history, were relegated to the category of what might have been.[15]

Not until the spring of 1862 did Confederate leaders contemplate using their cotton resources in alternate approaches to the Europeans. In July 1862 Davis offered Napoleon III of France 100,000 bales of cotton to break the northern blockade, and in December he tendered a barter arrangement to the British, which would have exchanged $300 million in cotton, tobacco, and naval stores for desperately needed manufactured goods. When these attempted bribes fared no better than the coercive embargo, the South sought to employ cotton holdings as the collateral for a variety of bond schemes. The most significant of these transactions was a loan secured by cotton from the French firm of Emile Erlanger and Company in 1863. That the South derived approximately $8.5 million after discounts and expenses from the $14.5 million loan demonstrated the costs of delay. The fate of both the South and its cotton was far more problematic in 1863 than in 1861 and therefore less able to inspire fiscal confidence.[16]

Having exhausted all other alternatives, the Confederacy turned belatedly in late 1863 to Stephens's and Toombs's suggestion of shipping cotton directly to Europe as payment for war matériels. Proponents of this policy contended that the central government should acquire the cotton and oversee both its transportation to Europe and the return of war matériels. Direct government involvement was designed to eliminate the perceived abuses of private blockade running. Beginning in April 1861, the government had encouraged private shippers to run the blockade and thereby demonstrate its ineffectiveness. Repeated demonstrations were expected to bring European condemnation of the blockade and perhaps diplomatic recognition or military intervention. Although none of these benefits transpired, private, often foreign, merchants amassed large profits and frequently brought luxury items of no value to the war effort back to the South from Europe. Jefferson Davis complained that Confederate commerce had been

15. Henry Blumenthal, "Confederate Diplomacy: Popular Notions and International Realities," *Journal of Southern History* 32 (May 1966): 169; Lester, *Confederate Finance and Purchasing,* 5–7, 196–97; Ball, *Financial Failure and Confederate Defeat,* 71–79; Samuel B. Thompson, *Confederate Purchasing Operations Abroad* (Chapel Hill, 1935), 4.

16. Case and Spencer, *United States and France,* 299–300; Judith F. Gentry, "A Confederate Success in Europe: The Erlanger Loan," *Journal of Southern History* 36 (May 1970): 157–88.

almost exclusively in the hands of aliens; that our cotton, tobacco, and naval stores were being drained from the States, and that we were receiving in return cargoes of liquors, wines, and articles of luxury; that the imported goods, being held in a few hands and in limited quantities, were sold at prices so exorbitant that the blockade-runners, after purchasing fresh cargoes of cotton, still retained large sums of Confederate money, which they invested in gold for exportation and in foreign exchange, and that the whole course of the trade had a direct tendency to impoverish our country, demoralize our people, depreciate our currency, and enfeeble our defense.[17]

In January 1864 President Davis and the Confederate Congress forbade the importing of luxuries and directed that one-half of the tonnage of private ships sailing to and from the South be reserved for government cargoes. Individual states were empowered to charter the other half of such vessels. In April the Confederate government also moved to purchase cotton, tobacco, and naval stores for direct shipment abroad. "Cotton which had failed as a political king was now to be put into service as a menial where it should have been put in the beginning."[18]

Ironically, the Confederacy confronted a scarcity of available cotton. Although the government owned 400,000 bales, most of it was stored on inland, often inaccessible, plantations. A flock of government agents fanned out over the countryside in a frequently chaotic, self-defeating purchasing spree. Not until August were government acquisitions consolidated into a coherent system, but this system never encompassed the large cotton trade through Matamoros, Mexico, which remained overwhelmingly in private hands. The Confederacy also encountered transportation problems. The first Confederate purchasing agents in Europe had quickly recognized the greater efficiency and economy of chartering or acquiring blockade runners for exclusive government use. Captain James D. Bulloch had employed the *Fingal* in this fashion in November 1861, and the Ordnance Department owned four steamers by 1864. Contracts were quickly negotiated for fourteen additional ships, only six of which reached Dixie before the war ended. Even with the ongoing dependence on private shipping, contemporaries ap-

17. Thompson, *Confederate Purchasing Operations Abroad,* 50–51, 96 (Davis); Ball, *Financial Failure and Confederate Defeat,* 91–94, 96–99.

18. Thompson, *Confederate Purchasing Operations Abroad,* 88–89; Owsley, *King Cotton Diplomacy,* 389 (king).

plauded the new system. By year's end, President Davis claimed that the government had exported 11,796 bales of cotton worth $2.1 million, three times the value that would have accrued under prior arrangements. Still, by late 1864 the South faced a much more effective Union blockade and a drastically reduced store of cotton, and in early 1865 northern victories rendered the system irrelevant.[19]

The same faith in King Cotton, assumptions of a short war, and apprehensions over central authority that delayed the most productive use of cotton combined with the Confederacy's resulting financial weakness to retard the formation of well-coordinated purchasing operations in Europe. Through at least the first two and one-half years of the war, the South's efforts at securing war matériels in Europe were characterized by "numerous officers, agents, business firms, and other individuals seeking, in a more or less independent fashion, to issue orders, to determine policies, to supervise finance, to purchase supplies, and to ship them to points of safety in the Confederacy." While government agents such as Captain James D. Bulloch of the Navy Department and Caleb Huse of the Ordnance Department were competent, resourceful, and surprisingly successful, the lack of clear central authority and policy often resulted in official Confederate agents bidding against one another and private contractors for matériels. This wasted limited resources and yielded exorbitant private profits. The lack of system also produced debilitating jealousy and damaging recriminations among Confederate agents and repeatedly left the government embarrassed by the actions of private contractors posing as official representatives of the South.

By mid-1863, Mason, Slidell, Bulloch, and virtually all of the South's competent representatives in Europe were pleading with Richmond for reform. Bulloch later observed that "nothing gave me so much harassing perplexity . . . as the supervision of the private contracts," and Henry Hotze, who oversaw Confederate propaganda in Europe, wrote to Secretary of State Benjamin in October 1863 that it was "undeniable that the credit of the Government has suffered most seriously by the clashing interests, the rivalries, and hostilities, sometimes the disgraceful public squabbles of con-

19. Thompson, *Confederate Purchasing Operations Abroad*, 19–20, 24; Owsley, *King Cotton Diplomacy*, 387–93; Spencer, *Confederate Navy in Europe* , 25–26; Stanley Lebergott, "Why the South Lost: Commercial Purpose in the Confederacy, 1861–1865," *Journal of American History* 70 (June 1983): 58–62, 69, 73–74.

tractors. . . . This great evil is by the many forms of authority . . . the want of precision and vigor." The Confederate government remedied most of these problems by giving Colin J. McRae general authority over the South's European purchasing and financial operations in September 1863 and by canceling all private contracts. McRae provided the needed precision and vigor; still, as with cotton's use and blockade running, his influence was brought to bear well after the time of decision had been reached both on American battlefields and in European capitals.[20]

This pattern of overconfidence in King Cotton and exaggerated expectations of European intervention also led to missed opportunities in Confederate propaganda efforts abroad. By the summer of 1861, Rost, Yancey, and Mann recognized the South's inferior ability to place its case before the European public. The North commanded a near monopoly of American war news; by contrast, the South lacked both a reliable flow of information and prosouthern newspapers as outlets for the Confederate version of events and issues. This lack of information was only part of the larger Confederate liability in communications, which sometimes required up to six months for dispatches to go from Richmond to London or Paris, a time lapse that seriously hampered Confederate diplomats. Although the southern commissioners solicited State Department attention to these matters, the response was belated. Not until mid-November 1861 did Richmond designate Henry Hotze to oversee Confederate propaganda work. Swiss-born, Hotze in the 1850s had migrated to Mobile, Alabama, where he became a naturalized citizen and an associate editor of the *Mobile Register*. Intelligent, cosmopolitan, and energetic, Hotze was one of Dixie's most able and active foreign agents.[21]

Hotze reached Europe on January 29, 1862. He quickly succeeded in inserting prosouthern materials into several British papers and in cultivating writers willing to aid the South. In May he initiated publication of the *Index*, a paper that ultimately provided the South with an effective news and public-relations organ in London and circulated more generally throughout the British Isles and France. But even as he improved the South's public

20. Thompson, *Confederate Purchasing Operations Abroad*, 11, 77, 83 (Bulloch, Hotze); Owsley, *King Cotton Diplomacy*, 384–86.

21. Charles P. Cullop, *Confederate Propaganda in Europe, 1861–1865* (Coral Gables, Fla., 1969), 18; Crook, *The North, the South, and the Powers*, 211; Jenkins, *Britain and the War for the Union*, 1: 136–37; Howard Jones, *Abraham Lincoln and a New Birth of Freedom: The Union and Slavery in the Diplomacy of the Civil War* (Lincoln, Neb., 1999), 42–43, 67.

posture, Hotze echoed previous complaints of a dearth of reliable and timely news from the South and woefully insufficient funding. Obtaining information remained a problem throughout the war, as the Union blockade significantly impeded the transmission of Confederate intelligence.[22]

In the crucial autumn of 1862, financial circumstances remained desperate. Hotze received no money from Richmond until January 1863. In the interim he was relegated to soliciting loans with mixed success from other Confederate agents. Among those agents was Edward DeLeon, a South Carolinian with experience as U.S. consul in Egypt who had been added to the Confederate propaganda contingent in April 1862 and provided with $25,000. DeLeon not only rejected Hotze's entreaties but also emerged as a bitter and injurious rival of both Hotze and John Slidell. In sum, delayed commencement, inadequate funding, and debilitating internal rivalries and bickering plagued still another facet of Confederate diplomacy.[23]

In addition to these fiscal, organizational, and personnel shortcomings, at least two central themes in the Confederate message were ill-suited to inducing European intervention. As did Mason and Slidell, Hotze emphasized the ineffective or "paper" nature of the Union blockade and the inevitability of southern independence. Historian Henry Blumenthal has observed perceptively that if the blockade were so porous, Britain and France had little incentive to intervene to obtain southern cotton. Similarly, the assumption of assured southern victory was as likely to produce European restraint as diplomatic intrusion and possible conflict with the North. Why intervene in the face of U.S. Secretary of State William H. Seward's repeated threats of war if one agreed with the December 13, 1862, pronouncement by the London *Spectator*: "We are assuming what all Englishmen now assume, that absolute subjugation of the South is a dream, that the war is a question of boundaries,—a question, as mathematicians would say, of maximum or minimum extent of the slave power"? Both British and French leaders echoed this refrain well into 1863, and at least one historian has contended, not altogether convincingly, that this "glittering illusion" was the "fundamental reason for England's inaction."[24]

22. Cullop, *Confederate Propaganda*, 18–54.

23. Ibid., 73–84, 132–35.

24. Blumenthal, "Confederate Diplomacy," 157, 162; Joseph M. Hernon Jr., "British Sympathies in the American Civil War: A Reconsideration," *Journal of Southern History* 33 (August 1967): 360 (*Spectator*); Sheldon Vanauken, *The Glittering Illusion: English Sympathy for the Southern Confederacy* (Worthing, England, 1988), 129.

When neither Confederate economic diplomacy nor southern propaganda realized the objective of European intervention, more traditional geopolitical calculations determined Dixie's foreign policy fate. Here, as in the economic realm, British and French decisions would prove decisive, and neither country was inclined toward rash actions. In London, Prime Minister Henry John Temple, Lord Palmerston, presided over a narrow Whig majority in the House of Commons, which he sought to avoid endangering with the American question. In Paris the mercurial Napoleon III confronted a divided public, and an overly prosouthern policy would have put him at odds with the bulk of French workers, liberals, and intelligentsia.

A much greater concern with European than American issues reinforced this caution in both Britain and France. At the time of the firing on Fort Sumter, Napoleon's foreign policy was overextended by involvements in China, Mexico, Austria, and Italy, and each of the latter three took precedence over the American war. Both of the French emperor's foreign ministers, Edouard Thouvenel and Edouard Drouyn de Lhuys, advocated a restrained and neutral policy. When asked about his sovereign's policy, Drouyn de Lhuys observed, "He has none; he awaits events." Given these domestic and foreign policy considerations, Napoleon would act only in concert with Britain.[25]

Therefore, the crucial decisions were left to Palmerston and his foreign secretary, Lord John Russell. As did generations of British leaders, they worried most about the European balance of power. To this primary consideration, they added the defense and control of Canada. Even more than with Napoleon, these diverse domestic and diplomatic calculations translated into a circumspect American policy. In October 1861, Palmerston declared that Britain should keep "quite clear of the conflict," and Russell advised Parliament, "For God's sake, let us, if possible, keep out of it." Acting on what historian Norman A. Graebner has characterized as "Europe's diplomatic tradition" of realism, Palmerston, Russell, Thouvenel, and Drouyn de Lhuys refused to recognize or align their nations with the Confederacy "until the South had demonstrated the power required to establish and maintain its independence." Only by the "Course of Events," Palmerston pronounced, could southern "independence . . . be converted into an Established Fact." Unless "their separate independence" was a "truth and

25. Spencer, *Confederate Navy in Europe*, 213 (Drouyn); Case and Spencer, *United States and France*, 316–73; Blumenthal, *Franco-American Relations*, 123–24, 133–49.

fact," the states of the Confederacy would not be "a bit more independent for our saying so unless we followed up our Declaration by taking Part with them in the war."[26]

During the late summer and fall of 1862, events appeared to portend this southern diplomatic and perhaps military triumph. In late August the Confederates routed the Yankees at the Second Battle of Manassas and General Robert E. Lee invaded western Maryland, threatening Baltimore and Washington. Appalled at the ever-mounting carnage, convinced that the North could not subdue the rebellion, and apprehensive over the possibility of a race war tied to the abolition of slavery, Russell initiated British cabinet consideration of mediation and sounded Paris on the possibility of joint action. Southern hopes soared when British Chancellor of the Exchequer William E. Gladstone proclaimed on October 7 that "there is no doubt that Jefferson Davis and other leaders of the South have made an army; they are making, it appears, a navy; and they have made what is more than either, they have made a nation."[27]

Before either London or Paris could act on these inclinations toward mediation, events dictated otherwise. On September 17, the war's most sanguinary single day, northern forces stopped Lee's invasion at the Battle of Antietam near Sharpsburg, Maryland, and forced the Confederates to retreat into Virginia. Five days later, President Abraham Lincoln issued the preliminary Emancipation Proclamation, declaring slaves freed on January 1, 1863, in those areas still in rebellion. Neither the North's demonstration of resiliency and ongoing military vitality nor the long-delayed declaration on slavery immediately diverted Russell and fellow British interventionists. The British press condemned Lincoln's pronouncement as a hypocritical and desperate attempt to incite a slave insurrection. The London *Times* sneered that Lincoln's real objective was a "servile war" in which the slaves would "murder the families of their masters," and *Punch* dismissed the proc-

26. Frank J. Merli and Theodore A. Wilson, "The British Cabinet and the Confederacy: Autumn, 1862," *Maryland Historical Magazine* 65 (fall 1970): 1242 (Russell and Palmerston quotes); Norman A. Graebner, "Northern Diplomacy and European Neutrality," in *Why the North Won the Civil War*, 66; Jones, *Union in Peril*, 197; Jenkins, *Britain and the War for the Union*, 2: 66 (Palmerston).

27. Jenkins, *Britain and the War for the Union*, 2: 172 (quote); Kinley J. Brauer, "British Mediation and the American Civil War: A Reconsideration," *Journal of Southern History* 38 (February 1972): 49–64.

lamation as "Abe Lincoln's Last Card; or Rouge-et-Noir." Russell shared this fear of servile insurrection and perceived Antietam as a further indication that the two sides were locked in an interminable stalemate doing unspeakable damage in the Americas, injuring international commerce, and threatening to suck others into the maelstrom.[28]

But during the remainder of the fall, the impact of both the battle and the declaration reverberated to the South's detriment. Even before Antietam, Russell had encountered stiff opposition to mediation within the British government. On September 29, the day before news of the northern victory reached Europe, George Gower, second earl of Granville and the lord president of the Queen's Council, warned Russell against holding "any bona-fide expectation of its [mediation] being accepted. . . . It would not be a good moment to recognize the South just before a great Federal Success—If on the other hand the Confederates continue Victorious as is to be hoped, we should stand better then than now in recognizing them. In any case I doubt, if the War continues long after our recognition of the South, whether it will be possible for us to avoid drifting into it."[29]

Following Antietam, British Secretary for War George Cornwall Lewis enunciated the most compelling challenge to Russell and his mediation policy. In a fifteen-thousand-word memorandum to the cabinet, the war secretary raised irrefutable legal and practical challenges to intervention. Most fundamentally, he asserted that the South had not established clear, unchallenged independence from the North. To undertake mediation in the absence of Dixie's autonomy would place Britain in an untenable political situation and a hazardous military position. Had the South's independence been sufficiently "clear," he wrote, "they and their English advocates would not be so eager to secure their recognition by European Governments." Prime Minister Palmerston agreed, asserting, "The whole matter is full of difficulty, and can only be cleared up by some more decided events between the contending armies." Reemphasizing the policy of caution, Palmerston and the cabinet rejected Napoleon's specific call in late October for joint intervention and with it the South's most promising opportunity for European intercession. "Characteristically," observed historian D. P. Crook,

28. Jones, *Union in Peril,* 164–80; Jones, *Lincoln,* 116 (*Times*); R. J. M. Blackett, *Divided Hearts: Britain and the American Civil War* (Baton Rouge, 2001), 29 (*Punch*).

29. Thomas, *Confederate Nation,* 181.

"southern diplomacy" had "played no part" in the British decision for abstention. By contrast, U.S. Secretary of State Seward's persistent threat of war against European meddlers hovered over British deliberations.[30]

Union opposition to slavery also impeded the southern diplomatic cause during the crucial months of late 1862. In January 1862 President Lincoln had predicted, "I cannot imagine that any European power would dare to recognize and aid the Southern Confederacy if it became clear that the Confederacy stands for slavery and the Union for freedom." Response to the preliminary Emancipation Proclamation in September 1862 and the final declaration on January 1, 1863, was far more complex than Lincoln had anticipated, but the North's antislavery stance ultimately strengthened its diplomatic position and weakened the South's. Although Russell, Gladstone, and the British press dismissed Lincoln's September declaration as a cynical war measure likely to incite brutal racial conflict, sizable segments of the British public increasingly applauded the North's official antislavery position. Beginning in December 1862, large pro-Union public meetings, composed largely of working people, endorsed the North's condemnation of slavery. Not all British workers favored the North; some advocated recognition of the South in hope of securing cotton and easing the suffering in the textile districts. But workers predominated in local Union clubs, while aristocrats and mill owners controlled pro-Confederate meetings. Henry Hotze recognized both the key role of British laborers and the burden slavery placed on Confederate diplomacy. The "Lancashire operatives," he lamented, were the only "class which . . . continues actively inimical to us. . . . They look upon us, and . . . upon slavery as the author and source of their present miseries."[31]

To have gained British intervention, the pro-South forces needed to

30. Jones, *Union in Peril,* 210–18 (Lewis); Howard Jones, "History and Mythology: The Crisis over British Intervention in the Civil War," in *The Union, the Confederacy, and the Atlantic Rim,* ed. Robert E. May (West Lafayette, Ind., 1995), 46 (Palmerston); Crook, *The North, the South, and the Powers,* 222.

31. James M. McPherson, "'The Whole Family of Man': Lincoln and the Last Best Hope Abroad," in *The Union, the Confederacy, and the Atlantic Rim,* 141 (Lincoln); Jones, *Lincoln,* 94 (Hotze); R. J. M. Blackett, "Pressure from Without: African Americans, British Public Opinion, and Civil War Diplomacy," in *The Union, the Confederacy, and the Atlantic Rim,* 78–90; Blackett, *Divided Hearts,* 28–29, 123–24, 230; Foner, *British Labor,* 1–78; Mary Ellison, *Support of Secession: Lancashire and the American Civil War* (Chicago, 1972); Kinley J. Brauer, "The Slavery Problem in the Diplomacy of the American Civil War," *Pacific Historical Review* 46 (August 1977): 439–69.

present a nearly unanimous voice; and the strong antislavery, pro-Union sentiment easily embodied the divided opinion sufficient to stymie inclinations toward mediation or recognition. Palmerston incisively described the dilemma. Slavery, he said, was the "great difficulty." How, he asked Russell, could their government "without offense to many People here[,] recommend to the North to sanction Slavery and to undertake to give back Runaways, and yet would not the South insist upon such Conditions[,] especially after Lincoln's Emancipation Decree[?]" Historian Reid Mitchell has asserted unequivocally, "The Emancipation Proclamation destroyed the possibility of European intervention in the Civil War. It established that what had looked to some liberals like a war for self-determination against a central government was actually a war of slavery against freedom."[32]

Determining how the French public responded to the Civil War and resulting economic suffering is even more difficult than for England, but here too, the South was clearly out of step with contemporary European attitudes opposing human bondage. In September 1863 Henry Hotze reported that antislavery feeling "had passed into, or has not yet ceased to be, one of those fixed principles which neither individuals nor nations permit to be called in question." French antislavery sentiment, he continued, was a "deep-rooted antipathy, rather than active hostility, against us." The following year, twelve important citizens of Tours wrote revealingly to John Slidell: "It is useless to make any appeal to the people of France. It may be to our interest to support you. There may be strong material and political reasons for a close alliance between us, but as long as you maintain and are maintained by slavery, we cannot offer you our alliance. On the contrary, we believe and expect you will fail!"[33]

Thus by early 1863, both the northern victory at Antietam and the official interjection of slavery into the foreign relations dialogue had undermined southern hopes for European intervention. By threatening stability and the balance of power and by dominating European attention, events on the Continent in 1863 further weakened Dixie's hopes for aid. Lasting from February through November, the Polish insurrection against Russian domination preoccupied both French and English policy makers. As the Polish

32. Jones, *Lincoln,* 129 (Palmerston); Reid Mitchell, "The Perseverance of the Soldiers," in *Why the Confederacy Lost,* ed. Gabor S. Boritt (New York, 1992), 117.

33. Owsley, *King Cotton Diplomacy,* 531 (Hotze); McPherson, "'The Whole Family of Man,'" 145 (citizens); Case and Spencer, *United States and France,* 316–33, 604–7.

crisis subsided, Denmark commenced a war with Austria and Prussia over the control of Schleswig-Holstein that lasted until mid-1864. Both northern and southern diplomats complained that European leaders were "far more deeply engrossed with the conferences, jealousies, and rivalries between the leading Powers of Europe than with the fate of constitutional government in America." On balance such preoccupation and its accompanying inaction aided the Union.[34]

As southern hopes for diplomatic recognition and European intervention faded in mid-1863, the Confederate response reflected the South's acute sense of honor and tendency to become irate at ostensibly less-than-equitable treatment. In a fit of "temper," Jefferson Davis ordered James Mason to leave London rather than submit to the continued British refusal to acknowledge the South's nationhood and independence. Even as Mason was quitting the British capitol, Davis and Secretary of State Benjamin expelled the British consuls from the Confederacy. The *Montgomery Advertiser* spoke for the Davis administration and the offended South: "If England, France, and Spain and other nations, desire representatives in the Confederacy to look after their own commercial interest and the interest of their citizens, let them take an honorable course and recognize the Confederate States as a nation."[35]

This collection of pro-Union developments did not entirely eliminate the possibility of European conflict with the North. Much of this possibility in 1863 and 1864 centered on southern efforts to build a navy in Europe. Hostilities between North and South followed two decades of remarkable innovation in naval science. Beginning in the 1840s, Europeans had developed steam-powered warships that were "propeller-driven, armored-plated, and equipped with rifled shell guns set in revolving turrets." Although the United States had not incorporated such changes into the federal navy prior to 1861, the Union possessed the capacity to construct such ships. When the war began, eight of the ten U.S. naval shipyards were located in the North. The Union quickly blockaded Pensacola in May 1861, leaving only the Gresport Navy Yard in Norfolk available to the Confederates. Despite ingenious

34. John Kutolowski, "The Effect of the Polish Insurrection of 1863 on the American Civil War Diplomacy," *Historian* 27 (August 1965): 566 (quote); Laurence J. Orzell, "A 'Favorable Interval': The Polish Insurrection in Civil War Diplomacy, 1863," *Civil War History* 24 (December 1978): 332–50.

35. Young, *Senator James Murray Mason*, 147–48 (temper); Hubbard, *Burden of Confederate Diplomacy*, 147–48, 151(*Advertiser*).

and tenacious efforts at domestic construction, by the war's end, the South had built only twenty-nine ironclads of widely varying quality and seaworthiness; by contrast, the North constructed sixty such ships and even sold some to foreign powers.[36]

Given this staggering deficit, Confederate Secretary of the Navy Stephen R. Mallory recognized both the potential importance of naval warfare to the South and the necessity of securing the ships in Europe. In May 1861 the secretary devised a two-pronged naval strategy and accompanying purchasing program. He first sought fast cruisers to attack the North's merchant marine; the attacks were designed to disrupt Union commerce and to disperse the Union fleet, thereby weakening the blockade. In addition, Mallory coveted a flotilla of ironclad rams to force open southern ports by challenging the northern blockade directly.[37]

Mallory complemented his strategic prescience with the brilliant appointment of James D. Bulloch as the South's first, and ultimately most important, naval official in Europe. Although a civilian in 1861, Bulloch had risen to the rank of lieutenant while serving fourteen years in the U.S. Navy and had added extensive experience as a captain for a New York shipping line in the 1850s. This combination of military and private background had afforded Bulloch a broad knowledge of naval technology and commerce, international law, and the Western Hemisphere's major sea lanes and harbors. Although hampered by inadequate finances, persistent harassment by northern agents, and the South's fragmented European organization, Bulloch's accomplishments led historian Warren F. Spencer to assert that he "served the Confederate cause better than any other agent abroad."[38]

Bulloch succeeded most spectacularly in the building and launching of the *Florida* and the *Alabama*. He did so by exploiting ambiguities in the British Foreign Enlistment Act, which allowed for the construction of naval vessels in British yards as long as the ships were equipped or armed beyond British territory or by persons unaware of the vessels' ultimate intended use. The *Florida* departed England in March 1862, and the *Alabama* followed in July. These two ships alone captured or destroyed nearly one hundred

36. Merli, *Great Britain and the Confederate Navy,* 5–7 (quote); Raimondo Luraghi, *A History of the Confederate Navy,* trans., Paolo E. Coletta (Annapolis, 1996), 27–28, 34–35, 53–55, 181–90, 346–47.

37. Merli, *Great Britain and the Confederate Navy,* 16–17; Spencer, *Confederate Navy in Europe,* 3.

38. Spencer, *Confederate Navy in Europe,* 17.

northern vessels and, together with some seventeen other Confederate raiders, caused northern insurance rates to double.

Ironically, the raiders succeeded too well. Russell and Britishers more generally recognized that, regardless of legal niceties, allowing the construction of southern naval ships on English soil conflicted with Britain's official neutrality and with the nation's long-term naval well-being. The *Southampton Times* castigated the policy as "inconsistent with our neutral position" and responsible for "the wanton destruction and the terrible havoc which these Confederate privateers have committed." Voicing the more extended view of British interests, the duke of Argyll stated that in "the first war in which we are engaged 'Alabamas' will certainly be fitted out against us from neutral ports. It will then be found important to be able to say that we did our best to protest against the legitimacy of such proceedings."[39]

Foreign Secretary Russell signaled the government's change of policy in April 1863 by seizing the *Alexandria,* a small wooden ship under construction in Liverpool. Henceforth, the British government would detain "vessels *apparently intended* for the Confederate service" even if conclusive proof were wanting. When the Court of the Exchequer rejected this interpretation of the Foreign Enlistment Act, "the British government after 1863 schemed to circumvent its own law." Although the *Alexandria* was eventually released, Russell, under intense northern pressure and against the backdrop of Union victories at Vicksburg and Gettysburg and ongoing European instability, detained and ultimately purchased the Laird rams. Armor-plated and equipped with turret-mounted guns, the rams occasioned great fear in the North and exaggerated hopes in the South. As with the *Alexandria,* their seizure indicated unmistakably that the British policy of neutrality had taken precedence over strict interpretation of the outmoded Foreign Enlistment Act—that Britain was not prepared to risk war with the North by adopting a prosouthern neutrality.[40]

Russell's seizure of the *Alexandria* destroyed Bulloch's British shipbuilding plan. The skilled Confederate operative perceived that subsequent efforts to launch southern ships "would result in their seizure and indefinite detention by the means of the interminable procedures of the court of the exchequer." Bulloch also recognized the bleak prospects for obtaining the rams; wooden ships might "evade the law," but the "object of armored

39. Merli, *Great Britain and the Confederate Navy,* 119.
40. Ibid., 176 (vessels); Spencer, *Confederate Navy in Europe,* 103 (circumvent).

ships" was "too evident for disguise." When Russell detained the rams in September, Bulloch conceded that "no amount of discretion or management on my part can effect the release of the ships." His only alternative was France, "where everything . . . would depend upon the secret purposes of the Chief of State," Napoleon III.[41]

The French emperor had broached the possibility of Confederate shipbuilding in France to John Slidell in October 1862, and Lucien Arman, a Bordeaux shipbuilder and intimate of Napoleon III, had renewed the overture in early 1863. Each asserted that both constructing and arming the ships were feasible as long as the vessels were officially being sent to another nation. His British prospects exhausted, Bulloch contracted with Arman for four cruisers in April 1863 and two ironclads in July. Although Bulloch erred in agreeing to arm the cruisers and in too openly visiting the construction site of the ironclads, larger French policy considerations once more dashed Confederate hopes. Union triumphs at Vicksburg and Gettysburg forecast a northern victory and threatened Napoleon's scheme for making Archduke Ferdinand Maximilian of Austria the emperor of Mexico; the Polish insurrection continued to convulse European politics; and Foreign Minister Drouyn de Lhuys, much like Russell in Britain, argued adamantly for a neutrality that avoided confrontation with the North. The outcome was virtually identical; the French government changed course and forced Arman to sell all six ships to other countries.[42]

Southern naval construction had run aground with a devastating finality. Confederates asserted that more equitable treatment, and with it the ability to construct a navy in Britain and France, would have altered the outcome of the war. Subsequent historians have disagreed. Specifically, they question whether the Laird rams were sufficiently seaworthy for an effective crossing of the Atlantic or whether the South had sailors adequately trained to maneuver them. More generally, Confederate financial weakness and the absence of coordinated purchasing operations made obtaining an adequate navy unlikely. Warren F. Spencer argues persuasively that "if a people need a navy, . . . they must possess their own resources to build, equip, arm and man those ships." Raimondo Luraghi concurs and adds that the purchase of a navy abroad was plagued by "too many imponderables"—the "first" being the fear of northern "strength among possible foreign producers."

41. Spencer, *Confederate Navy in Europe*, 104–5, 112.
42. Ibid., 111–13, 147–76; Case and Spencer, *United States and France*, 427–515.

But, even if the "myth of the rams' awesomeness" lacked substance, Union diplomats' belief in the myth and the conflict over Confederate shipbuilding had "created the most dangerous moment in British-United States relations since the *Trent* affair." When both Britain and France opted to restrict Confederate actions, the last real threat of European intervention or war with the North subsided. Considerations of power and national interest had prevailed. In the absence of Confederate battlefield victories, John Slidell's June 1864 observation was acute: "The weak have no rights; the strong no obligations."[43]

As the war ground to its devastating and seemingly inevitable conclusion following Vicksburg and Gettysburg, the Confederacy displayed its desperation by attempting to provoke a conflict between the Union and British Canada. In late 1863 Confederate Secretary of State Benjamin appointed Jacob Thompson and Clement C. Clay, former U.S. senators from Mississippi and Alabama respectively, and J. P. Holcombe, a law professor at the University of Virginia, as commissioners to Canada. Provided with $1 million, these inept emissaries engaged in extensive plotting, but failed to sway Canadian opinion toward the Confederacy and oversaw only one futile and largely counterproductive raid. On October 19, 1864, Lieutenant Bennett H. Young led an attack on Saint Albans, Vermont. Young and his Kentucky followers robbed three banks, wounded two people and killed another, and absconded with several horses and some $200,000. An American posse captured Young, and Canadian authorities apprehended four of the other Confederates.[44]

Although Canadian courts eventually released the raiders, the incident proved uniformly detrimental to the Confederate cause. U.S. Secretary of State Seward agreed with Senator Charles Sumner's assessment. "The whole proceeding," Sumner observed, "was a trap in which to catch the government of our country. It was hoped in this way the rebellion would gain the powerful British intervention which would restore its falling fortunes." Seward refused to take the bait. Instead, he skillfully utilized the attack to pressure Canadian authorities to restrict Confederate activities. Canadian

43. Spencer, *Confederate Navy in Europe*, 118–19, 217; Luraghi, *History of the Confederate Navy*, 348; Merli, *Great Britain and the Confederate Navy*, 212–17, 225 (Slidell); Wilbur Devereux Jones, *The Confederate Rams at Birkenhead: A Chapter in Anglo-American Relations* (Tuscaloosa, 1961), 115–17.

44. Robin W. Winks, *Canada and the United States: The Civil War Years* (Baltimore, 1960), 264, 272–76, 294, 298–301.

public opinion reacted negatively to the abuse of its neutrality, and Lord Charles Stanley Monck, governor general of British North America, thereafter refused to talk with the Confederate commissioners and worked more aggressively to forestall southern attempts to foment strife between Canada and the United States. To this end, the Canadian Parliament passed the 1865 Alien Act, providing for the fining and expulsion of foreign nationals acting from Canada against a friendly nation. The Confederates had been no more successful in drawing Britain into the war via this circuitous route than through direct appeals in Europe.[45]

The Confederates were similarly unable to forge an alliance with France in support of Napoleon III's scheme to install Archduke Ferdinand Maximilian as the emperor of Mexico. Together with Britain and Spain, France had intervened in Mexico in 1861 to collect unpaid debts. When it became clear that Napoleon's objectives stretched far beyond debt collection, the other two nations negotiated separate agreements with the Mexican government and withdrew their troops in April 1862. Thereafter, French soldiers occupied Mexico City in June 1863, and the following month, a French-controlled provisional government and assembly offered the crown to Maximilian. The ill-starred archduke accepted in the fall and in so doing raised southern hopes of a united front against the Union and an alternative approach to inducing French recognition.

John Slidell voiced the Confederate consensus when he announced to Maximilian's aide de camp that "without the active friendship of the South" the new emperor would "be entirely powerless to resist northern aggression." In another conversation, the southern emissary admitted that the South's motive in negotiating with Mexico "was not the expectation of deriving any advantage from an alliance per se, but from the consequences that would probably flow from it in another quarter"—that is the eliciting of French aid. Southerners assumed that French recognition of the South would assuredly accompany the Confederacy's protection of the puppet emperor. During late 1863, Maximilian reinforced these expectations by telling Slidell and two other southern agents that he agreed with the necessity of a Confederate-Mexican alliance and intended to make French recognition of the Confederacy a precondition to accepting the throne. He subsequently asserted that "the creation of this new state . . . will be . . . an absolute necessity for the Mexican Empire." Acting on this information, President

45. Winks, *Canada and the United States,* 303–34 (Sumner, 317).

Davis appointed William Preston, a former U.S. minister to Spain, as the Confederate representative to Mexico on January 7, 1864, and charged him with obtaining a treaty of commerce and friendship with Maximilian's government.[46]

Preston and his Richmond superiors quickly found their assumptions faulty and Maximilian's encouragement misleading. From the landing of the first European troops in Mexico, U.S. Secretary of State Seward had maintained a posture of restrained but obvious disapproval. As early as 1862, Jules Favre warned his fellow French legislators that the ending of the "terrible . . . gigantic" American war could lead Union armies to "rush into Mexico," and following northern victories at Vicksburg and Gettysburg and Seward's more pointed protests, this possibility appeared increasingly imminent. In February 1864, as Maximilian prepared to sail for Mexico, French Foreign Secretary Drouyn de Lhuys emphasized the need "to avoid all acts which would in the eyes of the United States constitute serious and founded complaints" and thereby "adversely affect the enterprise which we pursue in Mexico." Indeed, the French fear of northern power and hostility produced a response precisely opposite of that anticipated by the South. When combined with the Mexican project's growing unpopularity in France and the unsettled European backdrop, the Union threat prompted Napoleon to block Maximilian's overtures for an alliance with the Confederacy. By late spring 1864, all diplomatic doors had slammed shut, and neither Preston nor Slidell could gain access to the new Mexican emperor, much less negotiate the coveted alliance and obtain the accompanying French recognition. Characteristically, the desperate and unrealistic southerners pursued this doomed project well into 1865.[47]

Confederate diplomatic debacles in Canada and Mexico in 1863–64 were compounded by the collapse of Richmond's alliance with the Five Civilized Tribes in the Oklahoma Indian Territory. Even before the Confederacy had formulated a diplomatic strategy for dealing with the Cherokees, Creeks, Seminoles, Chickasaws, and Choctaws, secessionist governments in Texas and Arkansas sought to counter Union influence among these peoples. Both states dispatched commissioners, and in April 1861, Texans captured Forts

46. Owsley, *King Cotton Diplomacy,* 519–21, 523 (Slidell); Hubbard, *Burden of Confederate Diplomacy,* 162 (Maximilian); Crook, *The North, the South, and the Powers,* 340–41.

47. Case and Spencer, *United States and France,* 455, 566 (Favre and Drouyn); Kathryn A. Hanna, "The Roles of the South in the French Intervention in Mexico," *Journal of Southern History* 20 (February 1954): 7–14.

Washita, Arbuckle, and Cobb. Thereafter, the South appointed Albert Pike as its State Department representative, and between July and October 1861 he negotiated treaties of alliance with each of these tribes. In return for military aid and political allegiance, the South offered very generous terms. The Indians received guarantees of territorial and political integrity, representation in the Confederate Congress, control over their own trade, the opportunity for future statehood, and the legal right to hold slaves. The Confederacy also promised to provide annuity payments and to assume responsibility for all Native American damage claims filed against the United States.[48]

These magnanimous concessions signified no fundamental change in southern attitudes toward Native Americans. Military and diplomatic necessity, not the sudden acquisition of racial and ethnic tolerance, dictated the treaty terms. As historian Annie Heloise Abel notes, "The southern white man . . . conceded much, far more than he really believed in, more than he ever could or would have conceded, had he not himself been so fearfully hard pressed." Even as Pike negotiated these generous treaties, the Confederate Commissioner of Indian Affairs in neighboring Arizona ordered the Arizona Guards to *"kill all the grown Indians and take the children prisoner and sell them* to defray the expense of killing the Indians," and Confederate Brigadier General Henry H. Sibley made overtures to two governors of northern Mexican states to join him in fighting the Apaches and Kiowas. The Five Civilized Tribes recognized the discrepancy between prior southern actions and current promises, but Confederate pledges surpassed contemporary Union treatment or solicitations. Moreover, the geographic proximity of the Confederacy, the legalization of slavery, and early northern military reverses also argued for the Confederate alliance.[49]

Military events quickly demonstrated the fragility of the Confederate–Native American alliance. In March 1862 Union forces defeated a combined Confederate-Indian contingent at Pea Ridge, Arkansas, and in July 1863 the northern victory at the Battle of Honey Springs confirmed the Confederate

48. Annie Heloise Abel, *The American Indian as Slaveholder and Secessionist*, introduction by Theda Perdue and Michael D. Green (1915; reprint, Lincoln, Neb., 1992), 157–206; Kenny A. Franks, "The Implementation of the Confederate Treaties with the Five Civilized Tribes," *Chronicles of Oklahoma* 51 (spring 1973): 23–29.

49. Abel, *American Indian as Slaveholder and Secessionist*, 17–18; William H. Graves, "Confederate Indian Policy in the Southwest: Interest, Goals, Attitudes," *Mid-America* 66 (October 1984): 113, 116 (killing).

inability to protect its Indian allies or to control Indian Territory. The South also failed to honor its promises to supply military matériels and general annuities. Faced with the choice of diverting scarce resources from the eastern theaters, the South abandoned the Native Americans to their own devices. Without decisive military victories, the South was no more able to effect and sustain viable alliances in the American Southwest than in Europe, Canada, or Mexico.[50]

Having failed to realize any of the South's major foreign policy objectives, Davis and Benjamin in late 1864 resorted to the previously unthinkable: they dispatched Duncan F. Kenner, a Louisiana congressman, to Europe with an offer to emancipate the slaves in return for diplomatic recognition. Once again, Confederate timing was atrocious. Like other belated southern actions, the opportunity for this about-face had long since passed. Reluctant to act on much more compelling grounds in 1862 and 1863, neither Great Britain nor France dared risk armed conflict when imminent Northern victory appeared ever more apparent.

While formulating this last diplomatic effort, Secretary of State Benjamin echoed the South's repeated refrain of dismay and persecution in the face of persistent foreign policy reversals. John W. Daniel had complained characteristically that the Confederacy had "no worse enemies in the world than the British Government and the majority of the British nation. . . . All their diplomacy has been, and will ever be, employed to prolong the war, by preventing the interference of any other nation." James D. Bulloch subsequently described the French as even worse: "Every [French] pledge had been violated, and we have encountered nothing but deception and duplicity." Building on these sentiments, Benjamin asserted that the South had fought Europe as well as the North. Had the "contest . . . been waged against the United States alone, . . . it would long since have ceased." Britain and France had mistreated the South by tolerating the North's paper blockade and by denying the use of their ports to Confederate vessels with Union prizes in tow. How, he asked, could the European powers justify withholding recognition of a people who had fought so heroically for "their liberties and independence" against a foe who greatly outnumbered them, who practiced total and barbaric warfare against "our women and children," and who recruited "armies of mercenaries" from supposedly "neutral countries"? Still

50. Kenny A. Franks, "The Confederate States and the Five Civilized Tribes: A Breakdown of Relations," *Journal of the West* 12 (July 1973): 439–54.

unable to fathom why the recognition and support that seemed so logical and obtainable four years earlier had not materialized, Benjamin instructed Mason and Slidell to ask British and French officials for a "frank exposition" of the reasons for their pronorthern neutrality. Similarly, J. D. B. De Bow, who had written so confidently of King Cotton's power in the 1850s, could find no explanation for European actions: "God knows why & God only."[51]

Those historians emphasizing considerations of physical and political power have responded that God favored not just the military but also the diplomatic side with the larger battalions. Given the overall power differential between the North and South and the European diplomatic tradition of withholding recognition and aid until a rebelling state had clearly established its independence, the Confederacy's prospects were always pessimistic. The South never demonstrated its political and military autonomy to the satisfaction of the British, and neither the British nor the French dared to act in the face of repeated Union threats of war and ongoing European uncertainties.

In addition, the South's retention of slavery tragically conflicted with the sentiments and actions of the major Western European powers. An aspiring nation with the "peculiar institution" as the foundation for its political economy faced fundamental, if not insurmountable, obstacles to establishing a functional foreign policy relationship with Great Britain and France. Simply put, the "Southern cause . . . was a bad one." Southern inability to recognize the moral and, hence, diplomatic implications of holding others in bondage reflected the region's relative isolation from the larger cultural and intellectual trends of the Atlantic world.[52]

This same insularity contributed to unfounded Confederate optimism over the prospects of securing foreign recognition and the fatal southern misperception of the influence of King Cotton. Just as southerners vastly overestimated the economic and political influence of cotton, they greatly undervalued the importance of diplomacy and the necessity of securing substantial and sustained foreign assistance. This failure to appreciate the need to properly cultivate and solicit European support combined with Dixie's ongoing fear of centralized authority to impede a well-coordinated program of blockade running and purchasing abroad. Duplication of effort, waste of

51. Blumenthal, "Confederate Diplomacy," 161 (Daniel), 163 (De Bow); Merli, *Great Britain and the Confederate Navy*, 225 (Bulloch); Owsley, *King Cotton Diplomacy*, 532–33 (Benjamin).

52. Jenkins, *Britain and the War for the Union*, 2: 398.

scarce resources, private profiteering, and inadequate government supervision and involvement plagued both activities well into the war.

This combination of inherent weaknesses and diplomatic failures has led historians to criticize Confederate diplomacy harshly. Frank J. Merli, one of the closest students of southern efforts abroad, concludes that "a dispassionate evaluation of the evidence strongly suggests that the key element in the failure of the South was its inability to orchestrate all the instruments at its command to bring about a more forceful European response to the war." Henry Blumenthal, an even more stringent critic, asserts that southerners were "the tragic victims of their self-delusion." Blumenthal argues that only by immediately recognizing the importance of diplomacy and foreign aid, by employing cotton to obtain extensive credits early in the war, and by emancipating the slaves in 1861 could the South have overcome its inferiority in numbers, resources, and industrial capacity and obtained European recognition and assistance.[53]

While such criticisms and prescriptions have merit, they must be tempered by a more sympathetic, more historical appraisal of Confederate actions. King Cotton failed, but the power of the South's principal crop had been an article of faith among southerners since at least the 1840s and was widely accepted by northerners and Europeans as well. Southerners were overly confident of military victory and of European diplomatic recognition; but both British and French leaders also remained convinced until at least mid-1863 that the North could not reconquer the seceding states, and Seward and the key Union diplomats continued to be exceedingly apprehensive of possible European recognition of the Confederacy until about the same time. To be sure, southern purchasing and shipping operations in Europe lacked adequate coordination and central direction, but northern operatives complained correctly of precisely the same problems. At least a portion of the South's failures in this realm derived from the difficulty of putting an entirely new government in place. Moreover, southern fears of centralized governmental authority had been a hallmark of the region's political behavior and diplomatic perception since the colonial period. Similarly, expecting the South to have abolished slavery in 1861 in order to acquire diplomatic advantage is simply unrealistic. Southerners had gone to war to protect the

---

53. Frank J. Merli, "The Confederate Navy, 1861–65," in *In Peace and War: Interpretations of American Naval History, 1775–1984*, ed. Kenneth J. Hagan (Westport, Conn., 1984), 141; Blumenthal, "Confederate Diplomacy," 171.

peculiar institution because they could not imagine living with four million free blacks and because attacks on slavery were viewed as attacks upon the very integrity, value, and self-respect of southern society, polity, and economy. Perhaps even more than with King Cotton or centralized government, southerners could not have treated slavery differently and remained southern. To have done otherwise would have required them to transcend their life's experience—to have escaped their social, economic, and political milieu. In the last analysis, southerners failed to compensate for their deficiencies in population and resources through diplomacy precisely because they were southern.[54]

54. See Joseph A. Fry, *Henry S. Sanford: Diplomacy and Business in Nineteenth-Century America* (Reno, Nev., 1982), 50–59, for complaints by northern purchasing agents.

CHAPTER 4

Confronting the Reality of Dependence, 1865–1912

H ENRY GRADY, editor of the *Atlanta Constitution* and the most celebrated proponent of a New South, cut to the heart of the region's postwar condition while describing a funeral in northern Georgia: "They buried him in the midst of a marble quarry: they cut through solid marble to make his grave; and yet a little tombstone they put above him was from Vermont. They buried him in the heart of a pine forest, and yet the coffin was imported from Cincinnati. They buried him within touch of an iron mine, and yet the nails in his coffin and the iron in the shovel that dug his grave were imported from Pittsburgh. . . . The South didn't furnish a thing on earth for that funeral but the corpse and the hole in the ground."[1]

Contemporaries, both North and South, agreed with Grady's depiction of the South as a dependent, colonial region. Hamilton Fish, a U.S. senator from New York and secretary of state under Ulysses S. Grant, reputedly observed in 1860 that "the South was or would be splendid colonies to the North." Following the war, U.S. senator Chauncey M. Depew concurred. After noting that northerners had developed "all the great and sudden opportunities for wealth . . . in the Northwest States and on the Pacific Slope," he portrayed the "South [as] the Bonanza of the future" and advised "Go South, Young Man." Like Grady, Senator John Tyler Morgan of Alabama deeply resented the outcome of Fish's and Depew's vision. Morgan subsequently complained that the Northeast held the South in colonial "vassal-

---

1. Harold E. Davis, *Henry Grady's New South: Atlanta, A Brave and Beautiful City* (Tuscaloosa, 1990), 180.

age"—that a "Solid North" sought to make the South into the "Ireland of the American Union."[2]

In the wake of the epic conflict, the South faced heretofore unimaginable devastation. One of every ten white males, some 260,000, had perished. Union soldiers had left nine thousand miles of railroads in ruins. Defeated, emotionally spent, and physically weakened, veterans straggled home to find houses, barns, tools, fences, livestock, even entire towns destroyed. Real property values had declined by 50 percent, Confederate bonds and money were rendered worthless, and virtually no functioning banks survived.

Whereas the South had often acted in anticipation of a loss of liberties and resulting dependence prior to the war, the section's colonial status was tangible following the conflict. This dependency ran the gamut from personal and local relations to larger macroeconomic and political patterns. At the most basic level, poor farmers were increasingly drawn into the market economy, only to have their lives circumscribed by such arrangements as sharecropping, tenancy, and the crop-lien system. Devoid of capital, tenants, sharecroppers, and small landholders planted cotton or other money crops to try to meet their obligations to local storekeepers. This practice in turn left farmers dependent on others for food, clothing, and other necessities. These farmers joined larger landowners in complaining of being exploited by railroads and of having northeastern and British merchants determine the prices of their crops. Some farmers fled the countryside; those who remained felt "deeply humiliated at their growing dependence."[3]

This fundamental rural economic nexus symbolized numerous other developments. Lacking the necessary capital, skilled labor, technological community, and regional markets to compete with the more industrialized North, southerners had few alternatives to exchanging labor and raw materials for capital, expertise, and finished manufactured goods. The great bulk of southern industry involved extractive and first-stage processing of natural and agricultural materials; mining, lumbering, pig-iron and cotton textile production, and the making of cigars and plug tobacco constituted the most important endeavors. Over the five decades following the war, northern

---

2. C. Vann Woodward, *Origins of the New South, 1877–1913* (Baton Rouge, 1971), 114–15 (Fish and Depew); Joseph A. Fry, *John Tyler Morgan and the Search for Southern Autonomy* (Knoxville, Tenn., 1992), 47; see also Joseph J. Persky, *The Burden of Dependency: Colonial Themes in Southern Economic Thought* (Baltimore, 1992), 97–116.

3. Edward L. Ayers, *The Promise of the New South: Life after Reconstruction* (New York, 1992), 187.

capitalists increasingly acquired control over the railroads and most of Dixie's industry, save cotton textiles and North Carolina tobacco production. "Like other backward economies," observes historian Edward L. Ayers, "the South endured low wages, absentee ownership, and little control over national policy."[4]

Southerners argued with considerable merit that federal economic policy was consistently pronorthern. Protective tariffs aided northern and eastern manufacturers while forcing the agricultural South to pay more for finished products and machinery. Currency and national banking policies left southerners with insufficient supplies of money and credit. Pensions for Union veterans funneled funds collected nationally to areas north of the Mason-Dixon Line. Allocations for internal improvements conferred similarly disproportionate advantages to areas beyond the South.[5]

When combined with defeat in the war, the alleged horrors of Reconstruction, and southern white attitudes about race, these economic grievances, social dislocations, and federal policies made "The New South . . . an anxious place, filled with longing and resentment." The dominant and ultimately controlling political response of the Democratic Redeemers, who governed the South following Reconstruction, emphasized resistance to outside, "foreign" control, states' rights and restrained federal power, fiscal conservatism, unwavering white supremacy, and a "solid" Democratic polity. In short, they sought southern independence in political and racial matters. Southerners were more ambivalent about their economic relationship with the Northeast. While aggressively soliciting investors from outside the region, they also chafed at the accompanying loss of economic autonomy. Significantly, the Southern Alliance and the Populists, who provided the primary challenges to conservative Democratic rule, sought to liberate southern farmers. And stimulated by an aversion to monopolies, southern Progressivism in the early twentieth century targeted "the plutocracy of the Northeast" and often adopted a "sectional character, identifying the popular enemy with 'foreign' interests."[6]

These same tendencies were evident in most southern positions on foreign policy in the years from 1865 through 1912. Just as the experience of

4. Ibid., 22.

5. Woodward, *Origins of the New South*, 264–320; Richard F. Bensel, *Sectionalism and American Political Development, 1880–1980* (Madison, Wis., 1984), 60–103.

6. Ayers, *Promise of the New South*, viii (anxious place); Woodward, *Origins of the New South*, 371 (other quotes).

the war and Reconstruction was fundamental to southern domestic life, the regional ordeal and resulting devotion to the Lost Cause exercised a formative influence on the South's foreign policy perspectives. In the wake of the Republican North's military victory and the imposition of Reconstruction, loyalty to the Democratic Party was pervasive, and the overwhelming southern Democratic majority usually endorsed the same anti-Republican policies favored by the national Democratic Party. Southern concern for personal honor and manhood and ultimately the desire to demonstrate patriotic devotion to the reunited nation simultaneously looked backward to the Confederacy and forward to the nationalism that stimulated war with Spain in 1898. Even as southerners proclaimed their allegiance to the nation at war, the experience of military occupation and loss of political rights prompted many of them to decry the impact of U.S. imperialism on colonial subjects and to oppose territorial expansion at the turn of the century. Racial assumptions reinforced the South's objection to foreign policies that might incorporate nonwhites into the body politic.

Given their clear minority and dependent status, post–Civil War southerners were exceedingly apprehensive of national actions that enhanced central governmental and military power at the expense of states' rights and local control. Activist foreign policies not only promised to stimulate federal spending and raise taxes but also could help to construct a federal authority more capable of interfering with southern racial practices. Acting from these perspectives, the majority of southern congressmen recoiled from initiatives, such as an enlarged navy, that augmented federal power and spending, and southern Democrats were among the nation's strongest opponents of the acquisition of Hawaii and the Philippines. As the uneasiness over federal spending suggests, southerners continued to factor economic considerations into their foreign policy stands. Consistent with Dixie's staple agricultural, extractive, and first-stage-processing economy, most southerners remained committed to low tariffs and aggressive commercial expansion abroad.

As had been the case in the antebellum period, there was no unanimous southern definition of appropriate U.S. foreign policies. During the Gilded Age and early twentieth century, the conservative perspective described above predominated, but ironically, the most prominent and vocal southern commentator on U.S. foreign relations adopted an activist minority approach to many of these issues. By simultaneously adopting a minority position and forging to the front among southern foreign policy commentators,

John Tyler Morgan, U.S. senator from Alabama from 1877 to 1907, anticipated the role of J. William Fulbright a century later—with one crucial
difference. By the 1960s, majority southern opinion favored a more interventionist foreign policy and Fulbright argued for restraint.

Morgan was an unqualified economic expansionist, who supported constructing a new navy and an isthmian canal, endorsed war with Spain in
1898, and favored acquisition of Hawaii, Puerto Rico, Cuba, and the Philippines. Neither racial assumptions, potential competition for southern staple
crops, constitutional concerns, nor enhanced central power inhibited his un-
relenting imperial drive. Morgan fully shared the South's fears for its political and economic autonomy. But far more than the majority of his southern
contemporaries, who devoted their primary attention to domestic developments, he viewed foreign relations as the vehicle for achieving Dixie's economic independence and political equality. In so doing, he harkened back
to the antebellum nationalism and expansion that had often redounded to
southern benefit.

Following Appomattox, southerners resumed their antebellum search for
markets abroad. As the *Atlanta Constitution* observed in September 1900,
cotton was still king. During the late nineteenth century, the South continued to export raw cotton, but it also built cotton textile mills at a furious
pace; by 1900, 60 percent of the exports of U.S. cotton goods was produced
in the region. Southerners also sold tobacco products, timber, coal, and iron
abroad, but raw materials continued to constitute more than 80 percent of
Dixie's exports between 1870 and 1910. Over this same period, the South's
exports ranged from 15 to 20 percent of its output, compared to the national
and northeastern average of 5 to 6.[7]

Recognizing the centrality of the export market, numerous southerners
sounded the call for commercial expansion. Senator Morgan favored extending "the area of our trade throughout the known world, barbarous as
well as civilized." Only adequate markets were necessary to "bring . . .
wealth and strength that will build Alabama up into honorable rivalry with
the greatest states in the world." Senator Roger Q. Mills of Texas, who was
joined in the litany by Alabamians Joseph Wheeler and Hannis Taylor,

7. Walter LaFeber, *The American Search for Opportunity, 1865–1913*, vol. 3 of *The Cambridge
History of American Foreign Relations*, ed. Warren I. Cohen (New York, 1993), 175 (king); Peter
Trubowitz, *Defining the National Interest: Conflict and Change in American Foreign Policy* (Chi-
cago, 1998), 70.

agreed. Mills worried in the early 1880s that southern crops ran "far beyond the requirements of our home consumption." His stated solution was: "We must either have the foreign market or none." Focusing more narrowly on cotton goods, John F. Hanson of the Bibb Manufacturing Company of Georgia declared in 1898, "We must have the people of the whole wide earth for our customers. It is commercial conquest upon which we should be bent."[8]

Southerners sought to further this commercial conquest by sponsoring seven international expositions between 1881 and 1907. These gatherings began with the International Cotton Exposition in Atlanta and continued with others such as the World's Industrial and Cotton Centennial Exposition in New Orleans (1884–85), the celebrated Cotton States and International Exposition in Atlanta (1895), and the South Carolina, Inter-State, and West Indian Exposition in Charleston (1901–2). A circular explaining the need for the 1895 Atlanta exposition was fully applicable to all the others: "The answer is in the peculiar economic conditions now prevalent. The condition of the industrial world is expressed in one word— overproduction." This condition created the "absolute necessity for an expansion of trade beyond the limits of the home market."[9]

Advocates of commercial expansion argued that the protective tariff impeded "the large, free, liberal commerce" in southern agricultural goods. Southerners also contended that high duties on equipment for cotton and iron production blocked the growth of southern industry. Morgan charged in 1883 that these duties were directed at the "iron of the South that is your [Northeast] competitor, not the iron of England." Together with southerners' fundamental status as consumers of finished goods, these considerations led them to consistently favor lowering the tariff. With an eye on foreign

8. Fry, *Morgan*, 63, 73; William A. Williams, *The Roots of Modern American Empire: A Study of the Growth and Shaping of Social Consciousness in a Marketplace Society* (New York, 1969), 301 (Mills); Patrick J. Hearden, *Independence and Empire: The New South's Cotton Mill Campaign, 1865–1901* (DeKalb, Ill., 1982), 67 (Hanson); Tennant S. McWilliams, "The Lure of Empire: Southern Interest in the Caribbean, 1877–1900," *Mississippi Quarterly* 29 (winter 1975–76): 44–51; Tennant S. McWilliams, *Hannis Taylor: The New Southerner as an American* (University, Ala., 1978); Thomas D. Schoonover, *The United States in Central America, 1860–1911: Episodes of Social Imperialism and Imperial Rivalry in the World System* (Durham, N.C., 1991), 46–61.

9. Robert W. Rydell, *All the World's a Fair: Visions of Empire at American International Expositions, 1876–1916* (Chicago, 1984), 76 (answer); John E. Findling, "Opening the Door to the World: International Expositions in the South, 1881–1907," *Studies in Popular Culture* 19 (October 1996): 29–38.

markets, many southerners linked their campaign to the expansion of silver currency, another ostensibly domestic issue. They asserted that the coinage of silver would not only expand the money supply and reduce the South's dependence on northern sources of credit but also facilitate U.S. access to markets in Asian and Latin American countries with silver currencies. Morgan and other commercial expansionists further endorsed federal subsidies to expand the U.S. merchant marine, enlarge and modernize the navy, and construct an isthmian canal.[10]

The canal was Senator Morgan's pet project and the centerpiece to his blueprint for stimulating southern prosperity and autonomy. The senator began championing a canal in the early 1880s and remained its most ardent advocate until Theodore Roosevelt's seizure of the Panama route in 1903. Morgan perceived commercial expansion as the key to southern economic resurgence and to escaping northern and British dominance; the canal in turn was the essential avenue to foreign markets. Fellow southerners enthusiastically agreed with this facet of Morgan's expansionist blueprint, and the canal emerged by the 1890s as "the single most important foreign policy goal of southern politicians and commercial interests."[11]

While few southerners dissented from the goal of commercial expansion or questioned the sectional utility of a canal, considerations of race, domestic politics, optimum federal power, fiscal conservatism, and appropriate diplomatic restraint frequently took precedence over purely economic calculations and an outward-looking policy. Several issues illustrated this dynamic. Southerners favored the purchase of Alaska. A part of North America, the vast region was sparsely populated, could be acquired peacefully, and possessed great commercial potential. Expansionist prospects in Cuba and Mexico elicited much more ambivalent responses. When Cuban revolutionaries rebelled against Spanish rule in 1868, southerners expressed sympathy and favored recognizing Cuban independence but eschewed direct inter-

10. Fry, *Morgan*, 63; O. Lawrence Burnette Jr., "John Tyler Morgan and Expansionist Sentiment in the New South," *Alabama Review* 18 (July 1965): 163–82; Joanne Reitano, *The Tariff Question in the Gilded Age: The Great Debate of 1888* (University Park, Pa., 1994), 90, 101–2.

11. Fry, *Morgan*, 95–109, 199–238; August C. Radke, "Senator Morgan and the Nicaragua Canal," *Alabama Review* 12 (January 1959): 5–34; Marshall E. Schott, "The South and American Foreign Policy, 1894–1904: Regional Concerns during the Age of Imperialism" (Ph.D. dissertation, Louisiana State University, 1995), 265 (single). See also Marshall E. Schott, "The South and American Foreign Policy, 1894–1900: New South Prophets and the Challenge of Regional Values," *Southern Studies* 4 (fall 1993): 295–308. Subsequent citations will be to Schott's dissertation.

vention. Despite a long-standing southern desire to acquire the island, memories of Civil War combat were too vivid, the trials of Reconstruction were too immediate, and southern racial apprehensions were too pervasive. The *Wilmington (N.C.) Morning Star* doubted that "those who have watched the workings of reconstruction in the Southern States" would endorse "an incorporation of several millions of sable citizens into the 'grand brotherhood of the Union.'" Similar preferences for diplomatic restraint arose regarding U.S.-Mexican relations. Southern papers opposed the forceful annexation of territory in the 1860s, and party politics and sugar growers' fears of economic competition induced the majority of southern senators to oppose the 1884 commercial treaty with Mexico.[12]

Despite lucid arguments for potential southern benefits, strong objections also arose to greater U.S. involvement in the Congo in the mid-1880s. Morgan envisioned the region as an ideal dumping ground for the South's surplus cotton and surplus blacks, and he helped persuade the Arthur administration to extend diplomatic recognition to King Leopold II's African International Association (AIA) in 1884 and to send U.S. representatives to the Berlin West African Conference of 1884–85. The senator wielded no such influence with Grover Cleveland. Upon assuming his duties in March 1885, the new president promptly withdrew the General Act of the Berlin Conference, which recognized the AIA and guaranteed free trade in the Congo Basin, from Senate consideration. Significantly, Cleveland garnered prominent support from House Foreign Affairs Committee member Hilary A. Herbert of Alabama, who condemned U.S. involvement in the Congo as unwise meddling in European affairs and a violation of the two-spheres dimension of the Monroe Doctrine. Involvement in the Congo contradicted Herbert's maxim that the United States should be "attending to our own affairs and leaving other people and other nations to theirs in their own way."[13]

12. Richard E. Welch Jr., "American Public Opinion and the Purchase of Russian America," *American Slavic and East European Review* 17 (April 1958): 490–91; George H. Gibson, "Attitudes in North Carolina Regarding the Independence of Cuba, 1868–1898," *North Carolina Historical Review* 43 (January 1966): 43–53, 45 (*Morning Star*); Donald M. Dozer, "Anti-Expansionism during the Johnson Administration," *Pacific Historical Review* 12 (September 1943): 256–57; Edward W. Chester, *Sectionalism, Politics, and American Diplomacy* (Metuchen, N.J., 1975), 127.

13. Fry, *Morgan*, 77–79; Joseph O. Baylen, "Senator John Tyler Morgan, E. D. Morel, and the Congo Reform Association," *Alabama Review* 15 (August 1962): 117–31; Hugh B. Hammett, *Hilary Abner Herbert: A Southerner Returns to the Union* (Philadelphia, 1976), 140 (Herbert).

Southerners provided even more decisive opposition to another Arthur administration initiative, the 1884 Frelinghuysen-Zavala Treaty with Nicaragua. This pact granted the United States a two and one-half mile right-of-way for constructing a canal in return for a "perpetual alliance" and U.S. protection of Nicaraguan territory. Democratic opponents decried the European-style protectorate and the entangling alliance and objected to the ratification of a Republican treaty during the Arthur administration's final days. In January 1885 the treaty failed to obtain the requisite two-thirds by a vote of 32 to 23, and Cleveland subsequently withdrew this measure from Senate consideration. Of the 23 negative votes, 14 were cast by southern Democrats; of the 6 positive Democratic votes, 5 came from Morgan and four fellow Gulf Coast senators who concurred with the Alabamian's canal strategy. Party politics and the propensity for diplomatic restraint again took precedence over potential economic gain.[14]

Although Congressman Herbert and Morgan agreed on the U.S. need to construct a larger, more modern navy, majority southern opinion once more demurred. Herbert, first as a member of the House Committee on Naval Affairs from 1885 to 1893 and then as secretary of the navy during Cleveland's second term, served as the most effective southern proponent of a stronger navy. He initially argued that since weak nations were inevitably drawn into conflicts, only a credible navy could enable the United States to avoid wars. Later in the 1890s, he joined Morgan and Congressman Joseph Wheeler of Alabama in proclaiming naval power crucial to the stimulation and protection of American commerce, and as navy secretary he championed the move to a battleship navy and significantly increased the number of ships assigned to safeguard U.S. interests in East Asia. During this fifteen-year advocacy of the new navy, Herbert maintained a comparatively moderate tone. This tact proved most effective in attracting the support of a limited but crucial number of southern congressmen, the bulk of whom hailed from other Gulf states and envisioned the prospect not only of increasing trade but also of building shipyards to bolster their states' economies. Herbert's work prompted the *Saint Louis Republic* to characterize him as a "Southern man with Massachusetts Principles."[15]

14. Chester, *Sectionalism, Politics, and American Diplomacy*, 128; Fry, *Morgan*, 98.

15. Hammett, *Herbert*, 109–40, 182–98 (*Republic*); Thomas H. Coode, "Southern Congressmen and the American Naval Revolution, 1880–1898," *Alabama Historical Quarterly* 30 (fall/winter 1968): 89–110.

Herbert, like Morgan, had adopted a minority southern perspective on this issue. For example, when the House authorized the celebrated "ABC" cruisers, the *Atlanta, Boston,* and *Chicago,* in 1883, southerners voted 39 to 16 in opposition. Three years later, Congress approved construction of two additional cruisers by a margin of 151 to 72, with southerners casting 47 of the negative votes and only 22 of the positive ones. This basic pattern prevailed through the remainder of the century. Southern dissenters questioned the strategic necessity for a significantly expanded navy, objected to the expense, worried about strengthening federal power, and understood that the great bulk of the construction funds would be spent in the Northeast. Southerners also accused northern Republicans of building a navy to avoid lowering the tariff. With an eye toward Dixie's crushing social and economic needs, they contended for domestic rather than foreign policy priorities. Representative William C. Oates of Alabama branded an enlarged navy in conflict with the "spirit and genius" of the nation's representative system and an expedient device "to make permanent disposition of the surplus revenue, and thereby dispense with the necessity of revising the tariff and reducing taxation." Tom Watson declared that Georgians were less troubled by foreign threats than those of "an outrageous [federal] legislature that is taxing our people to death; which is putting labor under the heels of monopoly, and making corporations greater than the citizen."[16]

Similar apprehensions informed the South's position on pre-1890 expansionist projects in Hawaii. Motivated primarily by fears of injurious competition, representatives from Louisiana and other sugar and rice growing areas consistently opposed the 1876 reciprocity agreement with Hawaii. Southerners cast 10 of 12 negative votes in the Senate and voted 36 to 25 against the measure in the House. Throughout the 1880s, Senators Randall I. Gibson of Louisiana and Roger Q. Mills of Texas marshaled a vigorous southern campaign aimed at repealing the treaty. They complained that the pact jeopardized the South's access to domestic markets by allowing the duty-free entry of sugar and rice produced by cheaper contract labor, that the treaty facilitated the covert dumping of Asian goods in the United States, and that the arrangement was costing the nation millions in lost revenues. The *New Orleans Times–Democrat* editorialized representatively in

16. *Congressional Record,* 47th Cong., 2d sess., 3637; Ibid., 49th Cong., 2d sess., 2352; Coode, "Southern Congressmen and the American Naval Revolution," 99, 103 (Oates and Watson); Trubowitz, *Defining the National Interest,* 51 (Oates).

1881 that the treaty "encourages coolie or slave labor, defrauds the government of $2,800,000 of revenues a year, . . . opens up no new trade, [and] injures home interests." Only by adding an exclusive U.S. right to a coaling station at Pearl Harbor were advocates of the treaty able to secure Senate renewal of reciprocity in 1887.[17]

Characteristically, John Tyler Morgan broke with most of his southern compatriots and provided the most forceful arguments for reciprocity. Morgan touted the islands' intrinsic commercial wealth, which attracted $20 million annually in shipping, insurance, and mercantile fees. But he was most interested in strategic calculations, in "other and perhaps higher considerations." Both reciprocity and the Pearl Harbor proviso enhanced U.S. influence at the expense of the British and other Europeans. Since the islands provided the "only stopping place, in a distance of 20,000 miles" between the United States and Asian markets and were located on an almost "direct line of travel" between Central America and Asia, he deemed the archipelago crucial to commercial expansion and the optimum use of an isthmian canal. That Morgan and other expansionists coveted the islands did not escape the attention of southern opponents of reciprocity, who warned that the commercial relationship was a dangerous prelude to annexationist schemes.[18]

Their apprehensions were well founded. Alarmed by the McKinley Tariff of 1890, which removed Hawaiian sugar from the free list, and by the actions of Queen Liliuokalani, who sought to restore native control of the islands, a white minority of planter-missionaries staged the "revolution" of January 1893. U.S. minister to Hawaii John L. Stevens safeguarded the coup by landing American marines from the USS. *Boston* to prevent the Queen and her followers from reasserting control. The leaders of the new Hawaiian "republic" promptly negotiated a treaty of annexation with the United States, which President Benjamin Harrison forwarded to the Senate in February. The Senate failed to act on the pact, and it remained under consideration when Grover Cleveland began his second tenure as president in March. Both the actions of Minister Stevens and the blatant minority status

17. Gregory Lawrence Garland, "Southern Congressional Opposition to Hawaiian Reciprocity and Annexation, 1876–1898" (master's thesis, University of North Carolina at Chapel Hill, 1983), 5–8; Donald M. Dozer, "The Opposition to Hawaiian Reciprocity, 1876–1888," *Pacific Historical Review* 14 (June 1945): 164 (*Times-Democrat*).

18. Dozer, "Opposition to Hawaiian Reciprocity," 171; Fry, *Morgan*, 81.

of the Hawaiian government induced Cleveland to withdraw the treaty from Senate consideration and to oppose annexation of the islands.

The South staunchly resisted annexation, and southerners actively influenced Cleveland's decision. James B. McCreary of Kentucky, chair of the House Foreign Affairs Committee, urged the new president to delay consideration of the treaty until after his inauguration. Among Cleveland's cabinet members, Secretary of the Treasury John G. Carlisle from Kentucky, Secretary of the Interior Hoke Smith of Georgia, and Secretary of the Navy Hilary A. Herbert from Alabama all opposed adding Hawaii to the Union. These southern advisers also persuaded Cleveland to appoint James G. Blount, a former Georgia congressman, as a special commissioner to investigate the U.S. role in the Hawaiian revolution.[19]

While in Congress from 1872 through 1892, Blount had consistently questioned the need for an aggressive expansionist foreign policy and had rebuffed overtures from representatives of the new Hawaiian republic as he left the House. Therefore, the results of his investigation were hardly surprising. After four months of close research in the islands, he reported that the overwhelming majority of native Hawaiians opposed the revolution. A white minority had engineered the rebellion for economic gain, and Minister Stevens had rendered decisive and improper aid. The entire affair violated U.S. principles of self-determination, smacked of imperial rule, and offended his southern sensitivity to a people's loss of liberties. Cleveland agreed; the president opposed annexation and disposed of the issue by forwarding Blount's report and in essence the Hawaii question to "the broader authority and discretion of Congress."[20]

Ironically, Senator Morgan, chairman of the Senate Foreign Relations Committee, was a central wielder of that authority. Morgan held extended hearings on the Hawaiian affair and authored a report in late February 1894 endorsing annexation of Hawaii, which he termed "an American state . . . embraced in the American commercial and military system." No southern congressmen assented. Southern Democratic representatives voted 76 to 0 against an annexation resolution, and Congressman McCreary wrote a contrary measure ultimately adopted by the House. McCreary pronounced ei-

19. Tennant S. McWilliams, *The New South Faces the World: Foreign Affairs and the Southern Sense of Self, 1877–1950* (Baton Rouge, 1988), 22–23.

20. Ibid., 20, 23–24; Fry, *Morgan,* 83–84 (Cleveland); Carol E. Schott, "Racism and Southern Anti-imperialists: The Blounts of Georgia," *Atlanta History* 31 (fall 1987): 24–29.

ther a protectorate or annexation "inexpedient," branded "interference with the domestic affairs of an independent nation . . . contrary to the spirit of American institutions," and urged that the "people of that country should have absolute freedom and independence in pursuing their own line of policy."[21]

The range of southern arguments was instructive and clearly foreshadowed the region's response to the epic debate over imperialism at the turn of the century. Overwhelmingly Democratic, the South rejected virtually all Republican-sponsored measures, usually with some reference to Republican oppression during Reconstruction. The *Charleston News and Courier* opined that it would "go hard with [the Republicans] to give up Hawaii," just as "it went hard with them to get out [of] the South." To party politics and recollections of "foreign" interference, southerners added racial objections. According to the *Wilmington (N.C.) Morning Star,* Dixie had a "sufficient stock of mongrelism to last us the balance of this century, at least, without taking in the nut brown islanders of the South Pacific." Broadening the long-standing economic concern of sugar and rice growers, Senator Donelson Caffery of Louisiana feared that a Hawaiian colony might divert general northern investment and thereby cripple southern economic expansion. Southerners also continued to identify an expansionist foreign policy with a stronger military, an expanded central government, and the renewed possibility of forceful intrusion into local affairs. Representative Henry G. Turner of Georgia opposed any "occasion for a navy"; he counseled against an "imbroglio with England or with any other country." Finally, as they had done with reciprocity, southerners joined other anti-imperialists in warning that the decision about Hawaii provided a critical precedent, that acquiring the islands would make it "proper to annex Santo Domingo, or any other country that may send commissioners to propose annexation."[22]

In contrast to the 1850s, southerners no longer endorsed expansion into the tropics. With neither the augmentation of southern political influence nor the protection of slavery in the balance, racial concerns, potential economic competition, fear of enhanced federal power, and partisan politics

21. Fry, *Morgan,* 83–85 (quotes); Garland, "Southern Congressional Opposition to Hawaiian Reciprocity and Annexation," 12–13; Thomas J. Osborne, *"Empire Can Wait": American Opposition to Hawaiian Annexation, 1893–1898* (Kent, Ohio, 1981), 69–70.

22. McWilliams, *New South Faces the World,* 38 (*News and Courier*); Osborne, *"Empire Can Wait,"* 37 (*Morning Star*), 71–72 (final quote); Garland, "Southern Congressional Opposition to Hawaiian Reciprocity and Annexation," 9–20, 39 (Turner).

prevailed. Both the bases and the alignment of southern sentiment remained unchanged when President William McKinley revived the issue of Hawaiian annexation in late 1897. After McKinley and his Republican congressional lieutenants failed to muster the necessary two-thirds majority in the Senate to ratify a treaty, they turned to a joint resolution, which required only a simple majority vote in each house. Characteristically, Senator Morgan introduced the Foreign Relations Committee's resolution into Senate consideration. Once again he commanded meager southern support. Although Congress passed the resolution in early July 1898, southerners dissented by 57 to 18 in the House and 12 to 7 in the Senate.[23]

They reiterated previous reservations and protested that by resorting to a joint resolution, McKinley had employed an unconstitutional device to circumvent senatorial authority. This posture reversed antebellum southern Democratic support for the use of a joint resolution to annex Texas. Perceptions of sectional interest had changed and with them the Democratic South's willingness to circumvent the two-thirds Senate majority necessary to ratify a treaty. Without a hint of self-consciousness, given the recent implementation of the "Mississippi Plan" to exclude African Americans from his state's politics and society, Congressman John Sharp Williams objected to violating the national principle of self-government and appealed to the central southern concern of honor: "When," he declared, "a self-seeking oligarchy, or a mistaken patriotism, or a criminal covetousness . . . leads our country and . . . flag out in the endless race for conquest and domination, it has lost its honor and should be unfurled in disgrace." Dixie's representatives further emphasized that Hawaii constituted a strategic liability rather than an asset. Congressman Claude Kitchen of North Carolina flatly rejected the arguments for the islands' geographic importance. Were his imperialist adversaries to "Start in London, cross the English Channel, cross the Austrian Empire, cross Turkey, and stand in the palace of the Sultan," they would not have "traveled as far as from San Francisco to Honolulu," and yet they employed Hawaii's "proximity as a reason for annexation."[24]

Proximity had much to do with American concern over the Cuban rebellion against Spanish rule after February 1895. When the Cuban revolution-

23. *Congressional Record,* 55th Cong., 2d sess., 6019, 6712.
24. Osborne, *"Empire Can Wait,"* 85, 89, 102, 104, 110–12, 117–20; Schott, "South and American Foreign Policy," 65 (Williams); E. Berkeley Tompkins, *Anti-Imperialism in the United States: The Great Debate, 1890–1920* (Philadelphia, 1970), 105 (Kitchen).

aries launched a relentless guerrilla war against Spanish authority, they endangered $50 million in U.S. investments on the island and helped devastate U.S.-Cuban commerce. Prodded by the often-exaggerated accounts of the U.S. press, Americans also reacted with horror at Spain's allegedly cruel treatment of the Cubans. Most of this opprobrium was directed at General Valeriano Weyler y Nicolau and his attempts to segregate the rebels from the general population by herding the latter into concentration camps. This practice had little effect on the revolutionaries but killed thousands of civilians through disease and starvation. Intertwined with these economic and humanitarian considerations was the question of whether the Cuban efforts warranted U.S. recognition of their status as belligerents or as an independent state. Reflecting the well-established U.S. distaste for revolution and refusing to relieve Spain of the legal responsibility for protecting American property in Cuba, both Cleveland and McKinley declined to recognize either Cuban belligerence or independence.

Southern sympathy for Cuban suffering coincided with Democratic politics and the characteristic regional concern for honor and manhood. Often equating Cuba's suffering and resistance to outside domination to the South's experience during the Civil War and Reconstruction, southerners were among the most forceful advocates of U.S. recognition of Cuban belligerency and independence. Senator Morgan led the interventionist campaign in the Senate, where he condemned Spanish crimes "against all principles of humanity and Christianity," and particularly denounced General Weyler for plunging his "crime-stained sword into the bosoms of women and little children." The senator regularly implored Congress to recognize the Cubans and urged that the United States seek "peace, security, and, good neighborship with Cuba [even] if we have to fight for it."[25]

Congressman Joseph W. Bailey, Democratic minority leader in the House, mounted a similar campaign for Cuban recognition and ultimately for war. Bailey pointedly equated Cuban suffering with the South's experience during Reconstruction and condemned the Republican Party as the culprit—this time for its refusal to intervene rather than for its intervention and occupation of a neighboring region. Bailey rejected any thought of arbitrating "that bloody deed, the destruction of the *Maine.*" The Texan had "no sympathy for those rash, intemperate spirits who would provoke war simply for the sake of fighting," but he preferred to "follow them, and suffer

25. Fry, *Morgan,* 157; McWilliams, *Hannis Taylor,* 34–35.

all the miseries and misfortunes their heedlessness would bring than to follow those other contemptible and mercenary creatures who are crying for 'peace at any price.'"[26]

Bailey's and Morgan's professions of sympathy for the Cubans and claims of special insight into their suffering based on the Reconstruction experience must not be accepted uncritically. Although they and other southerners who employed the Reconstruction analogy truly sympathized with the loss of liberty suffered by Cubans or Filipinos who became U.S. colonial subjects, this sympathy was more abstract than real. These southerners had no genuine empathy for nonwhites, either within the United States or abroad, and the South's overwhelming opposition to territorial expansion and the inclusion of Hawaiians or Filipinos within the body politic graphically demonstrated the racial limits of that concern.

Regardless of the extent of genuine sympathy, examples of enthusiasm for moving beyond Cuban recognition to U.S. military intervention were also manifest across the South. Two of Dixie's most prominent papers, the *Atlanta Constitution* and the *Louisville Courier-Journal,* echoed Morgan's and Bailey's aggressive tone and message. The *Constitution* editorialized in November 1897 that the time had come "when Cuba should be wrested from Spain at all hazards." Following the destruction of the *Maine* in February 1898, diverse southerners called for war. More than seven hundred outraged Texans rallied in Dallas; reaction was so intense in Jackson, Mississippi, that the "town appeared to be in the midst of war hysteria"; and in South Carolina, would-be volunteers beseeched the governor for the opportunity to fight.[27]

Southern proponents of action on behalf of the Cubans often cited the opposition of Wall Street and powerful business interests and the debilitating influence of material considerations on the nation's honor and man-

26. Sam Acheson, "Joseph W. Bailey and the Spanish War," *Southwest Review* 17 (winter 1932): 153; Kristin L. Hoganson, *Fighting for American Manhood: How Gender Politics Provoked the Spanish-American and Philippine-American Wars* (New Haven, 1998), 72.

27. Martha Ashley Girling, "Southern Attitudes toward the Cuban Question, 1896–1898" (master's thesis, Mississippi State University, 1960), 11–12 (*Constitution*); John J. Leffler, "The Paradox of Patriotism: Texans in the Spanish-American War," *Hayes Historical Journal* 8 (spring 1989): 24; Donald B. Kelley, "Mississippi and the 'The Splendid Little War' of 1898," *Journal of Mississippi History* 26 (May 1964): 124; Harris Moore Bailey Jr., "The Splendid Little Forgotten War: The Mobilization of South Carolina for the War with Spain," *South Carolina Historical Magazine* 92 (July 1991): 194.

hood. Senator Wilkinson Call from Florida declared that "if this god of business is to be allowed to . . . suppress the manhood and courage of our people, . . . it would be an unwise and ruinous policy. There can be no prosperity in a country where there is no sense of patriotism and national honor." John Sharp Williams agreed and warned that if the American man became "nothing but a miserable money-making machine, . . . Chivalry is dead; manhood itself is sapped." Voting against the ever-vivid backdrop of southern history, a genuine concern for Cuban suffering, resentment of what seemed to be an example of dishonorable northern business influence, and an eye to embarrassing the McKinley administration, southern congressmen overwhelmingly endorsed resolutions to recognize Cuban belligerency.[28]

As war became more imminent after January 1898, southerners emphasized their willingness to fight for the United States and to demonstrate their loyalty to the nation. Foreign policy crises earlier in the decade had elicited similar responses. After New Orleans residents lynched eleven Italian citizens in March 1891, ex-Confederates rushed to volunteer for the threatened conflict. A Georgian requested the authority "in event of war with Italy . . . to raise a company of unterrified georgia rebels to invade rome disperse the mafia and plant the stars and stripes on the dome of St. Peters." In 1895 Hilary A. Herbert, who generally eschewed U.S. interventions abroad, endorsed Cleveland's confrontation with Great Britain over Venezuela's boundary with British Guiana. The navy secretary considered the war scare an opportunity for southerners to put aside "fratricidal strife" and to "stand for their country as one man."[29]

War with Spain provided another occasion for southerners to demonstrate their patriotism and to simultaneously affirm their manhood and honor as worthy successors of the Confederate cause. The post–Civil War generation of southerners had been reared in a society that revered the Lost Cause. According to this interpretation of the war, the South's soldiers had

28. Hoganson, *Fighting for American Manhood*, 47 (Williams); Hoganson, "The 'Manly' Ideal of Politics and the Imperialist Impulse: Gender, U.S. Political Culture, and the Spanish-American and Philippine-American Wars" (Ph.D. dissertation, Yale University, 1995), 146 (Call).

29. Gaines M. Foster, *Ghosts of the Confederacy: Defeat, the Lost Cause, and the Emergence of the New South, 1865–1913* (New York, 1987), 145 (Georgian); Hammett, *Herbert*, 205–6; J. Alexander Karlin, "The Italo-American Incident of 1891 and the Road to Reunion," *Journal of Southern History* 8 (May 1942): 242–46.

answered the Confederacy's call to arms with remarkable enthusiasm, courage, and devotion to duty, had followed superior leaders, and had been better fighters than their northern opponents. Only greater northern numbers had overcome southern military capacity and commitment to the cause. By contesting the Spanish, true sons of Dixie could exhibit similar qualities in defense of the United States while retrospectively affirming Confederate valor.[30]

This sentiment echoed throughout the South in early 1898. On February 17, the *Lynchburg News* proclaimed "the people of the South . . . as loyal to the flag of the Union as the people of Massachusetts or Illinois and if the United States should be unfortunately compelled to go to war with a foreign state, the men of the South would rush to the defense of the country with as much promptness and enthusiasm as the men of any other section." Representative Bailey predicted the approaching war would "forever efface from the memory of our countrymen those dreadful times of civil strife," and John B. Gordon, commander of the United Confederate Veterans, was confident that hostilities would lead "to the complete and permanent obliteration of all sectional distrusts, and to the establishment of the too long delayed brotherhood and unity of the American people."[31]

Southerners were delighted when ex-Confederate general Fitzhugh Lee, American consul general in Havana, defied Spanish authority and aggressively defended U.S. interests. The South also applauded as McKinley reinforced the theme of sectional reconciliation by making Lee and Joseph Wheeler, another former Confederate officer, major generals in the volunteer army and when the president subsequently traveled through the South in 1898, pointedly praising the section's contributions to the war effort. In terms indistinguishable from the proclamations of Bailey and Gordon, the president declared the conflict was "completing obliterating the sectional lines drawn in the last one."[32]

Only Wheeler saw action; and even his momentary reversion to an earlier campaign when he exclaimed, "We've got the Yankees on the run,"

30. Foster, *Ghosts of the Confederacy*, 145–49; Charles R. Wilson, *Baptized in Blood: The Religion of the Lost Cause, 1865–1920* (Athens, Ga., 1980); Rollin G. Osterweis, *The Myth of the Lost Cause, 1865–1900* (Hamden, Conn., 1973).

31. Richard E. Wood, "The South and Reunion, 1898," *Historian* 31 (May 1969): 416 (*News*); Acheson, "Bailey," 149; Ralph Lowell Eckert, *John Brown Gordon: Soldier, Southerner, American* (Baton Rouge, 1993), 329.

32. Eckert, *Gordon*, 329 (McKinley); Wood, "South and Reunion," 415–22.

failed to dampen the spirit of sectional unity. Southerners celebrated their heroes from the war of 1898 as the most recent examples of regional honor and manhood. They had met the expectations of an Alabama ex-Confederate that a "glorious" war record would "show not only to this country but to the world that the South had not degenerated." Significantly, southern commentary tied Dixie's heroes not only to the South's rightful place in a reunited nation but also to their Confederate forebears.[33]

In addition to affording the South an opportunity to affirm its loyalty, war with Spain promised to bolster the region's economy with extensive defense spending. Floridians campaigned vigorously and successfully to make Tampa the departure point for troops en route to Cuba. Miami and Jacksonville ultimately hosted troop camps, and even the tragic Chickamauga battlefield in Tennessee served as a camp for U.S. soldiers. Federal funds also built defense works in numerous southern coastal cities. For example, Benjamin R. Tillman secured a naval yard for Charleston, South Carolina, which together with its attached dry dock, machine shops, and other facilities brought at least $5.7 million to the state over a twenty-year period. While the spending was modest compared to that funneled into the South during the next century, it provided an important stimulus to local economies, and the pattern was prescient.[34]

Despite the verbal pyrotechnics directed at Spain, the professions of loyalty to the nation, the eagerness of many southerners to volunteer for combat, and the possibility of sectional economic benefits, the South was far from uniformly eager for war. Apprehensions abounded that Dixie would supply many fighting men only to receive in return a strengthened federal government, higher taxes, disrupted trade, ravished seaports, meager defense contracts, and territorial additions that yielded competitive agricultural products. With the Civil War and Reconstruction vividly in mind, the *Fayetteville (N.C.) Observer* warned that war would bring "death, wounds, suffering, colossal debts, and a strengthening of the central authority." The

33. John P. Dyer, *From Shiloh to San Juan: The Life of "Fightin' Joe" Wheeler* (Baton Rouge, 1961), 230; Foster, *Ghosts of the Confederacy*, 148 (Alabamian); John Pettegrew, "'The Soldier's Faith': Turn-of-the-Century Memory of the Civil War and the Emergence of Modern American Nationalism," *Journal of Contemporary History* 31 (January 1996): 61–63, 69; Nina Silber, *The Romance of Reunion: Northerners and the South, 1865–1900* (Chapel Hill, 1993), 161–96.

34. William J. Schellings, "The Advent of the Spanish-American War in Florida, 1898," *Florida Historical Quarterly* 39 (April 1961): 311–29; Francis Butler Simkins, *Pitchfork Ben Tillman: South Carolinian* (Baton Rouge, 1944), 352–53, 363, 365–68.

Charleston News and Courier predicted that the South would bear an inequitable share of this burden: "Its industries will be paralyzed, its commerce destroyed, its seaports shelled, its people killed and its burden of taxation increased." From New Orleans, the *Daily Picayune* agreed and elaborated on the dim prospect of Dixie deriving substantial "pecuniary benefits," since the South lacked "shipyards and . . . great factories" for producing needed matériels.[35]

Even as economic considerations provided a clear motive for some southern interventionists, a closer examination of the South's material calculations casts the region's unabashed bellicosity into doubt. Proponents of a gold standard in national monetary policy feared that war or the annexation of Cuba, Puerto Rico, or the Philippines might necessitate the expanded coinage of silver. In Alabama, for example, gold Democrats were significantly more cautious than their silver adversaries within the party. Floridians ultimately moved aggressively to take advantage of the war, but they did so only after expressing considerable angst over the possibility that hostilities would disrupt business and that the probable annexation of Cuba would result in injurious competition for the state's economy. All of Florida's "important newspapers were united in opposition to war" until McKinley called upon Congress for the authority to intervene. Only then, and especially after the passage of the Teller amendment renouncing U.S. intentions to annex Cuba, did the press "display any enthusiasm for war." Louisiana agricultural and business interests agreed that Cuban goods sheltered under the U.S. tariff umbrella would present ruinous completion, and Congressman William F. Lowe of Mississippi predicted that war would bring only yellow fever and a plunge in cotton prices. South Carolina senator Benjamin R. Tillman sneered that McKinley and the Republicans sought to protect American bondholders (who resided primarily in the North) rather than Cubans, and he asserted that his state had encountered "bonds of that kind . . . during the era of reconstruction." The *Manning Times* concluded that there was "absolutely nothing in it [the war] for southerners."[36]

35. Gibson, "Attitudes in North Carolina Regarding the Independence of Cuba," 61 (*Observer*); John Oldfield, "Remembering the *Maine:* The United States, 1898, and Sectional Reconciliation," in *The Crisis of 1898: Colonial Redistribution and Nationalist Mobilization,* eds. Angel Smith and Emma Dávila-Cox (New York, 1999), 46–47 (*News and Courier, Daily Picayune*).

36. William J. Schellings, "Florida and the Cuban Revolution, 1895–1898," *Florida Historical Quarterly* 39 (October 1960): 175; Marshall E. Schott, "Louisiana Sugar and the Cuban Crisis, 1895–1898," *Louisiana History* 31 (summer 1990): 271–72; Kelley, "Mississippi and 'The Splendid

Southern uneasiness over a conflict with Spain was not confined to those fearing detrimental economic effects or naval attacks. Two groups of southern "outsiders" added their voices to the counsels of caution. Populists and dissident Democrats denounced war as a conservative device for obstructing reform. Tom Watson predicted that hostilities would divert "the attention of the people from economic issues" and allow politicians to avoid questions "they dare not meet." He later observed that the "Spanish War finished" the Populists: "The blare of the bugle drowned the voice of the Reformer."[37]

Southern blacks agreed that war would obscure critical domestic problems, but they were primarily concerned with the ever-worsening state of the region's race relations. Prominent southern blacks such as Booker T. Washington and Representative George H. White of North Carolina, the only African American member of Congress, urged African Americans to support the war effort and thereby enhance their prospects for more equal treatment as citizens. But numerous other blacks cited atrocities, such as the February 1898 murder of black Republican postmaster Frazier B. Baker of Lake City, South Carolina, as more important than the alleged Spanish attack on the battleship *Maine*. Black skeptics found no reason why African Americans should fight "to bring other Negroes [in Cuba] under the flag that has never as yet protected those who are already here." Better that this combat be left to the South's "brave lynchers." Once the fighting commenced, African Americans decried the refusal of the southern press to acknowledge the heroic service of black soldiers in Cuba. To have done so might have disturbed the "repose of the Caste-Demon." Blacks also recognized perceptively that any decline of sectionalism would prove injurious to African Americans. A black Norfolk editor observed, "The Negro might as well know it now as later"; the "closer the North and South get together by this war, the harder he will have to fight to maintain a footing."[38]

Little War,'" 125; Stephen Kantrowitz, *Ben Tillman and the Reconstruction of White Supremacy* (Chapel Hill, 2000), 262–63; Bailey, "Splendid Little Forgotten War," 196 (*Times*); Girling, "Southern Attitudes toward the Cuban Question," 26–28; James M. Lindgren, "The Apostasy of a Southern Anti-Imperialist: Joseph Bryan, The Spanish-American War, and Business Expansion," *Southern Studies* 2 (summer 1991): 157.

37. C. Vann Woodward, *Tom Watson: Agrarian Rebel* (1938; reprint, New York, 1972), 334–35.

38. Lawrence S. Little, *Disciples of Liberty: The African Methodist Episcopal Church in the Age of Imperialism, 1884–1916* (Knoxville, Tenn., 2000), 100 (Caste-Demon); Willard B. Gatewood Jr., *Black Americans and the White Man's Burden, 1898–1903* (Urbana, 1975), 23–34, 111

The South's experience in raising troops for service in Cuba also illustrated the region's ambivalence about the war. By May 2, 1898, only eleven of South Carolina's seventeen militia companies were at full strength. The Richmond Volunteers' two lieutenants had withdrawn for "business reasons," and the Cantey Hill Rifles from Kershaw County voted not to serve and declared it was not "any part of their duty to throw down everything and volunteer to fight for we hardly know what." In Texas, entire companies voted not to fight when denied the right to elect their officers. One disaffected militiaman from Houston explained that he could "imagine nothing more galling and humiliating than a gentleman serving under such conditions" and asked if there were "not enough idle men, with no ties, to attend to this soldier business?" Alabama's governor encountered a similar response among his state's troops, who "enjoyed being lionized—dances, banquets, outings, parades—but such festivities did not automatically translate into a desire for combat or a commitment to bring the blessing of freedom to the Cubans." By the end of July, when Mississippi recruiters could not locate a sufficient number of local residents to fill the state's quota, they signed up the final three hundred volunteers in Chicago, Illinois.[39]

If not all southerners were enthusiastic about fighting in Cuba, the South was even less enamored with black soldiers being stationed in the region or assigned to Cuba. In March 1898 the Twenty-Fifth Infantry of black "buffalo" soldiers, which had been stationed in the West, was ordered to Cuba via the South. Other regular black units and volunteers followed and were located primarily at Chickamauga and subsequently in the Key West–Tampa area. White southern response was almost uniformly hostile. Congressman Samuel Robertson from Louisiana voiced southern fears when he predicted that African American veterans of combat in Cuba "will claim to be saviors of the country, and when they return it will be impossible to live in peace and quiet with them in the South." The *Tampa Morning Tribune* claimed that the "colored troops . . . have made themselves very offensive to the people of the city. The men insist upon being treated as white men are treated." A black sergeant furnished the alternate perspective: "It mattered not if we were soldiers of the United States, and going to fight for

(other quotes); Piero Gleijeses, "African Americans and the War Against Spain," *North Carolina Historical Review* 78 (April 1996): 188; Bailey, "Splendid Little Forgotten War," 196.

39. Bailey, "Splendid Little Forgotten War," 197; Leffler, "Paradox of Patriotism," 35–37; William Warren Rogers et al., *Alabama: The History of a Deep South State* (Tuscaloosa, 1994), 338; Kelley, "Mississippi and the 'Splendid Little War,'" 131.

the honor of our country, we were 'niggers' as they called us and treated us with contempt." These conflicting attitudes, together with prejudice on the part of white troops, led to numerous racial incidents. The most serious clash, the so-called Tampa Riot, occurred in early June 1898 and resulted in the wounding of twenty-seven black soldiers and several white Georgia troops and the destruction of saloons and cafes that had refused to serve the African Americans.[40]

Race also played a central role in the South's response to the U.S. suppression of the Filipino insurgents led by Emilio Aguinaldo. While opposing annexation of the archipelago, the *Atlanta Constitution* endorsed the campaign to "vindicate the authority of our flag." To "retreat under fire" would not only impugn national honor, it would also compromise Dixie's racial codes and practices by challenging white superiority and contradicting the contention that "History teaches us that the colored races cannot stand up in competition with the white race and live." Southern soldiers involved in this campaign reiterated the professions of loyalty and patriotism voiced in 1898, and they once again linked their motives and actions to a "holy love and reverence" for the Lost Cause.[41]

The vast majority of southerners were as unwilling to incorporate non-whites into the union as they were to accept a Filipino military victory. The prospect of adding Cubans or Filipinos to the body politic was no more palatable than annexing Hawaiians. After a visit to Cuba, James K. Vardaman declared the Cubans "a class of people that would cause hell itself to deteriorate. . . . of all the weak, weary and altogether worthless people that I have ever had the misfortune to come into contact with the Cuban is . . . the most terrifying. The American nigger is a gentleman and scholar compared with him." Southerners denounced Filipinos in equally disparaging terms. Senator John W. Daniel of Virginia dismissed the Philippines as a "witch's cauldron," peopled by a "mess of Asiatic potage," and warned that annexing the islands would confer full citizenship on their inhabitants: "All the various inferior tribes of that country" would gain equality with "a white-born American citizen" together with complete freedom to emigrate to the mainland, to vote, and to hold office. Sounding the same theme, Hil-

---

40. Schott, "South and American Foreign Policy," 169 (Robertson); Gatewood, *Black Americans and the White Man's Burden,* 43–54, 45, 47–48 (other quotes).

41. Christopher A. Vaughan, "The 'Discovery' of the Philippines by the U.S. Press, 1898–1902," *Historian* 57 (winter 1995): 311 (*Constitution*); Foster, *Ghosts of the Confederacy,* 151 (other quotes).

ary A. Herbert objected that the Filipinos were "not fitted to govern themselves, certainly not fitted to govern us," and Benjamin R. Tillman added the habitual refrain that southerners best understood the disastrous results of having "two races side by side that can not mix or mingle without deterioration and injury to both." Indeed, he said, "thoughtful" white men were "lying awake at night" in South Carolina tortured by the prospect of incorporating ten million "negroes . . . Malays, Negritos, Japanese, Chinese, [and] mongrels of Spanish blood."[42]

Southern opponents of annexing the Philippines reiterated many of the other arguments they had voiced against acquiring Hawaii. Holding outposts still farther removed from North America would compromise the United States strategically. Senator Horace Chilton of Texas bemoaned the probable increases in defense spending, the enlarged military establishment, and the likely "complications with the Powers of Europe." By interfering in a region of far greater material and military concern to the European nations, the United States was nullifying the Monroe Doctrine and its ban against European meddling in the Western Hemisphere and risking war "with the powers of the Old World at a place" of their choosing. Senator Hernando De Soto Money of Mississippi decried the "steady accretion of executive power" at the expense of Congress and the growth of a "great military establishment" and warned of the possible "use of these same soldiers . . . in our own land." Both Money and his constituents understood that a strong president might employ the military to interfere in southern race relations.[43]

Southerners also repeated the admonition that republican government and colonial empire were incompatible. Senator James H. Berry of Arkansas asserted, if "the doctrine that 'all just powers of government are derived from the consent of the governed' was true in 1861, it is true in 1898." Having fought for the Confederacy, Berry refused to impose a "carpetbag government" on the Filipinos. He and fellow southerners understood the "wrongs

---

42. William F. Holmes, *The White Chief: James Kimble Vardaman* (Baton Rouge, 1970), 82; Edwina C. Smith, "Southerners on Empire: Southern Senators and Imperialism, 1898–1899," *Mississippi Quarterly* 31 (winter 1977–78): 97, 99 (Daniel); Hammett, *Herbert,* 210; H. E. Mattox, "Hilary A. Herbert and the Paradox of an Anti-Imperialist Strong Navy Advocate," *The Southern Historian* 5 (spring 1984): 25; Simkins, *Tillman,* 356–57; Kantrowitz, *Tillman,* 263.

43. Smith, "Southerners on Empire," 100, 103 (Chilton); Leonard Schlup, "Hernando De Soto Money: War Advocate and Anti-Imperialist, 1898–1900," *Journal of Mississippi History* 60 (winter 1998): 329, 332.

and outrages that may be perpetuated even by Americans where they seek to govern by strangers and by military power an unwilling people." Other southerners were even more strident in tracing U.S. policy to crass northern political and material motives: "The black Republican party north" was simply waging another war "for the purpose of plunder & conquest & robbery," as it had done in "stealing our slaves & robbing the people generally."[44]

Finally, southern anti-imperialists challenged the economic utility of annexing the Philippines. Rice and sugar planters continued to worry about harmful competition if the Philippines was granted tariff equality and free access to the domestic American market. Nor could southern critics discern reciprocal commercial advantages in the Philippines, or by extension, in China. Access to China required at most a coaling station, certainly not a Philippine colony. Moreover, trade prospects in both Asian nations were greatly exaggerated. Senators Daniel and Donelson Caffery of Louisiana perceptively noted that the great bulk of U.S. exports flowed to Western Europe rather than to the less-developed areas of Latin America, Africa, and Asia. The latter regions lacked purchasing power, and their inhabitants were little interested in U.S. products. Caffery observed succinctly, "The surplus of civilization is consumed by civilization." By contrast, "a half-civilized man wants but little," and the "distant possessions would cost more in ten years for garrisons than they would yield in profit to the United States in a century." Chilton agreed: "Men may deceive themselves by daydreams about securing a great trade in China and Japan from the standpoint of the Philippines. But I have seen town-lot booms before."[45]

While their opinion had no influence on the South's congressmen, southern blacks also opposed territorial expansion. African Americans identified with Hawaiians, Cubans, and Filipinos as people of color and denounced U.S. suppression of the Philippine insurgency as "criminal aggression." Booker T. Washington declared that the Filipinos deserved independence. The Tuskegee educator questioned whether the U.S. government could do "for the millions of dark-skinned races to be found in Cuba, Porto Rico, Hawaii and the Philippine Islands that which it has not been able to do for nearly 10,000,000 negroes and Indians" already under Ameri-

44. Smith, "Southerners on Empire," 106, and Foster, *Ghosts of the Confederacy*, 150 (for Berry); Schott, "South and American Foreign Policy," 187 (black Republican).

45. Smith, "Southerners on Empire," 101; Schott, "South and American Foreign Policy," 199.

can jurisdiction. Always quick to strip away the hypocrisy in the imperialist claim of bearing the "white man's burden" to aid others, John Mitchell, editor of the *Richmond Planet,* noted that "with the government acquiescing in the oppression and butchery of a dark race in this country," it was "time to call all missionaries home and have them work on our own people."[46]

Agreeing with the conclusions, if not the rationale, of their black constituents, southern senators voted against the Treaty of Paris and the annexation of the Philippines by a margin of 15 to 10. Of the 10 senators voting yea, at least 4 acted inconsistently with their prior opposition to territorial imperialism. William Sullivan of Mississippi, Alexander S. Clay of Georgia, and Marion P. Butler of North Carolina accepted William Jennings Bryan's strategy of ratifying the treaty to end the war and then contesting the issue of imperialism in the 1900 presidential election; Samuel D. McEnery of Louisiana allegedly was promised a federal judgeship by the McKinley administration. Republicans William J. Deboe and Jeter C. Pritchard cast 2 of the remaining yes votes. More representative of the region's congressional opinion was the vote on Georgia senator Augustus O. Bacon's measure disclaiming any U.S. "intention to exercise permanent sovereignty, jurisdiction, or control" over the Philippines and pledging to free the islands when stability had been established. Eighteen southerners voted or were paired in favor of the Bacon amendment. Only 4 were opposed—Republicans Deboe and Pritchard, McEnery, and John Tyler Morgan, who held fast to his advocacy of territorial and economic expansion as the keys to achieving southern autonomy.[47]

Even as southern senators registered this resounding repugnance to territorial expansion, significant sectors of southern opinion were giving much greater credence to the arguments of Morgan and Wheeler and newer economic expansionists such as Daniel A. Tompkins. In fact, southerners had never ignored markets after 1865; rather, considerations of party politics, central governmental authority, race, and fiscal restraint had usually taken precedence over the long-standing southern pursuit of commercial expansion. By the 1890s, the South's industrial growth, primarily in the production of cotton textiles and secondarily in iron and steel and tobacco,

---

46. Willard B. Gatewood Jr., "A Negro Editor on Imperialism: John Mitchell, 1898–1901," *Journalism Quarterly* 49 (spring 1972): 48; Gatewood, *Black Americans and the White Man's Burden,* 185, 190.

47. McWilliams, *New South Faces the World,* 66–67; Smith, "Southerners on Empire," 91 n. 7, 94–97; Fry, *Morgan,* 177–78.

augmented the need for markets for staple agricultural goods. In the ten years after 1887, exports of coarse cotton from the United States to China increased by 121 percent, and by the turn of the century more than 50 percent of American cloth sold abroad went to China. The bulk of the cheaper varieties was produced in the South. In 1897, for example, Alabama's Cordova Mill exported its entire production to China, and a contemporary American traveler in North China and Manchuria simultaneously reported, "There was not a hole in the East where I did not find a Piedmont brand."[48]

Together with this growing industrial production came a renewed emphasis on a more outward-looking economic policy. The editor of *Dixie,* the region's largest trade paper, initiated the movement that led to the formation of the National Association of Manufacturers (NAM) in 1895. NAM concentrated on promoting foreign trade, and the next year, T. H. Martin of Georgia chaired a NAM committee charged with organizing an industrial exposition in Mexico City. Daniel A. Tompkins, a Charlotte textile manufacturer, was even more active and significant. An indefatigable organizer and publicist, Tompkins used his *Charlotte Daily Observer* to push hard for markets, marshaled support from other important textile producers throughout the South, and from 1902 to 1910 advanced his agenda from the executive committee of the American Asiatic Association, another commercial lobbying group. His position was uncomplicated: The United States had "developed her manufacturing interests to such an extent that her domestic market no longer absorbs her manufactured products." More specifically, the U.S. government needed "to insure the integrity of the Chinese Empire and protect our trade there."[49]

This pursuit of markets prompted Tompkins and most of his fellow textile manufacturers to favor retention of the Philippines and to endorse Secretary of State John Hay's efforts to protect the Open Door policy and equal access to Chinese markets. Senator John L. McLaurin of South Carolina

48. Hearden, *Independence and Empire,* 128–29 (Piedmont); LaFeber, *American Search for Opportunity,* 169.

49. McWilliams, *New South Faces the World,* 74–75; Hearden, *Independence and Empire,* 130–31; see also Martin J. Sklar, "The N.A.M. and Foreign Markets on the Eve of the Spanish-American War," *Science and Society* 23 (spring 1959): 145; Albert K. Steigerwalt, *The National Association of Manufacturers, 1885–1914* (Ann Arbor, 1964), 144–45; James J. Lorence, *Organized Business and the Myth of the China Market: The American Asiatic Association, 1898–1937* (Philadelphia, 1981), 17–18, 24–25, 34–35, 42, 52; Charles S. Campbell, *Special Business Interests and the Open Door Policy* (New Haven, 1951), 14, 17–20, 47, 60.

spoke for these interests in October 1899 when he declared that control of the Philippines "or at least of some portions is the only safeguard for our trade interests in the East. The abandonment of them means the dismemberment of China, its partition among the European powers, and the inevitable loss of our China trade." Senator Morgan agreed. "The South," he subsequently contended, was "more directly interested in our mastery and control of the commerce of Asia and the North Pacific than is any other section of the country." Key southern newspapers, such as Tompkins's *Daily Observer,* Richard H. Edmond's *Manufacturers Record,* Henry Watterson's *Louisville Courier-Journal,* and the *Atlanta Constitution,* joined the chorus. Joseph Bryan summarized their positions in the *Richmond Times:* The Philippines would become a *"pedis posito* in the East that will give us immense advantages in securing Eastern trade. . . . There is a prodigious market for our [the South's] wares in Japan, the Philippines, India, Australia, and most of all in China." The heightened sentiment for economic expansion was not confined to southern manufacturers. A Texas farmer called on "southern and especially Texas Populists [to] stand firm for a policy which will put us in touch with five hundred millions of Asiatic consumers. . . . Free commerce is what we want." Annexation of the Philippines, he declared, promised an escape from the "cruel and dishonest methods of gain heretofore imposed upon us in the South and West by the bondholders of Europe and New England."[50]

The South's response to Theodore Roosevelt's isthmian canal policy demonstrated the region's concern for economic expansion. Dixie had long since accepted Senator Morgan's argument of an isthmian canal's special relevance for the South. "Our southern states," he explained in 1903, "are still buried under the ashes of the great civil war, and . . . an isthmian canal is the best, if not the only hope of lifting them above the debris, through the energies of production and through commercial intercourse with the Pacific Ocean." By opening Latin American and Asian markets to the South's "peculiar crop of cotton . . . cheapest iron and steel and coal . . . and yellow pine," the project was "clearly sectional in its chief benefits." Morgan also preferred the Nicaraguan to the Panamanian route because the former was three hundred miles closer to southern ports and would bring sea traffic

50. Hearden, *Independence and Empire,* 135–36 (McLaurin); Fry, *Morgan,* 175; Lindgren, "Apostasy of a Southern Anti-Imperialist," 166; Williams, *Roots of Modern American Empire,* 428 (Texas farmer); McWilliams, *New South Faces the World,* 66 n. 47.

through the Gulf of Mexico rather than through the Windward Passage east of Cuba. As the *Mobile Register* noted, a Panama canal looked "towards the Atlantic coast and Europe." Convinced by the senator's tireless advocacy after 1880, most interested southerners endorsed his preference for the Nicaraguan route.[51]

When combined with Dixie's well-established Gilded Age apprehension over centralized authority, partisan anti-Republican tendencies, and uneasiness with diplomatic interventionism, this preference for Nicaragua might have yielded adamant opposition to Roosevelt's switch to Panama. But it did not. Persuaded by engineering considerations and the effective work of the Panama lobby, Theodore Roosevelt and the Republican-controlled Congress declared for the Panama route in 1902. When negotiations with Colombia failed to yield an American right-of-way, the president provided decisive military support for the Panama "revolution" of November 4, 1903. Two days later, Roosevelt recognized Panama as an independent country. On November 17, Secretary of State John Hay negotiated a treaty with Philippe-Jean Bunau-Varilla, granting the United States use of a ten-mile-wide canal zone in perpetuity in return for a $10 million initial payment, an additional $250,000 per year, and a U.S. guarantee of Panama's independence.

As a Republican president exercising vigorous executive authority, aggressively intervening abroad, establishing a protectorate, and opting for Panama over Nicaragua, Roosevelt had acted in ways that had produced adamant southern opposition to the Frelinghuysen-Zavala canal treaty of 1884 and the Hawaiian revolution of 1893. Although Morgan was outraged more by Roosevelt's choice of Panama than by his assertive policy, the senator couched much of his criticism in familiar southern refrains. He excoriated Roosevelt for performing a "caesarean operation by which a republic of Panama" was "taken alive from the womb of Columbia." By intervening with U.S. naval vessels and marines, Roosevelt had violated Colombian sovereignty; by recognizing a Panamanian government that was a "mere dummy" with no international standing, Roosevelt had acted prematurely and expediently. Although Senators Bacon, Daniel, Tillman, and Edward W. Carmack of Tennessee joined Morgan in lambasting Roosevelt, the Alabamian could not muster the nearly unanimous southern support necessary to block the treaty. The pact passed 66 to 14 in February 1904, with both senators from Arkansas, Florida, Georgia, and Louisiana, and one each

51. Fry, *Morgan*, 96–97.

from Kentucky, Mississippi, South Carolina, and North Carolina in the yes column. Seven southerners joined Morgan in intransigent opposition.[52]

Southern press opinion was even more ready to overlook Roosevelt's transgressions in return for the expected sectional benefits. Fifteen Louisiana newspapers favored passage of the treaty, and only three opposed it. The *Birmingham News* declared representatively that the "route [was] but an incident, the overshadowing necessity is a canal," and the *Montgomery Advertiser* demanded that "hair-splitting . . . cease, and digging . . . begin." From Louisiana, the *Crowley Daily Signal* reminded southerners that despite Roosevelt's "Bronco-busting, Hell-roaring style of statesmanship," his "practical" work in the "Panama affair meets with Southern approval." Moreover, agreeing with the president on Panama did not preclude attacking Roosevelt on the "nigger question." Projected economic gain had prevailed over other sectional considerations.[53]

On early-twentieth-century issues less likely to produce material gains, the South's dominant post-1865 foreign policy attitudes persisted. Jealousy over Senate prerogatives in the treaty-making process produced overwhelming bipartisan opposition to a series of ten arbitration treaties with Mexico and the major European states. In February 1905 the Senate voted 50 to 9 to require that arbitrated claims growing out of the agreement with France (and by extension out of the other nine pacts) be subject to two-thirds Senate approval. Southerners voted unanimously for this amendment. Dixie's concern for Senate restraint of the executive persisted. Southerners added a peculiar dislike and anxiety over the activist Republican president, who had invited Booker T. Washington for dinner at the White House, and a particular trepidation that the treaties might be used to force the payment of the South's repudiated state debts. Roosevelt pointedly castigated Senators Bacon, Morgan, and Thomas S. Martin of Virginia for "holding up the treaties." Six years later, southern Democrats were again instrumental in rejecting another set of arbitration treaties negotiated and submitted to the Senate by Roosevelt's Republican successor, William Howard Taft.[54]

52. Ibid., 231–35.

53. Howard R. Butler, "Public Opinion Concerning the Panama Canal as Reflected in Louisiana Newspapers of 1903 and 1904" (master's thesis, Louisiana State University, 1965), 57, 63, and Schott, "South and American Foreign Policy," 261 (*Signal*); Fry, *Morgan,* 233 (Alabama press quotes); Burton I. Kaufman, "New Orleans and the Panama Canal, 1900–1914," *Louisiana History* 14 (fall 1973): 333–46.

54. W. Stull Holt, *Treaties Defeated by the Senate: A Study of the Struggle between President and Senate over the Conduct of Foreign Relations* (1933; reprint, Gloucester, Mass., 1964), 204–12,

Bacon and Morgan also led the Senate opposition to Roosevelt's first attempt to implement his "corollary" to the Monroe Doctrine. Against the backdrop of European interventions to collect debts in Venezuela and U.S. determination to ensure unobstructed access to the projected canal, Roosevelt had proclaimed in December 1904 that "chronic wrongdoing" and insolvency in the Americas "could require intervention by some civilized nation." If the Monroe Doctrine were observed and European nations were precluded from performing such enforcement functions, the United States would have to serve as an "international police force." Roosevelt initially applied his corollary in the Dominican Republic, a nation plagued by civil war and staggering debts to both European and American creditors. Signed on January 20, 1905, the Dillingham-Sanchez protocol adjusted the Dominican debt and empowered the United States to guarantee Dominican sovereignty and to administer the country's customs houses. When it became apparent that the president intended to activate this agreement without consulting the Senate, Democratic protests forced the president to negotiate a second pact on February 7. It retained the debt adjustment and customs provisions, and while pledging to respect (rather than guarantee) Dominican sovereignty, it emphasized that attempted European control over the Caribbean nation would be interpreted as "an unfriendly disposition toward the United States."[55]

Roosevelt submitted this treaty to the Senate in mid-February, and the upper house spent most of the March 1905 special session debating the agreement. Unanimous Democratic opposition blocked its ratification; and Morgan and Bacon joined Arthur P. Gorman of Maryland, Henry M. Teller of Colorado, and Francis G. Newlands of Nevada as the most vocal censors of Roosevelt's incursions on Senate authority. Infuriated, the president withdrew the treaty from Senate consideration in mid-March and once more specified southerners as key obstructionists. Roosevelt complained, "Creatures like Bacon, Morgan, et cetra, backed by the average yahoo among the Democratic Senators, are wholly indifferent to national honor or national welfare." Together with other allegedly irresponsible politicos, they had undone Roosevelt's careful work: "The Senate adjourns. I am left

---

330–35 (Roosevelt, 209); Ronald F. Reter, "President Theodore Roosevelt and the Senate's 'Advice and Consent' to Treaties," *Historian* 54 (August 1982): 492–93; Fry, *Morgan*, 244–45.

55. Holt, *Treaties Defeated by the Senate*, 213–18; Richard H. Collin, *Theodore Roosevelt's Caribbean: The Panama Canal, the Monroe Doctrine, and the Latin American Context* (Baton Rouge, 1990), 341–426.

to shoulder all the responsibility due to their failure. Bacon, Morgan, Carmack and company go off, hoping that disaster will come to the country because the Republican administration will thereby be discredited."[56]

Roosevelt promptly circumvented the Senate by incorporating the treaty into an executive agreement, which did not require congressional approval and which remained in effect until February 1907, when the president belatedly obtained the treaty's formal ratification. This diplomatic sleight-of-hand confirmed southern fears of executive usurpation. Morgan declared that the "President has done exactly what the Senate refused to give him the authority to do." As with the arbitration treaties, southerners subsequently opposed two attempts by William Howard Taft to apply the "Dominican formula." Pacts with Honduras (1912) and Nicaragua (1912 and 1913) calling for loan agreements and customs collections failed to garner Senate approval. Partisan politics, fiscal restraint, apprehension over executive power, and uneasiness with diplomatic interventionism continued to underpin the South's foreign policy perspective.[57]

All of these concerns reflected the South's apprehensions over outside control in the half century after Appomattox. Conditioned to hate Yankees and Republicans, acting upon the experience of the Civil War and Reconstruction and subsequent devotion to the Lost Cause, wedded to states' rights and strict constructionism, confined within a colonial economy and beleaguered by the Republican Party's pronorthern economic policies, haunted by racial fears, and driven by the compulsion to maintain white domination, southerners were reflexively suspicious of Republican foreign policies. On the whole, the South had opposed initiatives that promised to benefit the Republican Party, to strengthen the executive or the military, to cost substantial sums, or to add territories populated by nonwhites or that produced goods competitive with Dixie's staple agriculture. In short, the South's basic foreign policy perspective was, like its domestic stance, conservative. Fiscal restraint, constitutional caution, racial anxiety, and political partisanship dictated this policy. While countering Republican initiatives, the South had provided the principal sectional opposition to and had articulated trenchant criticisms of what historian Michael H. Hunt has termed America's imperial policy of "national greatness."[58]

56. Holt, *Treaties Defeated by the Senate*, 212–27.
57. Fry, *Morgan*, 247; Holt, *Treaties Defeated by the Senate*, 237–40.
58. Michael H. Hunt, *Ideology and U.S. Foreign Policy* (New Haven, 1987), 19, 43–44.

Two influences in the 1890s altered this pattern. Dixie's desire to prove its loyalty to the nation and to demonstrate patriotism, valor, honor, and manhood worthy of heirs of the Confederacy prompted considerable, but hardly unanimous, interventionist sentiment in the years leading to the war with Spain and during the conflicts in Cuba and the Philippines. The second influence, the South's long-standing concern for foreign markets, had often played a secondary role to the aforementioned racial, fiscal, and political calculations. Still, southerners had never ignored the need to export their agriculture products, particularly cotton, which remained king; and by the turn of the century, economic considerations took precedence in specific situations. Economic expansionists such as John Tyler Morgan kept the need for foreign markets before the South and the nation. With the growth of southern manufacturing and the devastating effects of the panic of 1893 and the ensuing depression, Morgan's message commanded a greater following. This heightened economic consciousness was evident in the South's willingness to put aside partisan politics and the fear of executive usurpation to obtain the Panama Canal.

Despite these deviations, the South's fundamental foreign policy assumptions and interests remained largely unchanged as the half century following the Civil War neared its end. The election of Woodrow Wilson as president in 1912 transformed how Dixie acted on its principal assumptions and interests. The South welcomed Wilson, a Democrat and a man the region deemed one of its own, to the White House in 1913. As crucial southern backing for Jefferson, Jackson, and Polk had demonstrated, the South was willing to endorse an assertive foreign policy, particularly if the president was a southern Democrat who embodied no threat to the region's racial practices. Over Wilson's two terms, partisan politics, sectional pride, the responsibility of congressional leadership, devotion to the Lost Cause, conviction of nonwhite racial inferiority, and pursuit of low tariffs and commercial expansion led the South to provide the decisive support for Wilsonian foreign policies and in so doing to modify permanently the pattern of its post–Civil War response to U.S. relations abroad.

CHAPTER 5

Returning to the House of their Fathers, 1913–1920

WHEN THE DEMOCRATS elected Woodrow Wilson president in 1912 and carried both houses of Congress, southerners returned to the forefront of national politics and diplomacy for the first time since the 1840s. The first president since Lincoln of southern birth, Wilson appointed five other native southerners to his cabinet, and the congressional seniority system placed southern Democrats in key leadership positions in both houses. In early 1913 a journalist observed, "In Washington you feel it in the air, you note it in the changed and changing ways of business; you listen to evidence of it in the mellow accent with which the South makes our English a musical tongue; you hear strange names of men to whom leadership and importance are attributed, and if you ask, you almost invariably learn they are from the South." Edward M. House, Wilson's closest confidant on foreign policy, asserted correctly, "The South is clearly in the saddle, both in Congress and in the Administration." The sons of Dixie had returned to "the house of their fathers."[1]

Renewed southern influence proved exceedingly important. Scholars have asserted that Wilson and his followers "laid the foundations of a modern American foreign policy" and that he "established a conceptual framework for American foreign policy in the twentieth century." This Wilsonian search for a "New Diplomacy" could not have been undertaken without de-

1. Dewey W. Grantham Jr., "Southern Congressional Leaders and the New Freedom, 1913–1917," *Journal of Southern History* 13 (November 1947): 443 (journalist); David M. Kennedy, *Over Here: The First World War and American Society* (New York, 1980) (House); George B. Tindall, *The Emergence of the New South, 1913–1945* (Baton Rouge, 1967), 3 (fathers).

pendable and consistent support from the South. In all of his policies, ranging from reduction of the tariff to intervention in World War I and the
promotion of U.S. membership in a League of Nations, President Wilson
received essential backing from his southern followers. It was equally significant that in the course of rendering this critical support, the South transformed its post–Civil War perspective on U.S. foreign relations. Beginning
with the Wilson presidency, the majority of southerners discarded their opposition of the previous fifty years to an activist, interventionist foreign policy based on a strong military and directed by an assertive executive. A
resistant and vocal southern minority remained apprehensive at the prospect
of enhanced executive, federal, and military power; but over the ensuing five
decades, this revised, more activist southern viewpoint would prove crucial
to American foreign policies in World War II, the cold war, and Vietnam.[2]

Although Wilson had been gone from the South for twenty-five years
and had come to the White House via the presidency of Princeton University and the governorship of New Jersey, the South had claimed him as one
of its own from the time he first came to prominence as an author and academic in the mid-1880s. During his campaign for the presidency in 1912, a
Georgia editor characterized him as a man *"of southern blood, of southern bone
and of southern grit."* Born in Virginia and reared in Georgia and the Caroli-
nas, Wilson contended that "a boy never gets over his boyhood, and never
can change those subtle influences which have become a part of him. . . .
the only place in the country, the only place in the world, where nothing
has to be explained to me is in the South." Although Arthur S. Link, Wilson's foremost biographer, has questioned how peculiarly southern his political policies were, certainly a number of Wilson's diplomatic emphases were
consistent with previous southern goals. For example, his commitment to
low tariffs, to the free flow of American commerce and the expansion of

2. N. Gordon Levin Jr., *Woodrow Wilson and World Politics: America's Response to War and
Revolution* (New York, 1968), 1; Amos Perlmutter, *Making the World Safe for Democracy: A Cen-
tury of Wilsonianism and Its Totalitarian Challengers* (Chapel Hill, 1997), 28. See also Thomas J.
Knock, *To End All Wars: Woodrow Wilson and the Quest for a New World Order* (Princeton, 1995);
Lloyd C. Gardner, *Safe for Democracy: The Anglo-American Response to Revolution, 1913–1923*
(New York, 1984); Arthur S. Link, *Woodrow Wilson: Revolution, War, and Peace* (Arlington
Heights, Ill., 1979); Frank Ninkovich, *The Wilsonian Century: U.S. Foreign Policy since 1900*
(Chicago, 1999); David Steigerwald, *Wilsonian Idealism in America* (Ithaca, N.Y., 1994); and
Tony Smith, *America's Mission: The United States and the Worldwide Struggle for Democracy in
the Twentieth Century* (Princeton, 1994).

exports, to the preservation of national honor and international standing and credibility, to the prevention of imperial abuse by special (often business) interests, and to the declared (if not always practiced) avoidance of interference in the internal affairs of other nations, all had southern—even Jeffersonian—precedents.[3]

Certainly the new president did not lack for southern advisers. Five of his ten cabinet appointees were native southerners. Although Edward M. House of Texas lacked an official portfolio, he was Wilson's primary adviser on diplomatic policy. Wilson also appointed Walter Hines Page of North Carolina as ambassador to London, dispatched Thomas Nelson Page of Virginia to Rome, and sent William E. Gonzales, a Georgia publisher, to Cuba. And when the president worked with Congress on foreign policy, he dealt principally with southerners, who dominated the leadership positions. In the House, first Oscar W. Underwood of Alabama and then Claude Kitchen of North Carolina served as majority leaders; and the committee chairs included Henry D. Flood of Virginia in Foreign Affairs, William C. Adamson of Georgia in Interstate and Foreign Commerce, James Hay of Virginia and Stanley Hubert Dent Jr. of Alabama in Military Affairs, and Lemuel P. Padgett of Tennessee in Naval Affairs. In the Senate, Augustus O. Bacon of Georgia headed Foreign Relations; Joseph F. Johnston of Alabama, Military Affairs; and Benjamin R. Tillman of South Carolina, Naval Affairs.

This newly installed southern leadership represented a region that remained decidedly more poor, more rural, and more agricultural than the rest of the nation. In 1900 the South's personal income amounted to only 51 percent of the national average; by 1920, it had climbed to 62 percent. For these same years, southerners living in towns or cities of 2,500 or more inhabitants increased from 16 to 25 percent as compared to the national average of 40 and 50. In the countryside, cotton remained king, and the sharecropping of staple crops remained pervasive. Georgia provided a revealing example in which owner-operated farms had declined from 55.1 percent in 1880 to 34.6 in 1910. In 1913, an agricultural agent for the U.S. Census Bureau described the rural South as the nation's "most complete social problem." Sharecropping and tenantry had produced "poor agriculture, ex-

3. Arthur S. Link, "Woodrow Wilson: The American as Southerner," *Journal of Southern History* 36 (February 1970): 4, 13; see also Anthony Gaughan, "Woodrow Wilson and the Legacy of the Civil War," *Civil War History* 43 (September 1997): 225–42.

hausted soils, small crops, poor roads, decaying bridges, unpainted homes, and unkept yards."[4]

Southern industry featured the raising, extracting, and first-stage processing of agricultural goods and natural resources. Together with the region's railroads, these industries were increasingly controlled by northerners. Historian Dewey W. Grantham has observed that from 1880 to 1920, "a steady decline occurred in the fraction of nonagricultural wealth in the region owned by home-state residents." This ongoing colonial condition spawned an intense hostility toward "trusts" and monopolies, and railroads and insurance companies were often cited as the symbols of outside domination. When combined with the South's ever-present preoccupation with race, its long absence from sustained political influence in national affairs, and the resulting inequity in benefits, these socioeconomic conditions ensured that southerners thought of "their section as a unit within a larger unit," that self-conscious sectionalism informed their world view.[5]

When applied to foreign policy, this world view featured the long-established southern concern for foreign markets and the export of the region's agricultural products and textiles. Closely related to the search for markets was the desire to lower tariffs to facilitate trade, reduce the cost of manufactured goods to consumers, and curtail the power of northern trusts. Southerners also remained fearful of foreign policy initiatives that enhanced central political and military power. Racial assumptions, Dixie's traditional states' rights orientation, and the experience of Reconstruction led southerners to question the imperial domination of nonwhites and the potential military implications. These concerns also elicited southern apprehensions about conscription and the domestic legislation required to mobilize the nation for World War I.

But much more powerful considerations offset these misgivings and inclined both the southern public and its representatives to follow Wilson's activist foreign policy. Long out of positions of power, these southerners and their colleagues leading the crucial committees addressing domestic issues were well disposed to act in concert with Wilson. This inclination derived in part from their affinity for the president as a fellow southerner.

4. Dewey W. Grantham, *Southern Progressivism: The Reconciliation of Progress and Tradition* (Knoxville, Tenn., 1983), 321.

5. Dewey W. Grantham, *The South in Modern America: A Region at Odds* (New York, 1994), 6, 59.

More important was the South's collective belief that it had been treated unfairly during the previous fifty years of Republican dominance. Therefore, support for Wilson and his legislative agenda was tied to the South's desire to obtain its equitable share of federal assistance and patronage. Southerners also sought to demonstrate their ability to govern responsibly and effectively, and this led them to be far less rigidly tied to states' rights when in the majority and occupying positions of leadership than when relegated to the minority. As they had done during the Spanish-Cuban-American War, southerners also seized the opportunity afforded by World War I to affirm their patriotism and to act on the Lost Cause mythology. Building on their experience during the war of 1898, they fully recognized the potential economic benefits that accrued from defense spending.

Loyalty to the Democratic Party sealed overall southern allegiance to Wilson's policies. Representative John H. Bankhead of Alabama, a former Confederate soldier, likened the party to "something like an army in which the colonels must follow the lead of the general." While debating the repeal of the Panama Canal tolls in 1914, Congressman T. W. Sims of Tennessee agreed, "The President of the United States is the Court of last resort, and his decision on such questions is final and unanswerable and in this sense infallible." Alabama Republican Frederick Bromberg described this Democratic solidarity in less flattering terms: "Like monkeys the Democratic members of Congress dance to any tune that the hand at the organ chooses to grind out."[6]

Well-established southern foreign policy perspectives and influences were evident from the beginning of the Wilson administration. In fact, Wilson initiated his New Freedom legislative agenda by calling a special session of Congress for April 7, 1913, to lower the tariff. Southerners had argued since the 1790s that a high protective tariff aided northern manufacturing interests at the expense of the agricultural South and consumers generally and impeded the foreign commerce so crucial to Dixie's staple exports. Even more specifically, throughout the late nineteenth and early twentieth centuries southerners had also charged that the tariff fostered monopolies and benefited the "interests" at the expense of the "people" and

6. Tindall, *Emergence of the New South*, 8 (Bankhead); Robert H. Block, "Southern Congressmen and Wilson's Call for Repeal of the Panama Canal Tolls Exemption," *Southern Studies* 17 (spring 1978): 95 (Sims); Robert H. Block, "Southern Opinion of Woodrow Wilson's Foreign Policies, 1913–1917" (Ph.D. dissertation, Duke University, 1968), 71 (Bromberg).

aspiring southern industrialists. Fittingly, Wilson's key legislative lieutenants were Oscar W. Underwood of Alabama, chair of the House Ways and
Means Committee, and Furnifold M. Simmons of North Carolina, chair of
the Senate Finance Committee.

In addition to calling the special session, the president stipulated that
wool, food, leather, sugar, and cotton textiles be included on the free list,
lobbied effectively with individual Democratic congressmen and senators,
and made a dramatic public appeal for passage of the Underwood-Simmons
Tariff Act. The duties on sugar, the one southern agricultural item that had
received tariff protection over the previous fifty years, were ultimately
phased out over a four-year period. The ending of this duty, the absence of
protection for wool, cotton textiles, and pig iron, and reduced duties on iron
pipe and structural steel prompted considerable opposition in Louisiana,
Texas, North Carolina, and Alabama. Despite pressure from disgruntled
constituents, Underwood and Simmons skillfully guided the legislation to
passage. The House approved the tariff bill by 281 to 139, with only 5 Democrats (4 of whom were from Louisiana) in the negative column. The Senate
concurred 44 to 37, with only Louisiana's Joseph E. Ransdell and John R.
Thornton breaking Democratic ranks. The first reduction of the tariff since
the Civil War, the Underwood-Simmons Act set rates at 27 percent, approximately 10 percent lower than the Payne-Aldrich Tariff of 1909. While
the outbreak of World War I precluded a clear test of whether lowered
American rates would have stimulated foreign trade, the great majority of
southerners had embraced the region's and the Democratic Party's traditional low-tariff posture.[7]

Southerners also played a prominent role in promoting the independence
of the Philippines. Majority southern opinion had opposed annexing the
archipelago, and after 1902 William A. Jones of Virginia, ranking Democrat
on the House Committee on Insular Affairs, had regularly submitted reports advocating the islands' independence. Consistent with Jones's stance,
the 1912 Democratic platform had decried U.S. territorial imperialism as "an
inexcusable blunder" and pledged that the party would seek "an immediate
declaration of the Nation's purpose to recognize the independence of the
Philippine Islands as soon as a stable government can be established." Jones
introduced Philippine legislation in July 1914. The bill's preamble promised
eventual independence, and the measure stipulated that both houses of the

7. Arthur S. Link, *The New Freedom*, vol. 2 of *Wilson* (Princeton, 1956–65), 181, 194.

Philippine legislature would be elective and the insular senate would confirm the appointment of the governor general.[8]

The House passed this bill in October 1914, but more pressing issues related to Mexico and World War I delayed its consideration in the Senate until January 1916, when James P. Clarke of Arkansas voiced the more radical strain of southern anti-imperialism. Clarke's amendment to the Jones bill authorized Wilson to recognize Philippine independence and withdraw from the islands within two years. Clarke would have had the United States retain its naval bases and coaling stations and with them access to East Asian markets, and the senator urged Washington to guarantee the neutrality of the islands.

After consulting with President Wilson, Clarke subsequently modified his amendment by extending the time for U.S. withdrawal to four years and leaving this action to the discretion of the president. Stripped of the necessity for obligatory or immediate action, the revised Clarke proposal narrowly passed the Senate in February 1916. In the absence of active administrative support, even this emasculated measure failed to survive in the House. In May 1916, northern Democrats and Republicans revived the Jones Bill, and it subsequently became law in August. Wilson signed the legislation and praised it as fulfilling Democratic pledges to further self-government and independence. Significantly, southern cotton interests, with an eye on Philippine markets, had favored the Jones Bill with its more indefinite time requirements, and the final legislation was appreciably more moderate than either southern anti-imperialist rhetoric or Senator Clarke's original amendment. The responsibility of majority control and the reluctance to challenge the Democratic president were already evident.[9]

Wilson's call for the repeal of the exemption of U.S.-owned ships from paying Panama Canal tolls elicited a much less united response from southern congressmen. Congress had created this exemption while establishing the toll schedules in 1912, and Democrats had endorsed the legislation in their party platform. Great Britain promptly protested, asserting that the exemption violated the Hay-Pauncefote Treaty of 1901, in which the United States had pledged the canal would be open on "terms of entire equality" to

8. Peter W. Stanley, *A Nation in the Making: The Philippines and the United States, 1899–1921* (Cambridge, Mass., 1974), 179.

9. Ibid., 171–73, 179–80, 190, 215–25; Roy W. Curry, "Woodrow Wilson and Philippine Policy," *Mississippi Valley Historical Review* 41 (December 1954): 435–52.

"all nations." Following his election, Wilson accepted the British argument, thereby contradicting the party platform and his campaign speeches. He did so both out of a sense of fairness and a desire to maintain British support for U.S. policies in Mexico.[10]

The president worked initially with Representative William C. Adamson of Georgia, chairman of the Committee on Interstate and Foreign Commerce, who introduced a bill in early 1914 to suspend the exemption for two years. Wilson subsequently judged this action insufficient and requested Congressman T. W. Sims of Tennessee to sponsor a second bill canceling the exemption completely. Both measures faced stiff opposition. Northern Democrats with Irish constituents composed much of this opposition in the House, but the most significant dissenter was Oscar W. Underwood, Democratic majority leader. Underwood cited the need to comply with the party platform, but he was also concerned with the economic implications for Alabama. His hometown newspaper, the *Birmingham Age-Herald*, warned that bearing the cost of the tolls would jeopardize the sales of "Birmingham coal, Birmingham pig iron and Birmingham pipe sold to the Pacific coast states." Senator Joseph E. Ransdell of Louisiana elaborated the southern economic perspective. Ransdell declared the measure "fraught with friendship for railways," hostile to the "coastwise trade" that flowed particularly through New Orleans, and "seriously hurtful to the country, especially the South."[11]

Convinced of the legitimacy of his position and cognizant of the challenge to his leadership, Wilson demanded repeal in a manner that anticipated his rigid stand on subsequent foreign policy issues. On March 5, 1914, he placed the matter squarely before a joint session of Congress: "I ask this of you in support of the foreign policy of the administration. I shall not know how to deal with other matters of even greater delicacy and nearer consequence if you do not grant it to me in ungrudging measure." The president reinforced this compelling appeal by dispatching Secretary of the Treasury William G. McAdoo and Postmaster General Albert S. Burleson to Capitol Hill to wield the administration's patronage club. Wilson also worked closely with Congressmen Adamson and Sims in the House and Senators Simmons, Hoke Smith of Georgia, and John Thurston of Louisi-

10. Link, *The New Freedom*, 305.

11. Block, "Southern Congressmen and Wilson's Call for Repeal of the Panama Canal Tolls Exemption," 94, 97–98.

ana. Endorsing the president's position on equity and the practical necessity of maintaining good relations with Great Britain, these dutiful southern Democrats dismissed the tolls exemption as a sop to the "existing trust controlled monopoly" of the coastal shipping interests. Significantly, southerners on both sides of the debate appealed to the region's antagonism toward trusts and monopolies. These cumulative efforts yielded a vote for repeal of 247 to 162 in the House, with 11 southern Democrats and 2 Republicans dissenting, and 50 to 35 in the Senate, with 3 Dixie Democrats voting no.[12]

The South's response to tariff reduction, Philippine independence, and the Panama Canal tolls demonstrated the region's party regularity, racial assumptions, and persisting anti-imperialism. Economic considerations and concern for foreign commerce were also evident. But the Mexican Revolution and World War I constituted the most significant and revealing foreign policy issues of the Wilson era. Upon entering office in March 1913, Wilson confronted an ongoing and complex revolution in Mexico. In 1911, Francisco Madero had led the overthrow of Porfirio Díaz's dictatorship of nearly four decades. Soon thereafter, Victoriano Huerta deposed and murdered Madero. These developments deeply disturbed the new American president, who declared he would never "recognize a government of butchers." In addition to his moral objections to Huerta, Wilson feared that the new dictator's use of force provided an injurious example for other would-be Latin American revolutionaries. Disorder and violence might prevail rather than the preferred course of orderly, democratic change. Presuming that he could impose the latter, Wilson recognized that Americans had a substantial material stake in Mexico—nearly $2 billion in investments, or the ownership of approximately 43 percent of the nation's property value. Although the president never pursued narrow economic calculations and periodically denounced selfish American investors, he also castigated "foreign interests" that sought to "dominate" Latin America and pledged to expel the holders of "concessions" creating "intolerable" conditions. In practice, this policy, which combined "liberal opposition to imperialism and . . . missionary nationalism," served to safeguard American businessmen at the expense of the British and Germans.[13]

12. *Congressional Record,* 63d Cong., 2d sess., 6088–89, 10247–48; Link, *The New Freedom,* 310 (Wilson); Block, "Southern Congressmen and Wilson's Call for Repeal of the Panama Canal Tolls Exemption," 96–97, 99 (existing and sop).

13. Arthur S. Link, *Woodrow Wilson and the Progressive Era, 1910–1917* (New York, 1954), 109 (butchers); Levin, *Woodrow Wilson and World Politics,* 45 (imperialism and missionary nationalism); Derrel Roberts, "Mobile and the Visit by Woodrow Wilson," *Alabama Historical*

To preserve order, discourage revolution, promote constitutional government, and facilitate legitimate U.S. business interests, Wilson deemed Huerta's removal essential. The president initiated his anti-Huerta campaign by withholding diplomatic recognition and demanding that Mexico hold democratic elections to choose a new leader. When this led only to Huerta conducting and winning an election of his own, Wilson increased the pressure in February 1914 by revoking an embargo on arms sales to Mexico, thereby making weapons available to Huerta's rivals—particularly Venustiano Carranza and the Constitutionalist Party. This too failed to dislodge Huerta, and Wilson seized on a minor incident involving the arrest of American sailors in Tampico to claim an insult to U.S. "honor" and to request congressional authorization to use force if Mexico failed to render a suitable apology. On April 21, 1914, he acted on this authorization, ordering one thousand U.S. marines to occupy Veracruz, the principal port through which Huerta secured arms. The ensuing fighting left seventeen Americans and 126 Mexicans dead, with Huerta still clinging to power. Only a face-saving mediation by Argentina, Brazil, and Chile allowed Wilson to oust Huerta from office in August 1914 and to withdraw the American troops in December.

The South provided overwhelming support for Wilson's campaign to remove Huerta. Most of the national debate followed partisan lines, and southern Democrats rallied behind their president. Southerners responded positively to Wilson's idealism, to his anti-imperial declaration that the United States would "never again seek one added foot of territory by conquest," and to his tweaking of U.S. business interests for ostensibly opposing his Mexican policy. The *Atlanta Journal* applauded Wilson for making it "vividly clear that this government will not be used as a tool of particular interests," and the *Raleigh News and Observer* lauded his elevating the "moral over the material."[14]

Prior to the Tampico incident, southern legislators praised the president for resisting the use of force; thereafter, they voted almost unanimously to authorize armed intervention. Only 3 southern Democrats and 1 Republican voted against the congressional resolution in the House, and southern senators endorsed Wilson's policy 22 to 0. Southerners agreed that U.S. patience

---

Quarterly 27 (spring/summer, 1966): 88; Walter LaFeber, *The American Age: United States Foreign Policy at Home and Abroad since 1750* (New York, 1994), 279–80.

14. Block, "Southern Opinion of Woodrow Wilson's Foreign Policies," 32–33.

had been exhausted and that the maintenance of national honor demanded forceful action. Representative Pat Harrison of Mississippi proclaimed that "as much as my people desire peace they are unwilling to see the soldiers of this nation, once torn in civil warfare, humiliated and insulted." Following the occupation of Veracruz, Representative John Walker of Georgia characteristically mourned the fallen Americans, while denouncing the "mad and distracted Huerta" and declaring his support for war if it were required to defend "our flag, our uniform and our national honor." Only Dixie's smattering of Republicans and some Texans, most conspicuously Governor O. B. Colquitt, who preferred an even more aggressive remedy, criticized Wilson's policies.[15]

Republican and Texan pressure for more assertive intervention persisted when Huerta's departure led to neither order nor democratic government in Mexico. Not until October 1915 did Carranza defeat Pancho Villa and obtain de facto diplomatic recognition from the United States. Villa retaliated by leading a raid on Columbus, New Mexico, in March 1916 that left nineteen Americans dead. Amidst a clamor for war and intense political pressure, Wilson dispatched General John J. Pershing and a force that ultimately grew to ten thousand into Mexico to capture Villa. Pershing and his troops failed to locate Villa, but clashed with Carranza's forces in June, leaving nine Americans and thirty Mexicans dead. Despite even louder cries for war, Wilson halted the escalation. Difficulties with Great Britain and Germany took precedence, and Wilson was coming to realize the limits of the U.S. ability to affect the Mexican Revolution. After Carranza released several American prisoners and agreed to a joint commission on border relations, Wilson withdrew American troops in February 1917 and extended full diplomatic recognition to the Mexican government.

Just as they had done during Wilson's anti-Huerta campaign, southerners sustained his efforts to manage Carranza and Villa. Although a few southern Catholics objected to the recognition of Carranza in October 1915, the South joined the remainder of the nation in demanding intervention following Villa's raid into New Mexico. National honor was again at stake. Governor Thomas C. Rye of Tennessee proclaimed "The Old Volunteer State . . . ready for any emergency" that might be encountered in redressing

15. Ibid., 54 (Harrison), 64 (Walker); *Congressional Record*, 63d Cong., 2d sess., 6957–58, 7014; see also David J. Hellwig, "The Afro-American Press and Woodrow Wilson's Mexican Policy, 1913–1917," *Phylon* 48 (winter 1987): 261–70.

this "outrage." When Pershing crossed the Rio Grande, even such frequent critics as the *New Orleans Times-Picayune* and the Republican *Knoxville Journal and Tribune* applauded the decision. The *Times-Picayune* was convinced that Pershing's mission would be "supported by practically unanimous sentiment in and outside of Congress."[16]

This prediction proved accurate for the South. Representative John L. Burnett of Alabama represented the most ardent southern supporters by punching a fellow passenger on a Washington train for denigrating Wilson's Mexican policy as "cowardly." While Governor James Ferguson of Texas and Senator Duncan Fletcher of Florida began to lose patience and suggest a more extensive intervention, Democratic state conventions throughout the South, including Texas, endorsed Wilson's policies in 1916. Southern Democrats applied the "He kept us out of war" appellation to Mexico as well as Europe, and Henry D. Flood of Virginia announced that the Republican presidential candidate Charles Evans Hughes was "going to find it hard to get to the White House by way of Mexico." The following year the South acquiesced as Wilson withdrew U.S. troops and granted Carranza full diplomatic recognition. Among the minority of critics, the *Jacksonville Times Union* recognized correctly that "the Mexicans have steadily won" and the *Times-Picayune* asserted that "the punitive expedition will take its place alongside the expedition to Veracruz, the A.B.C. mediation, and the Mexican-American peace conference . . . of well meant but futile efforts to solve the Mexican problem."[17]

Wilson's failure to solve the Mexican problem resulted in part from the demands of coping simultaneously with the far greater challenges presented by war in Europe. Here again, majority southern reaction bolstered administrative policies, but throughout the period leading to war in 1917 there were also shrill dissenters voicing alternative and often traditional southern perspectives. Southerners reacted initially to the outbreak of hostilities in August 1914 out of a well-founded fear for the cotton trade. Over the fifteen years prior to 1914, cotton production had grown from approximately 4.5 million to 14 million bales and prices had risen to thirteen cents a pound. But with war threatening to disrupt exports to both Great Britain and the Continent, the cotton market collapsed precipitously. The major cotton exchanges closed on August 3, and by mid-October, prices had fallen to six to

16. Block, "Southern Opinion of Woodrow Wilson's Foreign Policies," 210, 212.

17. Ibid., 223, 231–32, 254, 259–60.

seven cents per pound, leaving Dixie vulnerable to a $500 million loss on its bumper 1914 crop.

Southerners demanded federal intervention. At the behest of the Southern Cotton Congress, two hundred southern agricultural and business leaders flocked to Washington for a cotton conference August 24–25, 1914. Spokesmen for this group, the National Farmers Union, and a southern bloc of congressmen called for the federal government to purchase southern cotton, extend needed credit, and deposit currency in southern banks for the planters' use. Wilson, Secretary of Agriculture David F. Houston, and Secretary of the Treasury McAdoo responded by tendering a federally owned and operated shipping line (which died in Congress), a federal cotton warehouse system with no credits, and a privately organized and ineffectual loan fund. They would go no farther and decried the South's other "perfectly wild and ridiculous" requests. When Wilson flatly rejected special-interest legislation or direct government subsidies, Governor Colquitt of Texas complained, "The President stood in the road and condemned the South, which made him, to heavier loss and more widespread misery than it has known in three generations. He vindicated an obsolete theory of political economy but he mighty near ruined the country by doing it." From Enterprise, Alabama, a lawyer warned Senator Bankhead, "If we do have to lose this crop, . . . I feel sure that the section will not get over it in 20 years, and I feel still more confident that the 'Solid South' will be broken."[18]

In the absence of administration action, British purchases and renewed exports to Germany and Central Europe gradually stabilized the market by mid-November 1914. The cotton exchanges reopened and prices rose to around nine cents per pound, only to have the market plunge to new lows in early 1915 when Germany declared a submarine blockade of the British Isles and Britain responded by banning all neutral commerce with Germany. Although the British pointedly omitted cotton from their contraband list, many southerners prodded the Wilson administration to ensure the safety of cotton exports. Senator James K. Vardaman declared that the British embargo had "destroyed" southern business and that German actions had not been "half so reprehensive and offensive." Hoke Smith, principal

18. Arthur S. Link, "The Cotton Crisis, the South, and Anglo-American Diplomacy, 1914–1915," in *Studies in Southern History*, ed. J. Carlyle Sitterson (Chapel Hill, 1957), 123 (wild), 128–29 n. 25 (Colquitt); Bruce E. Matthews, "The 1914 Cotton Crisis in Alabama," *Alabama Review* 46 (January 1993): 10 n. 26 (Ala. attorney).

spokesman for the cotton growers, grumbled at his "inability to obtain any real action from our Government" and threatened that unless Britain rescinded its orders in council, Congress would impose an arms embargo on shipments to the British and their allies. Mississippi senator John Sharp Williams warned the President of the strong anti-British feeling. It was "dangerous," he confided, "to tell my constituents that I can see something else besides cotton."[19]

This southern outcry was effective. Wilson and his advisers understood Dixie's economic dilemma and feared both the domestic political implications and the possibility of an arms embargo. The president assured Senator Simmons of North Carolina that he and the State Department were "constantly in communication with the British Government, pressing upon them our rights and the correction of their wrongs." Recognizing that an arms embargo or hostilities with the British, who controlled the seas, would completely destroy the cotton trade, Wilson and Edward M. House informed the British of the situation's "extreme urgency." London responded with a determination "to enter into any arrangement" that served to "make the price of cotton stable and prevent its collapse." Britain accomplished this by simultaneously declaring cotton contraband in late August 1915 and arranging to purchase sufficient quantities to sustain prices. With prices back to 12.5 cents by October, the cotton crisis had passed and decisive southern influence on both Washington and London was confirmed.[20]

In the wake of the crisis, many southerners, such as Hoke Smith, continued to believe that the president was devoting too little attention to King Cotton. But here again, a decisive majority of southern leaders had fallen into line, and in retrospect, the possibility of Dixie's congressmen helping impose an arms embargo was quite remote. In a vivid forecast of their response to wartime legislation, southern congressmen had departed from their states' rights tradition in demanding federal action on behalf of cotton. Fear of centralized authority had subsided markedly with a southern Democrat at the helm.

19. Anthony Gaughan, "Woodrow Wilson and the Rise of Militant Interventionism in the South," *Journal of Southern History* 65 (November 1999): 775 (Vardaman); Block, "Southern Opinion of Woodrow Wilson's Foreign Policies," 120 (Smith), 122 (Williams).

20. Timothy G. McDonald, "Southern Democratic Congressmen and the First World War, August 1914–April 1917: The Public Record of their Support for or Opposition to Wilson's Policies" (Ph.D. dissertation, University of Washington, 1962), 84; Link, "The Cotton Crisis," 135–36.

Considerations other than political regularity and the improved economic climate had influenced the South. From the war's outset, Dixie had been decidedly pro-Allied. In November 1914, a *Literary Digest* survey of newspaper editors found the South to be more pro-Allied than any other region of the country. Of 103 southern editors responding to the poll, 47 declared themselves as pro-Allied and 71 described their communities in similar terms. With few German-American citizens or communities, Dixie, unlike the Midwest, was home to virtually no backers of the Kaiser. The German forces' use of submarines and attack on Belgium reinforced the South's anti-German tendencies. For some southerners, a perceived German threat to the United States solidified the South's position as the nation's most pro-Allies region. Senator John Sharp Williams warned that Germany would not "rest satisfied" with "continental supremacy alone"; rather the "Royal House of Hohenzollern" sought "Germanic supremacy throughout the world."[21]

In addition to these specific conditions or issues, a growing strain of Anglophilia was replacing the South's nineteenth-century Anglophobia—a process that continued over the subsequent sixty years. Historians have attributed the "rapprochement," or "Anglo-American amity," that evolved after the mid-1890s to various influences. They have cited close economic ties; racial beliefs, such as "Anglo-Saxonism"; a common language, literature, and legal system; representative governmental institutions; British recognition of U.S. strategic dominance in the Western Hemisphere and support for the United States during the Spanish-Cuban-American War; and the settlement of nagging diplomatic controversies.[22]

Several of these considerations especially influenced the South. Britain easily remained the most important importer of southern products, an economic tie that sometimes rankled southerners but also compelled close economic relations. Among the British strategic concessions, the most gratifying to southerners was the Hay-Pauncefote Treaty of 1901, which

21. George Coleman Osborn, *John Sharp Williams: Planter-Statesman of the Deep South* (1943; reprint, Gloucester, Mass., 1964), 255; Tindall, *Emergence of the New South*, 38–40; Richard G. Eaves, "Pro-Allied Sentiment in Alabama, 1914–1917: A Study of Representative Newspapers," *Alabama Review* 25 (January 1972): 30, 43, 49, 55; James L. McCorkle Jr., "Mississippi from Neutrality to War (1914–1917)," *Journal of Mississippi History* 43 (May 1981): 95–96.

22. Bradford Perkins, *The Great Rapprochement: England and the United States, 1895–1914* (New York, 1968), 8–12; Charles S. Campbell, *The Transformation of American Foreign Relations, 1865–1900* (New York, 1976), 331 (amity).

cleared the way for a U.S. isthmian canal and its anticipated benefits for the South's economy. Racial considerations decisively reinforced economic, cultural, and institutional influences in aligning Dixie behind Britain.

Southerners were particularly receptive to the turn-of-the-century doctrine of Anglo-Saxonism, or the contention that "the civilization of English-speaking nations was superior to that of any other group of people." This Anglo-American "patriotism of race" and rationale for white supremacy held a special attraction for southerners, who were in the midst of legally disfranchising and segregating African Americans. Although the majority of southerners had recoiled at the prospect of empire in 1898–99, they agreed completely with the arguments for nonwhite inferiority in Rudyard Kipling's "The White Man's Burden." Southerners also had a great affinity for the English-speaking whites in South Africa. Despite marked differences in the development of Jim Crow and apartheid, both rested on an ideology of separatism and the term *segregation* had become common in both countries in the early twentieth century. With slavery and British abolitionism relegated to the past, racial beliefs and practices did much to align Dixie with a pro-British foreign policy.[23]

Writing in 1900, Virginian Philip A. Bruce captured the early stages of the rapprochement when he asserted that in traveling through Europe, he had "seen clearly that it is with Britain alone" that America had "much in common, whether in social or moral sentiments, political principles, or fundamental laws." Seventeen years later, John Sharp Williams reiterated the same sentiments: "It may be narrow, but I love my plantation better than any other plantation, my county better than any other county, my State better than any other State in the Union, and my country better than any other country in the world, and my race—the English speaking race— better than any other race. . . . Whence do we get our laws? Whence do we get our literature? Whence do we get our ethical philosophy? Whence do we get our general ideas of religions? From the people who sired our fathers before they came here." Bruce and Williams were representative of southern Anglophilia, but Woodrow Wilson was certainly America's most significant Anglophile. The president's admiration for "things British" included "political institutions. . . . manners, literature, and philosophy"

23. Stuart Anderson, *Race and Rapprochement: Anglo-Saxonism and Anglo-American Relations, 1895–1904* (Rutherford, N.J., 1981), 12; George M. Fredrickson, *White Supremacy: A Comparative Study in American and South African History* (New York, 1981), 241.

and certainly helped to predispose him to view British and German actions differently.[24]

German submarine warfare provided the occasion for such discrimination by jeopardizing U.S. economic interests and lives. In February 1915 Germany proclaimed a maritime blockade of the British Isles and threatened to sink Allied merchant vessels entering the war zone. With the sinking of the British liner *Lusitania,* Americans were confronted with the full implications of this policy. More than 1,200 persons died, including 128 Americans. Wilson's response was both resolute and unneutral. Determined to prevent "any abridgement of the rights of American citizens in any respect," the president declared that the "honor and self-respect of the nation" and the "whole fine fabric of international law" were imperiled. Perhaps the most fundamental of these U.S. rights was "the largest possible freedom of trade with all belligerents," but Wilson also believed that U.S. citizens had the right as neutrals to travel unmolested within the war zone.[25]

Following the German blockade proclamation, the president notified Berlin that it would be held "to a strict accountability" for any harm to Americans, a far more stringent standard than had been applied to British actions. The president's denunciation of the *Lusitania*'s sinking was even more explicit. He cited "the practical impossibility of employing submarines in the destruction of commerce in conformity with . . . the imperative rules of fairness, reason, justice, and humanity" and accepted international law. The latter required that unarmed merchant ships be warned and searched and the safety of the crew ensured before sinking. In essence, Wilson was demanding that Germany forego use of its submarines. Wilson subsequently contended that the proper application of international law precluded attacks not only on unarmed merchant vessels but also ones armed for defensive purposes and that Americans must be allowed to sail unmolested into the war zone aboard any merchant or neutral ship.[26]

---

24. Perkins, *Great Rapprochement,* 9–10 (Bruce); McDonald, "Southern Democratic Congressmen," 244–45 (Williams); Michael H. Hunt, *Ideology and U.S. Foreign Policy* (New Haven, 1987), 130 (Wilson); see also Tennant S. McWilliams, *The New South Faces the World: Foreign Affairs and the Southern Sense of Self, 1877–1950* (Baton Rouge, 1988), 90–93; George C. Herring and Gary R. Hess, "Regionalism and Foreign Policy: The Dying Myth of Southern Internationalism," *Southern Studies* 20 (fall 1981): 249–50.

25. McDonald, "Southern Democratic Congressmen," 134 (Wilson); Arthur S. Link, *The Struggle for Neutrality,* vol. 3 of *Wilson,* 105 (trade, Link's words).

26. Kendrick A. Clements, *The Presidency of Woodrow Wilson* (Lawrence, Kans., 1992), 124, 126.

Like most Americans, southerners were shocked and appalled at the sinking of the *Lusitania*. Edward A. Alderman, president of the University of Virginia, spoke for most Americans, north and south, in observing that people displayed "a sort of stunned amazement that such bold savagery and ferocity could mark the public policy of any great nation." In the immediate aftermath of the attack, the great majority of southern editors and political leaders approved of Wilson's demand that Americans be given the right to travel safely within or outside of the war zone. Many prominent southerners, such as Senators Duncan Fletcher of Florida, Morris Sheppard of Texas, and John K. Shields of Tennessee, reaffirmed their confidence in the president and urged their constituents to grant him the support and flexibility necessary to protect the national interest. The South, however, was not ready for war. Southerners may have been horrified at German actions, favored the Allied cause, and desired that commerce and travel remain unrestricted, but they also shrank from the prospect of war. Over the subsequent two years, Wilson and the nation realized the incompatibility of maintaining peace and safeguarding these rights.[27]

Texas representative Jeff McLemore and Oklahoma Senator Thomas P. Gore recognized the problem. In February 1916 McLemore offered a resolution directing the president to warn Americans against sailing on armed merchant ships, and Gore submitted a parallel resolution requesting the president to withhold passports from Americans planning to travel on belligerent ships and to further prohibit American travel on any ships transporting contraband. The Gore-McLemore resolutions generated impressive support and revealed the persistent southern ambivalence about an activist foreign policy and war. Representative Frank Park of Georgia opposed any policy that "would hurl the sons of the South to death and destruction because some fool or idiot or nonpatriotic rascal" wanted to risk his life aboard "a belligerent armed vessel." Among the most influential Democratic backers of the resolutions were Speaker of the House Champ Clark and Chairman of the Senate Foreign Relations Committee William J. Stone, both from Missouri, House Majority Leader Claude Kitchen from North Carolina, and Chairman of the House Foreign Affairs Committee Henry D. Flood from Virginia. Every Democratic member of Flood's committee also favored McLemore's position, as did frequent administration critics Hoke Smith and James K. Vardaman, both of whom contended that Wilson had

27. Block, "Southern Opinion of Woodrow Wilson's Foreign Policies," 129.

minimized British abuses and pursued an unneutral position toward Germany. [28]

As he had done with the Panama Canal tolls and the cotton crisis, Wilson took a forthright and inflexible stand—this time in opposition to Gore and McLemore. The president flatly refused to yield any American right of travel or by extension to compromise his definition of international law, and the vast majority of southern congressmen voiced their approval. Speaking for the administration, Carter Glass of Virginia rejected any "abject relinquishment of cherished National rights" and condemned any reproach of the president "for trying to preserve the dignity and prestige of the United States." The vituperative Virginian further announced: "A few cloakroom statesmen have jumped onto a political handcar bound for hell with the expectation that they would carry a trainload of Democrats along with them. I fail to find any coaches trailing after the handcar. There are some men, but precious few who seem to be willing to haul down the American flag and circumscribe the rights of American citizens on the high seas."[29]

The threatened revolt against the president collapsed meekly in the Senate, where the original Gore resolution failed even to come to a vote, and the House tabled McLemore's measure by a vote of 276 to 142, with southerners voting 98 to 13 on the side of the president. The margin of 9 to 1 was far greater than the next strongest 4 to 1 ratio among western Democrats. Of the 13 negative southern votes, Republicans cast 4 of them, and McLemore and other Texas Democrats cast 7 of the remaining 8. The southern-led "cloakroom struggle to sustain Wilson's diplomacy . . . had been successful." Southerners had again demonstrated their devotion to party regularity. They had also acted from a sense of patriotism and honor and the felt need to provide responsible support to the commander-in-chief. Representative Thomas Heflin of Alabama declared, "All the States of the South will join hands with the patriotic Representatives in other sections and show to the world an undivided country standing solidly behind the great President of the United States."[30]

In so doing, southerners responded to Wilson's explicit appeal for patriotic loyalty and national unity. From the spring of 1915 forward, the presi-

28. Gaughan, "Woodrow Wilson and the Rise of Militant Interventionism," 779.
29. Block, "Southern Opinion of Woodrow Wilson's Foreign Policies," 157–58.
30. *Congressional Record*, 64th Cong., 1st sess., 3720; McDonald, "Southern Democratic Congressmen," 139 (cloakroom), 152–53; Block, "Southern Opinion of Woodrow Wilson's Foreign Policies," 169–70 (Heflin).

dent countered opposition to his neutrality policies by portraying dissenters as threatening the nation's "vision of its united destiny," as "creatures of passion, disloyalty, and anarchy," who embodied the "gravest threats against our national peace and safety." An effective foreign policy dictated a united nation: "So long as one body of us is pulling in one direction and another body in another direction," the United States could do nothing "either for ourselves or for the world." As the region's response to foreign crises in the 1890s had graphically demonstrated, the South was peculiarly susceptible to an appeal to patriotism and loyalty. Dixie continued to feel compelled to demonstrate its devotion to the Union.[31]

Many southerners sympathetic to Gore-McLemore preferred to forfeit neutral rights rather than risk war and acted from a deep-seated fear of militarism and centralization and the conviction that northeastern industrial interests and monopolies would profit from war at the South's expense. These same apprehensions prompted mixed southern responses to preparedness or the preparation for possible entry into World War I. Southerners noted that northeastern Republicans sounded the initial call for preparedness in late 1914 and early 1915. Theodore Roosevelt was the most vocal private advocate, and Representative Augustus P. Gardner of New York campaigned aggressively for congressional action. In October 1914 Wilson dismissed the preparedness clamor as "good mental exercise," and in his Annual Message to Congress in December he asserted that there was no threat to "our independence or the integrity of our territory." Consistent with prior patterns, the administration's principal defense came from southerners—in this instance, Representatives James Hay of Virginia, Stanley Hubert Dent Jr. of Alabama, and Senator Kenneth D. McKellar of Tennessee.[32]

Following the German submarine proclamation in February 1915 and the sinking of the *Lusitania* in May, Wilson changed course and directed Secretary of the Army Lindley M. Garrison and Secretary of the Navy Josephus Daniels to recommend appropriate augmentation of U.S. military capacity. Working from the secretaries' recommendations, Wilson presented his preparedness program to Congress in December 1915. He proposed the construction of ten battleships, six battle cruisers, ten cruisers, fifty destroyers, and one hundred submarines over five years and the recruitment and main-

31. Gaughan, "Woodrow Wilson and the Rise of Militant Interventionism," 785–86.
32. Link, *Wilson and the Progressive Era,* 177; McDonald, "Southern Democratic Congressmen," 158.

tenance of a regular army force of nearly 142,000 and a reserve force, the so-called Continental Army, of 400,000.

Important southern opinion makers followed Wilson's lead. Consistent with their preference for Britain and the Allies, most southern papers warned of the German threat and favored increased U.S. military capacity. Henry Watterson posted "To Hell with the Hohenzollerns and Hapsburgs" on the masthead of his *Louisville Courier-Journal,* and the *Atlanta Journal* described the war as a "life and death struggle between democratic government and Prussian autocracy." Speaking for their customers, southern businessmen concurred. In a May 1916 survey, 265 of 280 businessmen reported that southern public opinion favored preparedness.[33]

These sentiments were far from unanimous; the South's strong post–Civil War apprehension over the militarism and centralization that accompanied war also persisted, especially in rural areas, where the Farmers Union was influential. These southerners remained convinced that eastern bankers and industrialists, and particularly munitions makers, were manipulating the nation's move toward war and would profit at the expense of the rural South and West. In the House of Representatives, Democratic Majority Leader Claude Kitchen led approximately thirty antipreparedness congressmen, some twenty of whom were from the South. Kitchen denounced "the big Navy and big Army program of the jingoes and war traffickers" and characterized the navy bill as an unprecedented "orgy of graft and plunder and profits on the part of ingenious, despotic, coercive, organized avarice." James K. Vardaman, the most adamant southern opponent of preparedness and war in the upper house, echoed Kitchen, declaring, "The traffickers in the spoils of war, the sharers of enormous profits of international commerce" had created the "unhealthy, abnormal, pernicious sentiment in favor of war." Representative Oscar Callaway's sectional perspective was even more explicit. Callaway dismissed the "preparedness agitation" of "the New Yorkers, Bostonians, and Philadelphians" as "self-interest and hypocrisy." They simply sought "'all they can get'" as "money is poured out along the Atlantic seaboard" and directed "to their locality."[34]

33. Tindall, *Emergence of the New South,* 39–40.

34. Ibid., 42; McDonald, "Southern Democratic Congressmen," 204 (Kitchen); Joseph E. Fortenberry, "James Kimble Vardaman and American Foreign Policy, 1913–1919," *Journal of Mississippi History* 35 (May 1973): 135 (Vardaman); Richard F. Bensel, *Sectionalism and American Political Development, 1880–1980* (Madison, Wis., 1984), 106–7 (Callaway), 111–15, 127–28; see also John Milton Cooper Jr., *The Vanity of Power: American Isolationism and the First World War, 1914–1917* (Westport, Conn., 1969), 26–27, 89–95, 235–36; Robert D. Johnson, *The Peace*

Although no other Democratic congressional leader joined Kitchen in outright public opposition to Wilson, Chairman James Hay and the southerners on his House Military Affairs Committee harbored similar concerns. Also recoiling at the prospect of enrolling African Americans into the military, Hay and his committee rejected the Continental Army and its 400,000 volunteers under the exclusive control of the national government. Hay formulated an alternative proposal that agreed to a regular army of 140,000 but substituted a 425,000-strong National Guard paid by the federal government and obligated to serve in time of war. After meeting with and converting Wilson to this basic dependence on the state-based National Guard, Hay guided his measure through the House, where fellow southerners voted 99 to 2 for the final bill.[35]

Southern leaders also managed the legislation expanding the navy. Following the Battle of Jutland in May 1916, which decisively demonstrated the superiority of battleships over cruisers, Senators Benjamin R. Tillman and Claude A. Swanson oversaw a revised bill reducing the building period from five years to three and specifying the construction of two additional battleships and battle cruisers during the first year. Among southern senators, only Vardaman voted against the bill, and southern congressmen endorsed it by a vote of 66 to 17, with Kitchen and fellow dissenters composing the minority.[36]

Kitchen and the rural progressives were more successful in determining the means for financing this increased defense spending. In typical southern fashion, the North Carolina Democrat turned to the income tax and aimed it at the Northeast. He asserted that "when the New York people are thoroughly convinced that the income tax will have to pay for the increases in the army and navy . . . preparedness will not be so popular with them as it now is." Going well beyond administration preferences, Kitchen and his

---

Progressives and American Foreign Relations (Cambridge, Mass., 1995), 43–46; Evans C. Johnson, *Oscar W. Underwood: A Political Biography* (Baton Rouge, 1980), 218–19, 246, 251–54; Milton L. Ready, "Georgia's Entry into World War I," *Georgia Historical Quarterly* 52 (September 1968): 256–58.

35. *Congressional Record,* 64th Cong., 1st sess., 8406; George C. Herring Jr., "James Hay and the Preparedness Controversy, 1915–1916," *Journal of Southern History* 30 (November 1964): 383–404; McDonald, "Southern Democratic Congressmen," 194.

36. *Congressional Record,* 64th Cong., 1st sess., 11384, 12700; McDonald, "Southern Democratic Congressmen," 202, 205.

Democratic followers passed legislation raising the basic income tax from 1 to 2 percent and the surtax on incomes over $2 million to 13 percent. The Revenue Act of 1916 also included a graduated estate tax, a specific tax on munitions profits, and taxes on corporate and surplus profits. Subsequent revenue bills in 1917 and 1918 imposed a 6 percent tax on the first $4,000 of income and 12 percent thereafter. Surtaxes could raise the levy to 77 percent on incomes over $1 million, to 65 percent on excess profits, and 25 percent on inheritances.[37]

The pattern of southern response established during the national debate about the protection of neutral rights and preparedness in 1915 and 1916 persisted as the nation went to war in 1917. On January 31 Germany declared unrestricted submarine warfare against all ships, belligerent and neutral, in the war zone surrounding Britain, France, and Italy and in so doing violated a series of assurances made following the sinking of the *Lusitania*. Three days later President Wilson broke diplomatic relations with Germany, and on February 26 he requested congressional approval for the arming of American merchant ships.

The South was again solidly behind its president. The bulk of the press, numerous state legislatures, and the great majority of southern congressmen sustained Wilson's position. On February 7, 1917, the Senate voted 78 to 5 to endorse the severance of diplomatic relations with Germany. Seventeen southerners voted with the majority; 2, Vardaman of Mississippi and William F. Kirby of Arkansas, opposed the action. Similar majorities prevailed on the armed-ship bill. It passed the House 403 to 14, with 111 southerners in favor and none opposed. The bill ran into a stubborn filibuster in the Senate, led by Robert LaFollette and three other midwestern Republicans. Although Vardaman and Kirby had spoken against the bill, neither participated in the filibuster. Momentarily successful, LaFollette's strategy necessitated that the issue be carried over to a special session of Congress, where the Senate voted 76 to 3 on March 8 to institute a new rule of cloture and to end the one-hundred-year-old practice of unlimited debate. In a significant revision of sectional practice and a clear forecast of Dixie's support for centralizing wartime legislation, southerners voted 20 to 0 for the cloture rule. Foreign policy and national defense had taken precedence over states' rights and the protection of local rights, particularly ones in which race was a re-

37. Grantham, *South in Modern America*, 77.

mote consideration. Wilson interpreted the Senate action as sufficient indication of support and on March 9 issued the order to arm U.S. ships.[38]

U.S. armed neutrality and the clear prospect of war failed to deter Germany. By March 18, German submarines had sunk three American ships in the war zone, and on April 2 President Wilson asked a joint session of Congress to declare war. The House did so with a 373 to 50 vote and the Senate with an 86 to 2 vote. Only Vardaman in the Senate, and Kitchen, McLemore, and 3 other southerners in the House voted against war. Those southerners favoring war variously cited items from Wilson's list of motives and objectives—to protect American lives, property, and neutral rights; to uphold freedom of the seas and international law; and to advance the interests of mankind by opposing autocracy and safeguarding and extending democracy.[39]

They also loudly proclaimed the South's patriotism. As they had done in the 1890s, southerners emphasized their devotion to the Union. Congressman W. W. Larsen of Georgia assured his colleagues that the "fires of patriotism burn bright in every [southern] home" and the South's "gallant sons can be counted upon to rally to the flag of our country with the same self-sacrificing patriotic devotion" as "those brave sons of the Confederacy who followed Gordon, Jackson, and Lee." The Reverend Randolph McKim pronounced the conflict a "Holy War" and harshly attacked pacifists as "weak-kneed, chicken-hearted, white livered individuals." "If the pacifists' theory" were correct, he thundered, "how could Robert E. Lee have been such a saint as he was?" The following July 4, Representative Robert L. Doughton of North Carolina was pleased to confirm that "the grandsons of the men who wore the blue and the grandsons of the men who wore the gray, are now marching with locked shields and martial step to the mingled strains of Dixie and the Star Spangled Banner."[40]

Larsen, McKim, and Doughton exaggerated the South's uniform commitment to the war. Although clearly embodying a minority response, many

38. McDonald, "Southern Democratic Congressmen," 219, 225, 231–33; Block, "Southern Opinion of Woodrow Wilson's Foreign Policies," 280, 282; Lamar W. Bridges, "Zimmermann Telegram: Reaction of Southern, Southwestern Newspapers," *Journalism Quarterly* 46 (spring 1969): 81–86.

39. McDonald, "Southern Democratic Congressmen," 246–47.

40. Block, "Southern Opinion of Woodrow Wilson's Foreign Policies," 302 (Larsen); Charles R. Wilson, *Baptized in Blood: The Religion of the Lost Cause, 1865–1920* (Athens, Ga., 1980), 172 (McKim); Grantham, *South in Modern America*, 81 (Doughton).

poor rural southerners demonstrated their lack of enthusiasm for the cause by requesting exemptions, refusing to register for the draft or report for induction, and deserting from army camps. They had decided that the war was being fought for economic and strategic objectives "extraneous to their own lives." More prominent southern dissenters articulated these and other reservations. Vardaman, together with representatives of the Farmers Union, continued to assert that northern industrialists and munitions makers were pushing the nation into a war that would harm the South and farmers. The Mississippi senator also questioned whether Germany was more responsible than Britain or France for the European conflict. Others, such as John L. Burnett of Alabama, refused to forgive Britain's interference with the South's cotton trade and reminded the nation that the British were the traditional enemy. McLemore objected not so much to fighting Germany but to doing so in an alliance with Britain and France that impaired U.S. independence. The most important southern opponent of war, House Majority Leader Claude Kitchen, provided the most trenchant analysis. Kitchen conceded that war was "sometimes necessary and imperative" but only if crucial national interests were in jeopardy. He found, he said, "no invasion is threatened. Not a foot of our territory is demanded or coveted. No essential honor is required to be sacrificed. No fundamental right is asked to be permanently yielded or suspended. No national policy is contested. No part of our sovereignty is questioned." Rather, the president was asking the United States to fight a war over European problems. Although these southern dissenters garnered minimal support in their home districts, they had raised a series of issues that historians have continued to debate.[41]

The southern senators' vote for cloture while considering the armed-ship bill was symptomatic of the willingness of Dixie's representatives to support war-related legislation that expanded federal and executive authority at the expense of states' rights. Congressman William B. Bankhead forcefully voiced majority southern opinion when he challenged the members of the House to find a theory or court decision "to the effect that the Constitution . . . in time of war can stand in the way of any measures necessary for the

41. Jeanette Keith, "The Politics of Southern Draft Resistance, 1917–1918: Class, Race, and Conscription in the Rural South," *Journal of American History* 87 (March 2001): 1361 (extraneous); Block, "Southern Opinion of Woodrow Wilson's Foreign Policies," 305 (Kitchen); Timothy D. Johnson, "Anti-War Sentiment and Representative John Lawson Burnett of Alabama," *Alabama Review* 39 (July 1986): 187–95; McDonald, "Southern Democratic Congressmen," 239–40.

saving of the life and very sovereignty of the government itself when in desperate peril." Senator Kenneth D. McKellar of Tennessee agreed and prodded the Senate to "get behind the executive, win this war, and work out all these academic questions afterwards." Acting from this perspective and the continuing force of party loyalty, southerners voted for a second, more restrictive antifilibustering resolution in 1918 and cast a total of only 21 negative votes in both houses against these cloture measures and six other major pieces of war legislation. Included among the latter were conscription, the Espionage and Sedition Acts; the Railroad Act, which provided for federal control of the roads; the Overman Act, which transferred significant discretionary powers from Congress to the executive; and the Lever Food Control Act, which empowered the federal government to control the production and distribution of foods, fuels, fertilizer, and agricultural implements and to set minimum prices on staples. Significantly, Asbury Lever of South Carolina, chairman of the House Committee on Agriculture, and southern senators, such as Furnifold Simmons of North Carolina, ensured that cotton, unlike wheat and corn, was not subject to federal price controls. Midwesterners railed at this sectional favoritism, and the issue helped the Republicans regain majorities in the congressional elections of 1918.[42]

Of these war measures, conscription most blatantly challenged southern traditions of individual liberty and voluntarism. Here too, the South ultimately sided with the president, but only after considerable debate, dissent, and administrative pressure. The most significant southern opposition came from Stanley Hubert Dent Jr. of Alabama, who had succeeded James Hay as chairman of the House Committee on Military Affairs. Dent and the six other southerners on his committee preferred to test a system of voluntary enlistment before resorting to the compulsory draft the Wilson administration proposed in April 1917. Dent argued for recognizing the "traditional history of the Anglo-Saxon race" and giving "every patriotic and loyal American citizen the right to tender his services to the government." Lurking behind southern arguments for tradition or constitutional liberties were

---

42. I. A. Newby, "States' Rights and Southern Congressmen during World War I," *Phylon* 24 (spring 1963): 34–50. Newby defines the South as the former states of the Confederacy for the purposes of voting statistics. See also Richard L. Watson Jr., "A Testing Time for Southern Congressional Leadership: The War Crisis of 1917–1918," *Journal of Southern History* 44 (February 1978): 22–24; Richard L. Watson Jr., "Principle, Party, and Constituency: The North Carolina Congressional Delegation, 1917–1919," *North Carolina Historical Review* 56 (July 1979): 307–8, 313–17.

fears about arming blacks and forcing whites to serve in integrated units. James K. Vardaman warned that drafting African Americans would place "arrogant strutting representatives of black soldiery in every community," and Representative James F. Byrnes of South Carolina was appalled at the prospect of the War Department assigning "a boy from South Carolina to serve . . . by the side of a negro from Indiana." If this occurred, he threatened ominously, Americans "would not have to go to Europe for war." Other southerners countered that a voluntary system would not meet the nation's emergency manpower needs and that the draft best promoted equity and democracy. Representative Thomas W. Harrison of Virginia traced the draft to the "Jeffersonian principles of equal rights for all and special privileges for none." It was the "only democratic system." These arguments, when combined with intense administration pressure and Wilson's assurances to southern congressmen that the draft would neither induct many blacks nor disturb southern labor patterns, left only 3 southern senators and 7 representatives voting against conscription.[43]

Party regularity, the need to demonstrate patriotism and legislative responsibility, and the crisis of war had helped induce the South's support for the Wilson administration, but Dixie also derived vast benefits from both the wartime boost to its economy and unprecedented federal defense spending. The federal budget expanded 2,600 percent from 1916 through 1919, and a significant portion of this increase went to defense spending in the South. The active influence of strategically placed southern congressional leaders, the energetic solicitations of southern communities, and the attractiveness of Dixie's climate combined to locate six of fifteen U.S. Army camps and thirteen of sixteen National Guard cantonments in the South. Every southern state, save Tennessee and Florida, landed at least one camp; and the demand for chemicals led to the beginning of industrial development in Tennessee and war prompted construction of several naval installations and the nation's principal naval air station in Florida.

This integral connection of federal defense spending to the South's economy, which traced its tentative beginnings to the war with Spain, became

43. *Congressional Record*, 65th Cong., 1st sess., 1550–51, 1557; Watson, "Testing Time for Southern Congressional Leadership," 20–21 n. 57 (Dent), 22 n. 61; Kennedy, *Over Here*, 159 (Vardaman); Newby, "States' Rights and Southern Congressmen," 41 (Harrison), 42 (Byrnes); Robert D. Ward, "Stanley Hubert Dent and American Military Policy, 1916–1920," *Alabama Historical Quarterly* 33 (fall/winter 1971): 182–86; John Whiteclay Chambers II, *To Raise an Army: The Draft Comes to Modern America* (New York, 1987), 153–66.

firmly established under Wilson. For example, Benjamin R. Tillman's pro-motion of the Charleston Navy Yard continued. The yard converted seven captured German ships, trained more than 25,000 naval personnel, and be-came the site of the navy's only clothing factory. Of greater import, the Newport News Shipbuilding and Drydock Company in the Hampton Roads–Norfolk area expanded its capacity by $9.5 million and became the nation's largest naval complex. Similarly, the nation's need for explosives led to the evolution of the massive DuPont chemical works in Hopewell, Vir-ginia, and the Tennessee Eastman Corporation in Kingsport. Fayetteville, North Carolina, won the battle for the $17 million allotted to build the na-tion's largest artillery base of 140,000 acres at Camp Bragg. Other southern cities, such as Houston, were also permanently transformed by the war. The conflict provided the occasion for deepening the Houston Ship Channel from twenty-five to thirty feet. When combined with the massive federal demand for cotton and oil, this improvement enabled Houston to greatly augment its warehousing, marketing, and financial facilities and to emerge as the world's largest cotton marketing and export center in the 1920s.[44]

In addition to these specific installations or projects, the war created an unprecedented demand for key southern products. After the initial decline in prices, King Cotton was "returned to his throne." The U.S. government alone purchased more than 500,000 bales of cotton for use in producing explosives, and the Army consumed 800,000 yards of cloth. Prices sur-passed thirty-five cents per pound by 1919, and the 1917–19 period was the best in history, culminating with the 1919 crop, which sold for $2 billion. Building army camps and wooden ships produced a comparable market for southern pine. The pine industry had slumped after 1907, and exports fell even farther with the beginning of the war. But as with cotton, the rebound was amazing. Between April 1917 and November 1918, the Southern Pine Emergency Committee furnished 1.9 billion board feet of lumber to the

44. Henry C. Ferrell Jr., "Regional Rivalries, Congress, and MIC: The Norfolk and Charleston Navy Yards, 1913–20," in *War, Business, and American Society: Historical Perspectives on the Military-Industrial Complex*, ed. Benjamin Franklin Cooling (Port Washington, N.Y., 1977), 59–72; John H. Moore, "Charleston in World War I: Seeds of Change," *South Carolina Historical Magazine* 86 (January 1985): 39–49; Watson, "Principle, Party, and Constituency," 310–11; Bruce A. Beauboeuf, "War and Change: Houston's Economic Ascendancy during World War I," *Houston Review* 14 (1992): 89–112; Daniel Schaffer, "War Mobilization in Muscle Shoals, Alabama, 1917–1918," *Alabama Review* 39 (April 1986): 110–46; Tindall, *Emergence of the New South*, 54–55.

government war effort. The southern oil industry received a similar stimulus from war-related demands, which absorbed existing excess capacity and underwrote additional development in Texas, Oklahoma, Louisiana, and Arkansas.[45]

If the South's pursuit of and benefit from defense spending was reminiscent of the Spanish-Cuban-American War, so too was Dixie's discomfort with having African American soldiers in its midst. James K. Vardaman could conceive "of no greater menace to the South" than inducting "millions of negroes" into the military and giving them arms. Southern apprehension over the potential disruption of its labor force compounded the region's uneasiness with the draft. But neither of these reservations prevented southern draft boards from discriminating blatantly in the number of blacks they designated for induction. Florida, Georgia, Louisiana, Mississippi, and South Carolina drafted more blacks than whites, and in the process frequently summoned black landowners while leaving landless African American workers on white properties undisturbed.[46]

Black soldiers also consistently experienced discrimination and substandard conditions while stationed in the South. Black units were rigidly segregated, as were the southern communities that adjoined the military installations. Only Camps Bowie and Meade provided acceptable treatment, and only Greenville, South Carolina, extended even minimal hospitality. The black soldiers more commonly received scant or inappropriate clothing and equipment; seriously overcrowded barracks or incomplete, tattered tents; and inadequate, unsanitary food and water. These ill-clad, ill-equipped, ill-housed, and ill-fed black soldiers were also disproportionately assigned to labor details—serving in some instances almost as southern chain gangs "to do work with a pick and shovel in the same state where they were previously working." In the most extreme instances, white officers in Virginia, Maryland, and Tennessee hired out the black soldiers to private contractors. From Camp Lee, Virginia, one black draftee reported, "They do not regard us as free citizens of the Republic, in the national army for the defense of our country and the principles of democracy." And the members of the Fifteenth New York Infantry, who had been stationed at Camp

45. Tindall, *Emergence of the New South*, 60 (King); Beauboeuf, "War and Change," 92; James F. Fickle, "Defense Mobilization in the Southern Pine Industry: The Experience of World War I," *Journal of Forest History* 22 (October 1977): 222.

46. Arthur E. Barbeau and Florette Henri, *The Unknown Soldiers: Black American Troops in World War I* (Philadelphia, 1974), 34–35.

Wadsworth near Spartanburg, remarked that they had trained in "Rectum, South Carolina."[47]

Not surprisingly, these conditions produced conflict. Although violence was narrowly averted at Camp Wadsworth, a deadly incident occurred in Houston in August 1917, when men from the First Battalion of the Twenty-fourth Infantry Brigade of black regulars clashed with white police and armed civilians. The black soldiers had gone into town in response to the jailing of one of their fellows. The "mutiny" left two black soldiers and seventeen whites, including five police officers, dead. The ensuing courts-martial and trials in state courts (an unusual development) resulted in the hanging of nineteen blacks and the sentencing of more than fifty to life imprisonment. A War Department investigator subsequently reported that the conflict was the virtually inevitable consequence of "racial" tension. Black soldiers had sought to assert "their rights as American citizens and United States soldiers." The local townspeople and police "resented the presence of colored soldiers and resented on the negro the badge of authority of the United States uniform." These same fundamental differences also contributed to the lynching of at least ten black veterans in 1919. James K. Vardaman again voiced the most extreme southern prejudice when he urged "every community in Mississippi . . . to organize and . . . pick out these suspicious characters—those military, French-women-ruined negro soldiers and let them understand that they are under surveillance and that when crimes similar to this [alleged rape] are committed, take care of the individual who commits the crime."[48]

As black soldiers elicited this extreme rhetoric and brutal southern attacks, the black press supported preparedness efforts and argued for African American loyalty designed to secure racial justice and full citizenship. African Americans also repeated earlier criticisms of the disparity between the nation's professed foreign policy objectives and its domestic racial practices. For example, James Weldon Johnson, who had been born in Florida and educated at Atlanta University before becoming a prominent New York journalist and reformer, denounced American "hypocrisy." Johnson excoriated a country that held up its "hands in horror at German 'atrocities'" while

47. Ibid., 90, 100; Lee Kennett, "The Camp Wadsworth Affair," *South Atlantic Quarterly* 74 (spring 1975): 210.

48. Barbeau and Henri, *Unknown Soldiers*, 31, 177.

ignoring the "wholesale murder of American citizens on American soil by bloodthirsty American mobs." He was equally critical of Wilson, "who still continues to talk about humanity, about bringing peace and righteousness to all the nations of the earth, but who has yet to utter one word against this outraging of humanity within the territory over which he presides." How, asked black editors, could the United States expect to prescribe for others without first conducting a diplomatic "house cleaning" and extending "full emancipation" to all of its citizens?[49]

Johnson and other African American critics were similarly disappointed when Wilson's peace program ignored issues of racial equity. The president believed that only a "peace without victory," a peace based on equitable treatment of the losers rather than a settlement based on political and military power could be enduring. But at the Paris Peace Conference between January and July 1919, the president found that neither vast U.S. military and economic power nor great personal popularity provided the leverage necessary to force British and French agreement to such a treaty. The resulting Treaty of Versailles declared Germany guilty of starting the war, stripped the Reich of its colonies, and ultimately saddled the losers with $33 billion in reparation payments. In addition, the treaty left France in control of the formerly German Rhineland and Saar coal mines and the Japanese occupying the Shantung Peninsula of China. The pact also omitted guarantees of both freedom of the seas and unrestricted freedom of commerce, as Wilson had advocated in his peace plans.

Unable to secure his preferred peace settlement, Wilson hoped the proposed League of Nations would remedy defects in the treaty. An integral part of the Treaty of Versailles, the League was designed to ensure orderly, peaceful change in the international community. Article 10, described by Wilson as the "heart of the [League] Covenant," required each member nation's pledge "to respect and preserve as against external aggression the territorial integrity and existing political independence of all the Members of the League." Since League members were to employ economic coercion or force to enforce this provision, U.S. membership and participation in this

49. Jonathan S. Rosenberg, " 'How Far the Promised Land?': World Affairs and the American Civil Rights Movement from the First World War to Vietnam" (Ph.D. dissertation, Harvard University, 1997), 61–62 (Johnson); William G. Jordan, *Black Newspapers and America's War for Democracy, 1914–1920* (Chapel Hill, 2001), 45–98.

international organization would have constituted a distinct departure from the nation's previous refusal to make binding commitments in Europe and Asia.[50]

While critics of the League questioned its potential interference with the Monroe Doctrine or U.S. tariff and race policies, the most fundamental objections focused on Article 10 and the maintenance of U.S. sovereignty and independence of action. Would the League be able to dictate American participation in a joint economic boycott or peacekeeping expedition? If so, would the president lose control of U.S. foreign policy or Congress forfeit its power to declare war? Approximately twelve "irreconcilable" senatorial opponents of the League cited such hazards as the basis for their unbending refusal to approve U.S. membership and the prospect of involvement in subsequent European wars. Henry Cabot Lodge, Republican chairman of the Senate Foreign Relations Committee, led a second, larger group of senatorial dissenters. Lodge and the "reservationists" informed Wilson as early as March 1919 that a contingent of Republicans would not vote for the League without the clarification of U.S. obligations and the preservation of an independent and sovereign foreign policy.

President Wilson rejected the Lodge reservations and failed to explain the obligations the United States would incur as a member of the League. Personal antipathy for Lodge, impaired health, and the conviction that compromise would subvert the League led Wilson to rebuff any congressionally initiated modification of the covenant. In the absence of such amendment, his contention that Article 10 constituted a "grave and solemn moral" but "not a legal obligation"—that it would be "binding in conscience only, not in law"—left both his opponents and many supporters dissatisfied and puzzled. Against this background of personal animosity, partisan politics, and genuine differences over appropriate international involvement, the Senate voted down the peace treaty and U.S. membership in the League in November 1919 and again in March 1920.[51]

The previous pattern of southern support persisted during Wilson's travail over the League. Although some commentators have cited this support as evidence of the South's proclivity for internationalism, the region's response derived primarily from partisan politics and a regional reverence for

50. Thomas A. Bailey, *Woodrow Wilson and the Great Betrayal* (1945; reprint, Chicago, 1963), 116; Clements, *Presidency of Woodrow Wilson*, 192.

51. LaFeber, *The American Age*, 327.

the southern president and his work. The *Greenville (S.C.) Piedmont* observed: "The South is heart and soul for the Treaty. It hasn't read it, but it has read some of the speeches of them darned Republicans." Forty percent of the pro-League resolutions adopted by state legislatures from 1917 through 1919 emanated from the South, and an April 1919 poll of editors by *Literary Digest* indicated a similarly broad-based southern endorsement of the League. Of the 285 southern respondents, 208 favored the League without change, 52 did so conditionally, and only 25 were opposed.[52]

Southern congressmen were equally positive. Like their constituents, they generally approved of Wilson's controversial decision to attend the Paris conference; and beginning in December 1918, southern senators delivered a series of set speeches praising the president and the League. Still, many southern senators were not completely comfortable with the League and its international obligations. Senator Oscar W. Underwood, for example, repressed private reservations in favor of his party and president. Nor did Underwood and all other southerners hold the president's version of the League sacrosanct. Unlike Wilson, Underwood and Senators Kenneth D. McKellar and Furnifold Simmons were willing to compromise and actively discussed this possibility with their Republican counterparts over the winter of 1919–20. Still, among southern Democratic senators, only Hoke Smith, James K. Vardaman, John K. Shields, and Thomas Hardwick publicly criticized the League. Smith and Vardaman were established critics of Wilson, and Shields was the one southern senator who could most legitimately be included among the irreconcilables. Many, but not all, southern Republicans also denounced the League. North Carolina was instructive: Marion P. Butler and John Motley Morehead censured the League, but one-half of the Republicans in the state legislature joined with the Democrats in passing a resolution endorsing the proposed organization. In short, the vast majority of southerners continued to furnish Wilson his most dependable foreign policy backing.[53]

52. Bailey, *Wilson and the Great Betrayal*, 48 (*Piedmont*); Dewey W. Grantham Jr., "The Southern Senators and The League of Nations, 1918–1920," *North Carolina Historical Review* 26 (April 1949): 199; Edward W. Chester, *Sectionalism, Politics, and American Diplomacy* (Metuchen, N.J., 1975), 180; Frank Abbott, "The Texas Press and the Covenant," *Red River Valley Historical Review* 4 (spring 1979): 32–41; Michael A. Nelson, "Arkansas and the League of Nations Debate," *Arkansas Historical Quarterly* 56 (summer 1997): 180–200.

53. Johnson, *Underwood*, 269–72; Grantham, "Southern Senators and The League of Nations," 192–204; Ralph B. Levering, "Public Culture and Public Opinion: The League of Nations Controversy in New Jersey and North Carolina," in *The Wilson Era: Essays in Honor of*

Southern senators demonstrated this allegiance in the decisive votes on the League. As the president and his southern senatorial brigade marched to the decisive engagement in November 1919, they confronted Republican congressional majorities for the first time during the Wilson presidency. Ironically, the same identification with and dependable support from the South that had been so crucial to Wilson's prior foreign policy turned into a liability when a "South-hating" sectionalism became the crucial issue in the 1918 congressional elections. Northeastern and midwestern Republicans emphasized the absence of price controls on cotton, the location of so many military training facilities in the South, and the southern influence on wartime tax bills in their successful efforts to unseat Democrats. Unable, therefore, to command partisan majorities for his foreign policy initiatives as he had done from 1913 to 1918, Wilson urged Democrats to reject the Lodge reservations, and southern senators complied. On November 19, the Lodge reservations failed by a vote of 39 to 55, and only 2 southern senators, Smith and Shields, ignored the president's directive. Wilson and the southern senators continued to reject compromise when the Senate voted again in March 1920. Of the 23 Democrats who remained loyal to the president in the 49 to 35 vote on the treaty with reservations, 19 hailed from Dixie. Five southern senators, Smith, Joseph C. W. Beckham of Kentucky, Duncan Fletcher and Park Trammell of Florida, and Joseph E. Ransdell of Louisiana, crossed party lines and voted for the League.[54]

Historian Dewey W. Grantham Jr., has argued persuasively that sectionalism played a crucial role in the defeat of the League. Grantham contends, "The Republicans distrusted Wilson because he was a southerner, because southerners were in his cabinet, and because southerner Democrats were in control of Congress. They believed Wilson was conspiring to aid the South." A former mayor of Charlotte cogently voiced the section's contem-

Arthur S. Link, eds. John Milton Cooper Jr. and Charles E. Neu (Arlington Heights, Ill., 1991), 178, 183–85.

54. *Congressional Record,* 66th Cong., 1st sess., 8786; Ibid., 66th Cong., 2d sess., 4599; Tindall, *Emergence of the New South,* 67 (South hating); Kennedy, *Over Here,* 241–44; Seward W. Livermore, *Politics Is Adjourned: Woodrow Wilson and the War Congress, 1916–1918* (Middletown, Conn., 1966), 169–76, 192–205, 245–47; Grantham, "Southern Senators and The League of Nations," 187, 192–93, 198; Leonard Schlup, "Senator J. C. W. Beckham and the Fight for Ratification of the League of Nations," *Register of the Kentucky Historical Society* 95 (winter 1997): 37–38, 48–49; Rayford W. Logan, *The Senate and the Versailles Mandate System* (1945; reprint, Westport, Conn., 1975), 83–84.

porary perception: "Lodge and his gang hate Wilson because he is a southerner and a democrat, and was President during the greatest war this country ever had." Other southerners excoriated Lodge and the Republicans for missing this rare opportunity for international progress. The *Louisville Courier-Journal* decried Lodge's reservations as a "pusillanimous instrument" devised in "contemptible malignancy and hypocrisy." John Sharp Williams, Wilson's foremost congressional supporter, denounced his opponents as "coarse grained jackasses," and Carter Glass later regretted the nation's failure to respond "when the greatest Christian statesman of all time summoned the nations of the earth to enter into a Covenant which contained the very essence of the Sermon on the Mount and was the consummation, as far as Christian nations could contrive, of the sacrifice on Calvary."[55]

But Wilson and the South also bore responsibility for the League's defeat. In both November and March, southerners had combined with the irreconcilables to reject compromise and U.S. membership in the League. The same partisanship and sectional solidarity that had been so crucial to Wilson's foreign policy prior to 1919 had also sustained the president in his unbending refusal to accept U.S. entry into the League on any terms other than his own. This combination of rigid presidential leadership and solid southern backing had previously enabled Wilson to dictate policy, but with the Democrats in the minority it led only to frustrating defeat. Dixie's loyalty to party and its southern president took precedence over any genuine understanding of and commitment to internationalism and was crucial to continued U.S. refusal to enter binding political agreements abroad.

The South's crucial role in the defeat of the League was indicative of Dixie's importance to the formation of U.S. foreign policy during the Wilson presidency. After fifty years in the political wilderness, southerners had returned to the house of their fathers and reclaimed seats of power. Southerners generally, and southern congressmen particularly, provided their southern-born president the most dependable and often decisive support for his foreign policies. Traditional southern devotion to a low tariff and export economy remained firmly in place, but the majority of southerners put aside

55. Grantham, "Southern Senators and The League of Nations," 204; Levering, "The League of Nations Controversy in New Jersey and North Carolina," 185 (Charlotte mayor); Schlup, "Senator J. C. W. Beckham," 47 (pusillanimous); Tindall, *Emergence of the New South*, 68–69 (*Courier-Journal*, Glass, and Williams).

their post–Civil War fear of foreign war and the accompanying centralization and militarism. A shrill minority of southerners voiced these apprehensions and warned as well that war would disproportionately benefit northeastern bankers and manufacturers and that wartime legislation such as the draft weakened states' rights. These heralds of traditional southern positions undoubtedly articulated the concerns of many of their fellows, but for the great majority of southerners other considerations outweighed such misgivings. Loyalty to the Democratic Party, sectional benefits from both federal patronage and defense spending, patriotism and the desire to demonstrate devotion to the nation, and the responsibility that accompanied positions of leadership and majority control in Congress proved decisive. Southerners sustained Wilson's repeal of the Panama Canal tolls exemption, loosening of imperial controls over the Philippines, intervention in Mexico, neutrality and preparedness policies prior to entry into World War I, and the president's conduct of the war and efforts at peacemaking.

In so doing, the South had diverged decisively from its post–Civil War pattern of opposition to an activist foreign policy characterized by a strengthened central government and military and aggressive intervention abroad. As had been the case in 1898 and would persist over the remainder of the twentieth century, southerners were determined to demonstrate their patriotism and willingness to fight for their country. Dixie also emerged from the world war devoted to the memory of Woodrow Wilson and his fight for the League of Nations. The South's subsequent support for U.S. membership in World Court and United Nations did not, however, constitute an endorsement of Wilson's understanding of constructive internationalism and its accompanying infringements on national sovereignty and need to "accommodate" national interests. Ironically, Dixie's most influential twentieth-century foreign policy perspectives would more closely resemble the unilateralist and independent internationalism advocated by Henry Cabot Lodge—Wilson's principal adversary.[56]

56. Knock, *To End All Wars,* 266–67; Steigerwald, *Wilsonian Idealism in America,* 35; Joan Hoff, "The American Century: From Sarajevo to Sarajevo," in *The Ambiguous Legacy: U.S. Foreign Relations in the "American Century,"* ed. Michael J. Hogan (New York, 1999), 183–231.

A hostile cartoonist attacks President Thomas Jefferson as a "Prairie Dog" being stung by a hornet with Napoleon's head. Jefferson is coughing up $2 million in an effort to purchase West Florida.

Library of Congress

President John Tyler sought to use foreign policy to safeguard the South and to align states' rights advocates behind his reelection in 1844.
Library of Congress

Fearful that Great Britain would side with the Confederacy, a northern cartoonist pictures "John Bull" arguing that King "*Cotton* is more important to me than *Wool*!!" *Library of Congress*

Senator John Tyler Morgan, Alabama, was the South's most prominent spokesman on foreign policy during his tenure in Washington from 1877 to 1907.
Library of Congress

During the presidency of Woodrow Wilson, a native southerner, the South regained a crucial congressional influence on U.S. foreign policy.
Library of Congress

White southerners endorsed the racial views that helped provide the rationale for President Wilson's intervention in the Mexican Revolution.
Library of Congress

Senators Carter Glass, Virginia, and Joseph T. Robinson, Arkansas, and Secretary of State Cordell Hull from Tennessee were consistent champions of President Franklin D. Roosevelt's foreign policies.
Library of Congress

Senator Tom Connally, Texas, was an important U.S. delegate to the San Francisco Conference that drafted the UN Charter and was equally critical to its ratification by the Senate.

Library of Congress

Representative Otto Passman, Louisiana, was the most severe southern critic of U.S. foreign aid programs during the 1950s and 1960s.

Arkansas Democrat–Gazette, LBJ Library

President Lyndon B. Johnson and his former mentor, Senator Richard B. Russell Jr.,
Georgia, disagreed vehemently over the proper U.S. military strategy in Vietnam.
LBJ Library Photo by Yoichi Okamoto

President Johnson confers with his commander in Vietnam, General William
Westmoreland. Westmoreland, a South Carolina native, has been described as embodying
the southern military tradition.
Library of Congress

Secretary of State Dean Rusk from Georgia and Senator J. William Fulbright, Arkansas, attempt to appear amiable prior to contentious Senate Committee on Foreign Relations hearings on Vietnam.
Library of Congress

'A Senator Fulbright to See You, Sire. Seems He Can't Reconcile Himself to Your Infallibility.'

Senator Fulbright, the most important senatorial critic of the Vietnam War, especially disturbed President Johnson, a fellow southerner and former senate colleague.
Boston Globe

While opposing the Vietnam War, the Reverend Martin Luther King Jr. personified African American ambivalence over U.S. involvement in Vietnam and an assertive foreign policy more generally.
Library of Congress

CHAPTER 6

Defending the Nation and Enacting the
Wilsonian Vision, 1920–1945

I N JANUARY 1936 Senator Tom Connally of Texas angrily rejected Gerald P. Nye's charge that Woodrow Wilson had lied to Congress: "Some checker-playing, beer-drinking back room of some low house" was the "only fit place" for such a calumny against "a dead man, a great man, a good man." Connally was confident that history would place Wilson above the "puny pigmies who now bark at his memory as Pike's Peak towers above the fog of an Arkansas swamp." Carter Glass of Virginia agreed that isolationist attacks on Wilson's memory constituted "miserable demagogy." In 1942, James F. Byrnes of South Carolina accepted the position of director of the Office of Economic Stabilization to "help Franklin Roosevelt achieve for the country the dream of Woodrow Wilson." As the war approached its end, Byrnes proclaimed "a particular pride in the strong support and active leadership which southern Democrats in the Congress have provided in matters involving international cooperation in war and in the peace."[1]

Indeed, the pursuit of the twenty-eighth president's goal of U.S. membership in an international organization gained the status of another southern "lost cause." Reverence for Wilson and hatred of the Republicans for blocking U.S. membership in the League of Nations constituted a principal component of the South's foreign policy perspective in the twenty-five years

1. Tom Connally, as told to Alford Steinberg, *My Name is Tom Connally* (New York, 1954), 214; Tennant S. McWilliams, "Jefferson, Wilson, and the Idea of the 'Militant' South, 1916–1945," (unpublished paper in possession of Joseph A. Fry), 19 (Glass); David Robertson, *Sly and Able: A Political Biography of James F. Byrnes* (New York, 1994), 368; see also Kendrick A. Clements, ed., *James F. Byrnes and the Origins of the Cold War* (Durham, N.C., 1982), 7.

after 1920. Just as supporting Wilson and his foreign policy initiatives had offered southerners an opportunity to demonstrate patriotism and legislative responsibility during the World War I era, the ongoing campaign to realize the martyred leader's vision provided the South with the vehicle for respectable participation in foreign policy decisions. Just as Wilson was a Democrat as well as a southerner, his erstwhile followers retained partisan politics at the center of the South's response to U.S. foreign policy. When the nation again faced international peril in the 1930s, the South provided another Democratic president his most dependable support for foreign policy initiatives. Politics, patriotism, and the South's sense of honor once more coincided. Economic considerations also remained fundamental; both foreign commerce and prospective defense spending influenced Dixie's attitudes and decisions, as did the ongoing strain of Anglophilia that had evolved after the turn of the century.

That economic calculations remained a primary consideration was predictable, since the South continued to lag behind the rest of the nation in virtually every socioeconomic category. World War I brought general prosperity and stimulated the development of industry, but good times were temporary, and the basic structure of the South's colonial economy was not altered. Agriculture and dependence on staple crops and their vulnerability to erratic market and price fluctuations still dominated Dixie's economy. By 1930, 67.9 percent of the South's population was still rural and 42.8 percent of its work force agricultural. Over the previous decade, the number of farm owners had fallen by 350,000, leaving approximately 60 percent of farm operators as tenants or sharecroppers, working the land of others at an annual per capita income of $189. Although the region was home to 28 percent of the U.S. population, it furnished only 15 percent of the nation's industrial wage-earners; and these workers remained overwhelmingly concentrated in extractive first-stage processing and low-wage export sectors such as textiles, lumber, and mining. These persisting patterns left overall wages at least 30 percent below the national average and per capita income amounting to only 53 percent of that earned by residents of other U.S. regions. Together with these substandard economic conditions went equally disturbing levels of spending for education and public health.[2]

2. Bruce J. Schulman, *From Cotton Belt to Sunbelt: Federal Policy, Economic Development, and the Transformation of the South, 1938–1980* (Durham, N.C., 1994), 3–5; George B. Tindall, *The Emergence of the New South, 1913–1945* (Baton Rouge, 1967), 111; William J. Cooper Jr. and

The depression of the 1930s further aggravated these often desperate conditions. Personal income plummeted. By 1931 the South's personal income payments fell to 67 percent of those in 1929 and the following year dropped to 55 percent, or $203 per year—compared to $408 nationally. Bank failures and the accompanying devastation for surrounding communities were widespread as southern banking resources declined nearly 31 percent from 1929 to 1934. "King Cotton was sick," Oklahoma City and East Texas were "drowning in a flood of oil," and in 1932 revenues from only one of Dixie's twenty-one major railroads met fixed costs. Federal programs helped to reduce the human suffering that accompanied this economic plunge. More than 4 million southerners were receiving federal aid by the fall of 1933, and over the ensuing six years nearly $2 billion in relief funds flowed to the South. These funds and the money from other programs such as the Civilian Conservation Corps, the Agricultural Adjustment Administration, and the National Recovery Administration brought help, many significant physical improvements, and the beginning of structural changes in southern agriculture and industry. Still, the South's economy remained colonial and predominantly rural and its social and commercial difficulties acute. In 1937 President Franklin Roosevelt designated the South as the "Nation's No. 1 economic problem," and the federal government's *Report on Economic Conditions in the South* described the South as a "belt of sickness, misery, and unnecessary death."[3]

Along with these all-too-familiar economic and social conditions, southerners retained their characteristic sectionalism and fear of outside, particularly federal, interference in political and racial issues. White southerners would tolerate no "'foreigners' . . . coming from outside to talk to 'their nigras,'" and they held fast to traditional states' rights positions and conservative fiscal beliefs in the 1920s. Although the Great Depression forced them to compromise the latter two positions temporarily, long-standing southern uneasiness with federal power and spending remained influential and regained predominance after World War II.[4]

In the wake of the election of Republican President Warren Harding in 1920, the South turned its attention to the Washington Naval Conference

Thomas E. Terrill, *The American South: A History* (New York, 1996), 604–7; Dewey W. Grantham, *The South in Modern America: A Region at Odds* (New York, 1994), 88–92.

3. Tindall, *Emergence of the New South*, 361 and 363 (first two quotes); Grantham, *South in Modern America*, 120; Schulman, *From Cotton Belt to Sunbelt*, 3 (last two quotes).

4. Schulman, *From Cotton Belt to Sunbelt*, 13.

of 1921–22. Harding and his secretary of state, Charles Evans Hughes, had sponsored the gathering of great powers in an effort to avoid a costly shipbuilding competition with Great Britain and Japan, to circumscribe Japanese aspirations in East Asia, and to mollify extensive U.S. sentiment for disarmament. Under Hughes's dramatic and skilled leadership, the conference produced three agreements promoting these objectives. In the Four-Power Pacific Treaty, the United States, Japan, Great Britain, and France eliminated the Anglo-Japanese Alliance of 1902 and agreed to maintain the territorial status quo and to consult if involved in a confrontation in East Asia. In return for Japanese concurrence, Great Britain agreed not to fortify Hong Kong and the United States pledged similar restraint in the Philippines, Guam, and Alaska. The Five-Power Naval Limitation Treaty stipulated a ten-year moratorium on the construction of capital ships and limits on overall tonnage of 500,000 for the United States and Great Britain, 300,000 for Japan, and 175,000 for France and Italy. Finally, the Nine-Power Treaty, which included these five nations plus China, Belgium, the Netherlands, and Portugal, codified the Open Door policy of international respect for China's sovereignty and territorial integrity.

Only the Four-Power Pact encountered significant opposition, and the response of southern senators suggested that political partisanship strongly conditioned their commitment to internationalism. Wilsonian devotees Carter Glass and Claude A. Swanson of Virginia, Furnifold Simmons of North Carolina, and Joseph T. Robinson of Arkansas augmented the unsurprising objections of the U.S. military and irreconcilable isolationists such as Senators William E. Borah of Idaho and Hiram Johnson of California. Glass dismissed the Washington Conference as a "cheap substitute for the League of Nations" and condemned the Four-Power Treaty as "nothing but a group intrigue . . . pregnant with war itself." No Republican project managed by Henry Cabot Lodge and supported by the senators who had so recently blocked U.S. entry into the League could gain the acerbic Virginian's vote.[5]

Glass's partisan and sectional response to the treaty was partially mitigated by the influence of Democratic minority leader, Oscar W. Underwood, who had served as a member of the U.S. delegation to the conference and spoke forcefully for the pact. Other southerners judged the effort at

5. Thomas N. Guinsburg, *The Pursuit of Isolationism in the United States Senate from Versailles to Pearl Harbor* (New York, 1982), 70–71.

disarmament consistent with Wilson's vision and eschewed partisanship. Mississippi senator John Sharp Williams observed, "I am a Democrat, a Bourbon Democrat, a plain blamed-fool Mississippi Democrat. I have no patience with Republicanism and I have no patience with partisanship in connection with international affairs. If a Republican President had sent the Versailles treaty to this body three-fourths of you Republicans would have voted for it, including the Senator from Massachusetts [H. C. Lodge]. If Mr. Wilson had sent these treaties to this body two-thirds of you Democrats would have voted for it, including . . . my poor little humble self." Neither Underwood's and Williams's influence nor the Senate Foreign Relations Committee's assurance that the treaty carried "no commitment to armed force, no alliance, no obligation to join in any defense" persuaded the majority of southern senators, who voted 15 to 9 against ratification. Still, this divided response yielded 9 of the 12 Democrats who crossed party lines to secure Senate ratification.[6]

Wilson's ongoing influence was even more apparent in the South's ardent endorsement of the World Court. Organized in accordance with Article 14 of the League of Nations Covenant, the Permanent Court of International Justice's Statutes were approved by the League Council in 1921 and circulated to potential members. In 1923 President Harding and Secretary Hughes recommended U.S. membership with four reservations that officially separated the United States from the League and precluded amendment of the court statutes without U.S. consent. When these restrictions failed to allay isolationist fears, Senator Claude A. Swanson added a fifth reservation in 1926 forbidding the court to "*entertain any request* for an advisory opinion touching any dispute or question in which the United States *has or claims an interest.*" Although many southerners, including Swanson, Glass, and Furnifold Simmons, decried the U.S. insistence on the court being disassociated from the League, southern senators voted 23 to 1 in favor of joining the court. They agreed with 14 other Democrats in the 76 to 17 vote to approve U.S. membership.[7]

6. *Congressional Record*, 67th Cong., 2d sess., 4497; George L. Grassmuck, *Sectional Biases in Congress on Foreign Policy* (Baltimore, 1951), 62–63 (Williams); Harold T. Butler, "Partisan Positions on Isolationism vs. Internationalism, 1918–1933," (D.S.S. dissertation, Syracuse University, 1963), 119–31 (121, no commitment); Guinsburg, *Pursuit of Isolationism*, 73; Evans C. Johnson, *Oscar W. Underwood: A Political Biography* (Baton Rouge, 1980), 318–23.

7. Guinsburg, *Pursuit of Isolationism*, 87–107; Butler, "Partisan Positions," 110; Henry C. Ferrell Jr., *Claude A. Swanson of Virginia: A Political Biography* (Lexington, Ky., 1985), 171.

When the other members of the court denied U.S. entry under the terms of the fifth reservation, the issue languished until 1935, when President Franklin D. Roosevelt consented to its reconsideration at the insistence of popular opinion and Arkansas senator Joseph T. Robinson. To the chagrin of Glass and others still hoping to realize a portion of Wilson's vision, neither FDR nor Senate Foreign Relations Committee Chairman Key Pittman exercised forceful leadership on behalf of U.S. membership. In the absence of administration influence, the court fell before Senators Borah's and Johnson's shrill opposition, radio priest Father Charles E. Coughlin's broadcasts, and William Randolph Hearst's isolationist newspapers. U.S. membership failed of passage by a vote of 52 to 37, with southerners endorsing the League by 17 to 5. The dissenters included Robert Reynolds of North Carolina, Huey Long of Louisiana, Park Trammell of Florida, Ellison Smith of South Carolina, and Richard Russell of Georgia. Reynolds and Long adopted agrarian insurgent and largely isolationist perspectives akin to those of Claude Kitchen, Tom Watson, and James K. Vardaman prior to World War I. Smith had broken with FDR on domestic issues, Trammell remained angry that court members had rebuffed U.S. entry in 1926, and Russell feared that membership on the court was a precursor to joining the League.[8]

The majority of southerners exhibited similar partisanship and ambivalent internationalism when considering foreign debt settlements and appropriations for humanitarian aid abroad. World War I and its aftermath had left U.S. allies and victims of the Central Powers owing the United States more than $10 billion. Handicapped by the devastation of the war, U.S. tariff restrictions, and irregular German reparations payments and convinced that the loans should be forgiven as part of the American contribution to the war, the Allies delayed repayment of this debt. Given the prospect of complete default and the need to help rejuvenate the international economy, the United States reached a series of agreements with the European nations after 1923. These settlements reduced interest rates from 5 percent to figures ranging from 3.3 percent for Great Britain to .4 percent for Italy and established a sixty-two-year repayment schedule.

Consistent with their Anglophile tendencies, southern senators and congressmen endorsed the agreement with Great Britain, but were adamantly

8. *Congressional Record,* 74th Cong., 1st sess., 1147; Guinsburg, *Pursuit of Isolationism,* 162–95; Paul Seabury, *The Waning of Southern "Internationalism"* (Princeton, 1957), 13; Gilbert C. Fite, *Richard B. Russell Jr., Senator from Georgia* (Chapel Hill, 1991), 176–77.

opposed to settlements with Italy, France, and Greece. Southern proponents of forgiving a portion of the debts argued that such generosity would promote good international relations and enhance the sale of southern exports. Agreeing with other American naysayers, opponents refused to shift the burden of retiring the debt to American taxpayers or to aid foreign leaders such as Benito Mussolini in Italy. They also added the sectional objection that northern banks, such as the House of Morgan, stood to benefit at the rest of the nation's expense. Some even recalled Confederate war debts, for which the South remained obligated, and stipulated that the Europeans should be treated in similar fashion. Finally, southern critics emphasized domestic needs: U.S. funds should go to debt-ridden cotton farmers or struggling southern manufacturers rather than as succor abroad.[9]

Southerners were even more opposed to additional foreign loans or to humanitarian aid during the 1920s. Southern Democratic congressmen voted in opposition on 70.8 percent of the roll-call votes on these initiatives, and southern senators were in the negative column 64.6 percent of the time. Southern representatives were 10 percent more negative than House Democrats overall and 57 percent more negative than House Republicans, and they were 6 and 44 percent more negative than Democrats and Republicans in the Senate. Congressman Fred L. Blackman of Alabama echoed the fundamental southern reservation regarding debt relief when he declared that "charity should begin at home and . . . before granting" huge sums abroad, "we should look after the immense suffering in this country." Numerous southerners also raised constitutional objections. Representative R. Walton Moore of Virginia found no authorization "affirmatively expressed" in the Constitution for foreign aid, and others denied that the General Welfare Clause applied to the use of U.S. taxes to promote foreign welfare. Although this voting pattern would change dramatically in the 1930s following Franklin D. Roosevelt's election, it forecast a significant strain of southern uneasiness with foreign aid in the 1930s and 1940s and eventual disaffection in the 1950s. It also spoke to southern partisanship in foreign policy and the region's unilateralist and nationalist rather than consistently internationalist tendencies.[10]

The South's virtually unanimous endorsement of immigration restriction

9. Butler, "Partisan Positions," 157–80, 250–67.

10. Ibid., 291–314 (quotes, 295, 302); Grassmuck, *Sectional Biases in Congress,* 97–99. Both Butler and Grassmuck define the South as the eleven states of the former Confederacy.

provided additional evidence of these perspectives. While nativism was a national phenomenon in the 1920s, the South had become the "most nativist part of the country." Given Dixie's adherence to political and Protestant fundamentalism, sympathy for prohibition, support for the Ku Klux Klan, and traditional suspicion of "outsiders," its claim to this dubious mantle was hardly surprising. Working from a vague definition of aliens, which included "immigrants, Catholics, Jews, Negroes, Communists, and Socialists," southern congressmen and senators voted 127 to 0 for the Johnson Immigration Act of 1924. This measure excluded Japanese immigrants and set European quotas of 2 percent for each national group residing in the United States in 1890. These votes were indicative of ongoing southern hostility to immigration, and southern congressmen voted in both 1937 and 1941 to deport illegal aliens. In the second instance, they favored expelling Jewish aliens even if they were being returned to perilous conditions in Europe.[11]

Both political partisanship and traditional southern economic arguments informed the South's position on tariff legislation during the interwar period. Despite the customary dissent of Louisiana representatives, who sought protection for sugar and rice, the protests of Florida senators on behalf of citrus and truck farmers, and the lobbying of Texas petroleum interests, southern Democratic senators and congressmen voted overwhelmingly against the higher Republican Fordney-McCumber Tariff of 1922 and the Hawley-Smoot Bill of 1930. Southern objections to protectionism reiterated the region's opposition to the artificial increase of the prices of manufactured and other consumer goods and the threat of jeopardizing access to export markets. As Oscar W. Underwood observed, exports and imports were "Siamese twins"—"kill one and you kill the other." The centrality of foreign commerce to southern economic well-being remained clear given the export of 58 percent of American cotton, 40 percent of its tobacco, and 50 percent of the naval stores. From 1926 to 1929, southern exports of $1.5 billion equaled 30 percent of all American exports and 20 to 25 percent of the South's economic production. Given Dixie's perceived need "to export

11. *Congressional Record*, 68th Cong., 1st sess., 6257–58, 6649; Robert A. Divine, *American Immigration Policy, 1924–1952* (1957; reprint, New York, 1972), 48; Grantham, *South in Modern America*, 104 (quotes); Butler, "Partisan Positions," 209, 319, 322–23; Alfred O. Hero Jr., *The Southerner and World Affairs* (Baton Rouge, 1965), 63. Hero defines the South as the eleven states of the former Confederacy. Because of his extensive and excellent use of public opinion polling, which does not always employ this same definition, he must be flexible. For example, Gallup adds Kentucky and Oklahoma to the eleven Confederate states.

or die," southern senators voted 16 to 3 against Fordney-McCumber and 17 to 5 against Hawley-Smoot. In the House, southern Democrats voted 88 to 6 and 70 to 10 against the two measures, while southern Republicans supported the bills 6 to 0 and 12 to 0.[12]

When the Hawley-Smoot Tariff and other initiatives from the Herbert Hoover administration failed to reverse the nation's economic descent, Franklin D. Roosevelt and the Democrats recaptured the White House and Congress in 1932. The Democratic victory returned southerners to positions of leadership in Washington. Although Roosevelt appointed Cordell Hull, a former Tennessee congressman and dedicated Wilsonian, as secretary of state, Claude A. Swanson of Virginia as secretary of the navy, and Daniel C. Roper of South Carolina as secretary of commerce, southerners did not regain the influence they had wielded in the executive branch under Woodrow Wilson.

But seniority enabled southern senators and congressmen to reclaim congressional dominance. First Joseph T. Robinson of Arkansas then, after 1937, Alben W. Barkley of Kentucky served as the Democratic floor leader in the Senate. In the House, Joseph Byrns of Tennessee, William B. Bankhead of Alabama, and Sam Rayburn of Texas served successively as floor leader and then Speaker between 1933 and 1940. Although the ineffectual Key Pittman of Nevada chaired the Senate Foreign Relations Committee until replaced by Tom Connally of Texas in June 1941, Pat Harrison, Walter George, Claude Pepper, Carter Glass, and James F. Byrnes were active and important committee members. Tennessee's Sam D. McReynolds chaired the House Committee on Foreign Affairs, and southerners also chaired the Senate Finance, Appropriations, and Military Affairs Committees, and the House Ways and Means, Military Affairs, and Naval Affairs Committees. During the crucial period from 1938 through 1941, southerners managed most of the administration's important foreign policy initiatives on the floor of Congress and provided the most dependable bloc of votes on their behalf. In so doing, southerners faithfully represented their constituents, who consistently expressed the strongest regional backing for Roosevelt and his cautious march toward war.

12. *Congressional Record,* 67th Cong., 2d sess., 12907; Ibid., 71st Cong., 2d sess., 10789–90; Johnson, *Underwood,* 327; Tindall, *Emergence of the New South,* 135 (export); Butler, "Partisan Positions," 149–50, 239–40; Charles M. Dollar, "The South and the Fordney-McCumber Tariff of 1922: A Study in Regional Politics," *Journal of Southern History* 39 (February 1973): 45–65.

Southern allegiance to the Democratic Party and devotion to lower tariffs persisted in the region's support for the Reciprocal Trade Agreements Act of 1934. Promoted aggressively by Secretary of State Hull, this measure left the Hawley-Smoot Tariff in place but empowered the president to reduce tariff rates up to 50 percent for nations willing to grant similar concessions to the United States. The act also included the most-favored-nation provision, which allowed for the broad extension of favorable tariff rates negotiated with any individual nation.

Other important southerners supplemented Hull's efforts by directing the hearings of an executive commission established by FDR to examine the trade issue. Vice-President John Nance Garner of Texas, Senators Joseph T. Robinson of Arkansas and Pat Harrison of Mississippi, and Congressmen Robert L. Doughton of North Carolina and James F. Byrnes of South Carolina dominated these proceedings. Doughton was aghast that the United States, in contrast to "practically every country" in Europe and several in South America, had failed to place "authority in the hands of the Executive branch" for the "purpose of removing trade restrictions." Ultimately, only two southern senators and one congressman broke with the regional consensus that lower tariffs would stimulate Dixie's exports and voted against the bill. Senator Huey Long and a Louisiana ally in the House sought to protect sugar, and Carter Glass objected to the measure's delegation of unilateral discretionary authority to the president. Glass endorsed the southern pursuit of markets but preferred to have the Hawley-Smoot rates reduced or repealed. Neither isolated southern support for protectionism nor constitutional concerns commanded appreciable influence as southerners provided the crucial votes to renew reciprocity in both 1937 and 1940. Between 1933 and 1945, southern senators cast 94.8 percent of their votes in favor of reciprocal trade. These votes proved crucial to the negotiation by 1947 of twenty-nine reciprocity agreements, which reduced the duties on 70 percent of American imports.[13]

The South's pursuit of export markets was also the principal motive for its backing of the Roosevelt administration's diplomatic recognition of Rus-

13. Peter Trubowitz, *Defining the National Interest: Conflict and Change in American Foreign Policy* (Chicago, 1998), 284 n. 130 (Doughton); Elmo M. Roberds Jr., "The South and United States Foreign Policy, 1933–1952," (Ph.D. dissertation, University of Chicago, 1954), 38–44; Rorin M. Platt, *Virginia in Foreign Affairs, 1933–1941* (Lanham, Md., 1991), 63–76; V. O. Key Jr., with the assistance of Alexander Heard, *Southern Politics in State and Nation* (New York, 1949), 353. Key defines the South as the eleven states of the former Confederacy.

sia in November 1933 and the Good Neighbor Policy toward Latin America. Mired in the Great Depression, southerners, like Americans generally, deemed the prospect of a Russian market for cotton goods more important than objections to the Soviet Union's Communist ideology. Indeed, southern newspaper editors provided the strongest regional support for recognition. Some declared that Russia would help preserve peace; others simply argued for trust in Roosevelt's judgment. But trade prospects were decisive. The *Dallas News*'s front-page headline boldly predicted, "RECOGNITION AID TO SALE OF TEXAS COTTON IN RUSSIA," and in October 1933, fifty-nine Texas papers endorsed recognition, compared to only two dissenters.[14]

Potential profits also drove southern support for efforts to improve relations with Latin America. Many southerners, such as Claude A. Swanson of Virginia, had criticized the Republican administrations of the 1920s for armed interventions and "imperialist departures" in Latin America, but Dixie's more general support for the Good Neighbor Policy derived from its association with the Democratic Roosevelt administration, with Secretary of State Hull's prominent role in its implementation, and with the search for markets. Both southern congressmen and Dixie's newspapers endorsed not only this commercial component of the Good Neighbor Policy but also the withdrawal of U.S. troops from Nicaragua and Haiti and the decisions not to intervene in Cuba or Mexico when confronted with disorder and the confiscation of American property.[15]

This virtually unanimous endorsement of Roosevelt's trade strategy was characteristic of the South's crucial support for the president's pre–World War II foreign policies. During the mid-1930s, both FDR and the South subscribed or at least assented to the isolationist "neutrality" policy designed to insulate the United States from war in Europe and Asia. When confronted with the Japanese attack on Manchuria in 1931–32, the German rearmament in 1935 and occupation of the Rhineland in 1936, the Italian invasion of Ethiopia in 1935, and the Spanish civil war in 1936, Congress passed and Roosevelt signed a series of neutrality laws between 1935 and

14. Peter G. Filene, *Americans and the Soviet Experiment, 1917–1933* (Cambridge, Mass., 1967), 266 (*News*), 290; Edward W. Chester, *Sectionalism, Politics, and American Diplomacy* (Metuchen, N.J., 1975), 203; Edward M. Bennett, *Recognition of Russia: An American Foreign Policy Dilemma* (Waltham, Mass., 1970), 131; Roberds, "South and United States Foreign Policy," 44–46.

15. Ferrell, *Swanson*, 180; Roberds, "South and United States Foreign Policy," 46–50; Platt, *Virginia in Foreign Affairs*, 79–109.

1937. Cumulatively, these measures forbade Americans to export arms or extend loans to belligerents, to travel in a war zone aboard ships of belligerent countries, or to arm merchant ships trading with belligerents. The last of these laws in 1937 allowed for the "cash and carry" sale of raw materials other than arms or munitions.

Like virtually all Americans, including the president, southerners were primarily concerned with the domestic economy in the period through 1938 and hoped that a neutral policy would enable the United States to avoid war. Therefore, southern congressmen agreed with the substance of FDR's policy. For example, Josiah Bailey of North Carolina "profoundly opposed" meddling in European affairs or fighting beyond the "neighborhood of our shores"; John L. McClellan of Arkansas declared the American people were "convinced" that they could not "reform the world"; Pat Harrison warned that if "we permit . . . carrying of guns on ships even for defensive purposes, we are likely to get into trouble"; Richard Russell of Georgia sought to avoid involvement in "Asiatic brawls" or "European quarrels" of "no remote concern to us"; and Harry F. Byrd of Virginia based his agreement with presidential policies on the assumption that they were "designed and will in actuality keep us out of war." Virginia's two principal newspapers, the *Richmond News-Leader* and the *Richmond Times-Dispatch,* agreed with the state's junior senator. The *News-Leader* admonished in 1933, "If Europe is mad enough to renew the war, the United States must be wise enough to remain neutral." The *Times-Dispatch* concurred, and asserted three years later "that the people of the United States are desirous above almost everything of staying out of the next war."[16]

In addition to agreeing with the essence of the neutrality policy, southerners were strongly inclined to follow the lead of their Democratic president. Representative Sam Rayburn spoke for the great majority of his regional contemporaries when he declared, "When the nation is in danger, you have to follow your leader. The man in the White House is the only leader this nation has." Rayburn subsequently asserted that "foreign affairs"

16. John R. Moore, *Senator Josiah William Bailey of North Carolina: A Political Biography* (Durham, N.C., 1968), 172; David L. Porter, *The Seventy-sixth Congress and World War II, 1939–1940* (Columbia, Mo., 1979), 29; C. Calvin Smith, *War and Wartime Changes: The Transformation of Arkansas, 1940–1945* (Fayetteville, Ark., 1986), 1 (McClellan); Martha H. Swain, *Pat Harrison: The New Deal Years* (Jackson, Miss., 1978), 220; Fite, *Russell,* 177; Ronald L. Heinemann, *Harry Byrd of Virginia* (Charlottesville, Va., 1996), 209; Platt, *Virginia in Foreign Affairs,* 145–46 (Richmond papers).

were "definitely an Executive function" and that Congress needed to avoid causing "embarrassment to those responsible for the foreign policy and its execution." Acting on these assumptions and their perception of the national interest, southerners voted almost unanimously for the neutrality legislation. Like the president, they refused to challenge the adamant isolationists. When Roosevelt subsequently sought greater discretion in implementing those measures, southerners again agreed. Tom Connally summarized this new position by objecting to the president being forced to make it "unlawful to export the tools of war to *either* side in a war." This rigid approach declared in advance that the United States would "exert no influence" and constituted a "form of unneutrality," by which America would "take the side of the strong and powerful against the weak."[17]

Southern Democrats also followed dutifully when Roosevelt and Hull reached their limit regarding restrictions on executive leadership and forcefully rejected the Ludlow amendment. Proposed by Representative Louis Ludlow of Indiana, this constitutional amendment would have required a national referendum for the declaration of war. In early January 1938, Speaker of the House William B. Bankhead signaled the president's and secretary's opposition, and on January 10, Bankhead read a letter from Roosevelt stating that the proposal would "cripple any President in his conduct of foreign relations, and . . . encourage other nations to believe that they could violate American rights with impunity." In the House's 209 to 188 vote to quash this effort, southern congressmen provided the decisive margin by opposing the measure 88 to 20.[18]

Only African Americans dissented significantly from this southern response to U.S. policy during the 1934–38 period. Blacks remained acutely conscious of the contradiction between their treatment at home and the U.S. defense of human rights abroad. One black southern schoolboy's response to his teacher's question regarding the proper punishment for Adolph Hitler spoke volumes: "I would paint his face black and send him to America immediately!" While generally agreeing that the United States should remain neutral and focus on domestic issues rather than foreign quarrels, blacks argued vehemently for an exception in the Italian-Ethiopian

17. D. B. Hardeman and Donald C. Bacon, *Rayburn: A Biography* (Austin, 1987), 100–1, 228; Connally, *My Name Is Tom Connally*, 220.

18. *Congressional Record*, 75th Cong., 3d sess., 282–83; Ernest C. Bolt Jr., *Ballots before Bullets: The War Referendum Approach to Peace in America, 1914–1941* (Charlottesville, Va., 1977), 153, 170–71, 173–74 (quote).

conflict, where people of color were under attack by a developed European nation. The *Richmond Planet* castigated American "hypocrisy" in withholding munitions from Ethiopia while selling oil and scrap iron to Italy. This clearly unneutral policy reinforced aggression and abetted Mussolini's "rape of Ethiopia." African American protests extended beyond editorial writing. Ethiopian support groups formed in Hampton, Virginia, and south Alabama, pickets demonstrated outside Italian-American stores in Mobile, and black schoolteachers were arrested in Birmingham for allegedly organizing boycotts of Italian-American businesses.[19]

Japanese and German advances in Asia and Europe soon confirmed Tom Connally's assertion that U.S. neutrality policy effectively placed America on the side of the aggressor nations and afforded the Roosevelt administration no viable means for aiding China, France, or Britain. In mid-1937 the Japanese moved beyond Manchuria and attacked China proper, signaling the beginning of World War II. Adolph Hitler and Germany added the European dimension to this international conflict by annexing Austria in March 1938, intimidating the western democracies at the Munich Conference of September 1938, absorbing Czechoslovakia in March 1939, and attacking Poland in September 1939.

Confronted with this perilous challenge, President Roosevelt cautiously altered the course of U.S. policy. Even as the nation moved steadily closer to war from the fall of 1939 to December 1941, FDR contended officially that the United States was seeking to avoid war by aiding the Allies—first Britain and France and, after June 1941, Russia as well. The president garnered his strongest, most dependable public and congressional support for this interventionist policy from the South. Just as they had done for Woodrow Wilson in the years leading to World War I, southerners rallied behind their Democratic president.

Amending the neutrality legislation constituted the first step in the refocusing of U.S. policy. Following the German attack on Poland in September 1939, the Roosevelt administration formulated legislation to end the arms embargo generally and to waive specifically the cash-and-carry requirement for Latin America. Tom Connally and James F. Byrnes managed

19. Mary L. Dudziak, "Desegregation as a Cold War Imperative," *Stanford Law Review* 41 (November 1988): 87–88 (Hitler); Platt, *Virginia in Foreign Affairs,* 150 (*Planet*); Brenda Gayle Plummer, *Rising Wind: Black Americans and U.S. Foreign Affairs, 1935–1960* (Chapel Hill, 1996), 48, 50.

the legislation in the Senate, and Luther A. Johnson of Texas oversaw floor work in the House. Southern spokesmen forcefully repeated FDR's contention that the current neutrality legislation unfairly discriminated against the British, whose control of the Atlantic Ocean would allow them to operate within the cash-and-carry framework. Just as the southern litany had earlier agreed with FDR in expressing the need for neutrality, voices from Dixie now followed the president's lead in calling for a more flexible, more pro-Allied policy. Democratic Majority Leader Alben W. Barkley recanted his earlier vote for the embargo; James F. Byrnes denounced the ban on the sale of weapons as an "unneutral act," which left the United States "taking sides with Hitler"; William B. Bankhead decried the "supreme and colossal mistake" of withdrawing the "management of foreign affairs" from the "hands of the President"; Kenneth D. McKellar urged the nation not to "avoid our world responsibility"; and Josiah Bailey of North Carolina proclaimed that he had "utterly changed" his "mind." While Bailey had not discarded his fear of an overly strong federal government, he realized that it was "better to give power to our own Republic than to yield to the power of a foreign nation and an alien dictator."[20]

Bailey's pronouncement was significant, since he had been among the most severe critics of Roosevelt's New Deal domestic legislation and along with Walter George of Georgia had been a target of FDR's unsuccessful attempt to secure more liberal Democratic nominees in the 1938 primaries. By the summer of 1939, Roosevelt had pointedly sought to mend relations with Bailey, Connally, Byrd, Glass, George, and Harrison. Bailey concluded in October 1939, "It may be that he [FDR] will realize that he cannot keep up with the left but can rely on the right." Indeed the support of these anti–New Dealers for the repeal proposition signaled the pattern over the next six years, in which southern Democrats of all stripes backed the president on foreign policy despite ambivalence and frequent opposition to his domestic programs. Only Harry F. Byrd of Virginia, Robert Reynolds of North Carolina, and John H. Overton of Louisiana spoke publicly against repeal, and only the latter two voted negatively in the Senate's 63 to 30 pas-

20. Irving Howards, "The Influence of Southern Senators on American Foreign Policy from 1939 to 1950," (Ph.D. dissertation, University of Wisconsin, 1955), 39 (Byrnes and McKellar); Porter, *Seventy-sixth Congress,* 41 (Bankhead); Moore, *Bailey,* 180, 186; Henry J. Walker Jr., "Beyond the Call of Duty: Representative John Sparkman of Alabama and World War II, 1939–1945," *Southern Historian* 11 (1990): 26.

sage of the revision. When the House followed suit 243 to 172, southerners voted 106 to 3 for revision.[21]

This virtually unanimous action by southern congressmen faithfully represented the opinions of their constituents. As Hitler tightened his grip on Austria in early 1938, a majority of southerners, as opposed to minorities from all other American regions, favored Anglo-American military actions "to maintain world peace." By fall 1938 and the convening of the Munich Conference, where Hitler began the absorption of Czechoslovakia, 60 percent of southerners (compared to 52 percent of midwesterners, 48 percent of northeasterners, and 45 percent of Plains States residents) predicted that the United States would be at war with Germany in their lifetime. After Germany's attack on Poland, an October 1939 Gallup Poll found that 77 percent of southerners, as opposed to 62 percent of all Americans, favored revision of the neutrality laws. Similarly, a *Richmond Times-Dispatch* poll determined that 75 percent of Richmonders endorsed FDR's suggested changes, and residents of the Virginia capital were busily organizing "Bundles for Britain" groups to send money, clothing, and other supplies to the embattled "Mother Country."[22]

The South maintained its position as the nation's most interventionist, pro-Allied region through the period leading to U.S. entry into war. In May 1940, 53 percent of southerners favored further revision of the neutrality acts to allow Britain to borrow money from the United States for the purchase of war matériel (compared to 41 percent in the next highest region); in June 1940, 70 percent of southerners endorsed aiding England even at the risk of war (compared to 54 percent in the next most aggressive region); in August 1940, 68 percent of southerners backed the destroyer-bases deal by which FDR traded overage American ships to Great Britain for strategic military locations in the Western Hemisphere (compared to 56 percent of northeasterners); in February 1941, 77 percent of southerners, compared to 54 percent of all Americans, sustained the passage of the Lend-Lease Bill to funnel war matériel to the British; in June 1941, 75 percent of southerners, versus 55 percent of their countrymen, agreed that U.S. Navy ships should be employed to safeguard vessels carrying cargoes to Great Britain; also in June 1941, 63

21. *Congressional Record,* 76th Cong., 2d sess., 1389; Porter, *Seventy-sixth Congress,* 89 (Bailey); Howards, "Influence of Southern Senators," 43; Roberds, "South and United States Foreign Policy," 58; Guinsburg, *Pursuit of Isolationism,* 237.

22. Hero, *Southerner and World Affairs,* 93; Platt, *Virginia in Foreign Affairs,* 153.

percent of southerners, and 50 percent of all Americans, believed the draft should be extended to retain men in the military for more than one year; and in September 1941, 88 percent of southerners replied that it was more important to defeat Germany than to stay out of war.[23]

This pro-British, anti-German attitude was reflected in the inability of either the German Foreign Institute, the most active Nazi organization in the South, or the America First Committee, the most important noninterventionist mass pressure group in the United States, to make appreciable headway in Dixie. Despite the region's practice of rigid segregation and oppression of blacks in ways that invited comparisons to Hitler and his attacks on Jews and other minorities, the vast majority of southerners unreservedly condemned the Nazis. Of the approximately one thousand members of the Nazi Party cited by the U.S. Army in 1946, only 2 percent lived or had resided in the South, and the region's principal concentration of German-Americans in northern Texas joined their neighbors throughout Dixie in rejecting all associations with the Nazis and their ideology. White southerners denied parallels between their treatment of blacks and Hitler's attacks on Jews. They argued that German persecution of Jews had legal sanction; the lynching of blacks did not. If any similarity of prejudice toward a despised minority was conceded, it was equated with activities of the Ku Klux Klan and discussion was confined to the 1920s. Black southerners, however, showed no hesitation in making the connection between their plight and the Jewish experience in Germany. As they had done since the late nineteenth century, African Americans exposed the hypocrisy of the U.S. position. Southern blacks subscribed to a 1938 editorial in *Crisis*, the journal of the National Association for the Advancement of Colored People (NAACP), that contended "the South approaches more nearly than any other section of the United States the Nazi idea of government by a 'master race' without interference from any democratic process."[24]

The South also proved to be "distinctly hostile territory" for the America First Committee. Not only did the organization fail to establish any influential chapters in Dixie, its organizers and proponents frequently suffered abuse and ridicule. Championing nonintervention and refusing to aid the

23. Hero, *Southerner and World Affairs*, 97–103; Platt, *Virginia in Foreign Affairs*, 157; Chester, *Sectionalism, Politics, and American Diplomacy*, 220.

24. Johnpeter Horst Grill and Robert L. Jenkins, "The Nazis and the American South in the 1930s: A Mirror Image?" *Journal of Southern History* 58 (November 1992): 667–94 (quote 689).

British resulted in the rejection of America First applications to open bank accounts, cost pro–America First attorneys business, and prompted radio stations to decline to broadcast America First speeches. In Sarasota, Florida, the young daughter of the America First chairperson was greeted with taunts from her classmates that she was "a German and so is your mother." And from Tarrant, Alabama, an embittered anti-interventionist complained that freedom of speech no longer existed "in this vast cultural desert called the South." One need only, "try to hold a Lindbergh meeting here and see what happens to it, or even to wear an America First button . . . . It is getting more like living in Germany every day."[25]

If these measures of popular opinion were not sufficiently indicative of the South's sympathies, Dixie's legislators left no doubt by backing FDR's increasingly interventionist decisions. Southerners provided crucial congressional leadership for the passage in September 1940 of the Burke-Wadsworth Bill establishing the nation's first peacetime draft. While reporting the bill from the Senate Military Affairs Committee and responding to advocates of a volunteer force, Lister Hill of Alabama quoted Woodrow Wilson's assertion that a draft would not be "conscription of the unwilling but selection from a nation that has volunteered *en masse.*" James F. Byrnes was confident that "the boys of the South" would volunteer but worried that those from the "populous centers of the country" might not be so patriotic, and Alabama congressman Luther Patrick subsequently contended that selective service had been necessary "to keep our Southern boys from filling up the army."[26]

Representative Beverly Vincent of Kentucky graphically demonstrated the South's willingness to fight when Martin Sweeney of Cleveland spoke disparagingly of the draft and Woodrow Wilson. Vincent refused to "sit by a traitor" and subsequently smashed Sweeney in the jaw when the latter swung at him. Young southerners volunteered in impressive numbers. In a representative instance, the entire Lepanto, Arkansas, high school football team joined the navy; and when one member failed the physical, he drank carbolic acid rather than risk being considered "yellow." Less impulsive actions were more important. As the vote on the draft approached, Josiah

25. Wayne S. Cole, "America First and the South, 1940–41," *Journal of Southern History* 20 (February 1956): 36–47 (quotes, 39, 42–43).

26. J. Garry Clifford and Samuel R. Spencer Jr., *The First Peacetime Draft* (Lawrence, Kans., 1986), 187 (Byrnes), 196 (Hill); John Temple Graves, *The Fighting South* (New York, 1954), 5 (Patrick).

Bailey assured Edwin "Pa" Watson, President Roosevelt's secretary, that southern Democrats would be "voting right and with the president on every question before the Senate, particularly conscription." Thereafter, the overwhelming majority of southern senators and congressmen voted for both the Burke-Wadsworth Bill and its extension the following summer.[27]

Southerners were equally critical to the passage of Lend-Lease in March 1941. In his State of the Union Address on January 6, 1941, President Roosevelt proposed to make the United States the arsenal of democracy by lending or leasing Great Britain matériels necessary to win the war and render American involvement unnecessary. The original appropriation was set at $7 billion, although the United States eventually provided more than $50 billion of matériel to opponents of the Axis. Amidst a din of isolationist protests, southerners minced no words publicly while simultaneously working effectively on the floor and in the cloakrooms. Carter Glass prescribed "doing anything that would beat hell out of Hitler" and believed "like David Harum in the Golden Rule, 'Do unto others what they would do unto you. But do it first.'" Claude Pepper asserted, "It is not written in the holy writ of Americanism that America should be a mere spectator at Armageddon." And Tom Connally again attacked Gerald Nye for criticizing Woodrow Wilson and FDR and this time dismissed the North Dakotan as a "Wilson hater and a Wilson vilifier, and a Wilson calumniator."[28]

Meanwhile, Speaker of the House Sam Rayburn alternately blocked hostile amendments with a curt "Not germane" and left the chair to work the floor where, according to one journalist, he employed "not only his finesse but both feet on his Democrats to keep them in line." On the other side of the Capitol, Walter George maneuvered masterfully from his chairmanship of the Senate Foreign Relations Committee and James F. Byrnes made the "[voting] checks, talked to the waverers, soothed the grumblers and shepherded the doubters into line." The cumulative efforts of these skilled debaters and managers resulted in southern Democrats providing the critical margin for passage in both houses. In the Senate's 60 to 31 vote, southerners were aligned 22 to 1, with Robert Reynolds the only dissenter. In the House,

27. Clifford and Spencer, *First Peacetime Draft,* 207 (Bailey), 214 (Vincent); Smith, *War and Wartime Changes,* 12.

28. Platt, *Virginia in Foreign Affairs,* 163, and Howards, "Influence of Southern Senators," 47 (Glass); Chester, *Sectionalism, Politics, and American Diplomacy,* 221–22 (Pepper); Howards, "Influence of Southern Senators," 46 (Connally).

southerners cast 104 of the 260 yes votes and only 4 of the 165 no votes. Two of these opponents were Republicans.[29]

Polls indicated that the South maintained its interventionist posture during the remainder of 1941. Southerners strongly endorsed President Roosevelt's decisions to provide protective convoys for Allied merchant ships and to direct U.S. naval vessels to "shoot on sight" at German submarines in the western Atlantic. This consistent southern interventionism as FDR moved the nation inexorably toward war has prompted historians to contrast the South with the Midwest, the nation's most isolationist region and to ponder Dixie's ostensible belligerence and internationalism. The South and Midwest might have been expected to agree on a noninterventionist foreign policy. Both were rural, poor, agricultural, often culturally provincial, and fearful of centralized government power. Why then was the South as interventionist as the Midwest was isolationist?

Carter Glass attributed the South's "attitude . . . to superior character and to exceptional understanding of the problem involved." Perhaps, but other explanations must be considered. Much has been made of the South's military tradition and unusual proclivity for war and personal violence. The evidence is suggestive but hardly conclusive. Southerners certainly reveled in the romantic lure that predated the Civil War and turned again in the 1930s to the mythical and psychologically compensatory Lost Cause and its portrayal of particular southern military inclination and capacity. Southerners also volunteered in large numbers and once more sought to demonstrate their devotion to the Union. Still, southerners have been no more likely to become military heroes in the twentieth century than other Americans, nor did the South exhibit a greater tendency than other U.S. regions for the genuine preparation or discipline that marked European military traditions. Appeals to patriotism and honor were more influential than true regional militarism.[30]

Other analysts have cited the South's propensity for personal violence,

29. *Congressional Record*, 77th Cong., 1st sess., 815, 2097; Warren F. Kimball, *The Most Unsordid Act; Lend-Lease, 1939–1941* (Baltimore, 1969), 206–7, 216–17; Hardeman and Bacon, *Rayburn*, 259; Robertson, *Sly and Able*, 297; Chester, *Sectionalism, Politics, and American Diplomacy*, 218.

30. Graves, *Fighting South*, 7 (Glass); McWilliams, "Jefferson, Wilson, and the Idea of the 'Militant' South," 1–39; Robert E. May, "Dixie's Martial Image: A Continuing Historiographical Enigma," *Historian* 40 (February 1978): 213–34; F. N. Boney, "The Military Tradition in the South," *Midwest Quarterly* 21 (winter 1980): 163–74.

another trait with antebellum precedents. Dixie's homicide rates have led the nation for much of the twentieth century, prompting sociologist John Shelton Reed to refer to a "culture of violence" in the region "below the Smith and Wesson Line." According to Reed, "Our people, black and white, have witnessed with some consistency and often at great cost to the belief that there are enemies who cannot or should not be appeased, conflicts that cannot or should not be negotiated. . . . in short, that there *are* things worth fighting for." As with the South's military tradition, this cultural pattern may have led southerners to have been particularly adamant in opposing the aggressors of the 1930s, but the connections of domestic violence to an interventionist foreign policy are not so readily demonstrated as those in other areas.[31]

Among other more tangible influences was the South's partiality for the British and recognition that Great Britain was defending American ideals and interests. Compared to the Midwest or Northeast, the white southern population was much more overwhelmingly Anglo-Saxon in origin. There were many fewer German-Americans, Italian-Americans, or Scandinavian-Americans who opposed or who were at least highly ambivalent about aiding the British. Unrestrained by constituents who opposed the nation's increasingly pro-British neutrality, southern congressmen were free to act on the Anglophilia that had become increasingly apparent after the turn of the century.[32]

Apprehensions over the Axis threat to the United States reinforced this Anglophilia. Carter Glass pronounced democracy in "mortal peril" and was convinced that it could "only be saved by quick and immediate aid" for those nations defending "both our welfare and our institutions." Harry F. Byrd agreed and called for "unstinted aid . . . to the gallant nation . . . which is today fighting for its very existence and for the preservation of American ideals." Representative Colgate W. Darden, also from Virginia, echoed the belief that "the survival of Great Britain offers the only opportunity to a long period of peace." And in an observation embodying the rationale that helped convince southerners to follow Roosevelt beyond economic aid to

31. John Shelton Reed, *One South: An Ethnic Approach to Regional Culture* (Baton Rouge, 1982), 141, 153; Sheldon Hackney, "Southern Violence," *American Historical Review* 74 (February 1969): 906–25.

32. Tennant S. McWilliams, *The New South Faces the World: Foreign Affairs and the Southern Sense of Self, 1877–1950* (Baton Rouge, 1988), 90–92.

challenge Germany in the Atlantic and Japan in the Pacific, Darden warned that it "would be fatal for us to assume that, having succeeded in Europe and the East," the Axis powers "will be content to leave unmolested the continents of the Americas."[33]

The Wilsonian legacy, economic considerations, and partisan politics complemented sympathy for Great Britain and strategic calculations. As Carter Glass and Tom Connally had made amply clear over the previous twenty years, countless southerners revered Wilson and his call for international involvement and cooperation—especially if the terms of the cooperation were not too clearly defined. In backing FDR, southerners once again believed that they were supporting and helping lead a cause of which they could be proud—a cause that allowed the South to defend democracy and the American way rather than forcing them to respond to criticism directed at lynching, sharecropping, or poorly funded educational and social services.[34]

Economic considerations strongly reinforced the South's desire to realize Wilson's goals. As had been the case prior to World War I, the outbreak of hostilities in Asia and Europe disrupted the South's export economy. With more than 50 percent of Dixie's cotton and 40 percent of its tobacco exported in the 1930s, the loss of markets in Britain and continental Europe, where the bulk of the cotton and tobacco was sold, and the possible alienation of Japan, the other primary purchaser of southern cotton, were devastating. By 1940 southern exports had fallen to one-half of the 1930 total of $1.4 billion. Countering aggressors and their nationalistic economic tendencies and restoring peace could also help recapture markets essential to regional prosperity. In the interim, southerners recalled the benefits derived from defense spending during World War I and recognized the potential stimulus that might be forthcoming. Surely Pat Harrison had both in mind when he asserted in 1941, "There can be no limitation on expenditures for our defense except what the job requires." Virginius Dabney, editor of the *Richmond Times-Dispatch,* was even more explicit in October 1940 when he declared that the difficulties in the agricultural sector "will be compensated

33. Rorin M. Platt, "The Triumph of Interventionism: Virginia's Political Elite and Aid to Great Britain, 1939–1941," *Virginia Magazine of History and Biography* 100 (July 1992): 346, 353, 358.

34. McWilliams, "Jefferson, Wilson, and the Idea of the 'Militant' South," 20–24.

for in part by the work which the manufacturing plants of the South are to play in the nation's gigantic defense effort" and by the sale of the "'critical'" raw materials located in Dixie.[35]

Although all of the foregoing considerations were influential, loyalty to the Democratic Party was most decisive. In the last analysis and in a pattern identical to the 1914–17 period, the South supported Roosevelt's pre–World War II foreign policy because he was a Democrat. Comparing the voting patterns of the South's congressional Democrats on defense spending and foreign fiscal policy for the period of Republican control through 1932 with FDR's tenure from 1933 through 1941 provides striking evidence of this partisanship. For the 1921–32 years, southern Democratic congressmen voted favorably 44.7 percent of the time for army legislation and 64 percent of the time for navy bills; southern Democratic senators voted favorably on 52.7 percent of the army measures and 63.3 percent of the navy appropriations. For the 1933–41 period, the House percentages were 87.5 percent for army and 95.5 for navy bills, and the Senate figures were 78.3 and 90.7, respectively. The pattern for foreign fiscal initiatives such as loans, humanitarian aid, or debt reduction, was similar. Southern congressmen voted favorably 29.2 percent of the time during the first period and 94.4 during the second; Dixie's senators registered 35.5 and 91.5 figures. In roll-call votes on measures to relax the neutrality legislation, southern Democrats voted favorably 85 percent of the time—7 points higher than the next highest Democratic region in the Border States, 60 points higher than Republicans from New England, and 80 points higher than GOP representatives from the Great Plains. Indeed, when examined over the entire interwar period, the "South was more Democratic than it was belligerent."[36]

Following the attack on Pearl Harbor, the stimulus of defense spending far exceeded southern expectations. As they had done during both the Spanish-Cuban-American War and World War I, southerners aggressively pursued the South's portion of the national bounty. More than a year before the Japanese planes appeared over Hawaii, the Southern Governors Conference had reminded Washington of the region's "vast reservoirs of natural resources and available labor" and their relevance to expanded defense in-

35. Swain, *Harrison,* 243; Virginius Dabney, "The South Looks Abroad," *Foreign Affairs* 19 (October 1940): 176; Trubowitz, *Defining the Nationalist Interest,* 135.

36. Grassmuck, *Sectional Biases in Congress,* 31, 36, 39, 91, 99, 125, 127, 152 (quote); Key, *Southern Politics,* 353–54.

dustries. Congressman Lyndon Johnson explained his objectives to a group of Texas editors in 1943. It was "essential," he lectured, to secure defense contracts for "small Texas manufacturing plants," not only to aid the war effort but also "to bolster those firms which have been producing only for civilian needs" and to expand these plants "for normal demands of the future." Over the course of the war, Johnson and many even more well-placed southern congressmen, such as Richard Russell and Harry F. Byrd, worked effectively to direct military bases and defense plants to their states. In their relentless pursuit of defense dollars, southerners received critical aid from President Roosevelt, who perceived defense spending as the mechanism for modernizing the South and looked "kindly on efforts to build the South during the war."[37]

When faced with the disasters and deprivation of the depression, southerners had sought and readily accepted New Deal domestic aid, but they had done so with trepidation—with the fear that with federal aid would come federal interference in southern politics and race relations. By the eve of war, threatened changes in race and labor relations and the changing outlook of the national Democratic Party prompted some southerners to fear a second "reconstruction." Governor Eugene Talmadge of Georgia railed against the New Deal as a "combination of wetnursin', frenzied finance, downright communism, and plain damn-foolishness"; and Carter Glass warned in 1938 that the South should "begin thinking whether it will continue to cast its 152 electoral votes according to the memories of the Reconstruction . . . or will have spirit and courage enough to face the new Reconstruction era that northern so-called Democrats are menacing us with."[38]

Unlike domestic programs, military spending was not accompanied by the menace of federal intrusion. Southerners understood and agreed with *Business Week*'s distinction between "military pump priming" and "welfare pump priming." The former did not "really alter the structure of the economy. It goes through the regular channels"; the latter, by contrast, "makes new channels. . . . It creates new institutions. It redistributes income." It could lead to unwelcome social and economic changes.[39]

37. Tindall, *Emergence of the New South,* 695 (governors); Schulman, *From Cotton Belt to Sunbelt,* 100 (FDR); Robert Dallek, *Lone Star Rising: Lyndon Johnson and His Times, 1908–1960* (New York, 1991), 228.

38. Grantham, *South in Modern America,* 127 (Talmadge); Schulman, *From Cotton Belt to Sunbelt,* 47 (Glass).

39. Schulman, *From Cotton Belt to Sunbelt,* 133.

Although military pump priming ultimately helped effect far greater social and economic changes than southerners expected, it also played a pivotal role in transforming the southern economy in the 1940s. As had been
the case during World War I, the South received more than its share of
military bases and training centers. Of the nation's 110 new camps, more
than 60 were constructed in the South. Salubrious climate, available space,
and congressional clout once more proved decisive. Together with the expanded or refurbished older facilities such as Fort Benning, Georgia, which
became the Army's largest basic training base, these 60 new camps embodied $4 billion or approximately 36 percent of the funds expended for military
installations on the continent. The South's military bases were so numerous
that one northern trainee decided "the whole draft business is just a Southern trick . . . put over by Southern merchants to hold the big trade they get
from the training camps." The construction of the Pentagon proved far
more significant than any of the 60 new camps. Begun in September 1941,
the world's largest office complex of more than 4 million square feet vividly
embodied the presence of the military and broader defense establishment in
the South.[40]

Another $4.4 billion or 17.6 percent of the national expenditures for de-
fense industries were spent in Dixie. Although this figure fell short of the
region's 28 percent of the nation's population, it produced far-reaching economic results. Several key manufacturing sectors benefited: shipbuilding,
especially at Newport News, Norfolk, Charleston, and Houston, but also at
Tampa, Mobile, Pascagoula, Beaumont, Wilmington, New Orleans, and
other cities on both the Atlantic and Gulf Coasts; aircraft plants in Dallas-
Fort Worth and Marietta, Georgia, and parts production in Dallas, Tulsa,
New Orleans, Nashville, Birmingham, and Miami; ordnance plants in Rad-
ford, Virginia, Choteau, Oklahoma, and Kingsport and Chattanooga, Tennessee; petroleum refineries in Louisiana and Texas; synthetic rubber and
steel, especially in Texas; uranium at Oak Ridge; and nonferrous metals in
Louisiana, Texas, and Alabama.[41]

40. Graves, *Fighting South,* 104 (trainee); Charles W. Johnson, "V for Virginia: The Commonwealth Goes to War," *Virginia Magazine of History and Biography* 100 (July 1992): 372–73;
Tindall, *Emergence of the New South,* 694; Grantham, *South in Modern America,* 172; Smith, *War
and Wartime Changes,* 35; Sarah McCulloh Lemon, *North Carolina's Role in World War II* (Raleigh, N.C., 1964), 12, 20–23; John R. Skates Jr., "World War II as a Watershed in Mississippi
History," *Journal of Mississippi History* 37 (May 1975): 131–42.
41. Tindall, *Emergence of the New South,* 696–701; Grantham, *South in Modern America,*
173–76; Cooper and Terrill, *American South,* 667–69; Schulman, *From Cotton Belt to Sunbelt,*

These defense dollars helped bring "more rapid and greater change to the South than it had experienced since the Civil War." Most immediately, wartime demand rejuvenated agriculture. One observer proclaimed under the title, "King Cotton Joins Up": "Overnight the South's great cotton surplus was lifted from the depths of 'economic problem number 1' into the realm of national blessing. . . . For clothing purposes alone, the average soldier consumes 124 yards of cotton a year." This increased demand for southern agricultural products tripled net farm income even as the farm population declined by 20 percent and urban areas grew by 30 percent, and the trend begun during the New Deal toward a more mechanized and diverse southern agricultural sector was reinforced. Of even greater long-term significance, industrial capacity grew by 40 percent between 1939 and 1947; the number of industrial workers increased by 50 percent, from 1.3 to 2.8 million; manufacturing surpassed agriculture in 1944 as the primary source of income; and per capita income increased by 140 percent.[42]

While some of this progress eroded with the end of the war, much of it wrought fundamental and lasting change. Together with the Tennessee Valley Authority, these newer industries, unlike the South's traditional low-wage, first-stage processing plants, produced a more sophisticated regional technological community and a much higher concentration of skilled managers and workers. With the growth of these higher-wage, higher-productivity industries, the center of southern manufacturing shifted from the Southeast and North Carolina toward the Southwest and Texas. Aircraft and ship construction, petroleum refining, and steel and nonferrous metal production were coming to replace textiles and tobacco. And with these changes, which could not have occurred without the war and massive federal subvention, came the less tangible experiences and perspectives that were also crucial to the positioning of the South for its postwar economic "take-off." To be sure, the South had not yet overcome its position as the "Nation's No. 1 Economic Problem," but it had narrowed the gap and with the outbreak of the cold war stood poised to profit from ongoing and unprecedented defense spending.

Cumulative southern efforts in attracting defense dollars helped spark

92–102; Neil R. McMillen, ed., *Remaking Dixie: The Impact of World War II on the American South* (Jackson, Miss., 1977).

42. Cooper and Terrill, *American South,* 667–69 (change); McWilliams, *New South Faces the World,* 133 (King Cotton); see also this chapter's notes 40 and 41.

the first volleys of the "Sunbelt-Frostbelt" battle. Responding to Congressman Clyde T. Ellis's complaint in 1940 that Arkansas was not receiving its equitable share of defense contracts, John R. McDowell of Pennsylvania voiced the growing concern of many northerners. McDowell railed that Ellis wanted "to tear down our factories, throw out of work our working men, close up our mines and our mills, and remove them to the wild hills of the Ozarks where the business and prosperity will rebound to the everlasting glory of the Ozark hillbillies."[43]

Together with this welcome economic stimulus and the beginning of northern protests came other unsettling domestic developments. As the war progressed, southern Democratic politicians became convinced that their influence in the party was declining in proportion to the enhanced importance in party calculations of the Congress of Industrial Organizations and northern black voters. Although southerners fought off soldiers' voting bills, anti–poll tax legislation, most efforts at unionization, and renewal of the Fair Employment Practices Committee, Dixie's conservative white establishment perceived such overtures as attacks on southern labor and race relations and threats to states' rights.

In an action that embodied both the conservative South's subsequent proclivity for using national security as a rationale for opposing unwelcome change and the section's discomfort with the Democratic coalition, Howard Smith of Virginia in the House and Tom Connally in the Senate sponsored the War Labor Dispute Act of 1943. This measure required unions in defense plants to give thirty days' notice before striking, forbade union financial contributions in federal elections, and authorized the president to seize any defense plant idled by a strike. Other southern conservatives, such as Josiah Bailey, Harry F. Byrd, and Richard Russell, loudly applauded the bill and helped pass it over Roosevelt's veto. Byrd had earlier berated Secretary of Labor Frances Perkins's alleged lack of courage in failing to prevent labor from impairing the defense effort and suggested she be replaced by a "two-fisted man"; Smith would have gone well beyond this law in confronting supposed "dictators at home," such as John L. Lewis of the CIO.[44]

Potentially unruly labor distressed white southerners, but nothing trou-

43. Smith, *War and Wartime Changes,* 20 (McDowell); Roger W. Lotchin, "The Origins of the Sunbelt-Frostbelt Struggle: Defense Spending and City Building," in *Searching for the Sunbelt: Historical Perspectives on a Region,* ed. Raymond A. Mohl (Knoxville, Tenn., 1990), 47–49.

44. Heinemann, *Byrd,* 217; Bruce J. Dierenfield, *Keeper of the Rules: Congressman Howard W. Smith of Virginia* (Charlottesville, Va., 1987), 96.

bled them so profoundly as the prospect of unruly blacks. With the increased opportunities for work in defense plants and service in the military had come growing restiveness on the part of southern blacks. In 1943 Howard Odum, a sociologist at the University of North Carolina, noted correctly, "It was as if some universal message had come through to the great mass of Negroes urging them to dream new dreams and to protest against the old order."[45]

Southerners responded harshly to these dreams and restiveness and to the presence of northern black soldiers stationed in the region. In addition to demanding that rigid segregation be observed on military bases, as well as in all other segments of society, this response took more drastic and shocking forms. Private Felix Hall was lynched at Fort Benning in April 1941. Four years later, Sergeant Isaac Woodward was dragged from a bus in South Carolina, while in uniform, by a local sheriff who blinded the recently discharged soldier by shoving a nightstick into both his eyes. In the four years that separated these two incidents, numerous other racial confrontations occurred.[46]

In 1941 a shooting spree between white military police and black soldiers broke out on a military bus in Fayetteville, North Carolina. The following year black soldiers rioted in Alexandria, Louisiana, when sixteen thousand African American troops were limited to a four-block section of the town's black neighborhood. And in 1943 African American soldiers engaged in armed conflicts with white civilian and military police at Camps Van Dorn and McCain in Mississippi and Camp Stewart in Georgia. Southern whites were similarly hostile to black efforts to secure equal opportunities and treatment in the region's defense plants. For example, in May 1943 the promotion of twelve African Americans to the job of welder in a Mobile shipyard induced white workers to riot and required army intervention to restore order. The next month four thousand of Beaumont's white shipyard and refinery workers attacked the town's black residential areas in an orgy of destruction that left three dead, hundreds injured, and extensive property damage.[47]

Incidents such as these starkly demonstrated the absence of significant

45. Tindall, *Emergence of the New South*, 716.

46. Bernard C. Nalty, *Strength for the Fight: A History of Black Americans in the Military* (New York, 1986), 164, 204–5.

47. Tindall, *Emergence of the New South*, 715; Robert J. Norrell, with the assistance of Guy C. Vanderpool, *Dixie's War: The South and World War II* (Tuscaloosa, 1992), 35–39.

progress in southern race relations. Therefore, it is not surprising that the responses of black soldiers echoed those of their predecessors who had trained in the South during the Spanish-Cuban-American War and World War I. "The white civilians hate us," one trainee observed, "and we in turn despise them." Another lamented, "You ain't in the United States now. This is North Carolina."[48]

Even as they acted to retain the domestic status quo in many areas, well-placed southern leaders recognized that war offered an opportunity to realize Woodrow Wilson's vision of international organization and cooperation. Here again, the Wilsonian "lost cause" and Democratic politics, together with the desire to enforce peace for nationalist reasons, were more important to most southerners than an abstract devotion to internationalism. Only a distinct minority favored any real surrender of national sovereignty to accomplish international cooperation. Although the most ardent and organized groups advocating internationalism between the wars had been centered in northeastern metropolitan areas, there was an active southern contingent. Founded in 1937 and thereafter directed by Keener C. Frazier, a political scientist at the University of North Carolina, the Southern Council on International Relations energetically promoted a Wilsonian agenda in the years before and during World War II. The council, which received both financial aid and educational materials for distribution from the Carnegie Endowment for Peace, published the journal *The South and World Affairs* and heartily endorsed both Hull's reciprocal trade policies and an activist, cooperative U.S. involvement abroad.[49]

While there is no evidence that Frazier and his dogged band of associates directly influenced their representatives in Washington, both groups agreed that Wilsonian internationalism was a "Southern idea," and southern Democrats played a central role in the nation's planning for a postwar peace organization and for U.S. membership in the United Nations. As early as the spring and summer of 1942, Secretary Hull proclaimed that "some international agency must be created which can—by force, if necessary—keep the peace among nations in the future." Convinced that the nation needed "to make better preparation for world peace than was made at the close of the First World War," Hull appointed an Advisory Committee on Post-War Foreign Policy, on which southerners composed one-half of the member-

48. Numan V. Bartley, *The New South, 1945–1980* (Baton Rouge, 1995), 8.
49. McWilliams, *New South Faces the World*, 121–34.

ship. Always fearful that his efforts would provoke a backlash of "sinister forces," like those that plagued Wilson's advocacy of the League, the secretary thereafter worked steadily but cautiously for a postwar peace organization. When Russia agreed at the Moscow Conference in October 1943 to participate in an international organization, the seventy-two-year-old Wilsonian considered it his greatest achievement. As his health declined over the remainder of the war, he assumed the role of senior adviser to FDR in the campaign for the United Nations.[50]

Southern congressmen also played key roles. Senator Josiah Bailey spoke for most southerners as early as June 1942 when he declared, "We were stupid in 1918, 1919, 1920, and 1921—terribly stupid, I might say criminally stupid. We had the world in our hand in 1918, and we had peace only for the asking." In March 1943, Senator Lister Hill of Alabama acted on this presumption by joining Republicans Joseph H. Ball and Harold H. Burton and fellow Democrat Carl A. Hatch in sponsoring the B2H2 Resolution. This measure called for the formation of a permanent international organization. In addition to providing relief and the framework for the peaceful resolution of disputes, the proposed organization was to possess an international police force to "suppress by immediate use of . . . force any future attempt at military aggression by any nation." Far too aggressive for the Roosevelt administration and Hull, who feared a divisive and destructive public debate, B2H2 was promptly dispatched to the Foreign Relations Committee, where chairman Tom Connally kept it safely under wraps for the next eight months.[51]

During this hiatus and much to the disgust of Connally and the surprise of longtime internationalists, J. William Fulbright, a freshman congressman from the "rube state" of Arkansas, proceeded to "grab the ball and run for a touchdown when they [the Senate]" had not been able to "cross the goal line in twenty years." On April 5, 1943, Fulbright submitted a more moderate, more general resolution favoring "creation of appropriate international machinery with power adequate to prevent future aggression and to maintain lasting peace, and as favoring participation by the United States therein." With the blessing of the Democratic leadership, the Fulbright Resolution received House approval in September.[52]

50. Ibid., 138 (idea); Robert A. Divine, *Second Chance: The Triumph of Internationalism in America during World War II* (New York, 1967), 51, 67 (Hull).

51. Moore, *Bailey*, 227; Virginia Van der Veer Hamilton, *Lister Hill: Statesman from the South* (Chapel Hill, 1987), 100–2; Divine, *Second Chance*, 92.

52. Hamilton, *Hill*, 101 (goal line); Randall B. Woods, *Fulbright: A Biography* (New York, 1995), 80.

Reassured by the strong House vote and polls indicating that 81 percent of Americans favored U.S. membership in a postwar peace organization, Roosevelt approved Senate action. In October, Connally formulated his own resolution, calling for the United States to join "in the establishment and maintenance of international authority with power to prevent aggression and to preserve the peace of the world." Although stronger than Fulbright's vision, Connally's statement was disappointing to the more aggressive internationalists seeking an international police force. Senator Claude Pepper of Florida disparaged the Connally Resolution as "an Old Mother Hubbard," which "covers everything and touches nothing," and complained of "shadows of those figures who contested with Woodrow Wilson about the League of Nations." Despite such criticism, the Connally Resolution passed, and together with the Fulbright pronouncement, put the United States officially en route to membership in the United Nations.[53]

Pepper's reference to Wilson presaged a remarkable Wilson "revival" during 1944 that identified the fallen hero and his League of Nations with the pursuit of peace. Numerous books and a popular movie praised the former president and his efforts for international organization and urged the nation to seize the opportunity so grievously lost after World War I. At their July 1944 presidential nominating convention, Democrats referred repeatedly to their former leader, and Josephus Daniels of North Carolina introduced a highly-acclaimed resolution pledging the party to "complete the tragically unfulfilled task."[54]

Southern Democrats acted on this pledge. Tom Connally served as one of the U.S. delegates to the San Francisco Conference in April 1945 that established the United Nations; and, together with McClellan, Hill, Barkley, Pepper, Chandler, and Fulbright, he worked energetically and effectively to assure Senate approval of the UN Charter. No southern senators dissented in the 89 to 2 vote to approve the charter and U.S. membership, and southern legislators agreed with the *Atlanta Constitution*, which noted, "If among the hosts there [in the Senate] was one of that gaunt, plain, tired old Presbyterian, with his Presbyterian inflexibility and stubbornness, it would not be strange."[55]

53. Divine, *Second Chance*, 145, 148.
54. Ibid., 213.
55. Ibid., 313–14; Roberds, "South and United States Foreign Policy," 93 (*Constitution*).

This unanimous and positive vote of Dixie's senators conspicuously misrepresented the attitudes of the South's African Americans. Southern blacks again exposed the discrepancy between the nation's professed ideals and its practices at home and abroad. No blacks were included in the official U.S. delegation to San Francisco, but Roosevelt appointed as consultant-observers Walter White, secretary of the NAACP; W. E. B DuBois, NAACP's director of special research; and Mary McLeod Bethune, NAACP vice-president and a distinguished southern educator. In addition, a remarkable meeting of white and black college students at the University of North Carolina selected an interracial delegation to observe the UN Conference and elected Charles Proctor of Fisk University to chair a standing committee intended to become a "permanent interracial organization of college students working in the interest of democracy, justice, and peace."[56]

White, DuBois, and Bethune attempted unsuccessfully to have the U.S. delegation and the conference address the issues of racial justice, labor rights, full employment, and colonialism. Secretary of State Edward R. Stettinius Jr., a Virginian, believed that his "job in San Francisco was to create a charter . . . not to take up subjects like . . . 'the negro's question.'" As postwar relations with Russia grew ever more tenuous, the secretary refused to alienate the United States's Western European allies by pursuing the colonial question. Domestic political constraints reinforced his refusal to address racial or labor issues. The UN Charter faced a senatorial gauntlet manned by southern Democrats, and Tom Connally never allowed the U.S. delegation to forget that he would brook no interference with the South's practices in the areas of race and labor relations or that the Senate would reject any infringement upon U.S. sovereignty. The absence of attention to race and other human rights issues led Howard University professor Rayford Logan to dismiss the charter as a "tragic joke." Bethune declared that the conference had illustrated in "bold relief" the "common bond" between African Americans and colonial peoples and that the "Negro in America" occupied "little more than colonial status in a democracy." Even though these champions of black rights met only frustration, "the experience reaffirmed for Afro-Americans the growing sense of an interrelationship between domestic and foreign affairs." With the dawn of the cold war, this

56. Plummer, *Rising Wind*, 134.

interrelation of civil rights and foreign policy would become increasingly important.[57]

The South's central role in the formation and ratification of the United Nations proved to be the high point of the region's support for Wilsonian internationalism. Convinced that they were pursuing the goals of the section's fallen hero, southerners had doggedly argued for U.S. membership in the League of Nations, the World Court, and finally the United Nations. In addition to this endorsement of participation in international organizations, the South had sustained its traditional devotion to low tariffs and the aggressive pursuit of foreign markets. Southerners had bolstered their case for an ostensible commitment to internationalism by providing President Roosevelt his most dependable and strongest backing as the nation moved to confront the threats of Germany and Japan and ultimately to war. As had been the case prior to World War I, the South had been the most consistently interventionist portion of the country.

These actions did not reflect an abstract understanding of and dedication to internationalism. In fact, the South as a whole was no more willing than the remainder of the nation to surrender sovereign powers to an international agency. This was abundantly clear in the region's response to the labor and race issues at the San Francisco convention. Rather the South's advocacy of the League, the World Court, and the UN embodied another "lost cause"— this time to enact the "southern idea" of the first southern president since the 1860s. Similarly, the South's support for Roosevelt's prewar policies, much like the region's backing of Wilson's pre–World War I stands, derived primarily from the region's partisan Democratic politics and ongoing need to demonstrate its patriotism and concern for the nation's security and survival. The responsibility that accompanied congressional leadership in the 1930s again influenced the South to follow executive leadership, as did the prospect and, after 1940, the real benefits of defense spending. In short, partisan politics, economics, and sectional pride were more influential than devotion to internationalism or a southern military tradition.[58]

57. Carol Anderson, "From Hope to Disillusion: African Americans, the United States, and the Struggle for Human Rights, 1944–1947," *Diplomatic History* 20 (fall 1996): 536 (Stettinius), 541–42 (Logan and Bethune); Plummer, *Rising Wind,* 152 (experience).

58. For commentary on the South's commitment to internationalism, see Alexander DeConde, "The South and Isolationism," *Journal of Southern History* 24 (August, 1958): 332–46; George C. Herring and Gary R. Hess, "Regionalism and Foreign Policy: The Dying Myth of Southern Internationalism," *Southern Studies* 20 (fall 1981): 268–77; and Charles O. Lerche Jr., *The Uncertain South: Its Changing Pattern of Politics in Foreign Policy* (Chicago, 1964), 257–71.

Indeed, the absence, or at least relative weakness, of a genuine southern commitment to internationalism would become even more apparent as the nation passed through the most intense period of the cold war. Over the years from 1945 through 1973, the South's nationalist and unilateral tendencies and devotion to a policy of containment of Communism based on a strong centralized military and directed by a powerful executive emasculated any argument for the South's peculiar attachment to international cooperation.

CHAPTER 7

Containing Communism and
Rejecting Internationalism, 1945–1973

B Y RESPONDING TO THE COLD WAR confrontation with the Soviet Union and China on the bases of distinctly southern perceptions and interests, Dixie sustained a practice established over the previous 150 years. While defending the region's customary post-1945 position in support of large defense appropriations and the use of force to promote foreign policy interests, Senator Richard Russell lectured a midwestern colleague that he would "be more military minded too if Sherman had crossed North Dakota," and the crusty Georgian similarly advised the Eisenhower administration that U.S. troops would be better used to counter the "red threat" rather than in an "undeclared war on the South" and its school systems. Congressman L. Mendel Rivers of South Carolina explored the lengths that some southerners were prepared to go in the unilateral opposition to Communism by justifying the use of nuclear weapons in the mid-1960s. He asserted that the United States was "merely postponing the final victory of Red China—unless the nation is prepared to risk the possible consequences of destroying her nuclear capability."[1]

Not all southerners would have been comfortable with the use of nuclear weapons, but the great majority would have applauded John C. Stennis when he placed patriotism and honor at the center of foreign policy considerations, Allen J. Ellender when he objected to U.S. foreign aid allocations,

1. Gilbert C. Fite, *Richard B. Russell Jr., Senator from Georgia* (Chapel Hill, 1991), 353, 363; Will F. Huntley, "Mighty Rivers of Charleston" (Ph.D. dissertation, University of South Carolina, 1993), 287–88.

and George Wallace when he disputed the viability of the less-developed nations created after 1945. In 1965, Stennis demanded that the Johnson administration "jerk this [antiwar] movement up by the roots and grind it to bits." The Mississippi senator also castigated CBS for publicizing "this deplorable and shameful activity on the part of those who have no regard for duty, honor, or their country." Ellender directed his protest over foreign aid spending toward Japan in 1956. "The Japs," he declared, "need no help." First, they were a "competent" rather than "backward" people, but more fundamentally, foreign aid was a "shameful expenditure of public funds." "Backward" people were no more deserving of U.S. economic or diplomatic support. After all, Wallace asserted, "All these countries with niggers in 'em have stayed the same for a thousand years."[2]

Like Russell, the great majority of southern representatives and their constituents were dependable backers of policies designed to contain Communism. Staunchly anticommunist, most southerners discarded all pretense of internationalism. They were consistently more pessimistic than other Americans about the long-term prospects for international peace and the ability of Third World, nonwhite countries to function successfully, were acutely sensitive to any threat of interference with southern race relations, and were more inclined to use force in the international arena. Based on these assumptions, most southerners and their representatives in Congress adopted a nationalistic policy that emphasized a strong and active military; uneasiness with arms control; hostility toward the United Nations, immigration, and foreign aid; a proclivity for tariff protectionism; and the endorsement of interventionism in less-developed countries. Many southerners continued to declare their allegiance to Woodrow Wilson and his principles, but Dixie's foreign policy positions seldom reflected a truly cooperative, liberal internationalism. Rather while supporting U.S. involvement abroad, this involvement needed to be on American terms. A unilateral emphasis characterized this independent international perspective.

Dramatic changes in the South's economy, society, and politics after World War II heightened southern insecurities and strengthened the region's preexisting foreign policy proclivities. While becoming significantly

---

2. Michael S. Downs, "A Matter of Conscience: John C. Stennis and the Vietnam War" (Ph.D. dissertation, Mississippi State University, 1989), 69; Thomas A. Becnel, *Senator Allen Ellender of Louisiana: A Biography* (Baton Rouge, 1995), 209; Dan T. Carter, *From George Wallace to Newt Gingrich: Race in the Conservative Counterrevolution, 1963–1994* (Baton Rouge, 1996), 7.

more mechanized, diversified, and productive, southern agriculture ceased to be the basis of the region's economy. The number of farmers decreased greatly; the size of farms grew; and King Cotton was dethroned. In 1950, 2.1 million southerners cultivated farms that averaged 93 acres; by 1975, the number of farmers had dwindled to 720,000, and their farms averaged 216 acres. Many persons, nearly 14 million between 1940 and 1980, left the land. By 1960, only 15 percent of southerners lived on farms, and by 1980 the number had decreased to 3 percent. By 1975, soybeans, livestock, poultry, tobacco, and dairy farming occupied much greater acreage, and cotton income failed to head any southern state's agricultural tally sheet.[3]

As agriculture declined in importance, the industrial and service sectors grew apace. Between 1940 and 1980, nonagricultural jobs increased from 7.8 million to 25.9 million, and the number of southerners working in manufacturing went from 1.9 million to 3.4 million. Although traditional industries such as textiles, coal, and steel grew, the bulk of the "boom" came in construction, food processing, consumer durables, and newer industries such as petrochemicals and defense-related endeavors. With industrialization came urbanization. By 1960, 58 percent of southerners had moved to the city, and by the 1980s the figure climbed to 75 percent—a population distribution much like the remainder of the country.[4]

This massive shift of people and economic emphases was a wrenching process. The post–World War II Civil Rights movement further intensified the white South's sense of displacement and anxiety. With the steadily increasing restiveness of southern African Americans, the erratic but growing presidential inclination to support racial reform, the activist federal courts, and the national and international focus on the issue, Dixie adopted a "resurgent southern sectionalism." Senator Russell again spoke for his fellow white southerners when he declared, "The white people of the Southern states . . . the most despised and mistreated minority in the country." Seeking to fend off what they viewed as radical social changes, southerners expressed this resurgent sectionalism through verbal pyrotechnics, political obstructionism, legal maneuvering, token integration, and violence—all of

---

3. Dewey W. Grantham, *The South in Modern America: A Region at Odds* (New York, 1994), 260; Numan V. Bartley, *The New South, 1945–1980* (Baton Rouge, 1995), 286.

4. Grantham, *South in Modern America*, 261; William J. Cooper Jr. and Thomas E. Terrill, *The American South: A History* (New York, 1996), 740.

which elicited even harsher northern and international condemnation and heightened solidarity within the South.[5]

The transformation of southern politics derived from and compounded the impact of these economic, social, and racial changes. The national Democratic Party's move leftward and greater solicitude for the interests of labor and especially for blacks led the South to defect from the New Deal coalition by the end of the 1940s. The South's rejection of the Democratic Party in presidential politics ensued with the Dixiecrat revolt in 1948 and Eisenhower's victory in five southern states in 1952 and culminated with Nixon sweeping the South in 1972. By the mid-1960s, the Democratic Party had also declined on the local level. From 1952 to 1968, the proportion of southerners who considered themselves Democrats fell from two-thirds to about one-half. Through the 1960s, southern Republicans held steady at about 20 percent with the remaining 30 percent becoming "independents." In a transformation as dramatic as the displacement of King Cotton, the Republicans supplanted the Democrats as Dixie's "traditional" party.[6]

Despite these vast changes, the new Sunbelt South exhibited many familiar characteristics. The South of the 1980s remained dependent, albeit less so, on the North economically. It also remained the nation's poorest region, with 25 percent of the country's population and 40 percent of its poor. The ranks of the southern poor contained America's highest proportion of poverty-stricken children, and poverty among blacks "remained especially pronounced." Indeed, areas of the Black Belt, Appalachia, and the Ozarks "more closely resembled Third World countries than the Sunbelt."[7]

Against this backdrop of far-reaching economic, social, and political transformation on the domestic front, southerners joined other Americans in responding to equally radical and troubling changes in the international arena. Even as southerners played a crucial role in the drafting and ratification of the United Nations Charter in the summer of 1945, the prospect of ongoing cooperation between the United States and the Soviet Union grew increasingly remote. Russia tightened its grip on Eastern Europe and showed no inclination to withdraw. Over the next year, a series of international confrontations starkly revealed that the wartime coalition would not

---

5. Grantham, *South in Modern America*, 194–212, 237 (Russell).
6. Bartley, *New South*, 389–87; Grantham, *South in Modern America*, 247 (traditional).
7. Bartley, *New South*, 444–45; Cooper and Terrill, *American South*, 733 and 742 (quotes).

survive the defeat of Germany and Japan. Joseph Stalin proclaimed an on-going conflict between communism and capitalism; the U.S.S.R. probed neighboring areas such as Iran and Manchuria; and U.S.-Russian disagreements over the control of atomic energy heightened tensions and further reduced the prospects for international cooperation. Crises followed in Greece, Berlin, and China from 1947 through 1949. The cold war had begun, and the United States responded with the containment policy designed to circumscribe Russian and ultimately all Communist expansion.

While reacting to the events of the early cold war between 1945 and 1953, the South established patterns that would persist over the next two decades. When confronted with this new foreign threat, southern devotion to internationalism and faith in the United Nations as a peacekeeping agency faded quickly and the region's anticommunism came to the fore. By August 1946, 74 percent of southerners predicted another war within twenty-five years; a year later the percentage had grown to 78 who foresaw war within ten years. Consistent with this pessimistic outlook concerning world peace and a determination to confront Communist threats, southerners emphasized a strong defense and the direct response to perceived Soviet threats rather than participation in the UN. Nationalism and unilateral action took precedence over international cooperation.[8]

Southern ambivalence toward foreign aid provided one of the early indicators of these attitudes. Southern congressmen adhered to the preferences of the Truman administration in 1945 by helping to extend the lending authority of the Export-Import Bank and authorizing $550 million for the United Nations Relief and Rehabilitation Agency. But they grumbled about the allocations. Tennessee senator Kenneth D. McKellar complained that the funds were being spent on industrial goods rather than southern agricultural "surpluses," and Congressman Graham Barden of North Carolina voiced the familiar southern priority of domestic over foreign needs by declaring that he thought more of his own "nation" than all the other forty-three members of the UN agency.[9]

The $3.75 billion loan to Great Britain in 1946 elicited a similar pattern of southern congressional complaints followed by strong majority support

---

8. Alfred O. Hero Jr., *The Southerner and World Affairs* (Baton Rouge, 1965), 105.

9. Elmo M. Roberds Jr., "The South and United States Foreign Policy, 1933–1952" (Ph.D. dissertation, University of Chicago, 1954), 111–12.

for the request of the Democratic president. Most southern papers and key representatives, such as McKellar and Senator Alben W. Barkley of Kentucky, endorsed the bill. Proponents emphasized that Great Britain was among the South's foremost southern export customers and that the British would help the United States promote its free-trade agenda. The continuing influence of wartime cooperation and Anglophile tendencies reinforced this primary economic motivation. Still, there were shrill dissenters. Senator Theodore Bilbo of Mississippi declared he was "tired of the idea of being a Santa Claus to the British." Harry F. Byrd of Virginia and Richard Russell were more important opponents; they objected to foreign aid generally and worried about its effect on the federal budget. Russell also voiced the South's nationalist and unilateralist inclinations. The Georgia senator had argued as early as 1943 that the United States should retain key military bases "fortified and developed with American money and sweat" during the war, and he refused to vote for this loan without territorial compensation from the British. Seven of 17 southern senators and 13 of 86 southern representatives registered these reservations by voting against the appropriation.[10]

As cold war divisions hardened during the late 1940s, the South's anticommunism, long tradition of party solidarity, and perceived economic interests took precedence over differences with President Harry Truman and northern Democrats, and Dixie's congressmen furnished crucial leadership and support for confronting international Communism and implementing containment. In the process, southerners gave increasing prominence to their resurgent fiscal conservatism and discomfort with foreign aid. In March 1947 President Truman requested a $400 million allocation to resist Communist expansion in Greece and Turkey. In appealing to Congress and the nation to shoulder this burden, Truman asserted expansively "that it must be the policy of the United States to support free people who are resisting attempted subjugation by armed minorities or by outside pressure." As he would do with the other key components of the early containment structure, Senator Tom Connally of Texas marshaled the Democratic forces from his chairmanship of the Senate Foreign Relations Committee. In the House, southerners contributed 86 positive and only 3 negative votes to the

10. Irving Howards, "The Influence of Southern Senators on American Foreign Policy from 1939 to 1950" (Ph.D. dissertation, University of Wisconsin, 1955), 96 (Bilbo); Fite, *Russell,* 194; Roberds, "South and United States Foreign Policy," 116–17, 346–48, 364–65.

287 to 107 margin. Only four of Connally's regional colleagues resisted his overtures.[11]

These impressive voting figures masked the concerns of several important senators, who, while disagreeing with one another, raised significant long-term questions about U.S. containment policy. Senator Claude Pepper of Florida, who had previously cautioned that a "get-tough" approach to dealing with other nations would only incite them to acquire "bigger sticks, and . . . begin that never ending vicious cycle of measure and counter-measure," deemed the Truman Doctrine too anti-Russian. He contended that rather than drawing territorial lines and intensifying the cold war, Congress should "rededicate this country to the United Nations and to its high purpose to maintain international peace and security." Senator J. William Fulbright harbored greater concerns over the Russian threat and acknowledged that in the short run Truman's application of the "ancient principle of balance of power" was the only recourse. However, Fulbright also shared Pepper's commitment to international cooperation. The Arkansan, who had previously argued for world government, suggested that a supranational European federation might be a viable alternative to an overly intrusive U.S. role. Despite his endorsement of an activist U.S. containment policy, Fulbright, whom Truman had characterized as "Senator Halfbright" and an "over-educated Oxford S.O.B.," worried appropriately about the fiscal implications of containment. "If we undertake the support of Greece and Turkey," he asked, "how and when can we stop the lavish outpouring of our resources?"[12]

Although Harry F. Byrd proceeded from a far more narrowly nationalistic perspective and from no real commitment to internationalism or the Wilsonian legacy, he shared Fulbright's fears over the ill-defined limits of the Truman Doctrine. The chronically obstructionist Virginian favored a hard line in confronting the U.S.S.R. and was emerging as a rigid cold warrior and proponent of extensive spending on U.S. military defense, but the Truman Doctrine seemed too open-ended and smacked too much of foreign aid. "In voting on military and economic aid to Greece and Turkey we

11. *Congressional Record*, 80th Cong., 1st sess., 3793, 4975; Roberds, "South and United States Foreign Policy," 147–48. The overall southern vote in the Senate was 18 to 4.

12. Thomas G. Paterson, "The Dissent of Senator Claude Pepper," in *Cold War Critics: Alternatives to American Foreign Policy in the Truman Years*, ed. Thomas G. Paterson (Chicago, 1971), 124; Roberds, "South and United States Foreign Policy," 147; Randall B. Woods, *Fulbright: A Biography* (New York, 1995), 126–27, 138.

are not voting for aid to these two nations," Byrd asserted correctly, "we are voting on a global policy . . . which will carry American dollars to many other foreign countries." Before undertaking "new and gigantic financial obligations," he said, the nation should assess its resources. Pepper and Byrd occupied opposite ends of the spectrum, and Fulbright fell somewhere in between, but all three expressed prescient concerns.[13]

Byrd's fears soon materialized in 1947 when Secretary of State George C. Marshall offered U.S. help in rebuilding war-torn European economies. Popularly known as the Marshall Plan, the European Recovery Program ultimately provided $13 billion to the Western Europeans. These dollars strengthened Western Europe against a possible Communist threat and helped reinvigorate the economies of the principal U.S. trading partners. The most successful U.S. foreign aid program of the postwar period, the Marshall Plan, like the British loan and Truman Doctrine, ultimately commanded strong southern congressional support. The region and its representatives were adamantly anticommunist and understood that a third of U.S. cotton and tobacco products were sold in Western Europe. House Minority Leader Sam Rayburn of Texas urged that the United States aid those in danger of being "smothered by Communism" and hoped that "this thing called isolation may not crawl out of the shadows and defeat the hopes of men and again break the hearts of the world." Mississippi senator James O. Eastland warned that failure to recoup these "historic markets" would destroy "the private enterprise system in the United Sates," and Representative Brooks Hays of Arkansas contended that "once Europe is rehabilitated, there will be automatically created a large market for the wide variety of goods produced on the farms and in the factories of the South."[14]

Not all southerners were convinced that these trade prospects warranted the expense. One Mississippian asked if defeated Confederate soldiers had appealed to the "victorious North for 'lend lease,' largess or even flour, of which it had plenty?" Senators Byrd, Ellender, Russell, Walter George of Georgia, Kenneth D. McKellar of Tennessee, Olin D. Johnston of South Carolina, W. Lee O'Daniel of Texas, and John J. McClellan of Alabama agreed. They criticized the size of the early allocations ($5.3 billion initially

13. Ronald L. Heinemann, *Harry Byrd of Virginia* (Charlottesville, Va., 1996), 249.
14. D. B. Hardeman and Donald C. Bacon, *Rayburn: A Biography* (Austin, 1987), 328–29; Roberds, "South and United States Foreign Policy," 155 (Eastland and Hays); Howards, "Influence of Southern Senators," 102–17.

and another $4.65 billion in 1949) and worried about the impact on the U.S. budget. These fiscal conservatives repeatedly and unsuccessfully attempted to reduce these sums, and in attacks that demonstrated the growing rift between the South and the Truman administration, often lambasted the State Department and its representatives for alleged mismanagement and inefficiencies. Despite this bickering, Democratic politics, economic calculations, and cold war fears prevailed, and the South fell in line behind the second major initiative of the evolving containment policy. The southern vote was 20 to 3 in the Senate and 82 to 7 in the House. Only Senators Byrd and O'Daniel and Representative Doughton voted against both the Truman Doctrine and Marshall Plan.[15]

In 1949 southerners also helped approve and implement the North Atlantic Treaty Organization (NATO), the third central component of containment in the 1940s. Signed in April, the NATO alliance, which included the United States, Canada, and ten Western European nations, was a collective security agreement stipulating that an attack on any one of the members was to be considered an attack on them all. Although the United States was not literally obligated to go to the aid of its allies, that was the clear understanding; and the treaty signified the formation of the collective ability to resist a potential Russian attack.

Southern senators voted unanimously to ratify the North Atlantic Treaty in July, but key legislators reiterated their growing objections to foreign aid—even foreign military aid—when presented with the Mutual Defense Assistance Act of 1949 later in the year. This appropriation funded the alliance by bolstering the military capability of the Europeans. The now familiar triumvirate of southern economizers in the Senate, Byrd, Russell, and George, sought to reduce the administration request for $1.3 billion. All three expressed concern for the nation's fiscal integrity. George believed it was time for the "American businessman . . . to make some money," and he worried that taxes would "go up, not down." Increased taxes would "weaken America," he said, and "if America is weakened, a great prop . . . back of the Atlantic community will be removed." From the House, the lesser-known Boyd Tackett of Arkansas echoed this theme and added his objection to Americans being taxed "to assist socialistic England."[16]

15. *Congressional Record*, 80th Cong., 2d sess., 2793, 3874–75; Roberds, "South and United States Foreign Policy," 151 (Mississippian); Susan M. Hartmann, *Truman and the 80th Congress* (Columbia, Mo., 1971), 63–64, 162, 164.

16. Roberds, "South and United States Foreign Policy," 170–71.

Administration supporters were equally familiar. Tom Connally again managed the legislation and chaired a series of combined meetings of the Senate Foreign Relations and Armed Services Committees. The crafty Texan helped bring his old ally Walter George into line by asking the Georgia senator if he would "let our friends be picked off one by one like pigeons in a shooting gallery for want of a few dollars of military aid." In the House, Speaker Rayburn shamed recalcitrant southern Democrats and Republican naysayers when he observed that "those who speak the loudest against communism are found wanting" when action was required. Connally and Rayburn held the majority of southerners in line, but the 7 negative votes from the South in the Senate and the 13 in the House were more than the total Democrat opposition from all other regions combined.[17]

The South endorsed President Truman's decision to send U.S. troops to repulse Communist North Korea's invasion of American-supported South Korea in June 1950. Senator Lyndon Johnson voiced the South's familiar call to honor and patriotism, as well as the region's staunch anticommunism and hardening cold war posture. Johnson termed Truman's action "courageous and essential" and declared, "The world has expected the United States to lead the free nations unafraid and unbullied. Now we are showing that we mean what we say." Over the first five months of the conflict, southerners joined the Texas senator in rallying to the cause, but when Chinese Communist forces came to the aid of the North Koreans in October and the war settled into a stalemate, both the southern public and its representatives grew impatient with Truman's decision to fight a limited war.[18]

Southerners had even greater difficulty than other Americans in adjusting to cold war constraints on the U.S. ability to pursue victory in traditional terms. Accustomed to virtually unbroken success in international affairs, all Americans bridled at the limits imposed by formidable adversaries such as Russia and China and the threat of nuclear war, but southerners voiced even greater frustration and a greater inclination to disregard these limits in the pursuit of victory. Simply containing Communist foes without clear military and political gains was not sufficient.

Public opinion polls revealed that southerners were more willing than

17. Ibid., 170–71 (Rayburn), 352–53, 366–67; Tom Connally, as told to Alford Steinberg, *My Name is Tom Connally* (New York, 1954), 339; Howards, "Influence of Southern Senators," 93–94.

18. Robert Dallek, *Lone Star Rising: Lyndon Johnson and His Times, 1908–1960* (New York, 1991), 383.

other Americans to attack the Chinese and North Koreans north of the thirty-eighth parallel that divided North and South Korea, to launch air and naval attacks on China, and even to use atomic weapons. In stands that forecast his attitudes on Vietnam, Senator Russell opposed a ground war with the North Koreans and Chinese and argued instead that the United States should bomb strategic targets in China until the Chinese withdrew and ended the war on U.S. terms. Senator John C. Stennis of Mississippi agreed and called upon Truman to pursue total victory, a demand he and numerous other southerners would repeat often over the next two decades. Stennis implied that this pursuit could include the use of atomic weapons, as he favored "hitting the enemy with everything we have until terms are met." Not only did southerners avow their primary faith in military force, some, such as Harry F. Byrd, asserted that the Korean War demonstrated the futility of foreign aid generally. South Korea's weakness after many years of U.S. aid revealed that American largess had not only failed to deter Communist aggression but also threatened U.S. solvency. "We cannot," Byrd proclaimed, "carry the world on our shoulders abroad and the New Deal on our backs at home without destroying the foundation principles of our democracy."[19]

Consistent with this demand for victory and willingness to expand the war to achieve it, the South supported General Douglas MacArthur in his confrontation with President Truman. When Truman dismissed the U.S. commander in Korea for refusing to accept the administration's decision for a limited war, 69 percent of white southerners, versus 55 percent of northerners, sided with MacArthur. Only 17 percent of southerners endorsed the president's decision, as opposed to 36 percent of northern residents. Several southern representatives, such as Byrd and Allen J. Ellender of Louisiana in the Senate and L. Mendel Rivers of South Carolina in the House, were publicly critical; other more liberal Democrats, such as Fulbright and Estes Kefauver of Tennessee, sided with Truman. Even more important, key southern leaders deftly disposed of the issue in an effort to avoid Republican political gains. Russell, Connally, and Rayburn, with the aid of internationalist Republicans, arranged for joint hearings of the Senate Armed Services and Foreign Relations Committees. The hearings were held in executive

19. Hero, *Southerner and World Affairs*, 112–13; Fite, *Russell*, 253; Downs, "A Matter of Conscience," 15 (Stennis); Heinemann, *Byrd*, 299.

session, no reports (either majority or minority) were issued, and the old soldier did indeed fade away.[20]

The South's preference for military solutions and demand for victory in cold war conflicts was evident in other international crises from 1954 through 1965. During the second Eisenhower administration, Senate Majority Leader Lyndon Johnson exercised the most significant influence on southern congressmen and hence the South's direct response to U.S. foreign policy. As a "liberal nationalist," Johnson understood both the need for a strong defense and the domestic economic benefits that the South derived from the military budget. He also agreed with Walter George, whom he succeeded in the mid-1950s as the South's principal spokesman on foreign policy, that bipartisanship was essential in addressing the nation's challenges abroad. In August 1956, Johnson declared that "politics stops at the water's edge when the security of our country is at stake." Finally, the ever-ambitious Texan's presidential aspirations required that he adopt clear, informed, and responsible foreign policy positions.[21]

Working within both this larger set of regional inclinations and his more personal considerations, Johnson skillfully marshaled southern support for Eisenhower's intervention to derail a left-leaning revolution in Guatemala in 1954. The following year he oversaw the passage of the Senate resolution giving Eisenhower the authority to defend the islands of Quemoy and Matsu against attack by the Peoples Republic of China. During the Middle East crisis of 1956, LBJ joined other southerners, who cared little for either President Gamal Abdel Nasser or vast increases in the growth of irrigated Egyptian cotton, in opposing U.S. funding of the Aswan Dam in Egypt. Following Nasser's seizure of the Suez Canal and the British-French-Israeli invasion of Egypt, LBJ artfully separated himself and the Democrats from the Eisenhower administration by opposing sanctions against Israel while he and southern senators simultaneously backed the Eisenhower Doctrine, which proclaimed that the "United States would use all means at its disposal

20. Hero, *Southerner and World Affairs,* 112; Roberds, "South and United States Foreign Policy," 220–21; Fite, *Russell,* 256–57, 263; Dallek, *Lone Star Rising,* 399–402; Burton I. Kaufman, *The Korean War: Challenges in Crisis, Credibility, and Command* (New York, 1986), 165, 167–69, 173–77.

21. Dallek, *Lone Star Rising,* 464 (liberal nationalist); Philip A. Walker Jr., "Lyndon B. Johnson's Senate Foreign Policy Activism: The Suez Canal Crisis, a Reappraisal," *Presidential Studies Quarterly* 26 (fall 1996): 998 (Johnson).

to preserve the integrity and independence of the nations of the Middle East."[22]

The South's proclivity for the use of force and adamant anticommunism remained prominent as the United States entered the decade of the 1960s. When polled in 1960, Dixie was more willing than the rest of the nation to confront the Soviet Union about access to Berlin, and over the ensuing ten years, southerners were consistently more opposed than other Americans to granting the People's Republic of China membership in the United Nations.[23]

Southerners also strongly supported President John F. Kennedy's abortive effort to overthrow Cuba's Fidel Castro with the Bay of Pigs invasion of April 1961. Senator George A. Smathers of Florida and Congressman L. Mendel Rivers spoke for a majority of southerners. Smathers, who admitted that Castro became "an obsession with me," described the Cuban government as a "bloody-handed left-wing dictatorship" headed by a "tyrant and megalomaniac . . . Fuhrer Fidel," and the senator prescribed an economic embargo and hemispheric "peace patrol" to block Cuban attempts to foment revolution in other Latin American countries. Rivers agreed that "further Communist imperialism . . . must not be permitted to spread"; the United States needed to disregard Russia's potentially hostile response and "clear the trash out of our backyard."[24]

When Kennedy moved to cleanse the U.S. backyard, he summoned Senator Fulbright, who had become chairman of the Senate Foreign Relations Committee in 1959, to the State Department on April 4, 1961. Fulbright met with the president, Secretary of State Dean Rusk, Secretary of Defense Robert McNamara, CIA chief Allen Dulles, and three members of the Joint Chiefs of Staff. After a briefing on the proposed invasion at the Bay of Pigs, Fulbright shocked this powerful group by warning that the United States could expect no positive outcome. If Castro were overthrown, the United

22. Dallek, *Lone Star Rising*, 478–79, 481, 511–13, 516.

23. Hero, *Southerner and World Affairs*, 125–26, 240–41; *Gallup Opinion Index* (hereafter cited as GOI), No. 8 (January 1966): 15; GOI, No. 17 (October 1966): 16; GOI, No. 45 (March 1969): 18; GOI, No. 65 (November 1970): 9. The Gallup Poll defined the South as the eleven Confederate states plus Kentucky and Oklahoma.

24. Brian L. Crispell, *Testing the Limits: George Armistead Smathers and Cold War America* (Athens, Ga., 1999), 159, 163; George A. Smathers Oral History, October 24, 1989, pp. 5–6, John Fitzgerald Kennedy Library, Boston, Mass. (hereafter cited as JFK Library); Huntley, "Mighty Rivers," 198–99.

States would be depicted as an imperialist invader of a small Latin American country; if he survived, the United States would appear impotent and ineffectual. Unfortunately, the influence of the invasion's proponents and bureaucratic momentum overwhelmed Fulbright's logic. On April 17, Castro's forces decimated the CIA-sponsored invaders, and on May 2, Walter Lippman proclaimed in the *Washington Post*, to the discomfort of the JFK administration, that Fulbright had been "the only wise man in the lot."[25]

Kennedy acted with much greater success to halt the activation of Soviet intercontinental ballistic missiles in Cuba in October 1962, and the South joined the rest of the nation in rendering virtually unanimous support. In the face of a naval quarantine and the threat of direct U.S. military intervention in Cuba, Soviet premier Nikita Khrushchev relented and removed the missiles. Both Fulbright and Richard Russell attended a briefing on October 22, just before Kennedy informed the nation of the Russian missiles and his proposed response. The young president must have been astonished at the Arkansan's advice, given his prior opposition to the Bay of Pigs operation. This time the senator joined Russell in arguing for a surgical air strike or conventional military invasion to ensure destruction of the missiles. Russell's stance was consistent; Fulbright's was an aberration, perhaps momentarily influenced by his senior colleague or even by Vice-President Lyndon Johnson, who also "favored an unannounced [air] strike" rather than the naval blockade, which, he said, would needlessly forecast "'our punch.'" Fortunately, Kennedy heeded the advice of more cautious advisers such as Secretary of State Dean Rusk. The steady Georgian argued persuasively for the quarantine on the grounds that "when two nuclear superpowers are at each other's jugular vein," it was imperative not to force the opponent "into a corner from which there is no escape." The president's rejection of the more bellicose southern posture in favor of Rusk's advice may well have avoided a nuclear exchange and World War III.[26]

Fulbright's condemnation of the U.S. invasion of the Dominican Republic in April 1965 was more characteristic of his uneasiness with the overly aggressive use of American power, especially at the expense of smaller, less-developed countries. Even in the cold war's most tense periods, Fulbright's

25. Woods, *Fulbright*, 267–69.

26. Ibid., 271–73; Robert Dallek, *Flawed Giant: Lyndon Johnson and His Times, 1961–1973* (New York, 1998), 87; Thomas J. Schoenbaum, *Waging Peace and War: Dean Rusk in the Truman, Kennedy, and Johnson Years* (New York, 1988), 314.

southern heritage and commitment to Wilsonian internationalism usually enabled him to look beyond rigid anticommunism and to gain an affinity for the nationalism and fear of outside domination that gripped Third World countries. Asserting that "the very word 'Yankee' still awakens in Southern minds historical memories of defeat and humiliation," he argued that southerners were particularly sensitive to foreign interventions.[27]

These sensibilities prompted his attack on President Johnson's decision to dispatch 22,000 U.S. and Organization of American States (OAS) troops to the Dominican Republic. Warned by American diplomats that former president Juan Bosch, an alleged Communist supported by Cuban-trained accomplices, was about to seize power, LBJ acted to forestall the "establishment of another Communist government in the Western Hemisphere." The president served notice that his administration was not about "to sit here in our rocking chair with our hands folded" while the "lives of thousands, the liberty of a nation, and the principles and values of all the American Republics" were at risk. As doubts arose regarding Bosch's Communism and the actual prospect of a radical takeover, Johnson astonished assembled reporters in early May by asserting that Americans had been in danger and that "some 1,500 innocent people were murdered and shot, and their heads cut off" prior to the U.S. intervention.[28]

Fulbright was incredulous. Increasingly distressed at the rapidly expanding U.S. involvement in Vietnam, he also objected to LBJ's rigidly anticommunist and interventionist Latin American policy. In his "Old Myths and New Realities" speech to the Senate the previous May, Fulbright had asserted that Castro's attempts to export his revolution posed no threat to the United States. Americans needed to recognize that democratic change and reform in Latin America would often involve violence and that the United States should tolerate and work with Communist nations that constituted no security threat. Not only did the U.S. intervention in the Dominican Republic conflict with this policy perspective, but hearings before the Senate Foreign Relations Committee also cast into doubt much of the administration's factual rationale for sending troops. On September 15 Fulbright charged in a Senate speech that U.S. diplomats had exaggerated the Communist threat and danger to American lives and property. The senator could

---

27. Randall B. Woods, "Dixie's Dove: J. William Fulbright, the Vietnam War, and the American South," *Journal of Southern History* 60 (August 1994): 548.

28. Dallek, *Flawed Giant*, 265–66; Woods, *Fulbright*, 379–80.

find no evidence that "Communists at any time actually had control of the revolution"; moreover, given professed U.S. adherence to the charter of the OAS, Johnson had "intervened . . . unilaterally—and illegally."[29]

Fulbright's attack had wide-ranging repercussions. LBJ was infuriated. He promptly unleashed administration supporters, who delivered harsh rejoinders, and the incident left personal and political relations between Johnson and Fulbright permanently embittered. This animosity between the president and the chairman of the Senate Foreign Relations Committee had critical implications for U.S. foreign policy formation during the Vietnam War. Significantly, two of the most prominent critics of Fulbright's position on the Dominican Republic were also southerners. Senator Russell B. Long of Louisiana praised the U.S. actions to block "another Cuba-type Communist takeover." Congressman Armistead I. Selden Jr. from Alabama agreed and appended to his remarks a list of seventy-seven "Communists participating in the Dominican rebellion." Selden also sponsored a House resolution endorsing unilateral "steps to forestall or combat intervention, domination, control and colonization . . . by the subversive forces known as international communism." This resolution, which faithfully represented southern preferences for staunch anticommunism, unilateral action, interventionism in the Western Hemisphere, and the decisive use of military force, passed by 312 to 52, with southerners voting 93 to 0 in favor and 9 other Dixie congressmen announced in support.[30]

The South complemented its endorsement of unilateral, often forceful interventions abroad with unswerving support for a strong military. Dixie's willingness in the mid-1950s to pay higher taxes for enhanced defense budgets derived both from the region's overt patriotism and its ongoing expectation of another major war. Calculations of sectional economic benefits reinforced foreign policy considerations. Southerners fully understood the economic stimulus Dixie had gained from World War II and were determined that the South continue to benefit from the infusion of federal defense dollars. Over the quarter century after 1945, the South developed a "political alliance with the Pentagon." Led by Senators Russell, Stennis, and Johnson, and Congressmen Carl Vinson and L. Mendel Rivers, southern

29. Woods, *Fulbright*, 334–36; *Congressional Quarterly Almanac* (hereafter cited as CQA), 1965, p. 517 (quote). Please note that the year refers to the year of coverage rather than to the date of publication.

30. CQA, 1965, pp. 517, 1004–5.

Democrats ensured that the defense budget remained virtually sacrosanct; in return, "fortress Dixie" became the home to seven of the nation's ten largest defense contractors, and federal spending (the most significant being for defense) far exceeded the region's tax payments. Indeed, defense spending became crucial to the evolution of the Sunbelt, and the defense bounty was central to William Faulkner's 1956 conclusion, "Our economy is no longer agricultural. Our economy is the Federal Government."[31]

The South's determination to capture a significant portion of the cold war defense bounty was evident in the wake of World War II. In July 1951 Congressman Albert Rains of Alabama signaled this resolve in an unsuccessful attempt to amend the Defense Production Act of 1950, the fiscal basis for fighting in Korea. Rains proposed that defense contracts be dispersed across the country to avoid the threat of nuclear attack. Although Rains's amendment failed, the support of the less-industrialized South and West (excepting Washington and California) versus the opposition of the more industrialized Northeast, Midwest, and Middle Atlantic was instructive. Five years later, Fulbright resumed the southern campaign to amend the 1950 act and thereby gain new defense projects at the expense of the "martial metropolises." With the congressional vote duplicating the 1951 sectional alignment, Fulbright also failed. Congressman Lenoir Sullivan of Missouri expressed the more industrialized regions' perspective when he protested against "moving a plant out of St Louis to a weed patch somewhere."[32]

Significantly, as the decade of the 1950s ended, the South had pursued defense dollars so successfully that it opposed any "reform" of the system of military procurement. Dixie's congressional influence and alliance with the Department of Defense had transformed the region from a humble solicitor of additional contracts into the target of complaints by the representatives of the older industrial regions. In 1959, Senators Jacob Javits and Kenneth Keating of New York and Senator Clifford Case of New Jersey proposed the Armed Services Competitive Procurement Act, designed to steer contracts away from the South. Keating lectured southerners, "Our country

31. Hero, *Southerner and World Affairs,* 84; Bruce J. Schulman, *From Cotton Belt to Sunbelt: Federal Policy, Economic Development, and the Transformation of the South, 1938–1980* (Durham, N.C., 1994), 135, 142, 145.

32. Roger W. Lotchin, "The Origins of the Sunbelt-Frostbelt Struggle: Defense Spending and City Building," in *Searching for the Sunbelt: Historical Perspectives on a Region,* ed. Raymond A. Mohl (Knoxville, Tenn., 1990), 55–56.

can't exist half rich and half broke any more than it could exist half slave and half free." Neither the Pentagon nor Richard Russell was impressed, and the bill died in Russell's Senate Armed Services Committee.[33]

Given the crucial contribution of defense spending to the southern economy, Russell's refusal to alter the system was predictable. His support for defense spending was echoed repeatedly by fellow southerners in opinion polls that indicated that the South was more comfortable with the level of cold war defense allocations than any other region. Both Russell and his constituents had good reason to be satisfied. The South's share of the nation's prime defense contracts had increased from 7 percent in 1950 to 15 percent in 1960 and 25 percent in 1970. From 1962 to 1972, defense dollars constituted more than 20 percent of income growth in Mississippi and between 10 and 20 percent in Texas, Alabama, Georgia, North Carolina, and Virginia. In the initial postwar period, weapons accounted for a smaller portion of southern contracts than those awarded to other regions; textiles, tobacco, coal, and food made up the difference. As the cold war persisted and military technology focused less on traditional weapons and more on missiles, electronics, and aircraft, the South's defense production moved away from the region's traditional low-wage, labor-intensive industries. Newer, more technologically sophisticated industries became the "engines" driving Dixie's economic expansion. Throughout this period of transition, the South's disproportionate share of military bases remained lucrative. In 1975, southern defense-related salaries amounted to one and one-half times the national average.[34]

Dramatic examples of the Dixie-defense coalition accentuated this pattern of general economic stimulus. By 1958, Carl Vinson and Richard Russell could boast of fifteen defense-related operations in Georgia, the most significant of which was Lockheed-Georgia, based in Marietta. The largest industrial concern in the Southeast, Lockheed operated in 55 of Georgia's 159 counties. Just up the coast in South Carolina, L. Mendel Rivers outdid his southern colleagues. One observer rightly characterized Rivers's district surrounding Charleston as "one of the most elaborately fortified patches of geography in the nation," and Vinson warned Rivers that if additional defense installations were located around Charleston, the area might sink into

---

33. Schulman, *From Cotton Belt to Sunbelt*, 144.

34. Ibid., 139–40, 149, 156; GOI, No. 50 (August 1969): 11; GOI, No. 71 (May 1971): 23; GOI, No. 88 (October 1972): 21; GOI, No. 93 (March 1973): 10.

the Atlantic. The warning was appropriate, for the list was daunting: an air force base; a naval station and shipyard; a marine corps air station; a mine warfare center; a naval hospital; and General Electric, McDonnell-Douglas, Avco-Lycoming, and Lockheed defense operations.[35]

The space program had even greater economic importance for the South. Prior to the Russian launch of *Sputnik,* southerners had exhibited little enthusiasm for space projects. Ironically, Congressman Albert Thomas from Houston had been one of the most severe critics of federal aeronautics programs. In the wake of the stunning Russian achievement, Senate Majority Leader Lyndon Johnson and Speaker of the House Sam Rayburn seized the issue and led the congressional campaign to establish the National Aeronautics and Space Administration (NASA) in 1958. NASA and the $60 million Manned Spacecraft Center (now Johnson Space Center) helped make Houston the Southwest's largest city and manufacturing center. The agency also transformed Huntsville, Alabama, from a sleepy textile town into a modern technological center and location of the Marshall Space Flight Center; and NASA led to the construction of other important installations at Cape Canaveral, New Orleans, and Bay Saint Louis, Mississippi. The space program went far toward fulfilling LBJ's search for a mechanism for building a New South of "science and technologically-based enterprise." The long-term impact of post–World War II defense spending reached beyond its boost to Dixie's economy and the regions inclination to support military spending and an interventionist foreign policy. By contributing to the Sunbelt phenomenon, these federal dollars influenced the population shift from the Northeast and Midwest to the South and West. This migration enhanced southern political power and strengthened its nationalist and unilateralist influence on overall U.S. foreign policy.[36]

The South's ambivalence toward arms control during the 1960s and 1970s reconfirmed the region's ongoing determination to maintain a strong military. Both the southern public and southern Democratic senators expressed significant reservations over the Limited Test Ban Treaty of 1963, in which the United States, Russia, and Great Britain agreed to confine nuclear test-

35. Schulman, *From Cotton Belt to Sunbelt,* 144; Fite, *Russell,* 319; Huntley, "Mighty Rivers," 218–32, 237 (quote), 285; see also Donald C. Harrison, *Distant Patrol: Virginia and the Korean War* (Chelsea, Mich., 1989), v–vi, 52–57.

36. Schulman, *From Cotton Belt to Sunbelt,* 147–49 (quote, 148); Michael J. Hogan, "Partisan Politics and Foreign Policy in the American Century," in *The Ambiguous Legacy: U.S. Foreign Relations in the "American Century,"* ed. Michael J. Hogan (New York, 1999), 356–57.

ing to underground explosions and to refrain from testing in the atmosphere, outer space, or underwater. Polls revealed that southerners remained the most pessimistic Americans concerning the possibility of peaceful coexistence with the Soviets, and southerners and westerners were the least supportive of the test ban agreement. Fulbright managed the treaty and argued eloquently on its behalf, but he could persuade only slightly more than half of his southern Democratic colleagues to support the agreement. In a positive ratification vote of 80 to 19, southern Democrats voted 12 to 9 in favor, and Kentucky's 2 moderate Republicans, John Sherman Cooper and Thruston B. Morton, also endorsed the treaty.[37]

Southern senators were also the strongest opponents of the 1968 Nuclear Nonproliferation Treaty. Signed by more than ninety nations, the treaty obligated the nations possessing nuclear weapons not to transfer them to other countries. After four days of debate and unsuccessful attempts by Republicans John Tower of Texas and Strom Thurmond of South Carolina and Democrat Samuel J. Ervin of North Carolina to add reservations, the Senate approved the treaty by 83 to 15. Of the 15 dissenters, 10 were southerners—7 Democrats and 3 Republicans. Twelve southern senators voted for ratification.[38]

The SALT I agreement (Strategic Arms Limitation Talks) elicited similar southern hostility toward any potential weakening of U.S. military power. Negotiated by President Nixon during his visit to Moscow in May 1972, SALT I included two basic parts. The defensive portion limited U.S. and Russian antiballistic missile systems (ABMs) to two sites: one for each capital and a second for an intercontinental ballistic missile launching center. The second or offensive segment froze both countries' land-based and submarine-launched missiles at existing levels—1,410 land-based and 950 submarine-launched for the Soviet Union and 1,000 and 710, respectively, for the United States. U.S. technological superiority and the weapons of Western European allies compensated for the numerical disparity. The Senate readily agreed to the defensive accord, but approved the arms agreement only after adding an amendment by Senator Henry M. Jackson of Washington. Jackson's proviso directed that any future SALT negotiations be based

37. Woods, *Fulbright*, 318–20; CQA, 1963, p. 686; George H. Gallup, *The Gallup Poll: Public Opinion, 1935–1971* (New York, 1972), 3: 1699, 1837.

38. CQA, 1967, pp. 162–68, 4-S. Please note that CQA page numbers containing a hyphen and *H* or *S* refer to tables of House and Senate votes collected at the end of each volume.

on the "principle of equality" and "not limit the United States to levels of intercontinental strategic forces inferior" to the Soviet Union. The Senate adopted this amendment by 56 to 35. Southern Democrats supported Jackson 16 to 1 (compared to all other Democrats, who were opposed 23 to 10), and southern Republicans agreed with the Washington hard-liner by 5 to 1.[39]

These same tendencies were evident in the support of southern senators for ABM systems. President Johnson requested $1.95 billion in 1968, and President Nixon sought another $904 million the following year. LBJ recommended the Sentinel System to insulate U.S. cities from potential nuclear attacks; Nixon shifted to the Safeguard System, designed to protect American missile sites. Both proposals cleared Congress only after bitter and prolonged debates—particularly in the Senate.

Southerners led both the pro- and anti-ABM forces. Just as they were doing relative to the war in Vietnam, Fulbright and John Sherman Cooper vehemently attacked the ABM proposals. Together with other opponents, they contended that U.S. missile capabilities far surpassed Russia's, that the ABM was technically flawed and therefore a great waste of money, and that a U.S. system would stimulate the arms race. Fulbright became so exercised in 1969 that he branded ABM supporters "stooges of the military." Since his fellow southern senators were the most consistent ABM supporters, he subsequently apologized. Richard Russell and Strom Thurmond in the Senate and Robert L. Sikes of Florida and George H. Mahon of Texas in the House responded by emphasizing the Soviet threat and Russian efforts to construct its own system. They also contended that a U.S. ABM network could save 20 million lives in case of attack and that an antiballistic capability was essential to future negotiations with the U.S.S.R. "Unilateral disarmament" in a "world of international banditry" was senseless, they contended. No "good fairy" was going to ride in on "a white horse . . . and bring disarmament and peace with a wave of her magic wand."[40]

During both the 1968 and 1969 debates, Cooper and Senator Philip A. Hart of Missouri submitted amendments seeking to delay or reduce the appropriations. Cooper's amendment of April 1968 to bar the use of funds for

39. CQA, 1972, pp. 589, 622–25, 62-S (quotes).

40. CQA, 1968, p. 457; CQA, 1969, p. 271 (quotes); Woods, *Fulbright,* 519–25; Richard C. Smoot, "John Sherman Cooper: The Paradox of a Liberal Republican in Kentucky Politics" (Ph.D. dissertation, University of Kentucky, 1988), 233–34.

deployment of the ABM until the secretary of defense certified that it was "practicable" failed by 28 to 31. Southern Democrats voted 10 to 1 in opposition, and southern Republicans split 1 to 1. The Cooper-Hart amendment of June 1968 proposing to delay Sentinel spending for a year elicited a similar response. It failed by 34 to 52, with southern Democrats voting 15 to 2 and southern Republicans dividing 2 to 2. The following August, Cooper and Hart attempted to restrict Safeguard funding to research and development rather than deployment. Once again, they failed by a vote of 49 to 51, with southern Democrats opposing the amendment 15 to 3 and Dixie's 6 GOP senators opposing 4 to 2. For the remainder of the Nixon administration, southern senators and congressmen continued to fend off efforts by Cooper and other critics of military spending to reduce ABM funding.[41]

The South's preference for a unilateral, nationalist foreign policy and its growing disillusionment with the United Nations were also evident in the region's rejection of any linkage of civil rights to foreign policy. In 1954, Senator John Bricker, a conservative Ohio Republican, sought to block the passage of domestic economic or social measures via international agreements or UN actions. His proposed constitutional amendment would have required a specific two-thirds vote of the Senate for any portion of a treaty or executive agreement to "become effective as internal law." Bricker was particularly apprehensive that the UN Charter, the Genocide Convention, or a proposed convention on human rights might provide the vehicle for the passage of a liberal domestic agenda.[42]

Conservative southerners shared his general apprehension, but were more specifically concerned about possible attacks on segregation. The Eisenhower administration strongly opposed the amendment as an unacceptable restriction on the president's authority in international relations, and both Walter George, the South's most influential spokesman on foreign relations, and Lyndon Johnson, the newly installed Democratic minority leader, agreed. Receiving only 42 of 92 votes, the amendment fell far short of passage in the Senate, where southerners voted 14 to 10 in opposition.[43]

The clear majority of southern senators subscribed to the George-

---

41. CQA, 1968, pp. 19-S, 34-S; CQA, 1969, p. 13-S.

42. Duane Tananbaum, *The Bricker Amendment Controversy: A Test of Eisenhower's Political Leadership* (Ithaca, N.Y., 1988), 155.

43. Ibid., 168.

Johnson bipartisan approach to foreign policy and to the belief that the executive should have wide latitude to direct foreign affairs, but the sectional alignment on an alternative measure was indicative of Dixie's distress over possible interference with southern race relations. Nineteen southerners voted for Senator George's amendment, which specified that an executive agreement could "become effective as internal law . . . only by an act of Congress." This proposal fell only 2 votes (61 to 30) short of the two-thirds necessary for passage, with only 4 southern senators (John Sherman Cooper, J. William Fulbright, Lister Hill, and Estes Kefauver) in the negative column. Lyndon Johnson had managed the vote so skillfully that he was able to follow the wishes of constituents in voting for the George proposal. Some historians suggest that he had assurance of at least 2 additional southern no votes had they been needed. Even allowing for a possible 6 southern senators in opposition, this vote demonstrated the region's overwhelming rejection of any international involvement or influences that impinged on southern race relations.[44]

The glare of both national and international spotlights intensified this southern distress. During late 1945 and 1946, whites had murdered blacks for voting or promoting civil rights in Georgia, North Carolina, Mississippi, South Carolina, and Texas, and four members of a black family were lynched in Georgia following an argument with a former white employer. These incidents and the region's rigid and oppressive caste system contributed to John Gunther's widely-read 1947 assessment that when traveling in the South, he felt as if he "wasn't in the United States at all, but in some utterly foreign land. . . . . That [the South] . . . is *the* problem child of the nation is of course indisputable. But how it resists being told so!" The report in October 1947 of President Truman's Committee on Civil Rights and the president's subsequent call for legislation to stop lynching, end the poll tax, and outlaw segregation in interstate transportation led many to see the South as the "nation's number-one moral problem and an embarrassment in cold war diplomacy."[45]

Civil rights activists consciously furthered this impression while attempting to highlight the inconsistencies in the nation's stand for freedom abroad and simultaneous enforcement of segregation of blacks at home. These pro-

44. Ibid., 155 (quote), 158–59, 168, 179–81; Dallek, *Lone Star Rising*, 435–37.
45. Grantham, *South in Modern America*, 198–99 (Gunther); Bartley, *New South*, 69 (embarrassment).

testers also linked the plight of African Americans to oppressed people in other lands and to other nonwhites seeking to escape from colonialism. In October 1947 the NAACP filed a petition, *An Appeal to the World,* with the UN Commission on Human Rights. Written by W. E. B DuBois, the appeal condemned southern racism by asserting, "It is not Russia that threatens the United States so much as Mississippi; not Stalin and Molotov but Bilbo and Rankin; internal injustice done to one's brothers is far more dangerous than the aggression of strangers from abroad." When the U.S. delegation to the UN refused to introduce the petition, Russia did so. Four years later the Civil Rights Congress, a Communist front, filed a similar petition with the UN, charging that U.S. treatment of blacks amounted to genocide. "The test of the basic goals of a foreign policy," the congress contended, "is inherent in the manner in which a government treats its own nationals and is not to be found in the lofty platitudes that pervade so many treaties or constitutions."[46]

With the UN headquarters in New York City, the international attention and negative implications for U.S. foreign policy were compounded by the mistreatment of nonwhite foreign diplomats, dignitaries, and students. For example, when Haiti's secretary of agriculture attended a meeting of the National Association of Commissioners, Secretaries, and Directors of Agriculture in Biloxi, Mississippi, he was blocked from renting a room or eating his meals at the conference hotel. And when President William Tubman of Liberia sought to cross Georgia by railroad, maintenance workers sabotaged his car.

Much to the embarrassment of the State Department and U.S. diplomats, the Soviet media regularly featured this unattractive side of U.S. race relations. Soon after World War II, *Pravda* asserted that the U.S. "Negro population, consisting of 13,000,000 people" continued to suffer "racial discrimination . . . in all its forms and in all branches of the economy and culture of the country." At the time of the Little Rock crisis in 1958, Soviet officials at the UN cited the incident while responding to U.S. criticisms of Russian repression of Hungary in 1956. Was it not hypocritical, they asked, for "white-faced but black-souled gentlemen [to] commit their dark deeds in Arkansas, Alabama, and other Southern states, and then . . . put on white

46. Mary L. Dudziak, "Desegregation as a Cold War Imperative," *Stanford Law Review* 41 (November 1988): 95, 97. The references are to Representative John E. Rankin and Senator Theodore Bilbo, both from Mississippi.

gloves and mount the rostrum in the UN General Assembly, and hold forth about freedom and democracy"? According to a Russian paper, "Fascist thugs of the Ku Klux Klan" were conducting "a savage hunt for Negro children because the latter plan to sit in the same classrooms with white boys and girls." The confrontations at Little Rock, Birmingham, Selma, and elsewhere elicited similar criticisms from other Communist bloc states and from western and neutral countries such as Brazil, Denmark, Great Britain, India, Indonesia, Ireland, Libya, and Nigeria. For example, the *Irish Times* opined that Little Rock had "given Communist propagandists the text for innumerable sermons to coloured peoples everywhere."[47]

Acutely conscious of the vulnerabilities created by the nation's racial record, the formulators of America's cold war foreign policy acted to improve the lot of American blacks at least in part from a foreign relations imperative. President Truman emphasized, "If we wish to inspire the people of the world whose freedom is in jeopardy, . . . we must correct the remaining imperfections in our practice of democracy." Truman's secretary of state, Dean Acheson, hardly a champion of black rights, asserted in 1952, "Our failure to remove racial barriers provides the Kremlin with unlimited political and propaganda capital for use against us in Japan and the entire Far East."[48]

When President Dwight D. Eisenhower reluctantly dispatched federal troops to protect black children in Little Rock in 1957, he lamented, it "would be difficult to exaggerate the harm that is being done to the prestige and influence, and indeed to the safety of our nation and the world. Our enemies are gloating over this incident and using it everywhere to misrepresent our whole nation." Secretary of State John Foster Dulles agreed, adding that "this situation is ruining our foreign policy. The effect of this in Asia and Africa will be worse for us than Hungary was for the Russians." The *Minneapolis Star* published a political cartoon that depicted the "Three 'R's" in Arkansas as "Race Hate," "Rights Denial," and "Red Propaganda Boost";

47. Paul G. Lauren, *Power and Prejudice: The Politics and Diplomacy of Racial Discrimination* (Boulder, 1996), 200 (*Pravda*); Michael L. Krenn, "'Unfinished Business': Segregation and U.S. Diplomacy at the 1958 World's Fair," *Diplomatic History* 20 (fall 1996): 593 (black-souled); Mary L. Dudziak, "The Little Rock Crisis and Foreign Affairs: Race, Resistance, and the Image of American Democracy," *Southern California Law Review* 70 (September 1997): 1670 and 1672 (final two quotes).

48. Dudziak, "Desegregation as a Cold War Imperative," 111–12 (Truman); Lauren, *Power and Prejudice,* 219 (Acheson).

and another periodical speculated that Arkansas governor Orval Faubus had "handed to the Communists the handsomest gift they could possibly have received." Five years later as rioters attempted to block the integration of the University of Mississippi, President John F. Kennedy lectured southerners, "The eyes of the nation and all the world are upon you and upon all of us." And in 1964, Secretary of State Rusk advised an enraged Strom Thurmond and his Senate Commerce Committee, "The biggest single burden that we carry on our backs in our foreign relations in the 1960s is the problem of racial discrimination."[49]

While white southerners were predictably uncomfortable with this outpouring of criticism and the prospect of outside intervention, they and many other Americans were also dismayed at the response of American blacks to U.S. cold war policies. In addition to protesting their oppression in the segregated South, blacks were noticeably less committed to the rigid anticommunist and antineutralist cold war posture adopted by most southerners. According to historian Brenda Gale Plummer, African Americans did not act from "isolationism" or "backwardness" but from "growing hostility" to the perception of the Truman administration "as more interested in the status quo overseas than in economic security and democracy at home." Only 23 percent of blacks (the majority of whom still resided in the South) favored the 1946 loan to Great Britain versus 43 percent of southern whites. In April 1947, 52 percent of southern whites but only 39 percent of southern blacks supported aid to Greece, and in 1950, 52 percent of southern blacks versus 36 percent of whites would have ended the Marshall Plan. Southern blacks were also less supportive than their white neighbors of U.S. intervention in Korea and were more inclined to view the conflict as a civil war. North Carolina civil rights activist Robert Williams thought "it was stupid to lose so many men for nothing."[50]

49. Azza Salama Layton, "International Pressure and the U.S. Government's Response to Little Rock," *Arkansas Historical Quarterly* 56 (fall 1997): 269 (Eisenhower); Cary Fraser, "Crossing the Color Line in Little Rock: The Eisenhower Administration and the Dilemma of Race for U.S. Foreign Policy," *Diplomatic History* 24 (spring 2000): 247 (Dulles); Dudziak, "Little Rock Crisis," 1671–72 (*Minneapolis Star* and Faubus); Thomas Borstelmann, "'Hedging our Bets and Buying Time': John Kennedy and Racial Revolutions in the American South and Southern Africa," *Diplomatic History* 24 (summer 2000): 443; Lauren, *Power and Prejudice*, 244 (Rusk); Schoenbaum, *Waging Peace and War*, 383.

50. Brenda Gayle Plummer, *Rising Wind: Black Americans and U.S. Foreign Affairs, 1935–1960* (Chapel Hill, 1996), 177, 184–85, 187, 206. For a different assessment of black responses, see Hero, *Southerner and World Affairs*, 504–43.

Southern blacks also identified with people of color seeking to escape the oppression of colonialism abroad. For example, numerous black organizations followed developments closely in India, South Africa, Liberia, and other emerging nations. African Americans and Indian news agencies exchanged information that supported their mutual antiracist and anticolonial positions after World War II, and Jawahahl Nehru and his sister, Vijaya Panet, directly criticized U.S. race relations. This close connection to Indian nationalists and the mutual opposition to imperialism were also manifest in the adoption by southern blacks of nonviolent strategies for advancing the Civil Rights movement. This common approach for seeking change was grounded not only in philosophy and domestic calculations but also a "sophisticated understanding of the global arena and a general critique of imperialism."[51]

By the end of the 1950s, southern black leaders such as Williams and the Reverend Martin Luther King Jr. were quite explicit in their linkage of the U.S. Civil Rights movement to anticolonial struggles abroad. Williams, who supported Castro's revolution in Cuba, contended, "Any struggle for freedom in the world today affects the stability of the whole society of man." King, who attended Ghana's independence celebration in 1957 and conducted a "study tour" of India in 1959, later characterized America's inner cities as a "system of internal colonialism." U.S. forays abroad, King contended, derived from "racist decision making"; American leaders refused to "respect anyone who is not white." In May 1961, King declared that U.S. policy makers failed to "understand the meaning of the revolution taking place in the world. There is a revolt," he observed, "all over the world against colonialism, reactionary dictatorship, and systems of exploitation. Unless we as a nation join the revolution and go back to the revolutionary spirit that characterized the birth of our nation, I am afraid that we will be relegated to a second-class power in the world with no real moral voice to speak to the conscience of humanity."[52]

As King learned firsthand in the late 1950s and early 1960s, the majority of southern whites had little sympathy for the aspirations of either African Americans or emerging Third World nations. The South's most powerful politicians opposed concessions on civil rights regardless of the international

51. Plummer, *Rising Wind,* 223.

52. Ibid., 296, 305; James H. Cone, "Martin Luther King Jr. and the Third World," *Journal of American History* 74 (September 1987): 462.

implications. Maintaining white supremacy at home easily took precedence even if it compromised the effectiveness of the nation's anticommunist stance abroad. Ironically, given this clear priority, southerners regularly castigated civil rights activists as subversives or communists. Both the Federal Bureau of Investigation and the Dies Committee investigated Mary McLeod Bethune. Faculty at historically black colleges, who shared the African American reservations about U.S. cold war policy, were frequently targeted and harassed, and other black institutions and activists were physically attacked and killed. All were equated with radical outside agitators—a practice that continued through the 1960s. According to one rural Georgia sheriff in 1962, "Some of these niggers down here would just as soon vote for Castro or Khrushchev."[53]

Southern congressmen and senators made the region's priorities abundantly clear. Like the Russians, Senator Herman Talmadge of Georgia compared Eisenhower's use of troops in Little Rock to the Soviet actions in Hungary; however, he drew quite different conclusions. While regretting the "destruction of the sovereignty of Hungary by Russian tanks and troops," he observed, "we are now threatened with the spectacle of the President of the United States using tanks and troops in the streets of Little Rock to destroy the sovereignty of the state of Arkansas." Senator James O. Eastland of Mississippi agreed that Eisenhower was seeking to "destroy the social order of the South," and he was convinced that "[n]othing like this was ever attempted in Russia."[54]

When the State Department and the United States Information Agency attempted to counter the international embarrassment occasioned by the Little Rock incident with a display at the 1958 Brussels World's Fair depicting U.S. race relations, southerners decisively objected. Talmadge informed Secretary of State John Foster Dulles that segregation was the province of individual states and "cannot by any stretch of the imagination be said to be one of legitimate concern to the citizens of other countries." L. Mendel Rivers warned that southerners were "not kidding around" and threatened "plenty of reaction on the Floor of the House" if the exhibit were staged, and his fellow South Carolinian, Strom Thurmond, assured Dulles that he

53. Borstelmann, "Kennedy and Racial Revolution," 445. The Dies Committee, chaired by Martin Dies of Texas, was the name of the House Un-American Activities Committee before it became a standing committee.

54. Dudziak, "Little Rock Crisis," 1685.

was speaking "for the great majority of the people of the South when I voice my emphatic objection to this kind of disparaging exhibit." Deferring to this "southern pressure," the Eisenhower administration removed the segregation portion of the "Unfinished Business" exhibit in midsummer 1958.[55]

Governor George Wallace of Alabama flamboyantly sustained these southern positions during the 1960s. In so doing, he embodied southern ties to the "radical right" movement in American politics and its rigid anticommunist foreign policies and linkage of civil rights and liberal social changes to an alleged international Communist conspiracy. Although racism was at the core of Wallace's appeal to alienated middle- and lower-middle-class white voters, "red-baiting . . . dominated every aspect" of his "anti–civil rights rhetoric." Wallace described the Civil Rights movement as a Communist plot, alleged that the Civil Rights Act of 1964 had been taken directly from the *Communist Manifesto,* and asserted that defenders of Martin Luther King and his "pro-communist friends and associates" were "the same people who told us that Castro was a 'good Democratic soul,' that Mao Tse-tung was only an 'Agrarian Reformer.'" In 1966 the governor even traced the origins of the nation's urban rioting to a strategy of attacking U.S. cities formulated during a "conference of world guerrilla warfare chieftains [meeting] in Havana, Cuba."[56]

Wallace's ties to the radical right extended beyond the similarity of their hysterical anticommunist foreign policy pronouncements. Any Wallace political rally attracted a motley assortment of radical right groups, including the John Birch Society, the Minutemen, the Ku Klux Klan, and the White Action Movement. Wallace received financial support from such wealthy southern reactionaries as H. L. Hunt and Leander Perez, and Asa Carter, the governor's principal speechwriter, was a Ku Klux Klan member and had been involved in right-wing politics since the 1940s. Wallace and Bill James Hargis from Tulsa were also mutual admirers. In the mid-1960s Hargis conveyed his right-wing evangelism to millions via some five hundred television stations and would have agreed completely with Wallace's contention that the "*international* racism of the liberals seeks to persecute the *international* white minority to the whim of the *international* colored majority."[57]

55. Krenn, "Unfinished Business,'" 600–1, 609.

56. Carter, *From George Wallace to Newt Gingrich,* 14 (red-baiting); Dan T. Carter, *The Politics of Rage: George Wallace, the Origins of the New Conservatism, and the Transformation of American Politics* (Baton Rouge, 1995), 161, 305 (Wallace).

57. Carter, *From George Wallace to Newt Gingrich,* 3 (Wallace), 10; Carter, *Politics of Rage,* 298–99.

Indeed the control of the United Nations by a majority of nonwhite nations intensified the South's disillusionment with the body by the early 1960s. Southerners, like most Americans, had been disappointed at the UN's failure to function either as an international peacekeeping organization or an effective instrument of U.S. containment policy in the decade after World War II. When bitter battles over trusteeships, the role of the Economic and Social Council, and membership for the People's Republic of China cast the "UN as a weapon in the East-West conflict," southerners grew suspicious of the body's utility for U.S. foreign policy. These suspicions changed to hostility as the initial U.S. domination of the UN diminished. Of the original fifty-one members of the UN, only three were from Africa, three from Asia, and seven from the Middle East. From 1955 through 1962, this geographic distribution changed dramatically when forty-eight new African and Asian nations gained membership, giving Afro-Asian countries a sixty to fifty-three majority over members from all other continents. Reacting to this change, Allen J. Ellender declared that he had never met "any Africans who have the capability to run their own affairs," and a South African official complained that "the complexion of the United Nations has changed from white to black." A much greater emphasis on colonialism, racism, and economic inequality accompanied this realignment of power. As the UN General Assembly passed the Declaration on the Elimination of All Forms of Racial Discrimination in 1965 or designated 1971 the International Year for Action to Combat Racism and Racial Discrimination, the majority of white southerners dismissed the United Nations as just another group of outside agitators.[58]

The South's low opinion of nonwhites and developing nations and its increasing refusal to support internationalist projects were also apparent in the region's growing opposition to foreign aid. Even as southerners provided strong support for the early containment policies, they had questioned the foreign aid components. This ambivalence turned to solid and often vehement opposition during the later Truman years and the remainder of the 1950s. By 1962 the South had become the region most critical of U.S. foreign aid policies.

Fiscal conservatism was a central consideration. Harry F. Byrd and Rich-

58. Gary B. Ostrower, *The United Nations and the United States* (New York, 1998), 72 (weapon), 125–27, 131, 147; Becnel, *Ellender*, 209; Lauren, *Power and Prejudice*, 233 (South African), 246, 252–53.

ard Russell continued to warn that the Soviet Union's strategy was to "bleed America white," and both asserted that U.S. funds were better spent on strengthening the nation's military. By the early 1950s, other southerners joined in this litany. Allen J. Ellender even detected "scandalous waste" in U.S. aid to Western Europe in 1951 and two years later suggested that much of the fear of Communism resulted from "outsiders who stir up trouble, especially the English and French who spread propaganda in the hope of scaring Congress into giving more economic aid." Louisiana congressman Otto Passman was even more blunt. In 1958 he informed a representative of the State Department, "Son, I don't smoke and I don't drink. My only pleasure in life is kicking the shit out of the foreign aid program of the United States of America."[59]

Intolerance of neutralism and commercial considerations were also influential. The South's opposition grew apace with the shift of much of U.S. aid from European nations to neutralist, less-developed countries in Asia and Africa. Southerners had little tolerance for neutralism in the cold war struggle. For example, when asked in 1957 if aid should be continued to India and other nations that had "not joined us as allies against the Communists," 54 percent of southerners, compared to 37 percent of northerners, were opposed. Southerners also worried that aiding these countries fostered competitors in the production of agricultural staples or in low-wage industries such as textiles. With no sense of irony in light of southern history or the contemporary southern wage scale, Herman Talmadge declared, "While unfair competition is closing the doors of numerous American industries, we continue to send our technicians and machines to foreign lands to provide the know-how to produce goods that will destroy markets for our own, due to the vast differential between slave wages and free wages." Similar concerns prompted Walter George and the southern-dominated Senate Appropriations Committee to argue forcefully in 1956 against helping Egypt build the Aswan Dam and with it the capacity to grow vast quantities of irrigated cotton. Southern racial views and practical politics solidified these anti–foreign aid inclinations. Former colonial nations that identified with and commented on the plight of African Americans excited southern enmity. India, Ghana, Indonesia, Egypt, and by extension other new nations

59. Fite, *Russell,* 252; Becnel, *Ellender,* 188; Allen J. Ellender Oral History, August 28, 1967, p. 28, JFK Library; Chester J. Pach Jr. and Elmo Richardson, *The Presidency of Dwight D. Eisenhower* (Lawrence, Kans., 1991), 165 (Passman).

incurred southern hostility in this fashion. Finally, after Eisenhower succeeded Truman, domestic political considerations no longer influenced southerners to support foreign aid allocations during the 1950s.[60]

Southern congressional voting paralleled the opinion polls and the assertions of Passman, Ellender, and Russell. Southern Democratic senators supported Truman on foreign aid increases 84 percent of the time, compared to 100 percent for northeastern Democrats and 90 percent for Democrats nationally. These senators voted against reductions in foreign aid allocations on 63 percent of the roll calls, significantly less than the Northeast at 99 percent or even the Midwest at 83. During the Eisenhower presidency, from 1953 through 1958, the South's endorsement of all measures fell to 59 percent and the votes against reductions to 40, compared to 75 and 54 for all Democrats in the upper house. Voting in the House on foreign aid authorizations from 1953 through 1962 was similar. Southern congressmen voted yes on only 48 percent of the foreign aid authorizations bills, compared to 66 percent of the entire House and 53 percent of the Midwest. The decline from 74 percent support in 1953 to 26 percent in 1957 and 40 percent in 1962 was the most dramatic among all sections.[61]

Dixie remained distinctly unenthusiastic about foreign assistance over the next decade. In 1963, Congress reduced President Kennedy's foreign aid request by 34 percent, a record during the program's fifteen-year existence. In the key procedural vote in the House, southern Democrats supported the reduction 58 to 32 and southern Republicans by 13 to 0. By contrast, all other Democrats voted 140 to 8 against the cuts and nonsouthern Republicans 143 to 16 in favor. Working particularly with fellow-Texan George H. Mahon, chairman of the House Appropriations Committee, and commanding greater support from southern Democrats generally, Lyndon Johnson neutralized Otto Passman and his crucial Foreign Operations Subcommittee on Appropriations. LBJ submitted less ambitious requests for fiscal 1965 and 1966 but also suffered the smallest percentage reductions in the program's history; he secured a $3.25 billion appropriation for 1965 (7.6 percent less than requested) and $3.22 billion (a 6.9 percent reduction) for 1966. The

60. Hero, *Southerner and World Affairs,* 203; Malcolm E. Jewell, *Senatorial Politics and Foreign Policy* (1962; reprint, Westport, Conn., 1974), 24 (Talmadge). Jewell defines the South as the eleven states of the former Confederacy.

61. Jewell, *Senatorial Politics,* 19; Charles O. Lerche Jr., *The Uncertain South: Its Changing Patterns of Politics in Foreign Policy* (Chicago, 1964), 68, 70, 72–73. Lerche defines the South as the eleven states of the Confederacy, plus Oklahoma, Tennessee, and West Virginia.

voting on the 1965 aid package was illustrative. Southern Democrats voted 46 to 46 on Passman's annual motion for sharp cuts, a decidedly different outcome than the 1963 vote. These 46 southern votes were decisive in the 208 to 198 rejection of the crusty Louisiana representative's assault on the foreign aid budget.[62]

Still, Johnson's victories were only relative ones. The majority of southern congressmen voted solidly against foreign aid appropriation bills throughout the 1960s. The southern Democratic delegation in the Senate, perhaps as a result of the senators' long personal associations with the president, occasionally voted in favor of foreign aid appropriations but more often voted narrowly against the administration. By the end of the Johnson era, foreign aid had become mired in the controversy over Vietnam, thereby inciting attacks from both traditional conservative critics, such as Passman, and former supporters, such as Fulbright, who had come to identify foreign military aid with the misapplication of containment. This combined opposition led Congress in 1968 to appropriate only $1.76 billion for fiscal 1969— both the lowest dollar figure to that time and the largest reduction (40 percent) of a president's request. Southern Democrats voted 40 to 19 against even this meager sum.[63]

Southerners grew even more intransigent under President Nixon. Southern Democrats voted 19 to 37 in the House and 5 to 11 in the Senate in opposition to fiscal 1970 foreign aid. Democrats overall voted 88 to 47 in favor. Interestingly, southern Republicans opposed the administration by 1 to 23 in the House and 1 to 3 in the Senate. In 1971, southern Democratic congressmen dissented by 23 to 46 and southern Republicans by 3 to 24. The latter vote is particularly telling since Republicans in the House reversed their previous pattern of solidly opposing Kennedy and Johnson proposals and voted 87 to 81 for the Nixon request. For the first time in the twenty-four-year history of the program, a foreign aid bill failed to pass when the Senate rejected the measure by 27 to 41. Southern Democrats voted 11 to 0 against. The southern rejection of foreign aid had become bipartisan and overwhelming.[64]

Continuing southern opposition to immigration also illustrated the ab-

62. CQA, 1963, pp. 98–99, 255–56; CQA, 1964, pp. 314, 636–37; CQA, 1965, p. 445; Herman E. Talmadge Oral History, March 10, 1966, pp. 20–22, JFK Library; Mike Mantos to Larry O'Brien, March 2 [1962], White House Staff Files, JFK Library.

63. CQA, 1968, pp. 604–5, 88–89-H.

64. CQA, 1969, pp. 44-S, 66–67-H; CQA, 1971, pp. 74, 387, 98–99-H.

sence of true internationalism in the region. Following World War II, southerners were more opposed than other Americans to proposals for admitting increased numbers of Europeans into the United States. Despite Dixie's strong opposition to Communism and active support for containment in the late 1940s and early 1950s, the South opposed extending a refuge to persons fleeing Eastern Europe. Even the Soviet suppression of the Hungarian revolt in 1956 prompted only 39 percent of southerners, compared to nearly 60 percent of the remainder of Americans, to favor President Eisenhower's recommendation to loosen entry restrictions for the refugees from this conflict.[65]

The South responded similarly to the Immigration Act of 1965, the most significant immigration legislation since the institution of the national origins system in the 1920s. The latter policy had set immigration quotas by country, based on the ethnic composition of the United States in 1890. This system resulted in more than two-thirds of non–Western Hemisphere immigrants being admitted from Britain, Ireland, Germany, and Scandinavia and most of the remainder from Eastern and Southern Europe. Asians were virtually excluded. Proposed by President Johnson, the 1965 reform eliminated the country-by-country quotas and set total non–Western Hemisphere immigration at 170,000. Over LBJ's objections, Congress added a 120,000 limit on immigrants from the Western Hemisphere.[66]

Southerners strongly opposed scrapping the quotas favoring Europeans from northern and western countries. Racial views took precedence over international cooperation. In national polls, only 40 percent of southern respondents (versus 58 percent in the East, 53 in the Midwest, and 51 in the West) favored ending the quota system, and Dixie's residents were the least inclined to increase overall immigration. In both the Senate and House, southerners led the opposition to LBJ's proposal. Strom Thurmond rejected the charge that the quota system was "racist or morally wrong." He argued instead that the "wish to preserve one's identity and the identity of one's nation requires no justification—and no belief in racial or national superiority." This desire was equivalent to the "wish to have one's own children, and to continue one's own family through them." Spessard L. Holland of Florida could not understand "Why, for the first time . . . the emerging nations

65. Hero, *Southerner and World Affairs,* 65–66.
66. Roger Daniels, *Coming to America: A History of Immigration and Ethnicity in American Life* (New York, 1990), 341–42.

of Africa" were to be "placed on the same basis as are our mother countries, Britain, Germany, the Scandinavian nations, [and] France?" Allen J. Ellender disdained all immigration when "almost four million" Americans were unemployed. From his critical position on the Senate Judiciary Committee, Samuel J. Ervin of North Carolina joined Republican Everett M. Dirksen of Illinois in holding the bill hostage until Johnson agreed to the 120,000 limit on immigrants from the Western Hemisphere. Even this concession failed to attract the support of southern representatives. In an affirmative Senate vote of 76 to 18, southerners cast 15 of the no votes; and in the House, southern congressmen registered 57 of the dissenting votes as the measure passed 320 to 69.[67]

The South's clear predilection for nationalism and unilateralism was also evident in the region's retreat from its two-hundred-year dedication to low tariffs and liberal international commerce. This retreat in part reflected Dixie's general rejection of international cooperation, but it also derived directly from the South's post–World War II economic development. The significantly reduced importance of agriculture in the southern economy diminished the relative influence of traditional free-trade proponents. Longstanding protectionist groups and other low-wage, low-technology interests simultaneously asserted increasing influence. Most prominent among these groups were Louisiana sugar producers, mountain coal companies, lumber interests, food processors, and especially textile firms. In addition, both the chemical and petroleum industries grew increasingly uneasy over the threat of foreign competition.[68]

Stronger protectionist sentiment emerged as early as the mid-1950s. Senators from South Carolina, North Carolina, and Georgia, the most important textile producing states, voted against the Eisenhower administration on reciprocal trade issues more than half of the time, and among these senators, support for reciprocal trade fell from 100 to 34 percent between 1947 and 1958. In an indication of more general protectionist trends, in 1955–56, southern senators voted 12 to 10 to reduce the president's discretion in determining when to increase duties on imports harming U.S. producers. This drift toward protectionism prompted Congressman Frank Smith of Mississippi to observe, "John C. Calhoun must be revolving in his grave today as

---

67. GOI, No. 3 (August 1965): 14–15; CQA, 1965, pp. 96, 462, 478–79 (quotes), 1012–13.
68. Hero, *Southerner and World Affairs*, 149–82; Alfred O. Hero Jr., "Changing Southern Attitudes toward U.S. Foreign Policy," *Southern Humanities Review* 8 (summer 1974): 277–78.

he sees the views about trade legislation of some of his [southern] successors."[69]

Calhoun surely grew ever more distressed during the 1960s and 1970s. Only after moving to safeguard textile, oil, and lumber interests against foreign competition was President Kennedy able to secure passage of his 1962 Trade Expansion Act. Textiles were the most prominent and powerful of these protectionist groups, and southerners were at the forefront of the textile defenders. Representative Carl Vinson of Georgia, a key organizer of a 128-member Textile Conference Group in the House, warned Kennedy, "Unless quotas are imposed that will provide the necessary protection to the textile industry," the Trade Expansion Act would incur the opposition of former southern supporters of lower tariffs. After JFK met with the Textile Conference Group and negotiated an interim long-term arrangement restructuring cotton imports, southern senators voted 13 to 2 and southern representatives 67 to 24 for the measure.[70]

Southerners had not reverted to their previous free-trade positions. The "Kennedy Round" of international trade talks following passage of the Trade Expansion Act did not yield substantive results until May 1967, when the United States agreed to cut tariffs by an average of 35 percent. Southerners were again among the protectionist protesters. The Southern Governors Conference unanimously endorsed appeals from the chemical and textile industries for import quotas. South Carolina senators Strom Thurmond and Ernest F. Hollings, North Carolina senator Samuel J. Ervin, and Representative Basil L. Whitener led the defense of textiles in Congress, and southern congressmen voted 84 to 2 for a bill reducing the import quota for extra-long staple cotton and banning its importation from Egypt and the Sudan. The following year, Hollings introduced an amendment for textile quotas, and Senate Finance Committee Chairman Russell B. Long of Louisiana sponsored a similar measure on behalf of oil. Neither gained passage.[71]

In 1970, southern congressmen overwhelmingly endorsed a measure the *National Journal* termed "the most protectionist act since the depression of

69. Jewell, *Senatorial Politics*, 28–29; Paul Seabury, *The Waning of Southern "Internationalism"* (Princeton, 1957), 23 n. 42 (Smith); "The Record of the 84th Congress," *New Republic*, October 15, 1956, 18–24.

70. Robert A. Pastor, *Congress and the Politics of U.S. Foreign Economic Policy, 1929–1976* (Berkeley, Calif., 1982), 109 (Vinson); Thomas W. Zeiler, "Free-Trade Politics and Diplomacy: John F. Kennedy and Textiles," *Diplomatic History* 11 (spring 1987): 127–42.

71. CQA, 1967, pp. 644–45, 658, 808, 811, 818, 84–85-H; CQA, 1968, p. 732.

the 1930's." President Nixon had submitted a trade bill to Congress that reestablished the president's authority to reduce U.S. tariffs, broadened assistance to businesses harmed by imports, and enhanced the executive's power to counter unfair trade practices. Over Nixon's objections, the House added textile and footwear import quotas, restricted oil imports, and required the president to impose import quotas on other items that the U.S. Trade Commission concluded were being seriously injured by imports (unless the executive deemed such action "contrary to the national interest"). Senator Thurmond; Representatives Wilbur Mills of Arkansas, James T. Broyhill of North Carolina, and John H. Buchanan of Alabama; and Governor Preston Smith of Texas were demonstrative advocates of protection for textiles and oil. It was "ridiculous," Broyhill contended, "to sit idly by while these major industries are being carved up as though we do not have the means to prevent it." Perceiving the House bill as the means, southerners voted 90 to 13 in favor (Democrats 66 to 11 and Republicans 24 to 2), compared to an overall vote of 215 to 165. Although the bill died in the Senate, the South had clearly become the nation's most protectionist region.[72]

Four years later, Nixon obtained his trade bill. Although the Trade Reform Act of 1974 was less protectionist than the House's 1970 measure, southerners in both the House and Senate strongly supported the president's bill. This did not signify a revival of free-trade sentiment. Rather it derived from the South's general support for Nixon and his restrained positions on civil rights, his ostensible partiality for states' rights, and his Vietnam policy, which combined aggressive use of force with U.S. troop withdrawals. The 1974 act also contained clear safeguards against injurious competition from imports. Congressional approval was required for the president to end nontariff barriers such as quotas, the process in which domestic industries gained relief from the detrimental effect of imports was made less rigorous, and the president received authority to impose import restrictions against nations that discriminated against the United States. The South's endorsement of these provisions was consistent both with its adoption of protectionism and its preference for unilateralism.[73]

During the first three decades of the cold war, the South had provided

---

72. Pastor, *Congress and the Politics of U.S. Foreign Economic Policy,* 127 (protectionist); CQA, 1970, pp. 1056 (Broyhill), 1059 (national interest), 72–73-H.

73. Edward S. Kaplan, *American Trade Policy, 1923–1995* (Westport, Conn., 1996), 87–99; CQA, 1973, pp. 833–45, 148–49-H; CQA, 1974, pp. 553–62, 78-S, 162–63-H.

the most consistent and predictable support for the nation's containment policies and the massive defensive budgets sustaining that doctrine. More pessimistic about the prospects for international peace, more comfortable with the use of force in the international arena, more receptive to appeals to patriotism and honor than other Americans, especially dependent on defense spending as an economic stimulus, and intensely opposed to radical change at home or abroad, southerners responded aggressively to the anticommunist crusade. Presidents from Truman through Nixon could depend on Dixie to sustain not only defense spending and harsh rhetoric but also military interventions.

While adopting the stance of cold warriors, the vast majority of southerners cast aside any pretense of internationalism. The South quickly became disillusioned with the United Nations after 1945 and persistently favored unilateral actions when U.S. interests were in question. As had been the case since 1789, race remained critical to the South's foreign policy perspective. Convinced of the inferiority of nonwhites and ever fearful of threats to the region's racial codes, southerners had no faith in an organization that increasingly incorporated Third World nations and provided a forum for Communists, neutralist opponents of the United States, and critics of Dixie's race relations.

Steadily increasing southern opposition to foreign aid embodied these racial reservations about the ability of nonwhites to use the funds wisely, as well as traditional southern fiscal conservatism and the reluctance to support potential competitors in low-wage manufacturing sectors or agriculture. Race and economics were evident in other southern positions. Southern racial biases were clear in Dixie's strong opposition to making the immigration laws less favorable toward northern and western Europeans. Southern uneasiness over foreign competition also contributed to a fundamental transformation in the region's approach to foreign commerce; for the first time in the nation's nearly two hundred years of existence, the South endorsed protectionism over free trade.

Unlike race and economics, partisan politics played a less decisive, or at least less clear, role in the South's responses to U.S. foreign relations after World War II. Responding to cold war imperatives, domestic civil rights policies, the benefits of national defense spending, and appeals to honor, patriotism, and anticommunism, the South supported the basic containment policies of both Democratic and Republican presidents. Because of the relative decline of the Democratic Party after 1960 and the "conservative coalition" of southern Democrats and Republicans throughout the period, the clearly partisan voting patterns of the 1920s, 1930s, and 1940s became far less prominent and less often decisive. Despite President Truman's civil rights initiatives, southern Democrats endorsed and managed congressional approval of the United Nations, the Truman Doctrine, the Marshall Plan, and NATO. Under the guidance of Walter George, Lyndon Johnson, and Sam Rayburn, southerners adopted a generally bipartisan, pro-Eisenhower stance on important issues during the 1950s. And from 1960 through 1973, the decided majority of southerners and their congressmen sustained the fundamental defense and Vietnam policies of Kennedy, Johnson, and Nixon, while expressing reservations about arms limitations and strategies of limited war in Vietnam. In fact, southerners took center stage during the American involvement in Vietnam. The war casts the South's post–World War II foreign policy perspectives into clear focus and provides an excellent case study of the region's ongoing influence on U.S. foreign relations.

CHAPTER 8

Taking Center Stage: Southerners and Vietnam, 1954–1973

I N ASSESSING THE U.S. experience in Vietnam under President Lyndon Johnson, Senator Herman Talmadge turned to an old Georgia saying to invoke the South's preference for military solutions to foreign policy issues and impatience with limited war: "You don't draw a pistol on a man unless you intend to use it, because if you do he might kill you." LBJ, Talmadge continued, should have "wrapped the flag around himself and thrown every resource our country had to conclude the war." Congressman L. Mendel Rivers from South Carolina agreed, stating, "Words are fruitless, diplomatic notes are useless. There can be only one answer for America: retaliation, retaliation, retaliation, retaliation! 'Quit the bombing.' I say, 'Bomb!'" In another characteristically southern assertion, Richard Russell, Talmadge's senate colleague from Georgia, made patriotism and honor a central consideration during the debate over the Gulf of Tonkin Resolution in August 1964. "Our national honor is at stake," he declared. "We cannot and we will not shrink from defending it. No sovereign nation," could do otherwise, he asserted, and "be entitled to the respect of other nations, or indeed could maintain its self respect."[1]

Georgia's two senators expressed essential facets of the South's response to U.S. involvement in Southeast Asia, a response that embodied the central

---

1. Herman Talmadge Oral History, July 17, 1969, p. 26, Lyndon Baines Johnson Library, Austin, Tex. (hereafter cited as LBJ Library); Michael Lind, *Vietnam, the Necessary War: A Reinterpretation of America's Most Disastrous Military Conflict* (New York, 1999), 118 (Rivers); Caroline F. Ziemke, "Senator Richard B. Russell and the 'Lost Cause' in Vietnam, 1954–1968," *Georgia Historical Quarterly* 72 (spring 1988): 50.

characteristics of Dixie's relationship to post–World War II American foreign relations. President Johnson and most southerners and their congressional representatives exhibited the South's traditional concern for personal and national honor and the region's enthusiastic patriotism so prominent in all foreign conflicts after 1865. The president and his southern neighbors remained rigidly anticommunist and retained their low regard for nonwhites—whether allies or foes. A significant majority of southerners continued to support military interventions abroad, to endorse liberal appropriations for defense, and for most of the war to grant the executive wide latitude in the foreign arena. Even more than other Americans, southerners had little patience for constraints on U.S. power and limited war. Once engaged militarily, they believed the nation should pursue victory as the only acceptable goal and outcome.

But even as the South established its reputation as the nation's most militaristic region and was represented by some of the nation's most fervent cold warriors, there were conspicuous dissenters. In one of his many speeches denouncing U.S. involvement in Vietnam, Senator J. William Fulbright of Arkansas compared it to the North's efforts to dominate the South: "Perhaps we Southerners have a sensitivity to this sort of thing [stalemate in Vietnam] that other Americans cannot fully share. We—or our forefathers—experienced both the hot-headed romanticism that led to Fort Sumter and the bitter humiliation of defeat and a vindictive Reconstruction." By sacrificing its idealism and respect for self-determination at the altar of empire, the United States risked, he said, "becoming a Sparta bent on policing the world." Although the Reverend Martin Luther King Jr. and Fulbright agreed on few domestic issues, King seconded the senator's indictment. In January 1966 King told his congregation at the Ebenezer Baptist Church in Atlanta, "America doesn't need to prove to one of the smallest countries in the world that it has the military power. . . . we will not stop communism with bombs and guns and bullets and napalm. We will stop communism by letting the world know that democracy is a better form of government . . . and by making justice a reality for all of God's children."[2]

2. Randall B. Woods, "Dixie's Dove: J. William Fulbright, the Vietnam War, and the American South," *Journal of Southern History* 60 (August 1994): 544, 548; Herbert Shapiro, "The Vietnam War and the American Civil Rights Movement," *Journal of Ethnic Studies* 16 (winter 1989): 128–29.

Ironically, LBJ and other key southern congressmen had opposed direct U.S. involvement in Vietnam in 1954 when the French appealed to the Eisenhower administration to forestall their imminent loss to Ho Chi Minh, a Communist and Vietnam's foremost nationalist, and his Vietminh resistance forces. After the French sought U.S. intervention to save their besieged troops at Dienbienphu in northwest Vietnam, Secretary of State John Foster Dulles met with congressional leaders on April 2 to request discretionary authority for the president to employ military force in fending off the Communists. When Dulles admitted that the Joint Chiefs of Staff and U.S. allies disagreed on the wisdom of intervention, that the British refused to cooperate, and that the French declined to ensure Vietnam's independence, the congressmen led by Russell and Johnson denied the request. Russell had complained the previous year that aid for the French was equivalent to "pouring [money] down a rathole," and Senator John C. Stennis of Mississippi had warned in January 1954 that the United States was "steadily moving closer and closer to participation in the war in Indo-China." When the Eisenhower administration sent Air Force technicians to service U.S. bombers being used by the French in February, Stennis declared presciently, "If our men are attacked, we will have to go to their aid. We could not stand back." On April 3, the day after Russell and Johnson had rejected the administration's overture, Stennis worried that the United States would be left virtually alone to confront the enemy, as had happened in Korea; and he could envision no "circumstances" in which "our land troops should go into Indochina and be committed in this war area."[3]

Ten years later, circumstances had changed dramatically. Johnson had attained his coveted goal of the presidency and with it the foreign policy challenges accompanying a rapidly deteriorating military situation in Vietnam. Following the French defeat in 1954, the United States had become the primary sponsor of the non-Communist and southern Republic of Vietnam in its struggle against Communist insurgents, known first as the Vietminh and after 1960 as the National Liberation Front or Vietcong, and the northern Democratic Republic of Vietnam. A decade of U.S. aid had staved off a Communist victory, but had done little to build a viable society, econ-

3. Ziemke, "Russell," 42; Michael S. Downs, "Advise and Consent: John Stennis and the Vietnam War, 1954–1973," *Journal of Mississippi History* 55 (May 1993): 89–90; Herbert S. Parmet, *Eisenhower and the American Crusades* (New York, 1972), 367. See also Thomas A. Becnel, *Senator Allen Ellender of Louisiana: A Biography* (Baton Rouge, 1995), 191, 209.

omy, or polity in the south. During the Eisenhower and Kennedy presidencies, Vietnam had remained a secondary, if increasingly important, issue; but as LBJ turned his attention to the condition of the American clients in late 1963 and early 1964, their situation was precarious. According to historian George C. Herring, "Military operations and the strategic hamlet program had come to a complete standstill. The government's authority was nonexistent throughout much of the countryside, and near anarchy prevailed in the cities." Therefore, Johnson, unlike his predecessors, faced the very real prospect of a complete Communist victory and a major defeat for the U.S. containment policy.[4]

The president could tolerate neither. His determination to prevail in Vietnam, to master his greatest foreign policy challenge, resulted from the basic international relations assumptions he shared with contemporary policy makers, from personal pride and ambition, and from his southern background. Most fundamentally, Johnson was a member of the "containment generation." He and his advisers, including fellow southerner Secretary of State Dean Rusk, believed that aggression had to be met with clear, unmistakable U.S. responses; appeasement led only to more serious confrontations. Declaring that there would be "No More Munichs" during his tenure, LBJ deemed tough, decisive stands such as the Truman Doctrine, the Marshall Plan, the Berlin airlift, and NATO as proper precedents to follow. In the absence of a firm U.S. stand, he believed, the North Vietnamese "want to take South Vietnam, and . . . Thailand, and . . . Burma, . . . and Sukarno-Indonesia, [and] . . . the Philippines, [and] . . . Hawaii. They'd like to come right back to Seattle." To lose a "war to communists" he said, in a "raggedy ass little fourth rate country" like Vietnam would incite "a mean and destructive debate" within the United States and cause America to "be seen as an appeaser" unable "to accomplish anything for anybody anywhere on the entire globe." Even as he moved to enforce containment and safeguard U.S. credibility, Johnson feared that an overly forceful reaction might draw Russia and China into the conflict and lead to a worldwide struggle or even a nuclear exchange. Therefore, he opted for a "limited war," designed to defeat the Vietnamese Communists without inciting a general conflagration.[5]

4. George C. Herring, *America's Longest War: The United States and Vietnam, 1950–1975* (New York, 1996), 125.

5. Thomas G. Paterson, "Bearing the Burden: A Critical Look at JFK's Foreign Policy," *Virginia Quarterly Review* 54 (spring 1978): 196 (containment generation); Eric F. Goldman, *The Tragedy of Lyndon Johnson* (New York, 1969), 451 (Munichs); Transcript of Congressional Briefing, February 16, 1965, p. 7, Congressional Briefings File, LBJ Library ("South Vietnam

Johnson's personal and southern qualities reinforced these general assumptions and shaped his approach to implementing foreign policy. Never as comfortable confronting international problems as he was exercising his virtually unparalleled domestic political skills, LBJ was convinced that the media and northerners generally doubted his abilities and criticized him unfairly because of his southern background. In moments of frustration he declared, "I don't think that I will ever get credit for anything I do in foreign policy because I didn't go to Harvard." Convinced that he faced "bigotry in the north against a southerner on . . . his ability to handle foreign relations," this first southern president since Wilson was bent on demonstrating that he was a "world statesman" rather than a "Texas provincial."[6]

LBJ's southern sense of honor, manliness, and patriotism fused with driving ambition to produce a rigid adherence to containment in Southeast Asia. A "profoundly insecure man," Johnson was terrified at the prospect of being called a "Coward! Traitor! Weakling!" or a "man without a spine" for letting "democracy fall into the hands of the Communists." He was determined not to be the "first American President to lose a war." Once committed to defeating Ho Chi Minh, Johnson could not admit that his policies might have been flawed either in conception or implementation. Like southerners more generally, his limited appreciation of other nations and societies left him "culture-bound and vulnerable to cliches and stereotypes about world affairs" and thereby unable to distinguish adequately among potential foes or to rethink the universal applicability of containment. His comment, "Foreigners are not like the folks I am used to," was indicative of the very provinciality he sought to surmount.[7]

Johnson's support for a strong military was also characteristically southern; ironically, together with that support came an uneasiness and suspicion born of his southern populism. Reflecting on information he had received

. . . Hawaii"); Doris Kearns Goodwin, *Lyndon Johnson and the American Dream* (New York, 1991), 252, 260 (Johnson); George C. Herring, "The Reluctant Warrior: Lyndon Johnson as Commander in Chief," in *Shadow on the White House: Presidents and the Vietnam War, 1945–1973,* ed. David L. Anderson (Lawrence, Kans., 1993), 96 ("raggedy ass" and limited war).

6. Goldman, *Tragedy of Lyndon Johnson,* 490; Robert Dallek, *Flawed Giant: Lyndon Johnson and His Times, 1961–1973* (New York, 1998), 86, 90.

7. Herring, "Reluctant Warrior," 108 (insecure man); Goodwin, *Johnson and the American Dream,* 253 (Coward); Dallek, *Flawed Giant,* 500 (American President); Waldo Heinrichs, "Lyndon B. Johnson: Change and Continuity" in *Lyndon Johnson Confronts the World: American Foreign Policy, 1963–1968,* eds. Warren I. Cohen and Nancy Bernkopf Tucker (New York, 1994), 26 (culture bound); Goldman, *Tragedy of Lyndon Johnson,* 447 (foreigners).

at the time of the Gulf of Tonkin incident in 1964, Johnson decided the "military had pulled a fast one on me there. I just can't fully trust the sons of bitches." His determination to control the military and to avoid a MacArthur-style challenge to civilian control strengthened his commitment to waging a limited war and his inclination simultaneously to micromanage on some levels while refusing to discuss and formulate an overall strategic mission in Vietnam. This compulsion for maintaining control also derived from Johnson's traditional southern belief that the president should be given broad-ranging, virtually unquestioned authority and support in foreign policy. Johnson had remarked of Eisenhower: "He is the only President we have, and I am going to support that President, because if I make him weaker I make America weaker." Senator Thruston B. Morton, a Kentucky Republican, vouched for LBJ's recollection. Morton recalled that during the Eisenhower years, Johnson had exhibited characteristic southern patriotism and support for the executive: "When the chips were down, he did nothing to negate or diminish the President's strength. . . . In fact, he tried in every way *I think* to support the flag." LBJ had supported Roosevelt, Truman, and Eisenhower and believed that he deserved the same backing from the public, press, Congress, and military.[8]

President Johnson received constant counsel and aid from another southerner, Secretary of State Dean Rusk. The two had developed a close personal relationship during the Kennedy years, when, as southerners who had risen from impoverished backgrounds, they frequently felt disdained and excluded by many of the Camelot contingent. They often joked about rural life and argued over who had been poorer. After working closely with the secretary of state, LBJ observed that Rusk had the "compassion of a preacher and the courage of a Georgia cracker"; he was a "loyal, honorable, hard-working, imaginative man of conviction," who "stood by me and shared the President's load of responsibility and abuse."[9]

Rusk, like so many other southerners, revered Woodrow Wilson, but unlike many of his regional brethren, he remained committed to his under-

8. Thomas J. Schoenbaum, *Waging Peace and War: Dean Rusk in the Truman, Kennedy, and Johnson Years* (New York, 1988), 431 (sons of bitches); Goldman, *Tragedy of Lyndon Johnson,* 489–90 (only President); Thruston B. Morton Oral History, September 13, 1974, p. 10, LBJ Library; John Sparkman Oral History, October 5, 1968, pp. 9–10, LBJ Library; Herring, "Reluctant Warrior," 97.

9. Schoenbaum, *Waging Peace and War,* 446; Thomas W. Zeiler, *Dean Rusk: Defending the American Mission Abroad* (Wilmington, Del., 1999), 132–33.

standing of internationalism, the centrality of international law, and the necessity of collective security. He believed that the United Nations and post-1945 collective security treaties embodied Wilson's vision and that world peace depended upon their defense. In his memoirs, he worried that his countrymen "do not read the UN Charter with the reverence with which we drafted it." The Georgia Wilsonian was convinced by 1963 that there were two contending forces in the international arena: "those who want the U.N. kind of world and those who are trying to tear it down."[10]

When Rusk assessed the situation in Vietnam, he readily identified the Viet Cong, North Vietnamese, and the People's Republic of China as the threats to a "U.N. kind of world" defined by law, self-determination, and constitutional government. Tracing the U.S. obligation back to the legal commitments of the Southeast Collective Defense Treaty of 1954, he argued in traditionally southern terms that the United States had given its "pledged word" and could not be "honorable in Europe and dishonorable in Asia." "The issue," Rusk proclaimed, was "a very simple one indeed. Hanoi, with Peiping's support and help" refused "to leave its neighbors alone." If the issue was simple, the implications were profound; the U.S. capacity "for organizing a peace" hung in the balance. Only by sustaining its "alliances" and "credibility" in both the Atlantic and Pacific could the United States repulse the Communist campaign of world revolutions and those who "would feel that they could with impunity move against" U.S. allies. Rusk concluded that "the issues in Vietnam are far greater than Vietnam itself, or even greater than Southeast Asia."[11]

Working from these perspectives, Johnson and Rusk steadily increased U.S. involvement in Vietnam. During the spring of 1964, U.S. efforts took the form of expanded covert operations against North Vietnam. When North Vietnamese torpedo boats attacked the destroyer *Maddox* on August 2 and allegedly attacked the *Maddox* and *C. Turner Joy* on August 4 in the Gulf of Tonkin, the president authorized a series of retaliatory air strikes against the North, but took no more general actions lest he imperil his reelection campaign. Safely reelected by record margins over Barry Goldwater

10. Zeiler, *Dean Rusk*, 86, 213; see also Schoenbaum, *Waging Peace and War*, 21, 265–67; Alan K. Henrikson, "The Southern Mind in American Diplomacy," *Fletcher Forum* 13 (summer 1989), 375–87.

11. Schoenbaum, *Waging Peace and War*, 423; Rusk Briefing for New Congressmen, January 13, 1965, p. 2; Rusk Foreign Policy Conference, May 22, 1967, p. 6, Congressional Briefings File, LBJ Library.

and faced with imminent political and military disintegration in South Vietnam, Johnson and his advisers initiated the Rolling Thunder bombing campaign against North Vietnam in February 1965. Over the next two years, the United States dropped some 161,000 tons of bombs on North Vietnam and 1 million tons on South Vietnam and ultimately employed 8 million tons of ordnance in Southeast Asia. Despite this unprecedented bombing campaign, Johnson was forced to deploy U.S. ground troops to avert the collapse of South Vietnam in the spring of 1965.

In July 1965 he approved the dispatch of 50,000 U.S. troops; by the end of the year, the number had increased to 165,000 and ultimately grew to nearly 450,000. Under the direction of General William C. Westmoreland, the United States pursued a policy of attrition designed to wear down the ostensibly weaker adversary, but by mid-1967 this strategy had led only to an enormously costly and unpopular stalemate. At least a portion of the popular unrest in the United States resulted from Johnson's refusal to discuss openly and clearly the war's operations and objectives with either Congress or the public. The result was a "covert full-scale war" devoid of either discernible military progress or clear public understanding and support.[12]

As they had done in every foreign war since 1865, southerners rallied to the cause. The eleven states of the former Confederacy provided nearly one-third of the soldiers who served in Vietnam, even though the South was home to only 22 percent of the nation's population. Approximately 28 percent of the military personnel who died in Vietnam were southern (15,437 of 55,622) and 27 percent of the Medal of Honor winners hailed from Dixie. Themes of honor, duty, patriotism, and anticommunism predominated in postwar interviews with southern veterans. Richard C. Ensminger, a Marine from North Carolina, observed characteristically, "I believe in God and country. When I went to Vietnam, I believed it was my duty to go over there and fight for my county. . . . I knew I had done something worthwhile." A Tennessee army veteran also spoke for his Dixie brethren when he voiced his resolve to "head off communism." General Westmoreland, a native of Beaufort, South Carolina, and in many ways the embodiment of the South's image of the honorable military tradition, argued in his autobiographical account of the war that U.S. soldiers should take "pride" in their performance and worried that the nation no longer valued "idealism, patriotism, and zeal." In a subsequent interview Westmoreland adopted the

---

12. Goodwin, *Johnson and the American Dream*, 281.

revealingly southern tact of comparing Vietnam's strategic battlefield characteristics to the Civil War.[13]

Florida senator George A. Smathers and his two sons, who were both serving in Vietnam, embodied these same southern perspectives on patriotic duty and service to country. While denouncing demands for U.S. withdrawal from Vietnam, Smathers acknowledged, "It has become difficult. . . . I wish my two sons were home and I wish that the sons of other parents were home. Nobody wants to be tied down there." But conceding to the North Vietnamese was unthinkable. The only alternative was to persevere and make them "hurt a little," since they would "not listen" if they believed they were "winning." These same emphases on military tradition, honor, and duty were also the principal themes in Vietnam veteran James Webb's widely-read and important novel *Fields of Fire.* Of southern heritage and a military family, Webb said he sought "to tell a story that would restore a sense of honor to the record of servicemen in Vietnam."[14]

The southern public's support for the war paralleled that of its soldiers and rested on the same regional values and assumptions exhibited by the Texas-born president and Dixie's warriors. In national polls, southerners were, compared to other Americans, the most inclined to believe in 1965 that the war would be won on the battlefield rather than through the "minds of native people living in that country"; were most sympathetic to the belief that "wars are sometimes necessary to settle differences"; were most in favor of going "all-out to win a military victory"; were most inclined to believe in June 1966 that the United States would secure "an all out victory"; were most supportive of bombing large North Vietnamese cities in February 1966, of bombing North Vietnam in October 1972 even as the war wound down, and of resuming bombing in January 1973 if no peace settlement were reached; were most willing to pay higher taxes to finance the war and to endorse higher levels of defense spending generally; were most critical of the publication in 1971 of the *Pentagon Papers*, questioning U.S. involvement in Vietnam; were most inclined to believe that China would enter the war

13. James R. Wilson, *Landing Zones: Southern Veterans Remember Vietnam* (Durham, N.C., 1990), 18, 28 (Ensminger); William J. Brinker, ed., *A Time for Looking Back: Putnam County Veterans, Their Families, and the Vietnam War* (Cookeville, Tenn., 1992), 58; William C. Westmoreland, *A Soldier Reports* (New York, 1976), 548, 559.

14. Brian L. Crispell, *Testing the Limits: George Armistead Smathers and Cold War America* (Athens, Ga., 1999), 190; Owen W. Gilman Jr., *Vietnam and the Southern Imagination* (Jackson, Miss., 1992), 29.

on the side of North Vietnam and the National Liberation Front; were least willing to allow the World Court or United Nations any role in peace negotiations; were least inclined to believe that the South Vietnamese could establish a stable government and most inclined to place that country under military leadership; were the least sympathetic to the various proposals after 1969 to withdraw all U.S. troops within a year; and were the least willing to concede that U.S. intervention in Vietnam had been a mistake.[15]

Country music, "an essentially southern art form," which found its primary appeal in the South during the 1960s and early 1970s, reinforced the statistical data amassed by George Gallup's interviewers. The southern country music audience expressed a clear preference for patriotic songs that endorsed anticommunism, personal bravery, fighting and sacrificing for freedom, commitment to honor and duty, and attacks on antiwar protesters. Several of the most popular recordings illustrated these preferences. During 1965, Tom T. Hall wrote "Hello Vietnam," which reached the top of the charts. In it a young man went to war because "we must save freedom in that foreign land or freedom will start slipping thru our hands." A second Hall song, "What We're Fighting For," declared that Americans "must fight to keep Communism from our door." The following year, "The Ballad of the Green Berets" rose to number two with its praise of "Fighting Soldiers from the Sky, Fearless men who jump and die." Later in 1970, Merle Haggard became President Richard Nixon's favorite country artist and the darling of prowar groups when he proclaimed in the number-one hit "Okie from Muskogee": "We don't burn our draft cards down on main street, but we like living right and being free." Haggard followed this song with "Fighting Side of Me," in which he directed protesters who were "running down our way of life fighting men have fought and died to keep" to support the nation or leave it. Among major country stars, only Johnny Cash questioned the U.S. involvement, defended the protesters' patriotism, and endorsed the withdrawal of U.S. troops. Although these sentiments attained only a distinctly minority voice among country entertainers and audiences,

15. GOI, No. 2 (July 1965): 17; No. 4 (September 1965): 12; No. 9 (February 1966): 6–7; No. 10 (March 1966): 10; No. 13 (June 1966): 7; No. 16 (September 1966): 10; No. 18 (November–December 1966): 11; No. 22 (April 1967): 22; No. 24 (June 1967): 5; No. 26 (August 1967): 7; No. 28 (October 1967): 18; No. 29 (November 1967): 4; No. 33 (March 1968): 6; No. 38 (August 1968): 11, 23; No. 52 (October 1969): 14; No. 53 (November 1969): 5; No. 56 (February 1970): 2; No. 61 (July 1970): 5; No. 69 (March 1971): 11–12; No. 71 (May 1971): 23; No. 72 (June 1971): 22; No. 74 (August 1971): 23–24; No. 88 (October 1972): 20; No. 92 (February 1973): 12, 17.

the fact that "What is Truth" and the "Viet Nam Talking Blues" achieved numbers three and eighteen positions on the charts indicated that southerners gradually tired of the war and its losses. Dixie remained supportive, but like the remainder of the nation grew weary of the sacrifices.[16]

The response of southern college students to the war affords additional insight. While far from quiescent, southern students were significantly less activist than those from other parts of the country. This response derived in part from the comparative conservatism they shared with their parents. A survey tracing overall student protests during 1967–68 found that 36 percent of responding southern institutions reported protests, compared to 49 percent in the Northeast, 44 percent in the Midwest, and 40 percent in the West. A May 1967 national mailing list of antiwar organizations, which were located primarily in towns or cities housing colleges, included ten in the Baltimore/Washington area, thirty in New England, thirty-four in northern California, Oregon, and Washington, but only eleven in the South. Similarly, 57 percent of the 1969 freshman class at the University of Kentucky believed that student protestors were not being disciplined sufficiently. And following President Nixon's "silent majority" speech in November 1969, 60 percent of southern college students polled approved of his handling of the war and 34 percent disapproved. These responses compared to an approval/disapproval rating of 52 and 43 among midwestern students and 36 and 58 among students in the East.[17]

The active hostility of southern communities and college administrators toward antiwar protestors reinforced this relative conservatism. Southern newspapers regularly denounced student protesters. The *Dallas Morning News* disparaged the "peacenik movement" and "leaping leftists" and admonished students at the University of Texas, Austin, that the institution's

16. Melton McLaurin, "Country Music and the Vietnam War," in *Perspectives on the American South: An Annual Review of Society, Politics, and Culture*, vol. 3, eds. James C. Cobb and Charles L. Wilson (New York, 1985), 146, 149, 150, 153–54; see also Ray Pratt, "'There Must Be Some Way Outta Here': The Vietnam War in Popular Music," in *The Vietnam War: Its History, Literature and Music*, ed. Kenton J. Clymer (El Paso, 1998), 168–89.

17. Durand Long and Julian Foster, "Levels of Protest," in *Protest! Student Activism in America*, eds. Foster and Long (New York, 1970), 83; Mailing List of Organizations Opposing the War in Vietnam—May 1967, Student Nonviolent Coordinating Committee Papers, 1959–72, Manuscripts Division, Library of Congress (hereafter cited as SNCC Papers); Mitchell K. Hall, "'A Crack in Time': The Response of Students at the University of Kentucky to the Tragedy at Kent State, May 1970," *The Register of the Kentucky Historical Society*, 83 (winter 1985): 40; GOI, No. 55 (January 1970): 16.

"purpose should continue to be higher education, rather than a political demonstration." The *Montgomery Advertiser* hurled similar epithets, such as "spoiled brats," "campus Jacobins," and "immature minds" favoring "appeasement and surrender" and described unrest at the University of Alabama as "campus theater of the absurd." Even Ralph McGill, the publisher of the more liberal *Atlanta Constitution,* questioned the judgment of "pacifist professors" and castigated "Doomsayers and defeatists." This southern hostility extended well beyond editorials. In October 1963, students at the University of North Carolina complained of local obstacles to their efforts to protest Vietnam developments. Campus police at Texas A&M arrested student protestors in 1966, drove them eighty miles from College Station, and warned them not to return. That same spring, Mississippi students noted the potential consequences of opposing the war when a Greenwood church was destroyed by arson following an antiwar prayer service. In 1967 an antiwar activist was shot in Austin, Texas, and in the wake of the U.S.–South Vietnamese invasion of Cambodia in April 1970, state police and National Guardsmen killed two students at Jackson State College in Mississippi. Two years later, police used high-pressure hoses to disperse students in Gainesville, Florida, who were protesting the U.S. mining of Haiphong Harbor.[18]

Indeed, the general response in May 1970 of Dixie's students to the invasion of Cambodia and the subsequent killing of protestors at both Jackson State and Kent State University augments this ideological profile. There were protests. More than one thousand students gathered to voice their discontent at the University of Kentucky, University of Tennessee students conducted a three-day strike, forty-five students were arrested at the University of South Carolina when they attempted to occupy the student union, and Georgia's state colleges suspended classes for two days. But among 445 southeastern college and university presidents responding to a national survey, only 7 or 1.6 percent reported a student or staff strike of a day or longer. This essentially equaled the protest activity of midwestern students but fell short of the 6 percent of campus disruptions in the Northeast and the 8 percent in the Pacific states. This same pattern held true for "peaceful"

18. *Dallas Morning News,* January 11, 1996, May 13, 1970; *Montgomery Advertiser,* April 13, May 12, 15, 23, 1970; *Atlanta Constitution,* March 15, 1966; Charles DeBenedetti, and Charles Chatfield, assisting author, *An American Ordeal: The Antiwar Movement of the Vietnam Era* (Syracuse, N.Y., 1990), 91, 152, 186, 280; Tom Wells, *The War Within: America's Battle over Vietnam* (Berkeley, Calif., 1994), 70, 543.

demonstrations and ones that damaged property. Dixie's universities reported the smallest numbers in both categories, again being roughly equal to the Midwest in percentage terms but far below the Northeast or Pacific states.[19]

Despite this overall support for the war and a military solution in Vietnam, the South was the region most critical of native son Lyndon Johnson's management of the war. When asked their opinion of his handling of the war, LBJ's fellow southerners consistently gave him a lower approval rating than did persons from other regions. Part of this dissatisfaction derived from the South's aversion to limited war and preference for decisive military solutions leading to victory in traditional terms. From Georgia, Senator Herman Talmadge observed that his constituents had "gotten sadly disillusioned" when their sons were sent off to war without the "full resources of our country" being "placed behind them." "They tend to become chagrined," he said, "and I am too." Texas congressman Wright Patman added that Johnson's neighbors had "wanted the President to be a hawk."[20]

In addition, Dixie's persistent uneasiness with an activist and powerful central government and most particularly the region's intense hostility toward Johnson's civil rights policies were also generalized into a low regard for his performance as president in both the domestic and international arenas. An exchange between Johnson's former colleagues in the Senate the day after he called for a voting rights bill in March 1965 was quite revealing. Lister Hill of Alabama asked Richard Russell what had "happened to that boy" he had "trained"? Russell replied, "I just don't know, Lister . . . . He's a turncoat if there ever was one." The Mississippi journalist Hodding Carter III reported in even more graphic terms that southerners roundly cursed Johnson as a "turncoat son-of-a-bitch," and Congressman F. Edward Hebert from Louisiana recalled that his constituents deemed the president "the most horrible man that ever lived." The vast majority of southerners agreed. When polled, a strong majority of Dixie residents opined in 1965 that John-

19. Richard E. Peterson and John A. Bilorusky, *May 1970: The Campus Aftermath of Cambodia and Kent State* (Berkeley, Calif., 1971), xii; Stephen H. Wheeler, "'Hell No—We Won't Go, Ya'll': Southern Student Opposition to the Vietnam War," in *The Vietnam War on Campus: Other Voices, More Distant Drums*, ed. Marc Jackson Gilbert (Westport, Conn., 2001), 154–55.

20. Talmadge Oral History, p. 26; Wright Patman Oral History, August 11, 1972, tape 2, p. 5, LBJ Library; *Montgomery Advertiser*, October 22, 1964, February 14, 16, 1965, January 4, 1966, April 2, 1968.

son was "pushing integration too fast," and they retained that conviction throughout his presidency.[21]

By contrast, the South was consistently more supportive than other regions of Richard Nixon's handling of the war. As with Johnson, Nixon's war policies were relevant. His geographically more aggressive bombing tactics, invasion of Cambodia in 1970, and mining of Haiphong Harbor in 1972 appealed to the South's preference for more assertive military tactics. But domestic considerations were again decisive. Nixon's "southern strategy" of opposition to forced busing to integrate schools, law-and-order approach to social issues, and strategic gestures toward federalism and states' rights shaped the South's perspective. As early as March 1969, 78 percent of southerners' "best guess" was that integration would be pushed "not so fast" or "about right" under the new president. Their "guess" was confirmed, and they responded with strong support for Nixon and his foreign policy.[22]

In aggregate terms, southern congressmen agreed with their constituents and provided dependable support for the American war effort. Still, within this overall support, southerners disagreed vehemently over tactics, international ramifications, and ultimate goals and in so doing established the contours of the painful national debate—even though Dixie's representatives continued to reflect distinctly southern perspectives.

These sharp differences among southerners had not yet arisen in August 1964 when President Johnson requested congressional approval of the Gulf of Tonkin Resolution, authorizing the president to take "all necessary measures to repel any armed attacks against the forces of the United States and to prevent further aggression." Uninformed about U.S. naval operations that might have incited the North Vietnamese attacks on the American destroyers and willing to accept LBJ's assurances that he was not contemplating escalation of the war, Senator Fulbright managed the resolution as chair of the Senate Foreign Relations Committee. Despite his uneasiness about U.S. involvement and opposition to the use of American ground forces, the Arkansas senator called for national unity and support for the president to

21. Dallek, *Flawed Giant,* 221; Hodding Carter III Oral History, November 8, 1968, p. 17; F. Edward Hebert Oral History, July 15, 1969, p. 48, LBJ Library; GOI No. 1 (June 1965): n.p. [5]; GOI, No. 14 (July 1966): 17; GOI, No. 35 (May 1968): 22.

22. GOI, No. 45 (March 1969): 2; *Dallas Morning News,* May 5, 14, 1970, February 11, 1971, January 17, 1973; *Montgomery Advertiser,* May 2, 14, 1970, February 24, 1971, April 12, 28, October 1, 29, December 6, 1972.

counter the "aggressive designs of North Vietnam and its Chinese Communist sponsor."[23]

From the opposite end of the southern Democratic foreign policy spectrum, Richard Russell worked closely with Fulbright to secure the resolution's passage. Russell agreed with Fulbright's opposition to the use of U.S. ground forces in Vietnam, and he too believed that Johnson shared this sentiment. Russell signaled his ambivalence with a successful amendment to the resolution empowering Congress to cancel the measure in the future without the possibility of presidential veto. But ultimately the Georgia senator was plagued by a conundrum that perplexed southern "hawks" for the duration of the war. American soldiers and sailors were in Vietnam and ostensibly under attack; national honor and credibility demanded a response and their safety dictated support. Russell proclaimed that "national honor" was at stake and only a vigorous reaction would safeguard "the respect of other nations, or indeed . . . self respect." Senator John C. Stennis, who after 1968 replaced Russell as the most crucial southern defender of defense appropriations, also sounded the deep southern devotion to honor and patriotism: "Our honor, our safety, and our security are at stake. . . . We dare not run away, certainly not while we are under attack."[24]

Within a year, these powerful southern senators, together with the rest of the nation, realized that LBJ had chosen to greatly expand rather than curtail U.S. involvement. When this escalation yielded only stalemate, Fulbright and Russell came to typify divergent southern responses to the war. The Arkansas senator emerged as the most significant southern, indeed the most significant congressional, opponent of the war. Like John Tyler Morgan, his predecessor as chairman of the Senate Foreign Relations Committee nearly a century before, Fulbright adopted a minority, nonetheless southern, perspective. A true devotee of Wilsonian internationalism, he believed that the U.S. refusal to accept UN mediation undermined international cooperation and organization. Fulbright's southern heritage also made him sensitive to issues of national self-determination and cultural autonomy and to what he considered the U.S. effort to impose its will on the Vietnamese. Accepting the South's traditional interpretation of Reconstruc-

23. Herring, *America's Longest War,* 136; Randall B. Woods, *Fulbright: A Biography* (New York, 1995), 355; Allen J. Ellender Oral History, November 9, 1971, p. 16, LBJ Library.

24. Ziemke, "Russell," 50; Gilbert C. Fite, *Richard B. Russell Jr., Senator from Georgia* (Chapel Hill, 1991), 439; Downs, "Advise and Consent," 94–95.

tion, recognizing the region's longtime position as an economic colony, and viewing the Civil Rights movement as the latest outside abuse of the South, the Arkansan compared the contemporary U.S. "arrogance of power" to previous northern attempts to dominate the South. In terms that echoed turn-of-the-century southern anti-imperialists, he warned that the United States could not practice imperialism abroad and preserve republicanism at home—that, he said, would be "contrary to the traditions which have guided our nation since the days of the Founding Fathers."[25]

As the prospect of a clear U.S. victory became more remote, Fulbright reminded that "Southerners have a sensitivity to this sort of thing [the stalemate or possibility of defeat in Vietnam] that other Americans cannot fully share. We—or our forefathers—experienced . . . the bitter humiliation of defeat." Convinced that "containment" had been transformed from its original purpose of combating Soviet power and expansion into a worldwide counterrevolutionary doctrine directed at emerging nations seeking to escape European colonialism, he feared that the Vietnamese were the victims of the "'fatal impact' of the rich and strong on the poor and weak." Confounded by Johnson's escalation of the war without substantive consultation with Congress, the senator decided that LBJ had deceived both him personally and the nation regarding Vietnam policies and decisions.[26]

Fulbright began to air his reservations about the war publicly as early as December 1964, when he declared U.S. involvement a mistake and warned that escalation was "senseless." Although he supported LBJ during the first half of 1965, the senator also asserted that the Vietcong would have to be included in any negotiated settlement, and he argued for a bombing halt if Russia would help broker a cease fire. In July, Fulbright joined Russell, John Sparkman, and John Sherman Cooper in writing a letter urging LBJ to halt the ever-increasing U.S. involvement. By early 1966, Fulbright recognized that the United States was unlikely to prevail militarily, and in February he chaired Senate Foreign Relations Committee hearings that elicited probing criticism of U.S. involvement and embarrassed a series of administration spokesmen, including Secretary of State Rusk. Also in February, Fulbright told a national television audience that the war was immoral and expressed regret over his role in the passage of the Gulf of Tonkin Resolution. The following December, the senator published *The Arrogance of Power*, in

25. Woods, "Dixie's Dove," 544.
26. Ibid., 548, 550.

which he called for negotiations, U.S. withdrawal, and the neutralization of Southeast Asia.[27]

In July 1967, Fulbright openly confronted Johnson at a meeting of senate committee chairmen with the president. He informed a shocked and infuriated Johnson that "what you really need to do is to stop the war. . . . Vietnam is ruining our domestic and our foreign policy." As 1967 ended, the Arkansas senator responded vehemently to Rusk's stubborn contention that American credibility would be jeopardized by a defeat in Vietnam. Fulbright declared that the nation's credibility and judgment had already been damaged irreparably by U.S. inability "to suppress this particular war of liberation." Even if the administration's dubious predictions of victory materialized, he contended, "we would still have little to be proud of and a great deal to regret," having fought an "immoral and unnecessary war" and squandered numerous "opportunities which . . . would have spared us and spared the Vietnamese the present ordeal." In March 1968, following the Communist attack on South Vietnam during the Tet offensive, Fulbright held two additional rounds of Senate Foreign Relations Committee hearings. In the first, the senator grilled Secretary of Defense McNamara about the events surrounding the Gulf of Tonkin incident and questioned the veracity of the Johnson administration in obtaining the crucial congressional endorsement; in the second, Secretary Rusk once more had to defend the administration's unsuccessful and deeply unpopular policies.[28]

Fulbright's bitter public dissent left him in a distinctly minority position among southern congressmen. Only three other southerners broke publicly with Johnson—Democrat Albert Gore of Tennessee and Republicans John Sherman Cooper and Thruston B. Morton of Kentucky. Gore shared Fulbright's conviction that the nation's reflexive anticommunist policies threatened the nation, even the world, with "disaster." He proclaimed in February 1966 that the commitment of combat troops was a "serious mistake that has increased . . . the danger of a major war." The real issue was "not defeat, retreat and surrender," he said, but rather the appropriate limitations of U.S. goals and the pursuit of a "tolerable political arrangement" and "honorable disengagement." Cooper, who, like Fulbright, rejected the assumption that U.S. security was at stake in Vietnam, contended that U.S. military involve-

---

27. Woods, *Fulbright*, 362.
28. Woods, *Fulbright*, 457; William C. Berman, *William Fulbright and the Vietnam War: The Dissent of a Political Realist* (Kent, Ohio, 1988), 27–29.

ment was therefore unwarranted and served only to raise the specter of the conflict "spreading into the third World War." He began questioning LBJ's bombing of North Vietnam as early as 1965 and ultimately called for its unconditional cessation as the first step toward meaningful negotiations with the enemy. Cooper was convinced that the United States controlled the "choice" for "peace." Halting the bombing involved potential hazards, but the possibility of a settlement "far outweighs any risk."[29]

In September 1967 Thruston B. Morton joined his fellow Kentuckian in urging an immediate end to the bombing of North Vietnam. Morton's assumption of an antiwar position was significant. In 1965 he had advocated a "firm policy" and "greater use of naval and air forces" against North Vietnam to avoid "similar problems in all of South and Southeast Asia and even in the Philippines, Taiwan and possibly Australia and New Zealand." By the summer of 1967, he had developed second thoughts. While denying that he was a "dove," who thought the United States should abruptly "pull out," he had become convinced that the "civil war" in South Vietnam posed insurmountable problems and that the North Vietnamese would not "negotiate while under fire." Morton hoped that restricted bombing and a significant reduction of search-and-destroy ground operations might bring the North Vietnamese to the negotiating table. The United States, he pronounced, cannot "obtain our objectives of peace in Vietnam" through military means, and the conflict stood in the way of "developing a set of ground rules" with the Soviet Union necessary for avoiding nuclear "holocaust."[30]

Although Gore, Cooper, and Morton provided sustaining arguments and votes, Fulbright shouldered the burden of congressional opposition to the war and endured savage attacks from conservative prowar forces. The senator's opposition to the war was highly significant. First, as chair of the Senate Foreign Relations Committee, his questioning of U.S. motives,

29. CQA, 1966, p. 384 (Gore); Robert F. Maddox, "John Sherman Cooper and the Vietnam War," *Journal of the West Virginia Historical Association* 11 (1987): 60–62; Draft, "Remarks on Vietnam" for the U.S. Senate, October 2, 1967, John Sherman Cooper Papers, Margaret I. King Library, University of Kentucky, Lexington, Ky.; see also Richard C. Smoot, "John Sherman Cooper: The Paradox of a Liberal Republican in Kentucky Politics" (Ph.D. dissertation, University of Kentucky, 1988), 226, 233–34, 236–38.

30. Thruston B. Morton to Joyce Spurlock, October 26, 1965; Morton to Robert Hubbard, August 24, 1967; Morton to Raymond Guinn, September 12, 1967, all in Thruston B. Morton Papers, Margaret I. King Library; Address of Thruston B. Morton, September 27, 1967, pp. 1–2, National Security File, LBJ Library.

strategies, and actions commanded extensive media coverage and comment. Second, his arguments were not just high-profile, publicly controversial copy; they were also forceful rational positions that proved persuasive and elicited responses from supporters of the war. Third, as a conservative establishment figure with an Oxford education and high rank in the U.S. Senate, the Arkansan could not be dismissed by being associated with younger, more radical, counterculture figures who also opposed the war. As historian Randall Woods has observed, Fulbright and his Senate Foreign Relations Committee hearings helped make it respectable for middle-class Americans to oppose the war. Fourth, the senator's probing questions and hearings also revealed administration inconsistencies and deceptions and contributed to the "credibility gap" that dogged the Johnson presidency. Finally, Fulbright's southern origins and conservatism enabled him to foster alliances with Russell, Sparkman, and Samuel J. Ervin and bring these and other key senators over to positions more critical of the war and extensive presidential power.[31]

Ironically, given Fulbright's racial views and opposition to the Civil Rights movement, African Americans constituted the largest bloc of southerners agreeing with his opposition to the war. During 1966, 35 percent of blacks opposed the war; by 1969, the figure had increased to 56 percent. Blacks were consistently more in favor of withdrawal and more opposed to escalation than whites. In 1966, 16 percent of blacks favored withdrawal versus 11 percent of whites, and 33 percent of African Americans favored escalation versus 48 percent of whites. By 1968, black percentages on withdrawal and escalation were 37 and 20; whites' preferences were 23 and 39. And in 1970, the black percentages for these categories were 57 and 10 compared to 37 and 29 for whites. This African American opposition derived from a priority on domestic, especially economic and racial issues; an identification with nonwhite opponents of outside colonial domination; and a growing sense that blacks were being drafted and serving and dying in Vietnam in numbers disproportionate to their place in American society.[32]

Black southerners were justified in believing that they were bearing a disproportionate burden of the fighting in Vietnam. Like African Americans

31. Woods, *Fulbright*, 411, 479.

32. Brenda Gayle Plummer, *Rising Wind: Black Americans and U.S. Foreign Affairs, 1935–1960* (Chapel Hill, 1996), 318; William L. Lunch and Peter W. Sperlich, "American Public Opinion and the War in Vietnam," *Western Political Quarterly* 32 (March 1979): 36. These are national figures.

nationally, southern blacks were more likely to be drafted. Between 1965 and 1970, blacks constituted just over 11 percent of the nation's men eligible for the draft. During that period, the percentage of African Americans drafted ranged from 13.4 percent (1966) to 16 percent (1967 and 1970) of the total number of draftees. At the height of the war in 1967, 64 percent of eligible blacks were drafted, compared to 31 percent of eligible whites.[33]

Although black poverty and inferior educational opportunities partially explained these numbers, the composition of southern draft boards was also crucial. In 1967, blacks filled only 278 of 17,123 positions on draft boards nationally, and no African Americans served on the boards in seven southern states. As Charles Evers, executive secretary of the Mississippi NAACP, argued in 1968, "Negroes were tired of having their sons and husbands sent off to Vietnam by all white draft boards." Within this unrepresentative institutional structure, some white southern draft board members were overtly and aggressively racist. Jack Helms, who headed Louisiana's largest draft board from 1957 through 1967, was a grand dragon in the Ku Klux Klan and characterized the NAACP as a "communist inspired anti-Christ, sex-perverted group of tennis short beatniks whose sole purpose is to cause strife in our beloved land." Civil rights activist Julian Bond's Georgia draft board chairman referred to Bond as a "nigger" and admitted that he had "always regretted" that the board had "missed him." Southern draft boards caught numerous other civil rights workers, who clearly received induction notices as punishment for challenging Dixie's racial practices and institutions.[34]

The inability of African Americans to join National Guard units compounded the inequalities of the draft. With access controlled by state and local officials, guard and reserve units essentially served as safe alternatives to service in Vietnam for middle-class whites. Although true nationally, this was especially the case in the South. For example, in Alabama, where blacks constituted 30 percent of the population, there were only ten African Americans among the state's 15,030 guardsmen. In Mississippi, blacks made up 42 percent of the population but contributed only one person to guard units compared to the 10,364 whites.[35]

Important southern black organizations and leaders protested these con-

33. James E. Westheider, *Fighting on Two Fronts: African Americans and the Vietnam War* (New York, 1997), 20–21; Shapiro, "Vietnam War and the American Civil Rights Movement," 136.

34. Westheider, *Fighting on Two Fronts*, 24–25, 28.

35. Ibid., 29.

ditions and questioned the consistency of United States principles, allegedly fighting for freedom in Vietnam while discriminating against minorities at home. In 1965 members of the Mississippi Freedom Democratic Party pronounced: "1. No Mississippi Negroes should be fighting in Vietnam for the White Man's freedom until all the Negro people are free in Mississippi. . . . 2. No one has a right to ask us to risk our lives and kill other colored people in Santo Domingo and Vietnam, so that white America can get richer." The following year, the Student Nonviolent Coordinating Committee (SNCC) equated the death of activist Samuel Younge to "the murder of people in Vietnam, for both Younge and the Vietnamese" were "seeking . . . rights guaranteed them by law." SNCC expressed "sympathy" for men "unwilling to respond" to the "draft" and to commit "aggression" in Vietnam and asked, "Where is the draft for freedom . . . in the United States?" When SNCC member Julian Bond endorsed this statement and asked if the "energy" employed in "destroying villages thousands of miles away" might not be better used in "building villages here," he was barred from taking a seat in the Georgia legislature to which he had been elected in 1965.[36]

The protests by the Mississippi Freedom Democrats, SNCC, and Bond were important, but paled in comparison to those of Martin Luther King Jr., the nation's most influential African American. As early as March 1965, King declared that the war was "accomplishing nothing," and over the remainder of that year he called upon the United States to suspend the bombing and pursue a negotiated settlement that included the participation of the National Liberation Front, China, and the Soviet Union. Continuing this dissent during 1966, King remained relatively restrained compared to SNCC or the Congress of Racial Equality. He hesitated to break completely with President Johnson, who had been critical to the successes of the Civil Rights movement, or to alienate more conservative groups in the black community such as the NAACP or the Urban League. That these relatively moderate positions failed to garner the support of King's own Southern Christian Leadership Conference (SCLC) until the spring of 1966 demonstrated the political sensitivity of opposing the war.[37]

36. SNCC Statement on Vietnam, January 6, 1966, SNCC Papers; Julian Bond Statement Prepared for Delivery, Georgia House of Representatives, January 10, 1966, SNCC Papers; Shapiro, "Vietnam War and the American Civil Rights Movement," 118–19 (Mississippi Freedom Democratic Party), 126; Clyde Taylor, ed., *Vietnam and Black Americans: An Anthology of Protest and Resistance* (Garden City, N.Y., 1973), 110 (Bond), 259.

37. Shapiro, "Vietnam War and the American Civil Rights Movement," 122–27 (King); Adam Fairclough, "Martin Luther King Jr. and the War in Vietnam," *Phylon* 45 (March 1984):

These differences of opinion demonstrated that southern blacks, like Dixie's whites, were hardly unanimous in their opinions about Vietnam. As had been the case during previous twentieth-century U.S. wars, the African American community agonized over the desire to serve its country, demonstrate patriotism, and enhance the case for civil rights and the disparity between the nation's stated foreign policy objectives and the treatment of domestic minorities. Southern black papers, ranging from the Democratic *Norfolk Journal and Guide* to the Republican *Atlanta Daily World,* extolled the bravery and patriotism of black soldiers and expressed great discomfort with SNCC and Julian Bond for appearing to endorse draft resistance. Although both papers doubted that Bond would have been expelled from the Georgia House of Representatives had he been white, the *Journal and Guide* described him as "rash" and "impolitic" and dismissed his stance as unacceptable to "patriotic, law-abiding American citizens." The *Daily World* agreed and castigated any actions that conveyed the "impression" that blacks were unwilling to bear their "share of responsibility . . . of military service."[38]

Clear evidence during 1966 that the war was being fought at the expense of civil rights reform and aid to the poor convinced both King and SCLC to abandon restraint. King moved toward a stronger, more public antiwar position in testimony before a Senate subcommittee in December 1966. He lamented, "The bombs in Vietnam explode at home; they destroy the hopes and possibilities for a decent America." "The chaos of the cities, the persistence of poverty, the degenerating of our national prestige throughout the world," he said, provided "compelling arguments" for peace.[39]

The nation's foremost black spokesman assumed a full-blown antiwar stance in his dramatic "Beyond Vietnam" address on April 4, 1967, at the Riverside Church in New York City. He branded his "own government" the "greatest purveyor of violence in the world today." "Our nation," he asserted, was "on the wrong side of a world revolution" and had supported governments in South Vietnam that were "singularly corrupt, inept, and

---

19–27. For the NAACP position on the relation of the Civil Rights movement to opposing the war, see John A. Morsell to Martin Kroll, April 27, 1967, and Morsell to Matthew Schechter, May 8, 1967, Records of the NAACP, Manuscripts Division, Library of Congress.

38. *Norfolk Journal and Guide,* January 22, February 5, 1966; *Atlanta Daily World,* January 8, February 2, 1966; *Jackson Advocate,* January 29, 1966; Arthur C. Banks Jr. and Finley C. Campbell (Morehouse College faculty) to editor, *Atlanta Constitution,* January 13, 1966.

39. Shapiro, "Vietnam War and the American Civil Rights Movement," 130 (King); Fairclough, "King and the War in Vietnam," 27–29.

without popular support"; had opposed a "revolutionary government seeking self-determination"; and had destroyed Vietnam's "two most cherished institutions: the family and the village." Rather than continuing to poison the soil of American thought and ignore domestic problems through aggression abroad, the United States government needed to halt the bombing, set a date for troop withdrawals, and negotiate realistically with both the North Vietnamese and the Viet Cong. King thereafter denounced the war in regular and vehement terms. Just two months before his assassination on April 4, 1968, he told his congregation in the Ebenezer Baptist Church in Atlanta, "God didn't call America to engage in a senseless, unjust war [such] as Vietnam. And we are the criminals in that war! We have committed more war crimes than any other nation in the world, and I'm going to continue to say it."[40]

Johnson was deeply distressed by criticism from both Fulbright, an old southern friend and colleague, and King and other African Americans, for whom the president believed he had risked much politically and accomplished much substantively; but LBJ was much more apprehensive of critics from the right—many of the most powerful of whom were southerners. While needing to retain conservative support for the funding of the war, LBJ feared "touching off a right-wing stampede" that might demand an invasion of North Vietnam or a reckless bombing campaign that would trigger a larger war with Russia or China.[41]

The most important of the southern conservatives was Richard Russell, Johnson's old friend and mentor who chaired the crucial Senate Armed Services Committee until January 1969. Hardly an unthinking hawk about Vietnam, Russell had opposed U.S. involvement in 1954 and rejected the domino theory, which predicted the loss of Vietnam to Communism would lead to the loss of the other nations of Southeast Asia. The Georgia senator also recognized the lack of genuine nationalism or initiative among the South Vietnamese and, with a sensitivity born of his southern agricultural roots, warned Johnson of the danger of forcing peasants off their land. "I don't know these Asian people," he observed, "but they tell me they worship their ancestors and so I wouldn't play with their land if I were you. You know, whenever the Corps of Engineers has some dam to dedicate in Geor-

40. Taylor, *Vietnam and Black Americans*, 82, 85–87, 92; Henry E. Darby and Margaret N. Rowley, "King on Vietnam and Beyond," *Phylon* 47 (spring 1986): 48.

41. Goodwin, *Johnson and the American Dream*, 282.

gia, I make a point of being out of state, because those people don't like economic improvements as much as they dislike being moved off their land." Despite these insights, Russell admitted in 1964 that since the United States was involved he could see no viable alternative: "As a practical matter, we're in, and I don't know how the hell you [LBJ] can tell the American people you're comin' out. . . . They'll just think that you've been whipped and you've been run; you're scared. . . . It'd be disastrous."[42]

Russell believed and most southerners agreed that once U.S. soldiers were involved, patriotism, national honor, and international credibility dictated complete national and congressional support, and he never wavered in voting for the appropriations requested to fight the war. He did, however, object to the Johnson-McNamara strategy of limited war, gradualism, and attrition. Russell railed at civilian interference with the military and called for an unrestrained, aggressive bombing campaign against North Vietnam's industry, ports, and transportation facilities. In January 1966, he characteristically advised Johnson, "For God's sake, don't start the bombing halfway. Let them know they are in a war. We killed civilians in World War II and nobody opposed. I'd rather kill them than have American boys die. Please, Mr. President, don't get one foot back in it. Go all the way." Four months later, he declared that the United States should "go in and win—or get out." To implement this unrestrained policy without fear of third-party interference, Russell recommended informing the Russians and Chinese that their intervention would lead to the U.S. response with nuclear weapons.[43]

Other southern conservatives echoed Russell's position—often from a far less thoughtful perspective. John C. Stennis, also on the Senate Appropriations Committee and Armed Services Committee (where he replaced Russell as chair in 1969), rejected limited war and demanded that the United States pursue "military victory." Like Russell, Stennis called upon the Johnson administration to "face and accept the risk involved and be prepared to meet Red Chinese military aggression," even if nuclear weapons were required. Following the Tet Offensive, Stennis reached the same conclusion as Russell: either the geographic restrictions on U.S. activities in North Vietnam, Cambodia, and Laos and the targeting restrictions on U.S. bomb-

42. Ziemke, "Russell," 62; Dallek, *Flawed Giant*, 102.
43. Russell Statement, "Meeting with Congressional Leadership," January 25, 1966, Meeting Notes File, LBJ Library; Fite, *Russell*, 449.

ing had to be removed or the United States should consider withdrawal. The choice was between a "hard-hitting war or no war at all."[44]

From his chairmanship of the Preparedness Subcommittee of Armed Services, the Mississippi senator held hearings in August 1967 examining the air war against North Vietnam. In marked contrast to Fulbright's hearings aimed at demonstrating the folly of the war, Stennis furnished a succession of prowar military witnesses a forum for excoriating Secretary of Defense McNamara and other civilians who were allegedly hampering the U.S. bombing campaign. Chairman of the Joint Chiefs of Staff General Earle G. Wheeler emphasized that bombing of North Vietnam was essential to winning the war in the South and that the cessation of bombing would be a "disaster." In a brilliant response, McNamara articulated the rationale for limitations on the bombing, opposed the campaign's extension, and contested bombing's effectiveness. If Stennis had intended to "get McNamara," as some observers believed, it worked. Faced with this public breech between the secretary of defense and the Joint Chiefs of Staff, Johnson moved to ease McNamara out by making him the president of the World Bank. But much to Stennis's consternation, the hearings did not force Johnson to abandon his overall strategy of limited war.[45]

The list of southerners agreeing with Russell and Stennis and expressing exasperation with Johnson could be greatly extended. Allen J. Ellender of Louisiana contended that the North Vietnamese should be "hit harder" and their "industrial and political centers . . . bombed by our forces if necessary." "The prestige and power of the United States have been laid on the line," he said. James O. Eastland of Mississippi noted that "a number of we Southerners" argued with LBJ for "not pressing for victory"—for not blowing the "fire out of North Vietnam." George Wallace echoed the militant southern inclination to defer to the Joint Chiefs of Staff, ascertain their recommendations, and then "get on doing it." When Wallace made Air Force General Curtis LeMay, known for his predisposition toward the use of nuclear weapons, his vice-presidential running mate in 1968, critics tellingly referred to them as the "Bombsey Twins." Like Richard Russell, A. Willis

44. Downs, "Advise and Consent," 97; Michael S. Downs, "A Matter of Conscience: John C. Stennis and the Vietnam War" (Ph.D. dissertation, Mississippi State University, 1989), 86–93, 100 (2d quote).

45. George C. Herring, *LBJ and Vietnam: A Different Kind of War* (Austin, 1994), 55–57.

Robertson of Virginia had initially opposed U.S. involvement, but once committed, he believed that "we ought to support the military" and follow "military advice" regarding strategy rather than deferring to civilians in the Defense Department. George A. Smathers of Florida considered "peaceful coexistence . . . part of the communist arsenal" and opined that Communists responded to only "one language; that is the language of strength and determination." Strom Thurmond concurred. According to Thurmond, "State Department people and some of the softies" had exercised undue influence; the militant South Carolina senator would have turned matters over to the air force and "won the war."[46]

Just as Russell and Stennis typified the majority southern position in the Senate, L. Mendel Rivers of Charleston, South Carolina, did so in the House. Like his Senate colleagues, Rivers provided unflagging support for defense appropriations while arguing for military control of tactical decisions and a virtually unrestrained bombing campaign. Declaring that he did not "give a damn about world opinion," he considered "definitive victory" the only acceptable objective. Rivers complained that Johnson had no plan for victory and that the administration's "inconclusive policy" was ineffective militarily and "destructive of the morale of our troops." In 1966 the South Carolina congressman called for the annihilation of Hanoi and Haiphong. If China intervened, he declared, "it would be foolish" not to retaliate with nuclear weapons.[47]

The pattern of southern congressional response to the war was evident in the consideration of Vietnam supplemental appropriation bills in both 1966 and 1967. Russell, Stennis, Ellender, Smathers, and Russell B. Long in the Senate and Rivers, George H. Mahon, and Robert L. Sikes in the House defended the appropriations and the U.S. presence in Vietnam while expressing frustration at the limitations on the bombing and ground operations. Fulbright and Gore declared the war a mistake and expressed their

46. CQA, 1966, p. 348 (Ellender); James O. Eastland Oral History, February 19, 1971, p. 21, LBJ Library; Dan T. Carter, *The Politics of Rage: George Wallace, the Origins of the New Conservatism, and the Transformation of American Politics* (Baton Rouge, 1995), 345, 360; Crispell, *Testing the Limits*, 188–89; Daniel T. Campbell, "Beyond George Ball: Doubts about American Intervention in The Vietnam Conflict, 1961–1965" (Honors thesis, College of William and Mary, 1994), 41–47 (Robertson); A. Willis Robertson Oral History, September 27, 1968, p. 22; Strom Thurmond Oral History, May 7, 1979, p. 21, LBJ Library.

47. Will F. Huntley, "Mighty Rivers of Charleston" (Ph.D. dissertation, University of South Carolina, 1993), 295–97.

fears that broader conflict with China or Russia might ensue. But in the end all southern Democrats, regardless of their position on the war, voted for the funding and in so doing allowed President Johnson to continue to pursue his limited war, which avoided both the calls for withdrawal and demands for more dramatic escalation.[48]

Southern congressmen continued to provide solid support for U.S. involvement in Vietnam during Richard M. Nixon's administration. Senators Fulbright, Gore, and Cooper remained the only prominent southerners actively seeking American withdrawal, while the overwhelming majority of their colleagues in both houses opposed all proposals to restrict funding for the war or to set a specific time limit on U.S. involvement. By April 1970 Fulbright dismissed Indochina as of virtually no importance to "American security or interests." The "central fact," he contended, "is that it does not matter very much who rules in those small and backward lands." Rejecting the concept of a monolithic Communist threat and the ongoing viability of containment, he concluded that the United States was "fighting a double shadow in Indochina"—"the shadow of the international Communist conspiracy and the shadow of the old, obsolete, mindless game of power politics." Although Cooper endorsed Nixon's policy of "Vietnamization," or gradual U.S. troop withdrawals, as a "clear change from past policies," he proposed after 1969 a series of amendments aimed at curtailing the use of U.S. troops and specifying the date of American withdrawal from the war. By July 1972, he declared that only the withdrawal of U.S. forces could secure the release of American prisoners of war.[49]

Fulbright and Cooper were significant figures in the growing minority congressional opposition to the war during the Nixon years, but John C. Stennis remained more representative of southern congressmen and their constituents. As chairman of the Senate Armed Services Committee, "the most influential position on military affairs on Capitol Hill," Stennis embodied the established southern role of safeguarding defense appropriations and became an intimate adviser to President Nixon. Usually informed in advance of Nixon's major Vietnam initiatives, Stennis backed Vietnamization, the bombing of Cambodia in 1969 and invasion of that country in 1970, the South Vietnamese incursion into Laos in 1971, and the U.S. mining of Haiphong Harbor in 1972. The Mississippi senator continued to denounce

48. CQA, 1966, pp. 153–54, 382–85, 391, 945; CQA, 1967, pp. 204–8, 10-H.
49. Woods, *Fulbright,* 559; Maddox, "Cooper," 67; see also Berman, *Fulbright,* 122.

restrictions on military decisions and actions; he could find "no precedent in all history for Congress to outline, limit, or define the perimeter of the battlefield." Violently opposed to antiwar activists, whom he regularly locked out of his office or committee hearings, and unswerving in his belief in the monolithic Communist threat, Stennis warned that any wavering in the support of the U.S. commitment would bring "unrestrained jubilation in Moscow, Peking, Hanoi, and every other Communist capital in the world."[50]

Southerners made these promilitary, prowar inclinations clear while responding to a number of other Vietnam-related issues. In August 1970 southern senators voted 22 to 0 against an amendment prohibiting the military from using "defoliant chemicals," or Agent Orange. The following year, Dixie's congressmen provided the decisive margin in a 200 to 198 vote, defeating an amendment that would have extended the draft by only one year rather than the two years sought by the Nixon administration. Southerners voted 75 to 21 against, with southern Democrats opposing 55 to 14 (compared to all other Democrats, who voted 119 to 40 in favor). Southerners also strongly opposed a motion directing President Nixon to furnish Congress a text of the *Pentagon Papers*, the secret Defense Department study leaked to the press by Daniel Ellsberg. And southerners were highly critical of the trial and murder conviction of Lieutenant William Calley for his role in the March 1968 massacre of unarmed civilians at the South Vietnamese village of My Lai. South Carolina senator Ernest F. Hollings criticized the army for prosecuting Calley and asked if all soldiers were to be "tried as common criminals" for a "mistake of judgment." Allen J. Ellender added that the South Vietnamese villagers "got just what they deserved." Following Calley's conviction in the summer of 1971, Herman Talmadge declared he was "saddened to think" that a person "could fight for his flag and then be court-martialed and convicted for apparently carrying out his orders." Representative Joe D. Waggonner of Louisiana believed that Calley had been made a "scapegoat," and William L. Dickinson of Alabama urged Nixon to grant Calley executive clemency and suspend his sentence. John R. Rarick of Louisiana agreed and pronounced Calley a "true soldier and a great American."[51]

50. Downs, "Advise and Consent," 105; Downs, "Matter of Conscience," 106, 122–23.

51. CQA, 1969, p. 853 (Hollings); CQA, 1970, p. 45-S; CQA, 1971, pp. 64, 66, 69–71, 267 (Rarick), 744 (Talmadge, Waggonner, and Dickinson), 38–39-H; Becnel, *Ellender,* 261.

Congressional votes on a series of Vietnam measures during the Nixon presidency further demonstrated the South's ongoing devotion to anticommunism and containment and reluctance to end U.S. involvement in Vietnam without a military victory. In the wake of Nixon's bombing campaign in Cambodia in the spring of 1969, the Senate sought to block such actions in Laos and Thailand by restricting the use of funds in the Defense Appropriations Bill. Southerners voted 17 to 5 (Democrats 12 to 5, and Republicans 5 to 0) to table an amendment by John Sherman Cooper and Mike Mansfield that would have limited support for local, non-U.S. forces in Laos and Cambodia. And southern senators cast 8 of 9 dissenting votes against a modified, but successful, version forbidding the use of U.S. forces.[52]

When President Nixon ordered U.S. combat troops into Cambodia the following April, Senator Cooper renewed his campaign to restrict the American military role in Indochina. Together with Senator Frank Church of Idaho, he offered an amendment to the Foreign Military Authorization Bill blocking expenditures to support U.S. forces, advisers, or combat aid for the South Vietnamese after July 1, 1970. The Senate approved the Cooper-Church amendment on June 30 by a vote of 58 to 37. Southern Democrats were opposed by 9 to 6 (compared to the overall positive Democratic vote of 42 to 11), and Southern Republicans voted 4 to 1 in the negative. When the more hawkish House voted 237 to 153 to table the Cooper-Church amendment, southern Democrats were aligned 67 to 8 with the majority and southern Republicans agreed by 27 to 0. By comparison, nonsouthern Democrats voted 112 to 32 in favor of the amendment. Southern Democrats even more decidedly opposed the McGovern-Hatfield amendment, which would have limited the number of U.S. troops in Vietnam to 280,000 after April 30, 1971, and mandated complete withdrawal by December 31, 1971. The Senate rejected the measure by a 55 to 39 vote, with southern Democrats aligned 15 to 2 against (as opposed to the remaining Democrats, who endorsed the proposal by 31 to 5).[53]

Cooper continued his antiwar campaign during 1971 and 1972. In 1971 he submitted an amendment requiring that all funds appropriated for U.S. actions in Indochina be directed toward American withdrawal. When the amendment was narrowly deleted from the foreign aid bill by a 47 to 44 vote, southern Democrats decided the issue by voting 11 to 3 for the deletion

52. CQA, 1969, pp. 454, 41-S.
53. CQA, 1970, pp. 89–90, 92–93, 932, 934–36, 946, 42–43-H, 46-S.

motion while remaining Democrats opposed the deletion by 30 to 6. In July 1972 the Kentucky Republican's call for an unconditional end to all funding after four months failed to reach a vote. The Senate instead passed by 50 to 45 a modified version submitted by Edward W. Brooke of Massachusetts that retained the four-month deadline but added the condition that all American prisoners of war had to be released prior to cessation of funding. Southerners voted 14 to 7 in the negative, with Democrats in opposition 8 to 6, and Republicans opposed 6 to 1. The Brooke modification of Cooper's amendment was the Senate's strongest protest against the war, but the House, as had become customary, rejected the end-of-the-war proviso. The distribution of votes was familiar. Within an overall vote of 229 to 177 against, southern Democrats voted 51 to 21 and southern Republicans voted 28 to 1 in support of President Nixon and the war.[54]

Despite this continuing support for the war, southerners agreed with their colleagues that Congress needed to reassert its position relative to the executive and to guard against future Vietnam-like involvements. In June 1969 Cooper amended a Fulbright "national commitments" resolution. Cooper's version stipulated that a treaty, statute, or concurrent resolution of both houses would henceforth be necessary for a U.S. commitment to use armed forces abroad or to promise to assist foreign nations with military or financial aid. The measure, which did not apply to Vietnam, passed 70 to 16, with all 24 southern senators voting or announced in favor, save Republicans Edward J. Gurney of Florida, Strom Thurmond of South Carolina, and John Tower of Texas.[55]

Three years later, in the midst of the North Vietnamese spring offensive of 1972, the Senate approved the War Powers Bill. With Fulbright overseeing the proposal in the Senate Foreign Relations Committee, William B. Spong Jr. of Virginia acting as the Democratic floor manager, and most significant, John C. Stennis joining Republican Jacob Javits of New York as the bill's principal sponsors, the upper house stipulated that without a declaration of war U.S. armed forces could be employed only to repel an attack or "immediate threat" on the United States or U.S. armed forces abroad or to protect U.S. citizens. Having committed U.S. forces, the president was required to report "promptly" to Congress, and the assigned forces had to be recalled after thirty days unless "Congress by specific legislation

54. CQA, 1971, pp. 65, 42-S; CQA, 1972, pp. 19, 38–39, 123, 462–63, 469, 80–81-H, 44-S.
55. CQA, 1969, pp. 177, 10-S.

authorized their continued use." Senator Stennis emphasized that, like the national commitments resolution, the War Powers Bill would not apply to Vietnam, but he stressed the need for this "safeguard" against the president risking "a war which the nation will not support." By clarifying the "role" for involvement through proper constitutional procedures, the president and military would be placed in a stronger position. Although Fulbright and the bulk of the Senate had less friendly intentions concerning the strength of the military, the Senate approved the bill by a 68 to 16 vote, with southern Democrats agreeing 12 to 2 and southern Republicans agreeing 4 to 3. The House passed a weakened version in August, which the Senate ignored.[56]

Congress returned to the issue in November 1973. Following the "peace" agreement with North Vietnam and the Viet Cong in January and the withdrawal of U.S. troops and release of U.S. prisoners in the spring, this final legislative commentary on the war was enacted. Both houses passed the War Powers Act over President Nixon's veto. The measure was identical to the Senate's 1972 version except for the extension of the deadline for notification of Congress from thirty to sixty days. In the Senate's 75 to 18 vote, southern Democrats were aligned 14 to 1 in favor and southern Republicans divided 4 to 4. The House's tally of 284 to 135 surpassed the necessary two-thirds by only 4 votes, with southern Democrats voting 53 to 20 and Dixie's Republicans aligned 14 to 21.[57]

The conclusion of American military involvement in Vietnam ended the first three decades of U.S. cold war foreign relations. The American experience in Vietnam cast the varied bases of the South's post-World War II foreign policy perspective into clear focus. The acute sensitivity to appeals to patriotism and honor, the steadfast opposition to communism, the inclination to give the executive broad authority in the foreign policy, the proclivity for the use of force and support for a strong national defense, the impatience with limited war and restraints on the military, and the disdain for nonwhites all served to align Dixie behind intervention and to sustain the region's support for U.S. involvement. Senators Russell and Stennis and Congressman Rivers embodied these traits and were instrumental in forging ongoing congressional backing for the war and the appropriations necessary to sustain the U.S. effort. Polling data, oral histories, the responses of col-

56. CQA, 1972, pp. 843–45 (Stennis), 68–69-H, 22-S. The 1973 version of this measure required the president to report to Congress within forty-eight hours.

57. CQA, 1973, pp. 940–41, 76-S.

lege students, and other cultural indicators such as the nature and popularity of country music in Dixie indicate that the majority of white southerners concurred with their prowar stands.

It was significant that Lyndon Johnson, a southerner terribly concerned with personal and national honor and credibility, led the nation to war, and once involved, his southern populist instincts contributed substantially to his suspicion of the military and his determination to fight a limited war. Johnson's Georgia-born-and-raised secretary of state, Dean Rusk, also viewed the war from a southern vantage point. More respectful of the military, as represented by figures as diverse as Robert E. Lee and George C. Marshall, Rusk was devoted to his interpretation of Wilsonian internationalism, collective security, and the rule of law in international affairs and was equally determined to repulse what he considered Communist aggression in Southeast Asia. Southerners also provided some of the most determined opposition to the war. Drawing on the same southern devotion to Wilsonianism, but interpreting it differently, and exhibiting traditional southern empathy for self-rule, cultural autonomy, and anti-imperialism, J. William Fulbright emerged as the most important and articulate congressional critic of the war. He was joined from the Republican side of the aisle by John Sherman Cooper, who agreed with Fulbright regarding the futility of the U.S. military effort and the need to reestablish the South's nineteenth- and early-twentieth-century determination to restrain an overly strong executive authority in foreign relations. And as they had done since the turn of the century, southern blacks reminded their neighbors in Dixie and the nation more generally of the contradiction and hypocrisy of oppressing African Americans at home while ostensibly fighting for human rights and personal liberties abroad.

Dixie's response to the U.S. loss in Vietnam reflected the South's previous experience with "coming to terms with defeat." As had been the case following the Civil War, southern leaders and most southern warriors were convinced that their cause had been honorable and patriotic. They also believed, as had their ancestors a century before, that the war had been winnable. Whereas proponents of the Lost Cause pointed to superior northern numbers and matériel, southerners in the 1960s and 1970s cited civilian restrictions on the military and faulty strategies. Had Johnson and McNamara permitted more extensive bombing or the invasion of enemy sanctuaries in North Vietnam or Cambodia, they asserted, U.S. power would have prevailed. The *Montgomery Advertiser*'s post mortem captured much of this sentiment. The *Advertiser* was confident that the war was "one we could have won, if winning had been our goal" and if we "had fought it as we knew how to fight." Assured of the correctness of the anticommunist cause and of containment and that the United States could have won the war, the South seems to have had many fewer second thoughts and harbored much less guilt about U.S. actions in Southeast Asia. Southern leaders have eschewed the "self-flagellation that became almost a national pastime as the United States backed out of Vietnam."[58]

American withdrawal from Vietnam marked the conclusion of nearly two centuries of U.S. foreign relations. A proper understanding of the formation of American foreign policy during these years must take into account the influence of domestic sectionalism, and the South has been the nation's most self-conscious region. Even before the ratification of the Constitution, southerners had come to see their colonies and then states as a section apart. Conditioned by an adherence to republican ideology, the long experience with staple agriculture and a colonial export economy, but most of all by their reliance on slavery as an economic and social institution, white southerners feared being cast into a minority and dependent condition. Although all these considerations remained crucial throughout the antebellum period, defending the peculiar institution grew ever more important after the mid-1830s. Secession, defeat in the Civil War, and the travail of Reconstruction confirmed the South's fears of dependence and a minority position within the national polity. Thereafter, devotion to the mythology of the Lost Cause and a simultaneous determination to prove that southerners could be both good Americans and meet the standards established by their Confederate ancestors further distinguished Dixie from other portions of the country. Widespread poverty and continued reliance on an extractive, low-wage, underdeveloped economy; one-party, Democratic politics; and the determination to maintain black segregation and disfranchisement confirmed southern sectionalism well into the 1960s.

Acting from a distinctive sectional perspective, the South consistently made its regional interests a prime consideration in responding to and attempting to influence U.S. foreign policy. Over the course of the nation's

58. *Montgomery Advertiser-Journal*, January 21, 1973; Gaines M. Foster, "Coming to Terms with Defeat: Post-Vietnam America and the Post–Civil War South," *Virginia Quarterly Review* 66 (winter 1990): 31–32; C. Vann Woodward, "The South Tomorrow," *Time*, September 1976, 98 (self-flagellation); James C. Cobb, *Redefining Southern Culture: Mind and Identity in the Modern South* (Athens, Ga., 1999), 83.

first 185 years, Dixie's attitudes about race, economic well-being, party politics, states' rights versus appropriate national power, patriotism, sectional pride, and personal, sectional, and national honor combined to determine public responses and the positions and actions of the South's political representatives. Although these responses, attitudes, and actions were never monolithic, majority southern opinion consistently exercised an important and at times decisive influence on U.S. foreign relations. Dixie's economic and political calculations frustrated Federalist tendencies toward closer relations with Great Britain and a declared, more general war with France in the 1790s; and the South provided the decisive momentum and leadership for war with the British in 1812. Southern political, economic, and racial assumptions were central to antebellum commercial and territorial expansion at the expense of the Spanish, Mexicans, and Native Americans. Ironically, when the South seized the opportunity to formulate an independent foreign policy, its essential southerness produced a flawed effort. Long-standing convictions regarding slavery, the economic and diplomatic influence of cotton, and states' rights and personal liberties combined with provincialism and a lack of understanding of the European political economy and diplomatic system to help defeat the Confederacy. During the five decades following the Civil War, the South looked warily upon the Republican-dominated foreign policy that grew increasingly assertive and imperialistic and was accompanied by a significantly stronger national executive and military. Southern protests failed to alter this pattern, but particular sensitivity to the experience of defeat and outside domination led southerners to articulate some of the more thoughtful objections to U.S. imperialism—even though these objections derived in part from unattractive racial prejudices.

With the election of Woodrow Wilson and the return of southern Democrats to power in Congress in 1913, Dixie reversed this fifty-year pattern of opposition to an assertive interventionist U.S. foreign policy. Sectional pride in Wilson, national security, Democratic Party politics, the perceived obligation to demonstrate patriotism and devotion to the Union and to maintain regional standards of honor and manhood, the desire to act responsibly in positions of leadership, an emerging Anglophilia, and the prospect of retaining markets abroad and attracting defense spending at home caused Dixie to amend its postbellum approach to U.S. foreign policy. This fundamental change was exceedingly important because the South provided the most consistent and dependable support for Wilson's foreign policies.

The reversal was equally important to the course of U.S. foreign relations through the end of the Vietnam War. Influenced after 1920 by pride in Wilson's memory and a determination to fulfill his goal of U.S. membership in an international organization, the South consistently fought for U.S. participation in the World Court, cooperation with the League of Nations, and membership in the United Nations. Southern influence was crucial to the American decision to join the UN. Similarly, Dixie, motivated by Wilson's example and the other considerations cited above, extended crucial support to Democrat Franklin D. Roosevelt during the crises of the 1930s and World War II. By the late 1930s, the South had become the most interventionist section of the country.

Southern willingness to sustain an interventionist foreign policy based on unprecedented defense spending and military strength and directed by an imperial president continued during the most intense period of the cold war from 1945 through 1973. Dependable southern support for the cold war policies of all the presidents from Truman through Nixon sustained a containment strategy ranging from general institutional commitments, such as the Marshall Plan and the North Atlantic Treaty Organization, to more specific actions, such as interventions in Korea, Guatemala, Cuba, the Dominican Republic, and Southeast Asia.

This post-1930 pattern of southern response to U.S. foreign policy did not derive from a genuine commitment to Woodrow Wilson's vision of internationalism. Although some southerners, such as Claude Pepper and J. William Fulbright, favored a cooperative involvement in foreign affairs and fundamental reductions in national sovereignty, the vast majority of southerners opted for a unilateralist posture that emphasized international involvement on independent, nationalist terms. Southerners warmly praised Wilson and harshly castigated Republicans and nonsoutherners for blocking the United States entry into the League of Nations. But Dixie never subscribed to Wilson's "revolutionary claim that the American national interest was inseparable from the larger international interest"—particularly if the latter infringed on American freedom of action either at home or abroad, on U.S. security, or Dixie's economic interests. Both the preference for a strong military and disillusionment with the United Nations after 1945 signaled the South's fundamental rejection of Wilsonianism. Similar inclinations were evident in Dixie's opposition to immigration reform, growing support for tariff protectionism, and rejection of foreign aid. The South's support for the war in Vietnam graphically demonstrated this unilateralism and interventionism, as well as the considerations with which the region determined its cold war attitudes on foreign policy. Indeed, Dixie concluded this nearly 185 years of responding to and influencing American foreign relations just as it had begun—by looking abroad through a distinctly southern lens and calculating the potential impact of national policies from a decidedly sectional perspective.[59]

Over the past three decades, significant elements of this sectional perspective have been adopted or have at least remained influential nationally. Observers of the late-twentieth-century American domestic developments have argued that southern social, economic, and political values have gained national acceptance—that a "southernization of America" has occurred. When applied to U.S. foreign policy, this argument yields suggestive patterns.

For example, Jimmy Carter, the first president from the Deep South since Zachary Taylor, conducted the most unpopular foreign policy in the post-Vietnam era. Although international events well beyond U.S. control contributed to the nation's rejection of his policies, it is ironic and instructive that many of his pre-1979 assumptions and actions both looked back toward Wilsonianism and conflicted directly with the South's well-established post-1945 foreign policy perspectives. Operating on the belief that American economic and military supremacy had eroded, Carter believed that U.S. policy needed to move beyond rigid anticommunism and containment. His administration sought to revamp a foreign policy that had yielded great power confrontation, support for authoritarian dictators, neglect of the Third World, and abuse of human rights. Carter pursued instead ongoing arms reduction agreements with the Soviet Union, recognition of and closer relations with the Peoples Republic of China, enhanced sensitivity to global human rights, and a North-South dialogue promoting development and understanding in Africa and Latin America. In brief, he adopted policies in conflict with the South's, and apparently much of the nation's, aggressive anticommunism, proclivity for unilateralism rather than cooperative internationalism, hostility toward Russia and China, lack of concern for less-developed countries, opposition to foreign aid, and proclivity for simple, often military solutions to foreign policy problems. Only in the last year of his presidency did Carter revert to a more traditional cold war stance.

59. H. W. Brands, "The Idea of the National Interest," in *The Ambiguous Legacy: U.S. Foreign Relations in the "American Century,"* ed. Michael J. Hogan (New York, 1999), 126.

In contrast to Carter, President Ronald Reagan's foreign policies, which corresponded much more closely to cold war southern preferences, earned far greater plaudits from the American public. While loudly praising American patriotism and honor, Reagan viewed the world in terms of an older, simpler East-West conflict, in which the United States needed to contain Russia and China and their evil communist advances. He deemed peace through military and ideological strength the key to U.S. foreign policy success, initially rejected all calls for disarmament talks with the Soviets, and significantly increased defense spending. When he ultimately moved toward a renewal of détente, it came in the guise of an American victory rather than a necessary compromise. Far less solicitous of the Third World, Reagan decried foreign aid and the United Nations, unilaterally intervened in countries from Nicaragua to Libya, and proclaimed the virtues of supporting anticommunist, authoritarian leaders.

This brief epilogue hardly substantiates that southern foreign policy attitudes have persisted as a coherent set of assumptions or that they have prevailed nationally in a post-Vietnam or, more recently, a post–cold war international environment. It does argue for the continuing value of examining sectional influences on the formation and implementation of U.S. foreign relations. This would especially seem to be the case as domestic and foreign critics have castigated George W. Bush, the most recent southern president, for his nationalistic emphasis on a missile defense system at the expense of longstanding arms limitation agreements, for the unilateral rejection of a global warming treaty, and for recommending the largest increase in defense spending since the Reagan years, even before the terrorist attacks of September 2001. In the wake of these attacks, the president has cultivated a broader, ostensibly more cooperative international coalition but on terms largely defined by the United States.

BIBLIOGRAPHIC ESSAY

The following sources were most essential in formulating the book's interpretive structure and arguments and examining the South's perspectives, actors, and votes. For a complete listing of sources, see the notes. William J. Cooper Jr. and Thomas E. Terrill, *The American South: A History* (New York, 1996), provide an excellent overview of southern history and a cogent explanation of the South's antebellum concern for liberty and honor; Edward W. Chester, *Sectionalism, Politics, and American Diplomacy* (Metuchen, N.J., 1975), traces the broad outlines of sectionalism and foreign affairs; Joseph J. Persky, *The Burden of Dependency: Colonial Themes in Southern Economic Thought* (Baltimore, 1992), explicates the region's ongoing sense of economic oppression; and Peter Trubowitz, *Defining the National Interest: Conflict and Change in American Foreign Policy* (Chicago, 1998), makes a cogent case for the centrality of domestic sectionalism in the formation of U.S. foreign policy. Where any ambiguity existed in secondary sources, the votes of southern senators and representatives on key legislation or treaties during the years through 1960 have been traced in the *Annals of Congress, Congressional Globe,* and *Congressional Record.* The *Congressional Quarterly Almanac* was consulted for the 1960–73 period.

Drew R. McCoy, *The Elusive Republic: Political Economy in Jeffersonian America* (New York, 1982), and J. C. A. Stagg, *Mr. Madison's War: Politics, Diplomacy, and Warfare in the Early Republic, 1783–1830* (Princeton, 1983), lucidly explain the place of republicanism in Jeffersonian foreign policy, and Peter S. Onuf links republicanism to sectionalism in "Federalism, Republicanism, and the Origins of American Sectionalism," in *All over the Map:*

Rethinking American Regions, Edward L. Ayers et al. (Baltimore, 1996), 11–37. Reginald Horsman, "The Dimensions of an 'Empire for Liberty': Expansion and Republicanism, 1775–1825," *Journal of the Early Republic* 9 (spring 1989): 1–20, demonstrates how expansion through 1820 was of particular benefit to the Jeffersonians and the South. Lawrence S. Kaplan's *"Entangling Alliances with None": American Foreign Policy in the Age of Jefferson* (Kent, Ohio, 1987); Kaplan's *Thomas Jefferson: Westward the Course of Empire* (Wilmington, Del., 1999); Delbert H. Gilpatrick's *Jeffersonian Democracy in North Carolina, 1789–1816* (New York, 1931); John H. Wolfe's *Jeffersonian Democracy in South Carolina* (Chapel Hill, 1940); Norman K. Risjord's *The Old Republicans: Southern Conservatism in the Age of Jefferson* (New York, 1965); and Robert W. Tucker's and David C. Hendrickson's *Empire of Liberty: The Statecraft of Thomas Jefferson* (New York, 1990) are also useful for the Jeffersonians.

For southern Federalists, see Stanley Elkins and Eric McKitrick, *The Age of Federalism* (New York, 1993); Norman K. Risjord, "The Virginia Federalists," *Journal of Southern History* 33 (November 1967): 486–517; George C. Rogers Jr., *Evolution of a Federalist: William Loughton Smith of Charleston (1758–1812)* (Columbia, S.C., 1962); Joseph W. Cox, *Champion of Southern Federalism: Robert Goodloe Harper of South Carolina* (Port Washington, N.Y., 1972); Lisle A. Rose, *Prologue to Democracy: The Federalists in the South, 1789–1800* (Lexington, Ky., 1968); and James H. Broussard, *The Southern Federalists, 1800–1816* (Baton Rouge, 1978). Richard R. Beeman, *The Old Dominion and the New Nation, 1788–1801* (Lexington, Ky., 1972), and John W. Kuehl, "Southern Reaction to the XYZ Affair: An Incident in the Emergence of American Nationalism," *Register of the Kentucky Historical Society* 70 (January 1972): 21–49, provide useful commentary on both parties.

The South and the War of 1812 are examined in Roger Brown's *The Republic in Peril: 1812* (New York, 1971); Norman K. Risjord's "1812: Conservatives, War Hawks, and the Nation's Honor," *William and Mary Quarterly,* 3d ser., 18 (April 1961): 196–210; Burton Spivak's *Jefferson's English Crisis: Commerce, Embargo, and the Republican Revolution* (Charlottesville, Va., 1979); Frank L. Owsley Jr.'s and Gene A. Smith's *Filibusters and Expansionists: Jeffersonian Manifest Destiny, 1800–1821* (Tuscaloosa, 1997); Robert V. Haynes's "The Southwest and the War of 1812," *Louisiana History* 5 (winter 1964): 41–51; Margaret K. Latimer's "South Carolina—A Protagonist of the War of 1812," *American Historical Review* 61 (July 1956): 914–29; Ronald L. Hatzenbuehler's "Party Unity and the Decision for War in the House of

Representatives, 1812," *William and Mary Quarterly*, 3d ser., 29 (July 1972): 367–90; Sarah McCulloh Lemmon's *Frustrated Patriots: North Carolina and the War of 1812* (Chapel Hill, 1973); and James Wallace Hammack Jr.'s *Kentucky and the Second American Revolution: The War of 1812* (Lexington, Ky., 1976).

For the 1815–60 period, essential context and much information on the South and foreign affairs can be found in William W. Freehling's *Secessionists at Bay, 1776–1854*, vol. 1 of *The Road to Disunion* (New York, 1990–); Charles G. Sellers's *The Market Revolution: Jacksonian America, 1815–1846* (New York, 1991); Michael A. Morrison's *Slavery and the American West: The Eclipse of Manifest Destiny and the Coming of the Civil War* (Chapel Hill, 1997); and Michael F. Holt's *The Rise and Fall of the American Whig Party: Jacksonian Politics and the Onset of the Civil War* (New York, 1999). The most important studies directed specifically at the South and foreign relations are Robert E. May's "Epilogue to the Missouri Compromise: The South, the Balance of Power, and the Tropics in the 1850s," *Plantation Society* 1 (June 1979): 201–25; May's *The Southern Dream of a Caribbean Empire, 1854–1861* (Athens, Ga., 1989); Ernest M. Lander Jr.'s *Reluctant Imperialists: Calhoun, The South Carolinians, and the Mexican War* (Baton Rouge, 1980); Douglas A. Ley's "Expansionists All? Southern Senators and American Foreign Policy, 1841–1860" (Ph.D. dissertation, University of Wisconsin, 1990); John McCardell's *The Idea of a Southern Nation: Southern Nationalists and Southern Nationalism, 1830–1860* (New York, 1979); and Edward P. Crapol's "John Tyler and the Pursuit of National Destiny," *Journal of the Early Republic* 17 (fall 1997): 467–91.

On the continuing importance of republicanism and the southern defense of liberty, see J. Mills Thornton III, *Politics and Power in a Slave Society: Alabama, 1800–1860* (Baton Rouge, 1978); William J. Cooper Jr., *The South and the Politics of Slavery, 1828–1856* (Baton Rouge, 1978); Kenneth S. Greenberg, *Masters and Statesmen: The Political Culture of American Slavery* (Baltimore, 1985); Harry L. Watson, *Liberty and Power: The Politics of Jacksonian America* (New York, 1990); Lacy K. Ford, "Republican Ideology in a Slave Society: The Political Economy of John C. Calhoun," *Journal of Southern History* 54 (August 1988): 405–24; and Morrison, *Slavery and the American West*. Thomas R. Hietala, *Manifest Design: Anxious Aggrandizement in Late Jacksonian America* (Ithaca, N.Y., 1985), and William Earl Weeks, *Building the Continental Empire: American Expansion from the Revolution to the Civil War* (Chicago, 1996), connect Jacksonian republicanism to the expansion of the 1840s. For southern concern for manhood and honor and the issues of violence and a martial society, see William R. Taylor, *Cavalier and Yankee: The Old South and American National Character* (New York, 1961); Greenberg, *Masters and Statesmen;* Bertram Wyatt-Brown, *Southern Honor: Ethics and Behavior in the Old South* (New York, 1982); Gregory S. Hospodor, "'Bound by all the ties of honor': Southern Honor, the Mississippians, and the Mexican War," *Journal of Mississippi History* 61 (spring 1999): 1–28; John Hope Franklin, *The Militant South, 1800–1861* (Cambridge, Mass., 1956); Robert E. May, "Dixie's Martial Image: A Continuing Historiographical Enigma," *Historian* 40 (February 1978): 213–34; R. Don Higginbotham, "The Martial Spirit in the Antebellum South: Some Further Speculations in a National Context," *Journal of Southern History* 58 (February 1992): 3–26.

For antebellum southern white relations with Native Americans, Reginald Horsman, *Race and Manifest Destiny: The Origins of American Racial Anglo-Saxonism* (Cambridge, Mass., 1981), develops the racial context. The expulsion of Indians from the Southeast can be traced in Michael D. Green's *The Politics of Indian Removal: Creek Government and Society in Crisis* (Lincoln, Neb., 1982); Ronald N. Satz's *American Indian Policy in the Jacksonian Era* (Lincoln, Neb., 1975); Arthur H. De Rosier Jr.'s *The Removal of the Choctaw Indians* (Knoxville, Tenn., 1970); J. Leitch Wright's *Creeks and Seminoles: The Destruction and Regeneration of the Muscogulge People* (Lincoln, Neb., 1986). Kenneth W. Porter's *The Black Seminoles: History of a Freedom-Seeking People,* revised and edited by Alcione M. Amos and Thomas P. Senter (Gainesville, Fla., 1996); and Daniel H. Usner Jr.'s *American Indians in the Lower Mississippi Valley: Social and Economic Histories* (Lincoln, Neb., 1998) address the white fears of a black-red alliance. For Native American–settler relations in Arkansas and Texas, see S. Charles Bolton, *Territorial Ambition: Land and Society in Arkansas, 1800–1840* (Fayetteville, Ark., 1993); T. R. Fehrenbach, *Lone Star: A History of Texas and the Texans* (New York, 1968); Dianna Everett, *The Texas Cherokees: A People between Two Fires, 1819–1840* (Norman, Okla., 1990); F. Todd Smith, *The Caddos, the Wichitas, and the United States, 1846–1901* (College Station, Tex., 1996); and Robert M. Utley, *The Indian Frontier of the American West, 1846–1890* (Albuquerque, 1984).

Students of Confederate diplomacy must still begin with Frank L. Owsley's *King Cotton Diplomacy: Foreign Relations of the Confederate States of America,* 2d ed., revised by Harriet Chappell Owsley (Chicago, 1959). Other important, more recent general accounts are Henry Blumenthal's "Confederate Diplomacy: Popular Notions and International Realities," *Journal of Southern History* 32 (May 1966): 151–71; D. P. Crook's *The North, the South, and the Powers, 1861–1865* (New York, 1974); Brian Jenkins's *Britain and the War for the Union,* 2 vols. (Montreal, 1974–80); Emory M. Thomas's *The Confederate Nation: 1861–1865* (New York, 1979), ch. 8; and Charles M. Hubbard's *The Burden of Confederate Diplomacy* (Knoxville, Tenn., 1998).

Although all of these studies address the failure of the King Cotton strategy and the crucial British and French decisions to withhold diplomatic recognition, the recognition issue is examined specifically in Howard Jones's *Union in Peril: The Crisis over British Intervention in the Civil War* (Chapel Hill, 1992); Lynn M. Case's and Warren F. Spencer's *The United States and France: Civil War Diplomacy* (Philadelphia, 1970); Frank J. Merli's and Theodore A. Wilson's "The British Cabinet and the Confederacy: Autumn 1862," *Maryland Historical Magazine* 65 (fall 1970): 239–62; and Kinley J. Brauer's "British Mediation and the American Civil War: A Reconsideration," *Journal of Southern History* 38 (February 1972): 49–64. For slavery as a consideration in European decisions, see Howard Jones, *Abraham Lincoln and a New Birth of Freedom: The Union and Slavery in the Diplomacy of the Civil War* (Lincoln, Neb., 1999); Kinley J. Brauer, "The Slavery Problem in the Diplomacy of the American Civil War," *Pacific Historical Review* 46 (August 1977): 439–69; R. J. M. Blackett, "Pressure from Without: African Americans, British Public Opinion, and Civil War Diplomacy," in *The Union, the Confederacy, and the Atlantic Rim*, edited by Robert E. May (West Lafayette, Ind., 1995), 69–100; and James M. McPherson, "'The Whole Family of Man': Lincoln and the Last Best Hope Abroad," in *The Union, the Confederacy, and the Atlantic Rim*, 131–58. Blackett, *Divided Hearts: Britain and the American Civil War* (Baton Rouge, 2000) insightfully examines the British debate about the American war.

The shortcomings of Confederate economic assumptions, fiscal policies, and European purchasing efforts can be followed in Samuel B. Thompson's *Confederate Purchasing Operations Abroad* (Chapel Hill, 1935); Frank J. Merli's *Great Britain and the Confederate Navy, 1861–1865* (Bloomington, Ind., 1970); Richard I. Lester's *Confederate Finance and Purchasing in Great Britain* (Charlottesville, Va., 1975); Warren F. Spencer's *The Confederate Navy in Europe* (University, Ala., 1983); Douglas B. Ball's *Financial Failure and Confederate Defeat* (Urbana, 1991); and Thomas D. Schoonover's *The United States in Central America, 1860–1911: Episodes of Social Imperialism and Impe-*

rial Rivalry in the World System (Durham, N.C., 1991). Charles P. Cullop provides a perceptive account of *Confederate Propaganda in Europe, 1861–1865* (Coral Gables, Fla., 1969).

Confederate efforts to enlist Native Americans as allies are examined in Annie Heloise Abel's *The American Indian as Slaveholder and Secessionist*, with introduction by Theda Perdue and Michael D. Green (1915; reprint, Lincoln, Neb., 1992); Kenny A. Franks's "The Implementation of the Confederate Treaties with the Five Civilized Tribes," *Chronicles of Oklahoma* 51 (spring 1973): 21–33; Franks's "The Confederate States and the Five Civilized Tribes: A Breakdown of Relations," *Journal of the West* 12 (July 1973): 439–54; and William H. Graves's "Confederate Indian Policy in the Southwest: Interest, Goals, Attitudes," *Mid-America* 66 (October 1984): 111–19.

C. Vann Woodward, *Origins of the New South, 1877–1913* (Baton Rouge, 1971), and Edward L. Ayers, *The Promise of the New South: Life after Reconstruction* (New York, 1992), provide superb treatments of the postwar South's domestic condition. Richard F. Bensel, *Sectionalism and American Political Development, 1880–1980* (Madison, Wis., 1984), and Trubowitz, *Defining the National Interest*, locate the South's sectional responses to U.S. foreign policy in a larger national context.

For overviews of the South's postbellum foreign policy perspectives, see Tennant S. McWilliams's pioneering and essential *The New South Faces the World: Foreign Affairs and the Southern Sense of Self, 1877–1950* (Baton Rouge, 1988); Marshall E. Schott's excellent study, "The South and American Foreign Policy, 1894–1904: Regional Concerns during the Age of Imperialism" (Ph.D. dissertation, Louisiana State University, 1995); Schott's "The South and American Foreign Policy, 1894–1900: New South Prophets and the Challenge of Regional Values," *Southern Studies* 4 (fall 1993): 295–308; and Chester's *Sectionalism, Politics, and American Diplomacy*.

Evidence of the Gilded Age South's opposition to an assertive foreign policy and imperialism can be gleaned from Schott's "South and American Foreign Policy (1995)"; Thomas H. Coode's "Southern Congressmen and the American Naval Revolution, 1880–1898," *Alabama Historical Quarterly* 30 (fall/winter 1968): 89–110; Gregory Lawrence Garland's "Southern Congressional Opposition to Hawaiian Reciprocity and Annexation, 1876–1898" (master's thesis, University of North Carolina at Chapel Hill, 1983); Thomas J. Osborne's *"Empire Can Wait": American Opposition to Hawaiian Annexation, 1893–1898* (Kent, Ohio, 1981); and Edwina C. Smith's "Southerners on Empire: Southern Senators and Imperialism, 1898–1899," *Mississippi Quarterly* 31 (winter 1977–78): 89–107.

Dixie's more aggressive tendencies, support for economic expansion, and in some instances, territorial acquisitions are explored in Tennant S. Mc-Williams's "The Lure of Empire: Southern Interest in the Caribbean, 1877–1900," *Mississippi Quarterly* 29 (winter 1975–76): 43–63; Patrick J. Hearden's *Independence and Empire: The New South's Cotton Mill Campaign, 1865–1901* (DeKalb, Ill., 1982); James M. Lindgren's "The Apostasy of a Southern Anti-Imperialist: Joseph Bryan, The Spanish-American War, and Business Expansion," *Southern Studies* 2 (summer 1991): 151–78; Joseph A. Fry's *John Tyler Morgan and the Search for Southern Autonomy* (Knoxville, Tenn., 1992); and Schoonover's *United States in Central America.*

Considerable scholarly attention has been devoted to the South's role in the Spanish-American War. Among the numerous state studies, see especially William J. Schellings's "Florida and the Cuban Revolution, 1895–1898," *Florida Historical Quarterly* 39 (October 1960): 175–86; Schellings's "The Advent of the Spanish-American War in Florida, 1898," *Florida Historical Quarterly* 39 (April 1961): 311–29; George H. Gibson's "Attitudes in North Carolina Regarding the Independence of Cuba, 1868–1898," *North Carolina Historical Review* 43 (January 1966): 43–65; Donald B. Kelley's "Mississippi and 'The Splendid Little War' of 1898," *Journal of Mississippi History* 26 (May 1964): 123–34; and John J. Leffler's "The Paradox of Patriotism: Texans in the Spanish-American War," *Hayes Historical Journal* 8 (spring 1989): 24–48.

For the influence of southern concern for manliness, patriotism, the Lost Cause, and sectional reconciliation, see Kristin L. Hoganson's *Fighting for American Manhood: How Gender Politics Provoked the Spanish-American and Philippine-American Wars* (New Haven, 1998); Gaines M. Foster's *Ghosts of the Confederacy: Defeat, the Lost Cause, and the Emergence of the New South, 1865–1913* (New York, 1987); John Pettegrew's "'The Soldier's Faith': Turn-of-the-Century Memory of the Civil War and the Emergence of Modern American Nationalism," *Journal of Contemporary History* 31 (January 1996): 49–73; and John Oldfield's "Remembering the *Maine:* The United States, 1898, and Sectional Reconciliation," in *The Crisis of 1898: Colonial Redistribution and National Mobilization,* edited by Angel Smith and Emma Dávila-Cox (New York, 1999), 45–64.

Willard B. Gatewood Jr., *Black Americans and the White Man's Burden, 1898–1903* (Urbana, 1975); Gatewood, "A Negro Editor on Imperialism:

John Mitchell, 1898–1901," *Journalism Quarterly* 49 (spring 1972): 43–50; and Piero Gleijeses, "African Americans and the War against Spain," *North Carolina Historical Review* 78 (April 1996): 184–214, provide excellent coverage of the responses of southern African Americans to war and imperialism at the turn of the century. See also James W. Geary's "Afro-American Soldiers and American Imperialism, 1898–1902: A Select Annotated Bibliography," *Bulletin of Bibliography* 48 (December 1991): 189–93, for citations to Gatewood's articles on black soldiers in Alabama, Florida, North Carolina, and Virginia during the war of 1898.

George B. Tindall's *The Emergence of the New South, 1913–1945* (Baton Rouge, 1967), Dewey W. Grantham's *Southern Progressivism: The Reconciliation of Progress and Tradition* (Knoxville, Tenn., 1983), and Grantham's *The South in Modern America: A Region at Odds* (New York, 1994) ably examine the domestic aspects of the Wilson years. Tindall also includes an excellent chapter on World War I. For the long-term significance of Wilson's foreign policies, see N. Gordon Levin Jr., *Woodrow Wilson and World Politics: America's Response to War and Revolution* (New York, 1968); Arthur S. Link, *Woodrow Wilson: Revolution, War, and Peace* (Arlington Heights, Ill., 1979); Lloyd C. Gardner, *Safe for Democracy: The Anglo-American Response to Revolution, 1913–1923* (New York, 1984); Thomas J. Knock, *To End All Wars: Woodrow Wilson and the Quest for a New World Order* (Princeton, 1995); Tony Smith, *America's Mission: The United States and the Worldwide Struggle for Democracy in the Twentieth Century* (Princeton, 1994); David Steigerwald, *Wilsonian Idealism in America* (Ithaca, N.Y., 1994); Amos Perlmutter, *Making the World Safe for Democracy: A Century of Wilsonianism and Its Totalitarian Challengers* (Chapel Hill, 1997); and Frank Ninkovich, *The Wilsonian Century: U.S. Foreign Policy since 1900* (Chicago, 1999).

In addition to the volume cited above, the following books and articles by Arthur S. Link, Wilson's foremost biographer, are highly informative: *Woodrow Wilson and the Progressive Era, 1910–1917* (New York, 1954); *The New Freedom*, vol. 2 of *Wilson* (Princeton, 1956–65); *The Struggle for Neutrality*, vol. 3 of *Wilson;* "Woodrow Wilson: The American as Southerner," *Journal of Southern History* 36 (February 1970): 1–17; and "The Cotton Crisis, the South, and Anglo-American Diplomacy, 1914–1915," in *Studies in Southern History*, edited by J. Carlyle Sitterson (Chapel Hill, 1957), 122–38.

Among other important studies focusing directly on Wilson's foreign policies and the South, Robert H. Block's "Southern Opinion of Woodrow Wilson's Foreign Policies, 1913–1917" (Ph.D. dissertation, Duke University,

1968) and Anthony Gaughan's "Woodrow Wilson and the Rise of Militant Interventionism in the South," *Journal of Southern History* 65 (November 1999): 771–808, have been especially helpful. Additional highly useful works include Timothy G. McDonald's "Southern Democratic Congressmen and the First World War, August 1914–April 1917: The Public Record of Their Support for or Opposition to Wilson's Policies" (Ph.D. dissertation, University of Washington, 1962); Block's "Southern Congressmen and Wilson's Call for Repeal of the Panama Canal Tolls Exemption," *Southern Studies* 17 (spring 1978): 91–100; and Roy W. Curry's "Woodrow Wilson and Philippine Policy," *Mississippi Valley Historical Review* 41 (December 1954): 435–52.

For the central role of southern congressmen during the Wilson years, see Dewey W. Grantham Jr., "Southern Congressional Leaders and the New Freedom, 1913–1917," *Journal of Southern History* 13 (November 1947): 439–59; I. A. Newby, "States' Rights and Southern Congressmen during World War I," *Phylon* 24 (spring 1963): 34–50; Richard L. Watson Jr., "A Testing Time for Southern Congressional Leadership: The War Crisis of 1917–1918," *Journal of Southern History* 44 (February 1978): 3–39; and Watson, "Principle, Party, and Constituency: The North Carolina Congressional Delegation, 1917–1919," *North Carolina Historical Review* 56 (July 1979): 298–323. Studies of specific congressmen include George C. Herring Jr.'s "James Hay and the Preparedness Controversy, 1915–1916," *Journal of Southern History* 30 (November 1964): 384–404; George Coleman Osborn's *John Sharp Williams: Planter-Statesman of the Deep South* (1943; reprint, Gloucester, Mass., 1964); Robert D. Ward's "Stanley Hubert Dent and American Military Policy, 1916–1920," *Alabama Historical Quarterly* 33 (fall/winter 1971): 177–89; Joseph E. Fortenberry's "James Kimble Vardaman and American Foreign Policy, 1913–1919," *Journal of Mississippi History* 35 (May 1973): 127–40; Evans C. Johnson's *Oscar W. Underwood: A Political Biography* (Baton Rouge, 1980); and Leonard Schlup's "Senator J. C. W. Beckham and the Fight for Ratification of the League of Nations," *Register of the Kentucky Historical Society* 95 (winter 1997): 29–55.

For useful state studies, see Milton L. Ready's "Georgia's Entry into World War I," *Georgian Historical Quarterly* 52 (September 1968): 256–64; Richard G. Eaves's "Pro-Allied Sentiment in Alabama, 1914–1917: A Study of Representative Newspapers," *Alabama Review* 25 (January 1972): 30–55; James L. McCorkle Jr.'s "Mississippi from Neutrality to War (1914–1917)," *Journal of Mississippi History* 43 (May 1981): 85–125; Bruce E. Matthews's

"The 1914 Cotton Crisis in Alabama," *Alabama Review* 46 (January 1993): 3–23.

There is no study of the growing southern Anglophilia at the turn of the century. For discussion of this historiographical gap and examination of the South's affinity for the British, see McWilliams's *New South Faces the World* and "Jefferson, Wilson, and the Idea of the 'Militant' South" (unpublished paper in the possession of Joseph A. Fry). National and some southern attitudes are explored in Bradford Perkins's *The Great Rapprochement: England and the United States, 1895–1914* (New York, 1968); Charles S. Campbell's *The Transformation of American Foreign Relations, 1865–1900* (New York, 1976); Stuart Anderson's *Race and Rapprochement: Anglo-Saxonism and Anglo-American Relations, 1895–1904* (Rutherford, N.J., 1981); and George M. Fredrickson's *White Supremacy: A Comparative Study in American and South African History* (New York, 1981).

In addition to Tindall's *Emergence of the New South*, several sources explore the benefits of defense spending for the South: Henry C. Ferrell Jr.'s "Regional Rivalries, Congress, and MIC: The Norfolk and Charleston Navy Yards, 1913–1920," in *War, Business, and American Society: Historical Perspectives on the Military-Industrial Complex*, edited by Benjamin Franklin Cooling (Port Washington, N.Y., 1977), 59–72; James E. Fickle's "Defense Mobilization in the Southern Pine Industry: The Experience of World War I," *Journal of Forest History* 22 (October 1977): 206–23; Daniel Schaffer's "War Mobilization in Muscle Shoals, Alabama, 1917–1918," *Alabama Review* 39 (April 1986): 110–46; and Bruce A. Beauboeuf's "War and Change: Houston's Economic Ascendancy during World War I," *Houston Review* 14 (1992): 89–112.

Arthur E. Barbeau and Florette Henri, *The Unknown Soldiers: Black American Troops in World War I* (Philadelphia, 1974); Lee Kennett, "The Camp Wadsworth Affair," *South Atlantic Quarterly* 74 (spring 1975): 197–211; William G. Jordan, *Black Newspapers and America's War for Democracy, 1914–1920* (Chapel Hill, 2001); Jonathan S. Rosenberg, "'How Far the Promised Land?': World Affairs and the American Civil Rights Movement from the First World War to Vietnam" (Ph.D. dissertation, Harvard University, 1997), address the African American experience during World War I and black responses to U.S. foreign policy.

Southern response to the Paris Peace Treaty and the League of Nations is examined in Dewey W. Grantham Jr.'s "The Southern Senators and the League of Nations, 1918–1920," *North Carolina Historical Review* 26 (April

1949): 187–205; Ralph B. Levering's "Public Culture and Public Opinion: The League of Nations Controversy in New Jersey and North Carolina," in *The Wilson Era: Essays in Honor of Arthur S. Link,* edited by John Milton Cooper Jr. and Charles E. Neu (Arlington Heights, Ill., 1991), 159–97; Frank Abbott's "The Texas Press and the Covenant," *Red River Valley Historical Review* 4 (spring 1979): 32–41; and Michael A. Nelson's "Arkansas and the League of Nations Debate," *Arkansas Historical Quarterly* 56 (summer 1997): 180–200.

The essential domestic backdrop for the 1920–45 period is provided in the relevant portions of Tindall's *Emergence of the New South,* Grantham's *South in Modern America,* and Cooper's and Terrill's *American South.* As with World War I, Tindall includes an incisive and important chapter on the South's relation to World War II. Bruce J. Schulman's *From Cotton Belt to Sunbelt: Federal Policy, Economic Development, and the Transformation of the South, 1938–1980* (Durham, N.C., 1994) is exceedingly helpful in understanding the role of federal spending (including defense spending) in southern economic progress.

The issue of southern "internationalism" after 1914 is a central concern of George C. Herring's and Gary R. Hess's "Regionalism and Foreign Policy: The Dying Myth of Southern Internationalism," *Southern Studies* 20 (fall 1981): 247–77; Paul Seabury's *The Waning of Southern "Internationalism"* (Princeton, 1957); Alexander DeConde's "The South and Isolationism," *Journal of Southern History* 24 (August 1958): 332–46; Charles O. Lerche Jr.'s *The Uncertain South: Its Changing Pattern of Politics in Foreign Policy* (Chicago, 1964); and Alfred O. Hero Jr.'s *The Southerner and World Affairs* (Baton Rouge, 1965). Hero's book is also an extremely informative compendium of public opinion data, congressional voting statistics, and southern attitudes through the early 1960s. McWilliams's *New South Faces the World* and "Jefferson, Wilson, and the Idea of the 'Militant' South, 1916–1945," cogently develop the southern devotion to Wilson and determination to enact his international vision. Robert A. Divine, *Second Chance: The Triumph of Internationalism in America during World War II* (New York, 1967), traces this process, including the contributions of key southerners.

In addition to Hero, several other authors have written extensive and highly useful studies on the South and foreign affairs for this era: George L. Grassmuck, *Sectional Biases in Congress on Foreign Policy* (Baltimore, 1951); Wayne S. Cole, "America First and the South, 1940–41," *Journal of Southern History* 22 (February 1956): 36–47; Rorin M. Platt, *Virginia in For-*

eign Affairs, 1933–1941 (Lanham, Md., 1991); Platt, "The Triumph of Interventionism: Virginia's Political Elite and Aid to Great Britain, 1939–1941," *Virginia Magazine of History and Biography* 100 (July 1992): 343–64; Elmo M. Roberds Jr., "The South and United States Foreign Policy, 1933–1952" (Ph.D. dissertation, University of Chicago, 1954); Irving Howards, "The Influence of Southern Senators on American Foreign Policy from 1939 to 1950" (Ph.D. dissertation, University of Wisconsin, 1955); David L. Porter, *The Seventy-sixth Congress and World War II, 1939–1940* (Columbia, Mo., 1979); and Chester, *Sectionalism, Politics, and American Diplomacy.* Also helpful are Thomas N. Guinsburg, *The Pursuit of Isolationism in the United States Senate from Versailles to Pearl Harbor* (New York, 1982); Johnpeter Horst Grill and Robert L. Jenkins, "The Nazis and the American South in the 1930s: A Mirror Image?" *Journal of Southern History* 58 (November 1992): 667–94; and Harold T. Butler, "Partisan Positions on Isolationism vs. Internationalism, 1918–1933" (D.S.S. dissertation, Syracuse University, 1963).

The ongoing debate over a peculiar southern militancy and proclivity for violence and war is carried on by McWilliams, "Jefferson, Wilson, and the Idea of the 'Militant' South"; May, "Dixie's Martial Image"; F. N. Boney, "The Military Tradition in the South," *Midwest Quarterly* 21 (winter 1980): 163–74; Sheldon Hackney, "Southern Violence," *American Historical Review* 74 (February 1969): 906–25; and John Shelton Reed, *One South: An Ethnic Approach to Regional Culture* (Baton Rouge, 1982).

For the African American perspective, see Brenda Gayle Plummer, *Rising Wind: Black Americans and U.S. Foreign Affairs, 1935–1960* (Chapel Hill, 1996); Bernard C. Nalty, *Strength for the Fight: A History of Black Americans in the Military* (New York, 1986); and Carol Anderson, "From Hope to Disillusion: African Americans, the United States, and the Struggle for Human Rights, 1944–1947," *Diplomatic History* 20 (fall 1996): 531–63. The black experience and other political, social, and economic developments, are examined by Robert J. Norrell, with the assistance of Guy C. Vanderpool, in *Dixie's War: The South and World War II* (Tuscaloosa, 1992); and in C. Calvin Smith's *War and Wartime Changes: The Transformation of Arkansas, 1940–1945* (Fayetteville, Ark., 1986); Sarah McCulloh Lemmon's *North Carolina's Role in World War II* (Raleigh, N.C., 1964); John R. Skates Jr.'s "World War II as a Watershed in Mississippi History," *Journal of Mississippi History* 37 (May 1975): 131–42; editor Neil R. McMillen's *Remaking Dixie: The Impact of World War II on the American South* (Jackson, Miss., 1977); Charles W. Johnson's, "V for Virginia: The Commonwealth Goes to War,"

Virginia Magazine of History and Biography 100 (July 1992): 365–98; and Jerry P. Sanson's *Louisiana during World War II: Politics and Society, 1939–1945* (Baton Rouge, 1999).

Biographies of several key southerners afford crucial details and perspective. See Henry C. Ferrell, Jr.'s *Claude A. Swanson of Virginia: A Political Biography* (Lexington, Ky., 1985); D. B. Hardeman's and Donald C. Bacon's *Rayburn: A Biography* (Austin, 1987); Virginia Van der Veer Hamilton's *Lister Hill: Statesman from the South* (Chapel Hill, 1987); Robert Dallek's *Lone Star Rising: Lyndon Johnson and His Times, 1908–1960* (New York, 1991); Gilbert C. Fite's *Richard B. Russell Jr., Senator from Georgia* (Chapel Hill, 1991); David Robertson's *Sly and Able: A Political Biography of James F. Byrnes* (New York, 1994); Randall B. Woods's *Fulbright: A Biography* (New York, 1995); and Ronald L. Heinemann's *Harry Byrd of Virginia* (Charlottesville, Va., 1996). See also the autobiographical *My Name Is Tom Connally* by Tom Connally, as told to Alford Steinberg (New York, 1954).

The Rayburn, Johnson, Russell, Fulbright, and Byrd biographies are also important to understanding the post–World War II period. In addition, see Thomas A. Becnel, *Senator Allen Ellender of Louisiana: A Biography* (Baton Rouge, 1995); Dan T. Carter, *The Politics of Rage: George Wallace, the Origins of the New Conservatism, and the Transformation of American Politics* (Baton Rouge, 1995); Robert Dallek, *Flawed Giant: Lyndon Johnson and His Times, 1961–1973* (New York, 1998); Brian L. Crispell, *Testing the Limits: George Armistead Smathers and Cold War America* (Athens, Ga., 1999); Will F. Huntley, "Mighty Rivers of Charleston" (Ph.D. dissertation, University of South Carolina, 1993); and Michael S. Downs, "A Matter of Conscience: John C. Stennis and the Vietnam War" (Ph.D. dissertation, Mississippi State University, 1989).

Numan V. Bartley, *The New South, 1945–1980* (Baton Rouge, 1995), traces the postwar South's domestic developments carefully and perceptively. See also, Grantham, *South in Modern America,* Cooper and Terrill, *American South,* and Schulman, *From Cotton Belt to Sunbelt.* Schulman remains especially important to understanding the regional impact of defense spending. Roger W. Lotchin, "The Origins of the Sunbelt-Frostbelt Struggle: Defense Spending and City Building," in *Searching for the Sunbelt: Historical Perspectives on a Region,* edited by Raymond A. Mohl (Knoxville, Tenn., 1990), 47–68, also explores this issue.

Hero's *Southerner and World Affairs* and "Changing Southern Attitudes toward U.S. Foreign Policy," *Southern Humanities Review* 8 (summer 1974):

275–94, are highly informative on the South's responses to trade policies, foreign aid, immigration, anticommunism, disarmament, and the United Nations. His most complete coverage of these issues ends with the early 1960s. Howards, "The Influence of Southern Senators on American Foreign Policy from 1939 to 1950," and Roberds, "The South and the United States Foreign Policy, 1933–1952," illuminate the South's support for the establishment of containment in the late 1940s. Malcolm E. Jewell, *Senatorial Politics and Foreign Policy* (1962; reprint, Westport, Conn., 1974); Lerche, *The Uncertain South;* Seabury, *Waning of Southern "Internationalism";* and Herring and Hess, "Regionalism and Foreign Policy," also examine and interpret the South's foreign policy perspectives during the 1950s, including the region's decisive rejection of internationalism. The *Gallup Opinion Index* and the *Congressional Quarterly Almanac* have been used to analyze aspects of the South's public and congressional attitudes on internationalism and the related issues noted above from the early 1960s (where Hero stops) through 1973.

On the central intersection of race and civil rights and the South's response to U.S. foreign relations, see Plummer, *Rising Wind;* Duane Tananbaum, *The Bricker Amendment Controversy: A Test of Eisenhower's Political Leadership* (Ithaca, N.Y., 1988); James H. Cone, "Martin Luther King Jr. and the Third World," *Journal of American History* 74 (September 1987): 455–67; Mary L. Dudziak, "Desegregation as a Cold War Imperative," *Stanford Law Review* 41 (November 1988): 61–120; Dudziak, "The Little Rock Crisis and Foreign Affairs: Race, Resistance, and the Image of American Democracy," *Southern California Law Review* 70 (September 1997): 1641–75; Michael L. Krenn, "'Unfinished Business': Segregation and U.S. Diplomacy at the 1958 World's Fair," *Diplomatic History* 20 (fall 1996): 591–612; Paul G. Lauren, *Power and Prejudice: The Politics and Diplomacy of Racial Discrimination* (Boulder, 1996); Azza Salama Layton, "International Pressure and the U.S. Government's Response to Little Rock," *Arkansas Historical Quarterly* 56 (fall 1997): 257–72; Thomas Borstelmann, "'Hedging Our Bets and Buying Time': John Kennedy and Racial Revolutions in the American South and Southern Africa," *Diplomatic History* 24 (summer 2000): 435–63; and Cary Fraser, "Crossing the Color Line in Little Rock: The Eisenhower Administration and the Dilemma of Race for U.S. Foreign Policy," *Diplomatic History* 24 (spring 2000): 233–64.

In assessing general southern responses to U.S. involvement in Vietnam, the *Gallup Opinion Index* and *Congressional Quarterly Almanac* provide useful data on public opinion and congressional opinions and votes. In *Vietnam, the Necessary War: A Reinterpretation of America's Most Disastrous Military Conflict* (New York, 1999), Michael Lind attributes the South's reaction to the war to an ethnically-based regional culture. Turning to key policy makers, the literature on Lyndon Johnson is virtually endless. I have used the following to think about his personality, policies, and actions in terms of his southern background: Dallek, *Flawed Giant;* Doris Kearns Goodwin, *Lyndon Johnson and the American Dream* (New York, 1991); Eric F. Goldman, *The Tragedy of Lyndon Johnson* (New York, 1969); George C. Herring, *LBJ and Vietnam: A Different Kind of War* (Austin, 1994); Herring, "The Reluctant Warrior: Lyndon Johnson as Commander in Chief," in *Shadow on the White House: Presidents and the Vietnam War, 1945–1975,* edited by David L. Anderson (Lawrence, Kans., 1993), 87–112; and Waldo Heinrichs, "Lyndon B. Johnson: Change and Continuity," in *Lyndon Johnson Confronts the World: American Foreign Policy, 1963–1968,* edited by Warren I. Cohen and Nancy Bernkopf Tucker (New York, 1994), 9–30.

Woods's *Fulbright* and "Dixie's Dove: J. William Fulbright, the Vietnam War, and the American South," *Journal of Southern History* 60 (August 1994): 533–52; and Fite's *Russell* are essential for understanding the South's two most important senators and the war. See also William C. Berman, *William Fulbright and the Vietnam War: The Dissent of a Political Realist* (Kent, Ohio, 1988), and Caroline F. Ziemke, "Senator Richard B. Russell and the 'Lost Cause' in Vietnam, 1954–1968," *Georgia Historical Quarterly* 72 (spring 1988): 30–71. Additional well-done studies focusing on crucial southern congressmen and the war include: Michael S. Downs's "Advise and Consent: John Stennis and the Vietnam War, 1954–1973," *Journal of Mississippi History* 55 (May 1993): 87–114; Downs's "A Matter of Conscience: John C. Stennis and the Vietnam War"; and Robert F. Maddox's "John Sherman Cooper and the Vietnam War," *Journal of West Virginia Historical Association* 11 (1987): 52–76. For Dean Rusk, see Thomas W. Zeiler, *Dean Rusk: Defending the American Mission Abroad* (Wilmington, Del., 1999); Thomas J. Schoenbaum, *Waging Peace and War: Dean Rusk in the Truman, Kennedy, and Johnson Years* (New York, 1988); and Alan K. Hendrikson, "The Southern Mind in American Diplomacy," *Fletcher Forum* 13 (summer 1989): 375–87. I have supplemented these studies with the oral history interviews with Allen J. Ellender, Thruston B. Morton, George A. Smathers, and John Sparkman and with White House Staff Files deposited in the John Fitzgerald Kennedy Library in Boston; with oral history interviews with Ellender, Morton, James O. Eastland, Wright Patman, A. Willis Robertson, Herman Talmadge, and Strom Thurmond and with Rusk briefings and press conferences, all housed in the Lyndon Baines Johnson Library, Austin, Texas; and with the John Sherman Cooper Papers and Thruston B. Morton Papers in the Margaret I. King Library at the University of Kentucky, Lexington.

Southern veterans provide their recollections in James R. Wilson's *Landing Zones: Southern Veterans Remember Vietnam* (Durham, N.C., 1990) and editor William J. Brinker's *A Time for Looking Back: Putnam County Veterans, Their Families, and the Vietnam War* (Cookeville, Tenn., 1992). Owen W. Gilman Jr., *Vietnam and the Southern Imagination* (Jackson, Miss., 1992), discusses southern writers and Vietnam and in so doing provides insightful observations on the "warrior South." On the South, country music, and Vietnam, see Melton McLaurin's "Country Music and the Vietnam War," in *Perspectives on the American South: An Annual Review of Society, Politics, and Culture*, vol. 3, edited by James C. Cobb and Charles L. Wilson (New York, 1985), 145–61; and Ray Pratt's "'There Must Be Some Way Outta Here!': The Vietnam War in Popular Music," in *The Vietnam War: Its History, Literature, and Music*, edited by Kenton J. Clymer (El Paso, Tex., 1998), 168–89. For southern students, see Mitchell K. Hall's, "'A Crack in Time': The Response of Students at the University of Kentucky to the Tragedy at Kent State, May 1970," *Register of the Kentucky Historical Society* 83 (winter 1985): 36–63; Richard E. Peterson's and John A. Bilorusky's, *May 1970: The Campus Aftermath of Cambodia and Kent State* (Berkeley, Calif., 1971); Charles DeBenedetti's and Charles Chatfield's, assisting author, *An American Ordeal: The Antiwar Movement of the Vietnam Era* (Syracuse, N.Y., 1990); and Tom Wells's, *The War Within: America's Battle over Vietnam* (Berkeley, Calif., 1994).

The southern African American responses to the war are explored in Plummer's *Rising Wind;* William L. Lunch's and Peter W. Sperlich's "American Public Opinion and the War in Vietnam," *Western Political Quarterly* 32 (March 1979): 21–44; Henry E. Darby's and Margaret N. Rowley's "King on Vietnam and Beyond," *Phylon* 47 (spring 1986): 43–50; Adam Fairclough's "Martin Luther King Jr. and the War in Vietnam," *Phylon* 45 (March 1984): 19–39; Herbert Shapiro's "The Vietnam War and the American Civil Rights Movement," *Journal of Ethnic Studies* 16 (winter 1989): 117–41; editor Clyde Taylor's *Vietnam and Black Americans: An Anthology of Protest and Resistance* (Garden City, N.Y., 1973); and James E. Westheider's

Fighting on Two Fronts: African Americans and the Vietnam War (New York, 1997).

For thoughtful discussions of the South's regional distinctiveness and influence on the remainder of the nation in the late twentieth century, see Peter Applebome, *Dixie Rising: How the South Is Shaping American Values, Politics, and Culture* (New York, 1996); James C. Cobb, "An Epitaph for the North: Reflections on the Politics of Regional and National Identity at the Millennium," *Journal of Southern History* 66 (February 2000): 3–24; Cobb, *Redefining Southern Culture: Mind and Identity in the Modern South* (Athens, Ga., 1999); and John Egerton, *The Americanization of Dixie: The Southernization of America* (New York, 1974).

INDEX